Carving Blocs

For my father
Sushil Kumar Datta
and
Sumit Sarkar
friend, comrade and historian par excellence

Carving Blocs
Communal Ideology in Early Twentieth-century Bengal

Pradip Kumar Datta

OXFORD
UNIVERSITY PRESS

YMCA Library Building, Jai Singh Road, New Delhi 110001

Oxford University Press is a department of the University of Oxford. It furthers the University's objective of excellence in research, scholarship, and education by publishing worldwide in

Oxford   New York
Athens   Auckland   Bangkok   Bogota   Buenos Aires   Calcutta
Cape Town   Chennai   Dar es Salaam   Delhi   Florence   Hong Kong   Istanbul
Karachi   Kuala Lumpur   Madrid   Melbourne   Mexico City   Mumbai
Nairobi   Paris   Sao Paolo   Singapore   Taipei   Tokyo   Toronto   Warsaw

with associated companies in

Berlin   Ibadan

© Oxford University Press 1999

ISBN 019 564739 8

Typeset by Rastrixi, New Delhi 110 070
Printed in India at Pauls Press, New Delhi 110 020
and published by Manzar Khan, Oxford University Press
YMCA Library Building, Jai Singh Road, New Delhi 110 001

Contents

	Acknowledgements	vii
	Abbreviations	viii
	Introduction	1
1.	Hindu Unity and the Communal Common Sense of the 'Dying Hindu'	21
2.	Muslim Peasant Improvement, Pir Abu Bakr and the Formation of Communalized Islam	64
3.	Burial of a Fakir, Calcutta 1924: Towards Communal Rupture	109
4.	'Abductions' and the Constellation of a Hindu Communal Bloc	148
5.	War Over Music: Meaning and Implications of the Riots of the 1920s and 1930	238
	Bibliography	297
	Index	311

Acknowledgements

Much of the exhaustion that follows the completion of a manuscript is soothed by the recollections of all those who contributed to its making. I wish to thank the following for helping me through suggestions, extending practical aid, giving encouragement, helping to maintain belief in the reversibility of communalism or for just being there: Chotopishi, Lalkaku and Kakima, Sambuddha, Pati, Dola, Sunil Kumar, Gautam Bhadra, Gyan Pandey, Neeladri Bhattacharya, Pasha, Debu, Bong, Joya Chatterjee, Tripti, Shikha, Prakash Upadhyaya, Dr Kanai Chattopadhyaya, Dr Swaraj Basu, Amita, Gregory, Prof. P.S. Gupta, Prof. B. De and all those who rallied under the banner of the People's Movement for Secularism during and after December 1992.

A special word of gratitude to Sumit and Tanika who provided indispensable emotional and intellectual support during the course of research and writing. I am especially grateful for their suspicion of fashions, which helped to maintain my conviction in independent thinking. My gratitude to them, above all, is for their solidarity in working towards a world without symbolic hatreds.

I am grateful to the Indian Council of Historical Research and the British Council Division for providing me with grants to do research in the U.K. I am also thankful to the staff of various libraries who have given unstinted help: Nehru Memorial Museum and Library (New Delhi), National Library (Calcutta), National Archives (New Delhi), West Bengal State Archives, Baghbazar Public Library (Calcutta), Bangiya Sahitya Parishad (Calcutta), Central Secretariat Library (New Delhi), Delhi University Library, India Office Library (London), School of Oriental and African Studies (London) and Centre for South Asian Studies (Cambridge).

I wish to thank those I interviewed, some of whom were literally fighting off death when I was recording them.

The responsibility for errors and opinions remains with me.

Abbreviations

BSP	Bangiya Sahitya Parishad (Calcutta)
BTAB	Bengal Tenancy Amendment Bill, 1928
CSAC	Cambridge South Asian Study Centre (Cambridge)
GOI	Government of India
GOB	Government of Bengal
GOI Home Poll.	Government of India, Home Department, Political Branch
GOI Home Judcl.	Government of India, Home Department, Judicial Branch
GOB Home Confidential, Poll.	Government of Bengal, Home Confidential, Political Branch. Political Department.
HMS	Hindu Mahasabha
IOL	India Office Library and Records (London)
KPP	Krishak Praja Party
NAI	National Archives of India (New Delhi)
N/K	Non-Cooperation/Khilafat movement
NL	National Library (Calcutta)
NMML	Nehru Memorial Museum and Library (New Delhi)
SOAS	School of Oriental and African Studies (London)
WBSA	West Bengal State Archives (Calcutta)

Introduction

Confronting Communalism: The Complicity of History?

History and communalism form a relationship that has been beset by suspicion in recent times. The necessity, even relevance, of the discipline of history in understanding and confronting communalism has been questioned by a large number of influential scholars, including Veena Das,[1] Gyanendra Pandey[2] and Partha Chatterjee.[3] The historical discipline, it is said, is complicit with communalism. The shared contour of their arguments is as follows: communalism is an integral product of the idea of the nation-state, which, in turn, is the outgrowth and main vehicle of modernity in the post-colonial world. At the same time, history writing is constitutive of the idea of the nation-state, for it provides the latter with its biography.[4] The intentions of historians, even when they are fervently poised against communalism, are self-delusive for they are condemned to collaborate with the very process of which communal politics is a consequence.

Das' argument, in particular, is important to consider. While Pandey identifies communalism as a product of modernity/colonialism

---

[1] Veena Das, 'The Anthropological Discourse on India: Reason and its Other', *Critical Events: An Anthropological Perspective on Contemporary India*, Delhi, 1995.

[2] Gyanendra Pandey, 'In Defence of the Fragment: Writing about Hindu-Muslim Riots in India Today', *Economic and Political Weekly*, vol. XXVI, nos 11 & 12, March 1991.

[3] Partha Chatterjee, *The Nation and its Fragments: Colonial and Postcolonial Histories*, Delhi, 1993.

[4] Although Das does not specifically talk about history in these terms (as does Pandey), she sees it as a part of the ontology of the State, the search for factual adjudication of communal conflicts being the way it suppresses religion and establishes its hegemony. By extension, a narration of its actions can only amount to its biography. *Critical Events*.

and then proceeds to simply equate them with historiography, Das advances a more subtle argument. She argues that in continuation with its colonial heritage, the contemporary Indian state constantly rehearses the notion that religious communities are irreconcilably divided, and that their rival claims can only be transcended and resolved by appealing to the 'objective' criteria of facts. Historians, who supply the facts, contribute to the suppressive tendencies of modernity by removing the state from the arena of religion altogether, relegating the latter to the private sphere and depriving it of its universal concern with 'suffering and redemption'.[5] This process produces communalism.

What concerns me is Das' model of history. It is based on an outdated idea of the historian as an arbiter of the past. Like a magistrate, the historian was supposed to adjudicate the substance of facts that made up the past. This notion was moored in the positivistic conception of 'facts' in which facts were equivalent to their meaning. Their significance depended on their verification, and once this was accomplished, they produced a stable and absolute truth about what they disclosed of the past. However, historiography, like history, moves on, and this idea has little relevance to the guiding principles of the historical discipline as it exists. In the latter, facts are not final; they exist in a constantly embattled state with other facts. The historical discipline is premised on an invitation to debate through research. Any bit of original research addresses itself to an existing body of facts and marshals, as counter-response, a rival spectrum of data. Underlying this process are a couple of assumptions. The first is that the past is composed of a large range of facts that can assume different significations when either new facts are unearthed and/or old facts are looked at in the light of their discovery. The second is the idea that factuality is not self-sufficient. Any historiography worth its salt will teach that it is the questions one puts to a period which determines factuality. More than most other intellectual pursuits, history has been grounded in the politics of choosing, emphasizing and collecting details.

But even this understanding does not quite capture the relationship of specificities to the historical discipline. Possibly the problem is with the word 'facts'. 'Details' may be a more apposite

[5] Ibid., p. 50.

description than 'facts'. For what it does is to remove the notion of the self-sufficiency of facts that accrue to them by virtue of its positivistic resonances. Conversely, the idea of details suggests an analogy with pictorial representation where it functions not only to create the representation, but is at the same time chosen by and appropriate to the overarching design/strategies of the picture. Details are not equivalent to themselves. Their valences alter according to the frame of reference in which they are placed, thereby providing them with flexibility. Further, historical conceptualization concerns not only the periods that are chosen for understanding, but pertains to the nature of evidence itself. The nature of historical evidence is not static. Unlike 'facts', details communicate the constant possibility of expanding the kinds of evidence and, what is equally important, allowing differences in their nature to be recognized. Anthropologically inspired 'deep structures' as well as discursive strategies; ideological formations and even a self-consciousness about historical narratives themselves — all of which are now integral parts of the discipline — need more flexibility of interpretation. They also involve examining new sorts of evidence (symbols, metonymies and so on) which are bound to be radically different from the nature of evidence provided by facts about political events.

At the same time, details are culled from narratives other than one's own, and are consequently verifiable. The 'bottom line' of the significance of details is not their expressive power, but that they establish that something had happened in the past. The verifiable specificity of details means that they are not individually plastic. Their import may change according to the narrative cast in which they are moulded, but it is equally true that, unlike artists, historians cannot invent their details. Consequently, historical details offer resistance to the freedom with which one seeks to marshal them for a particular argument or field of enquiry. Any line of interpretation has to reckon with the limits to meaning that details impose.

Details then, are not simply facts, but verifiable specificities that embody an interplay between the possibilities for expansive signification and an internal resistance to that very prospect. This dialectic defines the process of debate rather than the proclamation of absolute truths, as the distinctive basis for the historical discipline. The scope for reworking the significations of details allows them to yield fresh insights and be mobilized by different narratives and perspectives. This permits the space for interpretation necessary for debate. On the other hand, the limits that it places on the scope of interpretation, makes it certain that the debate will possess a minimum language of evaluation. In fact one can go further and say that the importance of verifiability ensures that there will be a debate in the first place. For it demands a minimum common discipline that sees to it that any particular interpretation of the past will always be addressed to another. The plurality of historical narratives does not produce a condition where voices speak of pasts that live in their own separated spaces, demanding not mutual appraisal but subscription to either one frame of reference or the other.

It is precisely the suppression of this function of history that allows Das to conflate the implications of Neeladri Bhattacharya's argument on the credibility of the BJP's claim on Ayodhya,[6] with that of Hindu communalism. Das argues that Bhattacharya shares common grounds with Advani when he tries to establish the real 'facts' about the possibility of Ram's birth there. The positive thrust of Bhattacharya's argument, read in the framework of details, concerns not only the issue of verifiability, but the questions that the alternate set of facts about Ayodhya raises about the course of Indian history. Above all, it is directed against Advani's proclamation that the Hindu claim to the Babri Masjid was not subject to contestation, since it was a 'belief'. The recourse to historical evidence was not meant to substitute this 'belief' by a matching absolutism of irrefutability. On the contrary, given the premises of historiography, it was a coded appeal to transfer the claim from the autocratic dictates of this 'belief' to the terrain of contestation, of which details provide a common, disciplinary language. Bhattacharya's contentions (or, for that matter, those of other secular historians) do not preclude a reply from the Hindutva representatives, but what they seek to do is to exclude the violence imbricated in the notion of an absolute belief.

But the wholesale rejection of history does more than perpetuate misconceptions about the latter and its resources for confronting communalism. It also prevents us from reflecting on the

[6] Neeladri Bhattacharya, 'Myth, History and the Politics of Ramajanmbhumi', in S. Gopal (ed.), *Anatomy of a Confrontation: The Babri Masjid-Ramajanambhumi Dispute*, Delhi, 1991.

nature of communalism. The latter is not a static formation: its structure of ideas, objects of address and motivations are constantly changing. Its established range of possibilities can only be grasped through the details that restructure it over time. Conversely, a jettisoning of historical understanding denudes it of its temporal particularities, and makes it an existential condition that can be redeemed only by interventions that live outside time by belonging to all time. Confronting communalism becomes a matter of invoking eternal verities alone. The act of blanketing communalism by rejecting history, in Das and Pandey, and, consequently, suppressing a whole host of questions pertaining to it, becomes apparent by contrast with the work of Partha Chatterjee who shares common grounds with them. The latter's more nuanced attack on history, accompanied by some characterizations of communalism, has the merit of opening out more specific avenues of exploration regarding the question of history and communal ideology.

While Das regards history as a method of proclaiming absolute truths by the State, Chatterjee[7] privileges historical narrative as the originative site for the production of communal ideology. There is a direct, causal relationship implied between the two by his definition of communalism as an ideology that forefronts the idea of origins by defining India as belonging to those whose religious origins and birthplace coincide in that country. This is a connection that seems insightful enough until we recall that the definition holds true for Hindu communalism alone. This formula cannot provide the basis for Muslim communalism which necessarily has to look elsewhere for its originative space. As a matter of fact, the purity of Islam, or rather, the definitive idea of Islam that its communal proponents advocate, derives less from the location of religious origins than from the idea of law and ethical behaviour. This qualification is necessary not simply to indicate the differentiated character of communalism and thereby underline the need to draw definitions that would be inclusive, but to also point out that communal ideology is not based on readings of the past alone.

A simple assertion of collective belonging is not sufficient for the needs of communalism. The very idea of belonging can be contentious. For instance, the claim that tribal ideologues often

[7] Partha Chatterjee, *The Nation and its Fragments: Colonial and Postcolonial Histories*, Delhi, 1994, pp. 76–115

make that they are the original inhabitants of the land can destabilize the equation between birthplace and religious origins. Moreover, the claim of belonging to a common place cannot tackle the problem of unifying diverse identities and interests concealed by religious nomenclatures. Communalism needs to employ a variety of ways to resolve the problems of unification. For instance, if a source for producing a stable collective subjectivity is by showing an unchanging historical predicament, another is provided by the trope of a unified character (for instance, the claim that Hindus are liberal). The foundation of this notion of collective personality is drawn from the area of 'culture' rather than that of history. For 'culture' and other related usages such as 'feeling', 'way of life' etc., can be expanded effortlessly to provide definitions that need not necessarily be stable, even as they emphasize the sense of a shared self. Within this scheme, history plays an important part in providing a resource for cultural interventions, rather than as something that determines it. In this connection it may be pertinent to mention that in nineteenth- and early-twentieth-century Bengal, it was possibly literature that was equally, if not more, responsible for the production of a communal mindset.

To invoke the powers of culture and literature is by no means a way of holding out a brief for history. But it helps to specify other important sites for the production of communal ideology. As a matter of fact, communal ideas derive from not only history and literature, but also religion, ritual, pamphlets, newspapers and the logic of events themselves, amongst others. The multiplicity of ideological locations rules out the possibility that any one of these could be reduced to being *the* originative source.

Communalism and Its Overwritings

Despite attempts, however limited, like Chatterjee's, there remains a relative absence of any elaborated definition of communalism and its processes. Communalism as an object of enquiry is dissipated into structural questions such as the march of modernity or even the idea of grand narrative itself. In a way this is understandable. Communalism is indissociable from rioting, the horror of which springs from the way brutalities are committed, and/or their justifications advanced, by those one sees everyday and even knows closely as relatives and friends. The intimacy of this violence cries out to be displaced in order for it to be made bearable. The affective response is reinforced by a certain lack within communalism. Unlike fascists, no one claims to be a communalist. Without a nomenclature denoting its specificities, communalism cannot elaborate its ideology. I will discuss this at greater length, but what is germane here is that its silence encourages the belief that communalism is an involuntary function of some other phenomenon. The nature of communalism encourages itself to be overwritten by other narratives.

Communalism possesses three broad explanations. There is firstly the symptomatic approach that focuses on the reality and modalities of communal violence, but sees it as the manifestation of a civilizational pathology. This is, of course, the essentialist view of the colonial administration that regarded communalism as the outgrowth of an unbroken and irreconcilable antagonism between homogeneous Hindu and Muslim communities. More influential are explanations that talk of communalism as the story of manipulation. The most forceful of these has been the nationalist allegation that communalism is the product of the colonial policy of divide and rule through which the natural brotherhood of Hindus and Muslims is destroyed by the creation of antagonistic vested interests. This is a story that has sometimes blended in with the economic one articulated mainly by orthodox Marxists and occasionally by colonial administrators. The former advances the idea of a mixed mode of production that combines capitalism with semi-feudal remnants, which creates a structural latency that allows those seeking to preserve their privileges to manipulate class conflict through communal disorder. Sharing an analogous framework is the community oriented approach. The economic variant of this is provided by Sugata Bose who concentrates on specifying macro-level economic dislocations. He argues that communal conflicts were a mediated consequence of the Great Depression, which sundered the symbiotic bonds between Muslim peasants and Hindu moneylenders. The former acted as Muslims because they were tied by religious bonds.[8] The classic statement of the communitarian approach is provided by the early work of Partha Chatterjee. Developing the notion of an economically

[8] Sugata Bose, *Agrarian Bengal; Economy, Social Structure and Politics, 1919–1947*, Cambridge, 1986.

homogeneous Muslim peasantry, Chatterjee defines this class as constituting a community. Communal conflicts are then seen as acts of peasant communitarian resistance to oppressive socio-economic relations, which are appropriated by elite politicians through defining them in communal terms.[9]

The essentialist and structural-latency readings are united in precluding the possibility of communal ideologies and institutions inflecting or transforming the social formation of which they are a part. Both encourage a reading of communalism as symptomatic. However, while the essentialist view is clearly unable to explain anything beyond a presumed civilizational peculiarity, the idea of structural latency — whether in the Marxist or communitarian versions — marks an advance in specifying the preconditions for the growth of communal formations. This is important for it implies a split between the social structure and that which is created by it, that is, communalism. Through this route it raises the crucial question regarding the agency by which communalism is produced, even if the answer is narrowed down to the crude utilitarianism of manipulation. However, even this hesitant, reductive quest for specifying communalism has tended to disappear in the new wave of explanations motivated by the anti-modernist, specifically anti- nation-state, turn. The tendency towards de-recognizing communalism has been carried to its logical end in a recent article by Dipesh Chakrabarty.[10]

Chakrabarty provides some right-sounding epithets against communalism, but that is all that he offers by way of specification. In fact, he goes further to say that communalism is no different from instances of ethnic discrimination available all over the world; hence, communalism should be renamed racism in order to prevent the 'orient' from looking 'peculiar'. I will not stop to consider the politics of naming, whereby communalism is called racism, rather than the other way, for what is at stake is the reality of communalism itself. Earlier studies had simply dissipated the visibility of communalism; this one argues for its disappearance. Although the article specifically compares communal identities with caste identities, the general import of the argument

---

[9] Partha Chatterjee, *Bengal 1920–1947: The Land Question*, Calcutta, 1984.
[10] Dipesh Chakrabarty, 'Modernity and Ethnicity in India: A History for the Present', *Economic and Political Weekly*, 30 December 1995.

suggests that communalism is equivalent to any other collective identity, since all are indiscriminately part of the triumph of modernity. This has pernicious consequences. Precisely because it is so firmly coincident with the metanarrative of modernity, communalism is normalized as part of a contemporary existential condition. If colonial essentialism had naturalized communalism by seeing it as revelatory of a civilizational dilemma, Chakrabarty resorts to a structural naturalization of communalism by presenting it as a phenomenon that is really a problem with an omnipresent, omnipotent modernity.

To be fair to Chakrabarty, he attempts a return to the historical specification of communalism. He does this by creating a split between communalism that is already formed in the crucible of modernity on the one hand, and, on the other, the historical context in which it becomes visible. This split is determined by Chakrabarty's commitment to the notion of 'hard', bounded collectivities that can admit of no transformation: they can only work out their own internal logic, separated from the workings out of other collective identities, merely coexisting with them. This obviously means that Chakrabarty also advances a particular idea of relationship between communalism and its context, in which the former can only *manifest* itself in a context, but not change or be *transformed* by it. What remains unexplored in this overarching determinism, is the self-activity of communal formations in providing explanations for their world and the multiple challenges posed by their contexts, rather than just for themselves. Without a recognition of this, it may be observed, we cannot even begin to grapple with the power, let alone define the limits, of communalism.

Possibly the more fundamental problem lies in the obsession with the singularity of collective identities. This allows different identities to be seen as separately bounded, sealed off from mutual interactions and mutually repetitive. It makes it impossible to understand the dynamic aspects of an identity formation. Once seen as singular and exclusive, the history of collective identities can only provide passive backdrops for one another. A different range of possibilities emerge once communal formations are seen as a part of a field in which they have to perforce relate to other collective identities (other than its binary in 'Hindu' or 'Muslim'), such as class, gender or caste affiliations. For what we then behold are the vulnerabilities of that identity, the ways in which its 'hardness' has to mediate, compromise, inflect and suppress in order to produce tentative unities that proclaim themselves to be bounded monoliths. In other words, the discursive claims of boundedness have to be seen in relationship to the many ways they grapple with the pressures, spaces and needs of their context which constantly poses the claims of other identities. Thus, in my period of study, communal formations have to deal with the problems of class identity that spring from land relations, even as they are compelled to confront the new norms of womanhood as these emerge in domestic and public spaces.

As a matter of fact, while any given cross-section of time may yield a spectrum of several 'hard' identities, to see them as part of a simultaneously happening social process is to recognize their boundaries to be overlapping and contestatory. They inhabit a shared time and space, which define them as part of a social field of multiple identities. These identities do not merely coexist, but address each other. Collective identities may be separate, but they are also relational. The modern condition then sketches out more problematic and paradoxical lines of movement in which 'hard' collectivities are constantly threatened by an inherently fluid social structure. Communal identities are structured by an internal tension. It is within this particular incertitude of contemporary identity formations, that the violence, horror and power of the communal logic need to be located.

Communalism in the Nineteen-twenties

The coupling of modernity with homogeneity has now become a common sense of academic life. The problem with epochal periodizations such as the 'modern' is that they tend to project the concerns of the present, backwards into the past. No doubt the present is unavoidably involved in the way we imagine the past, but epochal periodization which includes the contemporary historian in their time frame, tend to imagine the past in a direct line of continuity with the present. This is because the past becomes a necessary part of the self-recognition of the historians and their world. There is, in the case of the communalism-as-modernity argument, an obvious correspondence between the history of a world governed by notions such as governmentality and western categories of thought on the one hand, and on the other hand, the burden of a unified capitalist system, the 'no-exit' experience of which has been doubly reinforced by the constriction and failure of proletarian revolutions. History has at no time appeared so imprisoned by the triumphs and failures of its human subjects.

Neglected in these characterizations is the integrity of the past, involving an understanding of change that is not unidirectional and a historical process that is not internally homogeneous. It is necessary to recognize that the past need not necessarily possess the same structure of social and cognitive relations as the present, precisely because the past contains its own range of possibilities. Epochal periodizations need to reckon with more complex ideas of change that emerge from readings of smaller units of time. Limited time spans tend to reveal more of the contestations that underlie any major change, thereby allowing for a possibilistic notion of change.

The twenties in Bengal (and, if we go beyond the confines of this book, large parts of the sub-continent as well) indicate that the modern world is not simply made up of administrative homogeneity and 'hard' identities. The axis of this turbulent period was provided by the oscillation between the anti-colonial nationalism of the Non-cooperation/Khilafat movement which began the decade, and the consolidation of separate and antagonistic communal identities which culminated in the unprecedented communal violence of the mid-twenties. But these happenings were only the most noteworthy within a spectrum of mobilizations. The general spread of political consciousness meant a new self-consciousness of identities other than 'nationalist' and 'communal', many of which were already operational, but not previously known as objects of mass social and political mobilization. Consequently, these two affiliations were ruptured and challenged by emerging commitments to class and gender and the expansion and consolidation of inherited ones thrown up by low-caste assertions and sectarian differences.

The twenties raise some general questions. Located within this field of syncopated growth of multiple affiliations, the phenomenon of 'hard' religious boundaries can only be defined as a claim. This encourages an examination of such claims to ask how and why they were constructed, their relationship to rival claims and the unstable ways in which they were enunciated and organizationally consolidated.

A key feature of this process is that collective identities are very different from individual identities. The latter operate simply as frames of affiliation, each with its own distinctive range of people who belong to different social segments. These can, and often do, coexist in the same person without causing too many internal ruptures. Thus, someone who is a Hindu in ritual life can still have professional/personal relationships with Muslims or homosexuals. On the other hand, in the twenties at least, collective identities find it hard to operate on the basis of coexisting claims. Precisely because they are aligned to the acquisition of political power, and, in the case of communalism, to emerging as the sole political and social power, they need to be based upon, and produced through, ideologies. Ideological interventions remould the nature of identities as they exist at personal levels, seeking to make them exclusivist.

However, this drive runs against the differentiated nature of identity formations. Collective identities, contrary to the implications of the 'hard' identity argument, are not simply versions of the same thing. Each of them possesses separate social and political limits and possibilities. To take some obvious instances: while caste identities offer the opportunity of taking into account both cultural and economic disparities, class based affiliations provide the possibility of tackling vertical social divisions regardless of caste and communal divisions; communalism, on the other hand, has the advantage of submerging all sorts of vertical social divisions; the objects of the two are correspondingly different: while one lends itself to the changing economic relations, the other is confined to altering and reifying institutions of symbolic differentiation. In its bid to emerge as the comprehensive and decisive explanation for social relations, communalism has to confront the challenges of rival identities. Consequently, it needs to engage in a multiplicity of relationships with them, in order to neutralize their alternative structures of possibility and absorb them into itself.

Typically, communalism possesses an appropriative relationship with other social allegiances. These consist of several discursive and organizational strategies. A key one is that of displacement, whereby the claims of a particular identity are so relocated within communal discourse that its implied meanings are utterly transformed: this will be noticed in the way Hindu communalism structures gender images (ch. 2). Sometimes rival identities are simply suppressed or, in a more sophisticated manner, included in the concerns of communalism through their metonymic extensions. The Bakr establishment, for instance, includes the peasant through elaborating the ideas of improvement associated with the peasantry, even as it silences the claims of the peasant identity by simply not appealing to it in an overt fashion (ch. 3). Or, at other times, concerns that flow from commitments to other affiliations are straightforwardly re-oriented, which is the way the discourse around the 'dying Hindu' works (ch.1). It is by grappling with these appropriative strategies that one can discover the self-activity of communalism. Unravelling the different transactions of communalism can show us the ways in which communal identities attempt to actively acquire a social space for themselves and, in the process, also illuminate their tension spots.

While the success of communalism in actually appropriating its others stems from its ideological self-activity, what is significant is the role of conjunctures. Communal movements appear to come in waves, which is possibly a reason why the widespread analogy with fever seemed plausible to administrators and nationalists. In our times, Hindu communalism has acquired a solid institutional stability through the Rashtriya Swayamsevak Sangh, but even so, what the latter shares with the communalism of the twenties is that its communal worldview becomes publicly legitimized only during the peak points of its mobilization. This is partly the consequence of a lack of elaborated ideas, a feature I will discuss below. At this point however, what needs to be noted is that the importance of conjunctures for communalism indicates the complexity of the communal process — even if its reliance on the former suggests an inherent insufficiency. Let me elaborate with the instance of the relationship between caste and Hindu communal identities. It was the threat of the declassification of low castes as Hindus with their consent — an event which would provide Muslims with greater administrative patronage on account of the resulting inflation in the proportion they made up of the population — that marks the beginning of Hindu communalism expressed in the campaign that Hindus were dying. The latter was used as an imperative for inter-caste unity. At this stage however, the Muslim was perceived less as a threat than as a model for emulation. However, in another conjunctural moment in the twenties, the Muslims had emerged as an important political force in the Khilafat movement. This coincided with a new campaign that emanated from one of the low castes called the Rajbansis, based on the alleged abduction of Hindu women by Muslim *goondas*. This campaign was immediately taken up by upper-caste Hindu communalism, which could now claim to have produced a united caste bloc against the Muslims.

Communalism as an Ideological Process

A crucial aspect of the self-activity of communalism is the nature of its ideology. However, despite Savarkar's exposition of Hindutva, communalism lacked an elaborated ideology in the twenties. In fact, it is interesting to note that even the Hindutva of the post-1980s is marked by a relative absence of texts.[11] The reason for this must be sought in a fundamental feature of communalism noted earlier — especially that of Hindu communalism — which is its unsayability. Communalism cannot enunciate its ideology openly and explicitly elaborate the absolute importance of the antagonism between Hindus and Muslims. This is partly the consequence of censorship and state action (although Section 156a, through which colonial law prescribed punitive action for those spreading hatred between communities, was more often invoked as a threat than actually implemented). But more important was the self-censorship that was the consequence of the way communalism related to anti-colonial nationalism.

The latter, in order to pose as an alternative to colonial rule, had to be seen as existing above the realm of social differences and conflict, even if it drew on many of its energies. Communalism shared the all-in-unity structure based on a transcendental appeal to nationalism. However, unlike anti-colonial nationalism, the 'transcendental' appeal of communalism had, necessarily, to be, moored in social antagonism. It could not be regarded as being on a par with anti-colonial nationalism in embodying the possibilities of freedom for all those who lived within the sub-continent. It was precisely this inability that gave to communalism the powerful negative association of sectarianism. In fact, communal politics

[11] Tapan Basu et al. *Khaki Shorts Saffron Flags: A Critique of the Hindu Right*, New Delhi, 1993, p. 36.

regarded itself in this period as a supplement to nationalism. The normal justification of the Hindu Mahasabha was to claim that its role was to safeguard the rights of Hindus to which the Congress could not pay adequate attention, because of its different priorities. It was an argument that attempted to assuage the impression of sectarianism. Of course, while this justification testified to the desire to rise above the bondage of being seen as sectarian, it could not mitigate the effects of the actual campaign against the Other which was the real stuff of communal mobilization.

This had important consequences. The self-denial of its explicit objectives produced a situation in which communalism could only imply what was its principal characteristic. It could communicate the antagonism of Hindu and Muslim only through inferences. The core of this was provided by fragmentary discursive units that conjured up vivid images and circulated in that form as social common sense. I am using the word 'image' here to indicate a specific kind of symbolism. Unlike a literary symbol that allows for a vast range of meanings, some of which can even be contradictory, communal common sense offers a limited polysemy in which all the meanings are non-antagonistic and in fact reinforce each other in their orientation towards a common objective. In many ways, it resembled common social stereotypes. Like the latter, communal imagery possessed a vivid brevity that made it ideal for oral circulation, in addition to providing a reference point for any discourse that impinged on communal relations.

A classic instance of this was the common sense of (mainly mofussil) Hindu women being abducted by Muslim goondas. Like a stereotype, it spread its insinuation to cover all Muslims, holding them responsible for constant criminality and rapaciousness, while conversely creating a picture of Hindu weakness. However, what was interesting was that it went beyond the limits of a stereotype. Each component of this image — such as its reference to women or to land relations through invoking the mofussil — referred to separate anxieties. In the end, it became a composite point for mobilization of a large range of tensions including inter- and intra-caste relations, the threatened position of zamindars and the mofussil bhadralok, as well as the whole problem of gender relations. All the while it created a new political bloc that brought together those committed to collaboration with colonialism, on the one hand, and to revolutionary terrorism, on the other hand.

What was produced in this process was a communal bloc through which communalism generalized itself across the social and political spectrum and, indeed, attempted to become co-extensive with society itself (ch. 4).

Given the imagistic basis of communal ideology, there may be an impression that it is purely discursive in nature. This is not true. For instance, although the abductions campaign acquired its real power and impact from repetitive newspaper reports, these were based on actual allegations of such occurrences that had been reported from various places. The variety and nature of these events were overdetermined by the discursive structures provided by the communal campaign. But this was only one type of communal imagism. In other cases — as a matter of fact, in the more spectacular instances of communal mobilization — the logic of events dominated over the discursivities that surrounded it. The latter simply reinforced and extended the meaning of the event. What is interesting however, is that the communally conflictual events themselves possessed an imagistic structure, through which they galvanized multiple social anxieties and corresponding identities.

Riots are a case in point. Riot issues, such as *go-korbani* or music before mosque, are imagistic in nature and possess certain discursive features. The objection to the killing of a cow, or to music being played before a mosque, are public spectacles based on images. Moreover, analogous to printed material, these spectacles can be replicated across time and space. But what distinguishes them is the fact that they are symbols that impinge on actual spatial relations: music is objected to in front of a mosque that is normally located in a busy street. Even more important is the fact that the violence they create restructures the social relations of whole cities and towns. The sheer logic of riots compels the comprehensive transformation of social relations into Hindu versus Muslim (ch. 5). There is another sort of event that communalizes without producing physical violence. For instance, there was a contention that arose over the burial spot of a pir. The conflict imaged the question as to who governs sacred space. This issue realigned social tensions within Calcutta, and began to outline some of the questions that underlay partition itself, namely the relationship between religious identity and spatial boundaries (ch. 3).

The multiplicity of reference points is not something born with the image, but accretes to it over time. These images gain their richness of meaning as they circulate in a discursive terrain, or as they produce new developments in political and social relations. The accretive character of communalism indicates that it compensates for the lack of an elaborated ideology by producing an ideological process.

A crucial aspect of the ideological process of communalism is that it is not about the formation of a single identity. While talking of communalism, it is often forgotten that it is composed of both Hindu and Muslim varieties. The singular way of looking at communalism informs not only the communally biased view that Muslim communalism is the only representative of the general phenomenon, but also newer kinds of historiography that see the origins of communalism in exclusively discursive structures. For instance, Gyanendra Pandey boils down both communalisms to the same discursive paradigm that comes from a colonial discourse which speaks of bounded and eternally antagonistic Hindu and Muslim communities.[12] In an obvious sense what Pandey says is no doubt true, but the obviousness leaves out a great deal. Besides seeing colonialism as the great originary, the problems of which I will discuss later, the commonalities do not exhaust the meanings of Hindu and Muslim communalisms. Moreover, what is missed out is that, while there are undoubtedly common features between the two communalisms (the most self-evident aspect of which is antagonism — without which there would be no communalism), these possess different contextual meanings and occupy separate positions of importance in the two communalisms.

Consider, for instance, the common moorings of the two communalisms in a social-Darwinist view which makes the idea of antagonism crucial to existence itself.[13] In this view, social resources are limited and, consequently, different races in their struggle for existence are condemned to appropriate each other's resources. The key justification for communalism in my period is, however, not domination but parity. Hindu communalism looks for parity in physical terms. The importance of the body is, of course, in

---

[12] Gyanendra Pandey, *The Construction of Communalism in Colonial India*, Delhi, 1990.

[13] I have drawn a great deal of my observations on the social-Darwinist underpinnings of communalism from Aziz Al Azmeh, *Islam and Modernity*, London, 1992.

keeping with the vitalist and organicist notions of social Darwinism. But for Hindu communalism it had a more direct resonance in that it was preoccupied by numbers. As I have mentioned, the possibility of low castes declassifying themselves as Hindus was a motivating anxiety behind the origins of Hindu communalism. On the other hand, Muslim communalism looked for equivalence in the economic sphere. This was impelled by the relatively disadvantaged positions of both Muslim professionals and peasants. Moreover, even the ways in which they sought to produce the inflexibility of their boundaries were different. While Muslim communalism could use certain normative texts, this did not mean that they could simply deploy an inherited commonness. Possessing the advantage of a common text, it suffered from the accompanying problem of the antagonism that sectarian interpretations of the Koran and Hadis produced. At the heart of any species of Islamic self-consciousness lay the question as to who was a true Muslim. This meant that, willy nilly, Muslim communalism had to draw upon schismatic energies, that is, from one of the existing schools of Islamic thought, even as it tried to broaden its appeal by the process of antagonism with Hindus and through petitions to such broad platforms as Muslim 'feeling' and 'sentiment'. This gave to it a 'fundamentalist' complexion which has stayed with it till today. On the other hand, Hindu traditions did not provide its communalism with a normative text. But it endowed an alternate resource. This was the notion of *adhikar bheda*, which defined Hinduism by its lack of a singular self-definition. By itself however, pluralism could hardly produce the notion of a single Hindu collective body that could bind the low castes to itself by antagonism with religious others. Consequently, Hindu communalism had to stress the central importance of organization that could, as it were, centralize pluralism.

These are simply some indicators of how dissimilar similarities can be. What they do indicate is the importance of respecting the differences between the two communalisms. It is through detailing the ways in which the two communalisms constitute themselves in relationship to all the tensions and self-affirmations that mark Hindu and Muslim as identities, as well as the corresponding process of impacting on one another, that a full account of the two communalisms can emerge — one that will include the similarities and be able to go beyond them. My effort has been to maintain the integrity of this ideological process in the way that I have arranged my chapters. While for the most part I have tried to show Hindu and Muslim communalism in their separate and mutual interactivity, in the last chapter on riots I have brought them together, since, ironically, it is in riots that the two resemble each other most closely. This also provides the opportunity to focus on the traditions of mutuality that, paradoxically, accounts for the intensity that animates their antagonism.

I have consulted official records, pamphlets, biographies, newspapers, besides conducting interviews with survivors from this period. My effort has been directed towards mining these as sources for different representational strategies as well as for information on events that they provide. I feel that the division currently made between factuality and representationality cannot account for the full explanatory power of sources. Recently the relationship between discourse and event has been explored by Shahid Amin, but the problematic that he sets himself, that is, the representational status of events is not one that I share.[14] Instead, what I wish to explore is the power and logic of a phenomenon in which modes of discursive representation and the structure of events articulate themselves through each other. To reiterate a point made earlier, representationality is crucial for communal mobilization, because it deals so centrally with stereotypes, images and rhetorical structures, even as it draws all these from actual events and seeks to explain social contexts through its imagistic power. This understanding has, for instance, informed the way I have used newspapers. I have explored the social logic of events and the ways in which they have been represented. The persuasiveness of newspapers does not arise from obeying the autonomous logic of a discursive system. On the contrary, they are based on a complex interplay between two kinds of guiding ideas. While their significance lies in the way they represent events, they have to also obey the explicit public commitment to verifiability of its reports. Consequently, on the one hand they provide a window into the processes by which events are converted into symbols; on the other hand, because the onward rush of events can never be symmetrically aligned to the logic of communal discourse or be exhausted

---

[14] Shahid Amin, *Event, Metaphor, Memory: Chauri Chaura 1922–1992*, Delhi, 1995.

by it, newspaper reports also offer an opportunity to step outside the frame of communal representation and look at it from other perspectives, thereby providing a more complete introduction to the contestation within communalism, and between it and rival developments. My handling of newspapers is, as I have said, only an instance of my general approach. And at this level, to elaborate an imperative I have mentioned earlier, this method is important if we are to avoid underestimating communalism on the grounds that its facts are wrong, or being rendered paranoid (or enthusiastic, as the case may be!) by the apparent comprehensiveness and intensity of its symbolic universe.

1

Hindu Unity and the Communal Common Sense of the 'Dying Hindu'

I

One of the first markers of difference between Hindu and Muslim I learned as a child, was the 'fact' that Muslims bred faster. According to 'common knowledge' this was because they married four times. I did not question this assertion till much later, when it provided a key plank for the 'liberators' of the 'Ram Janambhoomi'. The proliferation of Muslims, they argued, would enable them to overrun the country. But a little research showed that this assertion was not commensurate with the actualities of population growth ratios. The 'fact' that I had picked up innocently now expressed communal paranoia. It raised a question: from where did this intensity come?

It may be disconcerting to begin a study of the past with the anachronism of a contemporary problem. I offer this autobiographical fragment because the history of early-twentieth-century Bengal allows us to map the complex history of this simple fear. Writing to Madan Mohan Malaviya about his impressions of a talk with a British statesman aboard a ship, sometime during the communally charged period of the mid-twenties, Lajpat Rai reported the following: 'The chief hope [of the British] seemed to have so far been on the chance of thinning their [the Hindus'] numbers with a view to make them politically impotent.'[1] What interested me was not the veracity of this report. Rather, it was the confirmation that a person engaged in the mobilization for an

---

[1] Cited in Indra Prakash, *Hindu Mahasabha: Its Contribution to Indian Politics*, New Delhi, 1966, p. 20.

exclusive Hindu constituency, was preoccupied with Hindu numbers. A more decisive fact followed in the tracks of the last. In the course of a speech at Patna given in 1925, Swami Shraddhanand declared that he had been seized by the problem of the imminent extinction of Hindus only after reading a book by one U,N. Mukherji entitled, *Hindus — A Dying Race* (hereafter ADR).[2] Later, I learned that it was in 1912 that Mukherji had actually met Shraddhanand to convince him of his thesis.[3] Mukherji's own book had been published three years earlier, in 1909. Equally surprising was its connection with a Hindu Mahasabha publication that came out seventy years later, called *They Count Their Gains — We Calculate Our Losses*. In the foreword, the book — which tried to create a scare of the growing population of Christians and Muslims — stated that the title was derived from a quotation of Bhai Parmanand.[4] It was wrong: actually the title cited the concluding lines of one of Mukherji's texts. Taken in relation to all that had been produced on this subject, it was clear that this was not simply the case of a discourse outliving its author. What I was confronted by was a text that had become 'common sense'. It circulated an antagonistic notion of communal relations in different contexts while reworking its meanings.

At stake was more than simply the tenacity of the preoccupation; it was an understanding of one of the primary sources of communal power — its ability to perpetually renew itself through the reiteration of stereotypes, without necessarily sounding repetitive. Moreover, although the relationship between different, stereotypical 'observations' seemed random, as say, the juxtaposition of Muslim fertility with either their superior sense of enterprise or their greater propensity for violence, the fact of their mutual proximity defined them as part of a network of meanings. They created a disposition that complemented an ideological line, without appearing to be interested. Their authority lay precisely in their sense of being a product of social·'good sense'.

Proximate to the phenomenon of common sense but not reducible to it, was the related objective of producing a collective Hindu

---

2 Shraddhanand said that U.N. Mukherji had also motivated him to start the Sangathan. *Amrita Bazar Patrika*, 17 June 1925.
3 J.F.T. Jordens, *Swami Sharaddhanand*, Delhi, 1981, p. 134.
4 Indra Prakash, *They Count Their Gains — We Calculate Our Losses*, New Delhi, 1979.

Self. As is apparent from the instances given, the demographic common sense functioned as a trope of extinction. This prospect was deployed like a prophecy, a warning that underlined the need to reform Hindu society in order to unify it. The growth of population and, in broader terms, social empowerment itself, could only be achieved by producing a single collective body of Hindus. Of special interest here is the fact that because of the permeable nature of common sense, that is, the way it so easily insinuates itself into different discourses and contexts, we are able to track the growth of Hindu communal thought on the subject of an alternative Hinduism, not in a single, definitive line of development, but as a multiplicity of discourses and ideological orientations. These proliferate within the parameters of recurrent themes, but what we get is the process of mutual borrowings, reorientations and contestations.

II

Summing up the effects of the census, Kenneth Jones states, 'Religions became communities mapped, counted, and above all compared with other religious communities.'[5] Although the next fruitful step would have been to consider the momentous importance of the census for communalism, Jones simply goes on to describe the census preoccupations of those seeking to produce a Hindu identity. However, evidence indicates that the census shaped communalism. H.H. Risley, Home Secretary, Government of India, who had proposed the partition of Bengal in 1903, speculated: 'Can the figures of the last census be regarded in any sense the forerunner of an Islamic or Christian revival which will threaten the citadel of Hinduism or will Hinduism hold its own in the future as it has done through the long ages of the past?'[6] Risley's comments were overdetermined by the 'calculations' made by O'Donnell, the census commissioner for 1891. On the basis of slower growth rates of Hindus, O'Donnell leapfrogged

---

[5] Kenneth Jones, 'Religious Identity and the Indian Census', in N.G. Barrier (ed.), *The Census in British India: New Perspectives*, New Delhi, 1981, p. 81.

[6] Cited in Lajpat Rai, 'The Depressed Classes', in Vijay Chandra Joshi (ed.), *Lala Lajpat Rai: Writings and Speeches, Vol. I, 1888–1919*, Delhi, 1966, p. 162.

across simple logic to deduce the number of years for Hindus to disappear altogether!⁷ Even as late as the 1911 Census, when it had become absolutely transparent that such speculations could arouse intense communal animosity, similar observations were made by officials.

A year earlier, an even more blatant act of colonial engineering had been proposed. E.A. Gait, the census commissioner, issued a circular proposing 'tests' to establish Hindu identity. These involved a fourfold query: whether the respondents worshipped the 'great Hindu gods'; if they were allowed entry into temples and permitted to make offerings to the shrine; whether the Brahmins who administered to them were 'degraded' or even recognized as Brahmins by their supposed caste members, and, finally, to what degree the respondents were untouchable. There was a sharp analytic acumen working here. The questions were designed to confirm both Brahminical exclusiveness as well as low-caste resentment of discrimination. They were designed to encourage the detachment of low castes from the 'Hindu' category, thereby isolating the upper castes who had threatened British power during the Swadeshi movement. Horrified, U.N. Mukherji observed in *Hinduism and the Coming Census*, that the tests: 'will break into two communities those that had hitherto been regarded as one'.[8]

The general impact of the census raises the question of the colonial origins of communalism. After what I have said, the answer seems foreclosed. But is it? Lucy Carroll has made a distinction between caste associations that sprung up to claim privileges before each census and withered away thereafter, and those which in their more permanent and evolving history, testified to more long-standing sources of collective aspirations.[9] Without elaborating the obvious answers as to whether there existed 'Hindu/Muslim' identities prior to colonialism, it may be observed that the census explains only the stabilization of these identities around new orientations (of the sort mentioned by

---

[7] *Census of India, 1891, Vol. III, Bengal*, C.A. O'Donnell (ed.), Calcutta, 1893.
[8] All citations to the Gait Circular are drawn from the appendix to U.N. Mukherji, *Hinduism and the Coming Census: Christianity and Hinduism*, Calcutta, 1911.
[9] Lucy Carroll, 'Colonial Perceptions of Indian Society and the Emergence of Caste(s) Associations', *Journal of Asian Studies*, vol. XXXVII, no. 2, Feb. 1978.

Jones), backed up by institutional facilities such as reserved educational and employment quotas. But it does not explain much of what the texts discussed below revealed: how, for instance, were relations of untouchability tackled by upper-caste representatives, especially the communalists. And, underlying this, the different responses to the census itself. Or, how the 'common sense' around the census became co-extensive with the encouragement of a communal world-view. It soon became clear that what these texts suggested was not an anthropologized history of collective affiliations, a stable, collective self that was inherited from an unchanging past or from an originative power-knowledge formation, but an unfamiliar ideological terrain that retained its marks of apparently improvised and dislocated growth.

Recently the idea of communities as monolithic has become current, drawing its influence from two apparently opposed notions. The paradox is illustrated by Gyanendra Pandey's recent book.[10] His thesis is framed by the notion of discrete communities, which were (mis)represented in colonial discourse. What we have here is an interlocking of two disparate assumptions: one, the colonial notion of pre-given communities that possess their internal histories. These discrete historical entities are seen as the 'truth' of these communities by Pandey. On the other hand, he also adheres to the colonial power-knowledge argument, by stating that these communities were stereotyped by colonialism. Pandey's entrapment by these two registers of colonial effects arises from his general assumption that communities are based on an inner logic.

It may be remarked that the larger point is missed, which is a specification of communalism itself. The specificity of the latter emerges only when it is placed in relationship with other ideas of community that grew up in reference to the census. This requires an understanding of communalism that sees it as an ideological field which is fraught with inner tensions, in which it wrestles with the claims of other collectivities. This involves inner conflict as communalism seeks to retain those elements of its constituency that threaten to defect to other claims. What we get then is a picture of communal identity formation as it is constantly engaged in the process of displacing or actively opposing the claims of other

---

[10] Gyanendra Pandey, *The Construction*.

identities. In short, the communal process has to be understood in its full movement between stabilization and dispersal.

III

U.N. Mukherji's main contribution, the ADR, was serialized in *The Bengalee* during the month of June in 1909, a period that found this paper in a communal temper.[11] It was published twice as a book in 1910 and sold at 4 annas, which was an easily affordable price for its English language readership. The author followed this up by writing the *Coming Census*, a Bengali translation of which he distributed 25,000 copies free of cost. Another 25,000 copies of a modified Bengali version of ADR called *Hindu Samaj*[12] were also distributed free.[13] The main criticism of Mukherji's thesis was launched by Sakharam Ganesh Deuskar, an important Extremist leader of the Swadeshi movement. But bigger fears blunted its edge. These had a double source. On the one hand, Ameer Ali's petition on behalf of the London branch of the All India Muslim League (made in the context of the Morley-Minto reforms of 1909),[14] called upon the authorities to effectively detach the lower castes as a bloc from the category of Hindus. On the other hand, increasing demands were made by influential sections of the so-called Backward Castes for autonomous and preferential treatment.[15] It was, therefore, a sign of the times that Mukherji was invited to guide a specially constituted 'Social Conference' of the Provincial Congress in 1911.[16]

Moreover, the debate on the census was acquiring a nation-wide importance. It had started featuring as a public issue in Punjab

---

[11] *Bengalee* carried daily reports on the Titagarh riots which had occurred in January 1909. Further, it campaigned against Ameer Ali's petition (see below). It also published serialized articles on Hinduism.

[12] U.N. Mukherji, *Hindu Samaj*, Calcutta, 1910.

[13] I have taken these figures from Deuskar (publication details given below). Papia Chakravarty provides contradictory figures. The latter claims that 50,000 copies of *Hindu Samaj* were distributed free. *Hindu Responses to Nationalist Ferment*, Calcutta, 1992, p. 32. I have opted for Deuskar's figures, since they seem more in keeping with Mukherji's practical disposition.

[14] Cited in Chakravarty, *Hindu Responses*, p. 44.

[15] Sekhar Bandopadhyaya, *Social Mobility in Bengal in the Late 19th and Early 20th Centuries*, Ph.D. Thesis, Calcutta University, 1985, p. 401.

[16] Ibid., p. 424.

since the previous century. But the appearance of Lajpat Rai's 'The Depressed Classes' in *The Modern Review* in July 1909 — barely a month after the publication of ADR — provided a sense of shared concern, not least because Rai advocated similar recommendations. More importantly, the census concern marked the beginning of a relationship between the communal politics of the two provinces, that was to acquire a common organizational structure in the twenties.

Given the importance of the ADR, it would be useful to start with a brief summary. Proceeding from O'Donnell's warning cited above, Mukherji asserts that the fundamental cause for the decline of Hindu numbers was due to the poverty of their peasantry. Conversely, the Muslim peasants were buying up land. In Calcutta, the labour market and petty artisanal enterprises were being taken over by immigrants, since Hindus (implying the Bengali variant) were prevented by caste rules from changing their inherited occupations and competing with them. Muslim immigrants were religious, hard-working and ate well; Hindu low castes drank liquor, were unkempt and lazy.

Mukherji proceeds to contrast singular English and Hindu societies. The latter was characterized by immense gradations of caste. In contrast, social classes in England were bonded by sharing the same feelings on common occasions provided by sports, war and Church activities. This accounted for the overwhelming organizational power possessed by their society. Islam had also produced a sense of commonness through masjid congregations. As a matter of fact, their reform movements of the 19th century were responsible for both their ability to acquire wealth, as well as for their unity under British rule. Hindus however faced disaster from three sources: Morley's equivocating reply to Ameer Ali's petition; the pulverization of Bengali industry by the British; and, now, dispossession of land by Muslims. The cause of their helplessness, Mukherji reiterates, lay in their caste exclusiveness.[17]

The fulcrum of the argument rests on inversion; disunity and accompanying lassitude is contrasted with vigour and unity. Interestingly, while two Others are deployed to provide inverted models for Hindus, the English is displaced by the Muslim. This slide is

---

[17] I have consulted U.N. Mukherji's serialized articles on 'A Dying Race' in the *Bengalee*, June 1909. All citations are drawn from here.

crucial. England presents an awesome prospect. Englishmen 'had reduced the art of making money into something like an exact science, [being] men in possession of every possible information . . . with all the advantages that capital and combination could secure . . .'. The tone is lyrical. Figures of completion abound: 'Hundreds of years', 'exact', 'every', 'all'. The English may have provided a model, but the lyricism also confessed to the impossibility of attaining it. Hindus could not match the investment in either capital or knowledge.

There is a feeling of disenchantment here. In the years preceding 1909, the prospect of rivalling British industry (in addition to elements of its administrative machinery, such as the Swadeshi arbitration courts that had tried to provide an alternative to the judiciary) had enthused the Swadeshi movement. But it was becoming clear by 1908 that all these initiatives were collapsing.[18] Yet nationalism had not lost its sense of outrage. Mukherji declares: 'If ever there was an unequal fight it was this'. The Swadeshi movement had left anger in addition to disenchantment, making it doubly impossible to regard the English as a model.

But the shutting out of one possibility opens out another: 'There is nothing in the laws that specially affects the Hindus unfavourably', Mukherji states, adding: 'The superiority of the . . . Mohammedans is entirely due to their religious revival and systematic moral training . . . .' The contrast here is absolutely crucial: England as a model is unattainable because it is a different country; the Muslims are a viable model because they belong to the same country and to the same conditions. If the latter could attain their power in these circumstances, then Hindus, too, could follow suit by reforming themselves. What is interesting is the compulsion to make the Muslim into a model. Mukherji does not specify how the Muslims had suffered under colonialism: his argument *needs* the superiority of the Muslims to be unalloyed by any consideration of disabilities, in order for his model to be an emulative one. Mukherji's assumption here is that power can be acquired in a situation of colonial supremacy simply by controlling one's subjectivity.

But England and Islam are not equivalent. The construction of Muslims as the prime antagonist of Hindus involves an alternative

[18] See Sumit Sarkar, *The Swadeshi Movement in Bengal 1903–1908*, New Delhi, 1973, pp. 135–6.

path of ideological and political activity. The core of this was contained in the area of religion. It was a sphere that had been 'guaranteed' by Queen Victoria's Proclamation of 1858, to be autonomous of the administration. This 'freedom' was referred to by all parties as a kind of Directive Principle, and it encouraged a vast range of initiatives for the production of a society autonomous of the colonial dispensation. During the popular mobilization for the Swadeshi movement the autonomous space had expanded to a notion of 'Society'. Tagore distinguished between 'rashtra' and 'samaj', identifying the latter as the province for independent enterprise. The defeat of Swadeshi naturally shrank the domain of this autonomy. It was this limited area that Mukherji appears to be addressing through the model of Islamic reform movements. The latter offers an alternative path of self-development through the sphere of religion. This had certain advantages. Self-reform needed no movement against a powerful colonial presence but could be carried out on an everyday basis.

Mukherji depicts the locus of the Islamic renaissance as the village masjid. Every Friday, prayers were followed by a *waz* or an address by a preacher which consisted of 'simple morality, simply told'. All this, it is reiterated, was done independent of any central organization. The greatest contribution of Islamic Reform movements, according to this representation, lies in producing the drive to self-organization and autonomy.

It should be remarked here that Mukherji skirts the borders of stereotyping. His picture of an integrated, grassroots monolith of Islam, is close to the stereotype of Islamic 'fanaticism'. More immediately, this image is derived from a famous passage in Hunter's history, which our author approvingly cites.[19] But it would be self-defeating for Mukherji to identify his argument with the stereotypical, for the latter denotes final, ontological conditions. On the other hand, the object of self-reform involves change. Mukherji thus carries out a more subtle exercise. He appropriates the weight of antagonism that stereotypes offer, while orienting these to the object of reform.

---

[19] In the citation of Hunter made by Mukherji in ADR, the former states how Muslims were no better than 'circumcised low caste Hindus', who had become dangerous after their reform movements, since Islamic 'first principle' means 'a religion of intolerance and aggression', part XVIII, *Bengalee*, 25 June 1909.

On the basis of his 'observations', Mukherji asserts that the cause of Muslim proliferation lay in the desire of Hindu widows for Muslim males. It is a claim that recalls the project of nineteenth-century Hindu reformers of widow remarriage who had put forward the untrammeled sexuality of the widow as an argument for their remarriage.[20] But, in a significant shift, Mukherji alters the proposed object of the change. Instead of putting the main emphasis on the reform of the widow's condition, Mukherji focuses on the need to reform the Hindu male's condition, so that the latter feels motivated to prevent widows from escaping the folds of the Hindu community. Unable to afford remarriage, Hindu peasants were powerless to prevent the proliferation of widows. This shift allows him to reorient the reformist concerns of the nineteenth century to the path of economic reform. Further, he claims that Muslim wealth gave to them a 'superior physique'. This argument enables Mukherji to harness the anxious energy generated by sexual stereotypes of the potent Muslim and effete Hindu to a condition which, since the Drain-of-Wealth theory, had been recognized as man-made and remediable.

There is a sub-text of Social Darwinism here, which condemns collectivities to eternal competition. Within this scheme, the Muslim has a double and complementary function. He is a threat to the continued existence of Hindus as well as a figure of aspiration. Mukherji's strategy is to make the superiority of Muslims a spur to defeat their silent machinations by self-reform. The encoding of hopeful expectations within fear provides a powerful world-view. It is a structure of expectations that was attractive not only for catering to the diminished possibilities of its time but, equally important, also for re-inscribing immediate political and social challenges.

Let me begin with one already touched upon, namely, the utility of the Muslim in providing a release from the cul-de-sac scenario at the end of the Swadeshi movement. Concerns that were integral to it, such as economic self-reliance, the cultivation of the body, organization through faith, could now be revived in this encounter with the new domestic enemy. Of course, the space for initiatives

[20] See, for instance, Mahesh Chandra Deb. For him however, the resultant evil was that of infanticide (of illegitimate offsprings), not flight to a Muslim. 'A Sketch of the Condition of Hindoo Women', *Awakening in Bengal in Early Nineteenth Century (Selected Documents), Vol. 1*, Gautam Chattopadhyaya (ed.), Calcutta, 1965, p. 104.

on these lines had attenuated after Swadeshi but, in the context of a perceived lack of alternatives, the figure of the Muslim becomes even more precious. Secondly, there was the problem of a shift in the linguistic composition of Calcutta's population. Mukherji's figures indicate that Muslims formed only a part of the overall deluge.[21] Because Mukherji does not elaborate this observation, the chauvinistic anxiety produced by a declining proportion of Bengalis, is relocated in the Muslim. Finally and most significantly, the Hindu's condition is signified overwhelmingly by the low castes. This has much larger consequences than the relatively straightforward one of displacement. It needs separate consideration.

IV

Mukherji's representation of the low-caste condition inverts that of the idealized Muslim. Consider the following characterization of the low-caste Bagdi as 'eternally poor . . . lazy, thriftless, unreliable'. Thus: 'There is no object for which they can unite . . . ', nor can they resist the hegemony of the Brahmins who decide untouchability rules. Low-caste movements for self-assertion, such as the ones launched by Vaishnavs and Kartabhajas, are absorbed by Brahminism. They assert their superiority over those lower in the hierarchy, increasing the centrifugal tendency amongst themselves as a whole.

Interestingly, Mukherji dismisses caste associations as forces militating against Hindu unity, indicating thereby, a bias against them for remaining outside the pale of Brahminical appropriation. He does not consider their Improvement ideology, their growing prosperity and a commitment to combination, or anti-Brahminism — all of which characterized the powerful Namasudra movement, for instance.[22] Ironically these are some of the attributes he

[21] It shows that the population profile of Calcutta had 1 Bengali Hindu to 25 Bengali Muslims and 100 upcountrymen, without including the Chinese, Marwaris etc. . . . The Census states that out of a total of 949,144 persons in Calcutta and its suburbs, 615,419 were Hindus and 286,576 Muslims. The majority of the population (about 68.1 per cent) were immigrants. But 52.2 per cent came from Bengal itself. J.R. Blackwood, *Census of India, 1901, Calcutta, Town and Suburbs*, vol. VII, part IV, Calcutta, 1902. Obviously neither set of figures could service Mukherji's arguments.
[22] Sekhar Bandopadhyaya shows how the Namasudras started taking to settled agriculture and profitable occupations in the nineteenth century. In

recognizes as worthy of emulation in the Muslims. He cannot, however, admit the value of caste associations, since it would irreparably damage his framework of Hindu unity. There was an inner, driving necessity to create this image of low-caste dependency.

His framework of comparing the Muslim peasant with low castes, saves Mukherji from having to refer to upper-caste conditions. The visible social and economic privileges of the former would have disastrously complicated the master metaphor of impending death for all Hindus. On the other hand, it permits Mukherji to make outrageously false assertions, such as the claim that Muslims were more advanced in education than Hindus! But there was an even more productive implication. The relationship between the low castes and Muslims was complicated. Prospects for an alliance were counterbalanced by indications of antagonism which became pronounced in the years that immediately followed the publication of this pamphlet.[23] Mukherji's framework of comparison, given the role the Muslim played in his thought, was designed to encourage the growth of the second tendency. Thus, although Mukherji mentions the attack on the Rajbansis in the 1907 riots, he suppresses the antagonism articulated against the upper-caste Swadeshi volunteers by low castes. On one occasion, Namasudra organizations had even proclaimed loyalty to the Crown![24]

V

Antagonism against Muslims, however, was not perceived as a sufficient condition for the integration of Hindus. Equally, Hindu society itself had to be restructured. This preoccupation had a long lineage. The key imperative was taken from Vivekananda (who was Mukherji's direct predecessor in thinking out ways of producing an integrated Hindu society). It concerned egalitarianism.

---

the latter half of that century, Guruchand, their ideologue and leader, produced an anti-Brahmanical ideology committed to self-improvement, 'Social Mobility in Bengal'.

[23] Namasudras and Muslims engaged in mutual rioting at Khulna in 1889. Bigger riots between them broke out in 1911, 1923–5 and 1938. In 1908 however, they made common cause against the upper castes, being politically aligned in their opposition against the Swadeshi movement. Bandopadhyaya, ibid., pp. 345–8.

[24] Cited in Bandopadhyaya, ibid., pp. 356–7.

With Vivekananda, Mukherji shared an attenuated definition of egalitarianism as denoting the suspension of untouchability — although it should be added here that Mukherji lacked Vivekananda's profound discomfort with upper-caste discrimination.[25] Nevertheless, Mukherji recommended the same institutional solution of education. It may be remarked that the suspension of untouchability demanded spatial intimacy. And it was this prerequisite that made education (with its sharing of space between the teacher and the taught) of the low castes an essential recommendation. But what was also possible to see in Mukherji's analysis were two other ideas that drove his vision of Hindu society as a gigantic pedagogic enterprise.

The first concerned the Brahmins whose importance exceeded their role as traditional educators. They also produced the self-image of the low castes. For instance, a low caste had to prostrate 'himself like a log of wood whenever he saw a Brahmin'. This, Mukherji argues, was responsible for their low self-esteem which, in turn, caused immorality to flourish and motivation to success, flounder. However, because Brahmins were themselves internally divided by region and sub-classifications such as *gotras*, they had become irresponsible. 'He [the Brahmin] claims superiority over all, but admits of no obligation or duty to any', admonishes Mukherji. Clearly, his strategy was not to question Brahmanical supremacy. On the contrary, he identifies the latter as a resource that needs to be utilized by Brahmins themselves.

It may be remarked that there were many roles devised for Brahmins in this period, all of which were posited on the need to make them the active vanguard of society. As stated, Mukherji followed Vivekananda in suggesting an extension of the pedagogic role of Brahmins. Unlike Vivekananda, however, Mukherji did not strike a utopian note. While emphasizing the inherited caste identity of Brahmins, Vivekananda also argued for Brahminhood as an

---

[25] While upholding an integrationist view of caste relations, Vivekananda also proclaimed that 'a time will come, when the Shudra of every country, with their inborn Shudra nature and habits — not becoming in essence Vaishya or Kshatriya [types of the financier and warrior respectively], but remaining as Shudra — will gain absolute supremacy in every society'. He beheld its prefigurement in socialism, anarchism and nihilism. 'Modern India' (translated from a Bengali contribution to the *Udbodhan*, March 1899), Swami Vivekananda, *Complete Works*, vol. IV, pp. 468–9.

ideal that must be realized by all.[26] Mukherji avoids making distinctions between the ideal and social meanings of Brahminism, protecting, thereby, the inherited preserve of Brahmins. But it also allows him to offer a more ambitious plan. By calling for the education of all castes by the Brahmins, Mukherji proposes a broader vista of hegemonizing low castes directly without losing their caste identity.

At the same time, Mukherji's greater preoccupation with education *per se*, allows him to move away from Brahmin exclusivism. In *Hindu Samaj*, published a year and a half after ADR, Mukherji begins to consider the whole of educated Bengali society as his vanguard, which, in effect, meant mobilizing the entire upper-caste Bhadralok. However, the shift away from Brahminism was incomplete, for, as we will see below, he valorized institutions that were traditionally associated with Brahmanical learning.

Paradoxically, while education allows for the reconstitution of social hierarchy, it also allows for egalitarianism. The prospect of Brahmins/upper castes teaching lower orders would break spatial taboos, thereby preparing the grounds for equal access to shared space, which is an important aspect of egalitarianism. But there is also another implication. Mukherji's word for pedagogy is 'training'. 'A trained man is superior to a man who is not trained', he declares. What he has in mind is a militarized society which reproduces a sameness of subjectivity. It is this ideal of sameness (as sharing) that had marked the picture of England and post-Reform Islam. It is realized in his model of pedagogy provided by the German *Volkschule*, which compulsorily removes 'differences between untouchable or respectable, rich or poor amongst the boys and girls . . . [since they possess] the same book, the same education, the same rules'.[27]

But there was also a new sensitivity to the question of pluralism in *Hindu Samaj*. Despite the greater imaginative stimulus offered by the prospect of sameness, he expresses a preference for the

---

[26] Vivekananda proclaimed that, 'the whole work is to raise the Chandal up to the Brahmin [ideal]'. Vivekananda warned that the process must be gradual. 'The Future of India', *Complete Works*, vol. III, p. 295. I should add here that there were others who envisioned a crucial role for Brahmins as 'disinterested intellectual leaders'. These included Satishchandra Mukherji and the Rabindranath Tagore of the Swadeshi period. The latter changed his views considerably after 1907. Sarkar, *Swadeshi*, p. 107.

[27] Mukherji, *Hindu Samaj*, p. 9.

relatively differentiated educational system of England because it allowed for the variations of denominational education. This model of Mukherji's is accompanied serendipitously with a patriotic imperative. He recommends internalizing this system through reformed *Tols* which would shed their Brahmanical exclusiveness.

The discrepancy between the worship of sameness and the invocation of pluralism pointed to a structural problem in the construction of a new Hindu society. This was posed in its starkest form in the pamphlet that Mukherji wrote after ADR.

VI

The prescriptions of the ADR assumed that there would be time to consolidate an integrated Hindu society: the latter faced only threats and apprehensions of a cleavage. By 1910 the comfort was over. The Gait Circular, released that year, posed an immediate challenge. The desperation that Mukherji felt was expressed in a major shift in his approach. In *Coming Census*, Mukherji relinquished the competitive framework of relationship with an Other based on the ideal of Sameness and Organization. Instead, *Coming Census* celebrates and valorizes difference with the Other.

There is only a single Other of Hinduism in *Coming Census*, which is Christianity (elided quite easily with England). This is obviously dictated by the need to address his arguments to the colonial authorities. However, there is no real qualitative distinction in Mukherji's treatment of the Christian and the Islamic, in so far as both are made to signify a similar social structure. In *Coming Census*, Mukherji reiterates his characterization of England with a major shift in methodological assumptions: he now deals with the normative rather than the observational. He asserts that the church is riven with differences between sects and schools. Despite this, 'All of them have one thing in common, they are all organizations.'

In contrast, Hindus are not only internally differentiated, but also, this condition derives from an idealization of pluralism. For one, there is no central authority; a Brahmin, according to Mukherji here, has no dictatorial powers since he is not ordained; nor is there any central ecclesiastical authority. In fact, there can never be a centralized authority because of the norm of pluralism. Most Hindus, argues Mukherji, call themselves *Pancha Dewata Upashak*, that is, followers of five gods. Thus no Hindu is pitted against his fellow by sectarian intolerance.

Mukherji affirms the *status quo* here. Hinduism is effectively portrayed as a utopia where problems of power are absent. It is a system that possesses 'belief without authority'. The idealization of the pluralism of beliefs allows Mukherji to conceal the asymmetries of caste relations. Untouchability is itself justified by translating it into a relationship of hygiene. Mukherji claims that a Brahmin draws water with his own *lota* (metal mug) instead of employing a low caste, because of sanitary precautions.

The basic concept that Mukherji draws upon is that of *adhikar bheda*, the orthodox idea which claims that every doctrinal path is equally valid, since all lead ultimately to the goal of realization. This concept was a rich one since it legitimized not only the plurality of doctrinal worship, but also caste differences. Of profound importance was the turn that Vivekananda had given to it. Vivekananda needed a sense of temporal purposiveness that was an essential precondition of organizing Hindus as a collectivity. Consequently, he integrated adhikar bheda with a theory of stages. Each religious path was seen as a stage in the development towards self-realization, a strategy that combined teleology with an additive structure, so that no path, whether of renunciation or social activity would be lost.[28]

Clearly, Mukherji turned away from this reconciliation of pluralism with organized purposiveness. The reason lay in his compulsion to justify the lack of definitiveness in actually existing Hinduism. He could ideologically preempt the separation of low castes, by showing them to be constitutive of the structure of internal differentiation that defined Hinduism itself. But the very nature of this contingency throws light on a deep structural problem that underlay the Hindu communal project. The invocation of variety as a normative principle could not neutralize the actual social contradictions that intensified when social groups constituting the full range of differences among Hindus were brought together. The principle of variety could only legitimize

---

[28] The most comprehensive exposition of this is to be found in his essay 'Bhakti Yoga', where he distinguishes between two broad stages (with many sub-stages in between). These are 'preparatory Bhakti' (associated with the worship of personal gods/symbols in which the Ultimate is seen to be incarnated), and 'Para Bhakti or supreme devotion' *Complete Works*, vol. III.

such divisions; it could not resolve them. Hindu communalism not only failed to mobilize the low castes, but remained plagued by other internal differences.

The imperative of unity meant that the principle of variety existed in constant tension with the need to give Hinduism a single, obsessive focus. Consequently, Hindu communal thinking could not do without fear and desire of the Other. The most impressive testament of this is offered by *Coming Census* itself which provides, as we have seen, the most 'liberal' statement of a Hindu communal thinker. While explaining the reasons for Hindu pluralism, Mukherji curiously supplies negative reasons. As contrasted to the English, he argues, Hinduism had a huge population that was not serviced by education. This was the result of Muslim domination for seven centuries. Hinduism had lain 'fallow' in that period. Education, the centralized power of State control, the 'fallen' state of Hinduism: all that was articulated in ADR and suppressed in the dominant argument of this text, comes out to assert the importance of making a monolithic Hinduism, demonstrating thereby — from a different path — the criticality of the contradiction between unification and pluralism that Mukherji faced and bequeathed to his followers.

We shall have the opportunity to see the unfolding of this contradiction later. Meanwhile, our original starting point — that is, of the overtly communal response to the census — needs to be considered. The next step in its evolution is a critique of the ADR.

VII

By 1910, the year he wrote his critique of ADR, Sakharam Ganesh Deuskar was already, unlike U.N. Mukherji, his antagonist, a highly revered leader. In 1905, this domiciled Maharashtrian introduced the Shivaji Utsav (a festival started by Tilak, which had mobilized Hindus against colonial rule at the cost of alienating the Muslims) in Bengal, following this up with authorship of *Desher Katha*, an indictment of British rule that became a standard reference book for Swadeshi activists. Deuskar's pamphlet, *Bangiya Hindujati Ki Dhangshanmukh?* (Are Hindus Heading Towards Destruction ?), was written as a rigorous statistical and political critique of ADR.[29]

[29] Sakharam Ganesh Deuskar, *Bangiya Hindujati Ki Dhangshanmukhe?*,

Deuskar admits that while the Hindus grew slowly during 1872–81 (by 3.65 lakhs), the Muslims increased at a greater rate (by 5.18 lakhs). However, between 1891–1901 Hindu numbers accelerated. These figures refuted Mukherji's claims, since both caste structure and the level of poverty remained constant during the period of accelerated growth. Alternatively, Deuskar traces the 'fallowness' of the 1871–81 period to the ravages of malaria. Even more effective is Deuskar's implication that Mukherji was deliberately whipping up anxiety. Deuskar underlines the fact that Mukherji did not specify O'Donnell's calculation that it would take a lengthy 650 years for the Hindus to disappear altogether: a figure that would not harmonize with the prospect of their immediate disappearance that ADR paints. Further, instead of an incidence of 232 per thousand for numbers of educated Hindu *muchis* (cobblers), Mukherji derived a paltry 8 per thousand.

Deuskar also offers an alternate set of reasons for the slower growth rate of Hindus. The important ones include the prohibition on widow remarriage, which was spreading to the Sanskritizing low castes. There was also a cultural cause, inasmuch as 'Bengalis' had declined physically because of westernization. The problem with these explanations is that the discourse of rigorous statistical explication and the more speculative one of causative factors, do not coalesce. Except possibly for one that concerns the prohibition on widow remarriage, and that is discussed with a measure of empirical persuasiveness by Mukherji. On the other hand, the East-West schema Deuskar offers as explanation involves such an abrupt switch from the physical to the cultural (without the mediations that Mukherji makes), that it seems more an excuse than an explanation.

Deuskar's critique represents a paradox. Its rigour played a valuable role in highlighting, by implicit contrast, the series of displacements and suppressions that advanced Mukherji's argument. On the other hand, these absences are also part of the reason for Mukherji's effectiveness. They allow his argument to call for fundamental changes, while permitting it to avoid questions that could imply internal social dislocations or threats to privilege. In fact, the looseness of Mukherji's argument defines it less as a foray

---

Calcutta, 1910. Other details are provided by Chakravarty, *Hindu Responses*, p. 35.

into the art of making logical and empirically verifiable statements, than as a network that orchestrates (and suppresses) key concerns of an emerging Hindu communal constituency. Its value is highlighted by its flexibility, which allows it, like a magnet passing through metal filings, to draw in various kinds of discourses that had become part of the common sense of the Swadeshi movement, into another seemingly coherent stream of argumentation, so that an alternate world-view can be produced, fattening itself on the traces of older ones. An identity emerges then, not as simple nomenclature alone, but as a many-faceted 'world', where a network of causality is comprehensive enough to link, for instance, economic problems with those of religious reform. Moreover this is accomplished without surrendering the major source of popular energy for the production of such communities, that is, of stereotypes. We have seen how the model of inverted characteristics exacerbates the load of anxiety, while the careful avoidance of ontological fixity paves a credible path for reformist desire to fulfill itself. But this does not move the vision away from the parameters of stereotyping. In fact, it makes stereotypes sophisticated and flexible, enlarging them so that they can conjure up a world-view. Ultimately, ADR leaves the reader with a pictorial evocation: a dying (low-caste) Hindu, self-divided and physically weak, surrounded by an already overwhelming and progressively expanding numbers of Muslims, who, in their self-engineered growth, suck out the life-blood of their rivals. A contest between two bodies, two personalities, two societies, two histories.

VIII

The specific analysis of the census in ADR does not appear to have exercised a major influence. It was Deuskar's critique of the analytic basis of Mukherji's claims that was possibly responsible for this. On the other hand, the census became a popular reference point and featured in conjunction with many of the concerns that were broached by the ADR. The detachment of the census from the arguments advanced in the ADR, can be seen in the concerns of *Hindu Samaj*, which, even while featuring the census at its commencement does not link up with the rest of ADR. The growing autonomy of the concern with the census had, as we will see, enormously productive consequences for Hindu communalism.

Henceforth, it developed its own history, entering into varied relationships with ideas that did not apparently have much to do with it. A good place to begin an understanding of its ambivalent development is Digindranarayan Bhattacharya's work.

Interestingly, U.N. Mukherji was Bhattacharya's mentor. Mukherji penned a highly laudatory 'Preface' to the most important work of Bhattacharya, *Jatibhed*.[30] The author of ADR had emerged as an authority on caste relations. After the withdrawal of the Gait Circular, he was invited to address the United Bengal Provincial Congress held at Faridpur in 1911, 'to improve the status of the Namasudras and other "depressed classes" and to bring them into the fold of organized Hinduism'.[31] Further, Mukherji went on to build a network of contacts with low-caste leaders, especially with Damodar Das, a representative of the Mali caste.[32] Bhattacharya also belonged to this network, but went beyond the limits set by Mukherji. Although there are traces of communal competition in *Jatibhed*, the invocation of an external Other is not crucial to Bhattacharya's argument, for it really focuses on caste oppression.

Jatibhed received acclaim from people like Tagore, Sir Surendranath Banerjea, Sir P.C. Ray and even Swami Shraddhanand. A reason for the consensus among Calcutta's *haute intelligentsia* can be found in the general lessening of upper-caste apprehensions about Muslims. The withdrawal of the Gait Circular was succeeded by the reunification of Bengal in 1911. At the same time, communalized Muslim leaders like Ameer Ali were displaced by young, anti-British ones epitomized by Fazlul Huq. The latter sought to come closer to the Congress. This trend was to crystallize in the Lucknow Pact of 1916 and culminate in the Non-Cooperation/ Khilafat movement. The increasing companionability in communal relations was not, however, accompanied by a cementing of relations between the two caste blocs. Namasudra demands for de-classifying themselves from the Hindus remained, while the announcement of the Montagu-Chelmsford Committee to study reforms triggered off demands for separate electorates.[33]

---

[30] Digindranarayan Bhattacharya, *Jatibhed*, Faridpur, 1912. Citations and references are drawn from this edition.
[31] Bandopadhayaya, *Social Mobility*, p. 424.
[32] Manindranath Mandal, *Bangiya Jana Sangha*, [Bengali Peoples Association], Khajuri village, Midnapore, 1923.
[33] Bandopadhyaya, *Social Mobility*, pp. 234, 460.

However, an equally important reason for the general commendation of *Jatibhed* was that it gave to the voice of reform a substantial rural identity. For instance, Mukherji's attitude to the rural low castes is managerial; distanced. He claims authority on the basis of 'objective' knowledge of an urban upper-caste observer. Bhattacharya's tone, by contrast, is that of a person in the thick of battle. Maybe this difference had something to do with their lives. While Mukherji belonged to the upper echelons of Anglicized Calcutta Bhadralok society, being a son-in-law of Sir Surendranath Banerjea and a member of the Indian Medical Service, Bhattacharya hailed from Serajgunj, a small town in Pabna district, and belonged to a Vaishnav family that traced its lineage to an associate of Chaitanya himself. He remained an organic intellectual, choosing to work in the interiors, addressing meetings and engaging in reform work.

At this level, he could be regarded as a vector through whom the urban reformer intellectuals could establish a connection with the rural intelligentsia. But there was a more important contribution he made to a long-standing process of the construction of a Hindu society. It was Vivekananda who marked a crucial shift in the history of the discourse on Hindu society, by subordinating the imperative of reform to the importance of integrating Hindu society.[34] He sought to 'develop', rather than reform Hinduism. What possibly prompted Vivekananda was the fate of the Brahmo Samaj, whose radical critique of Hinduism led to its marginalization. By the first decade of the century, a crisis — possibly stemming from a sense of alienation — appears to have gripped the reformers themselves. Many Brahmos began turning to Vaishnavism. Vivekananda had himself been a member of the Sadharan Brahmo Samaj. The implicit relationship of mass nationalism with Hinduism possibly intensified the migration. Bepin Chandra Pal, the extremist, moved away from Brahmo belief in *Nirakar*, the attributeless absolute, to writing treatises on the importance of symbolism.[35] Possibly the

---

[34] Vivekananda proclaimed, 'I do not believe in reform; I believe in growth'. He reinforces this assertion with a refusal to interfere with objects of reform, thereby ironically coming up with a status quoist belief: 'This wonderful national machine has worked through the ages.... Who dares to say whether it is good and how it shall move?', 'My Plan of Campaign', *Complete Works*, vol. III, p. 214.

[35] Pal believed that the turn to anchoring Brahmo Samaj in Hindutva

most celebrated convert was Bejoy Krishna Goswami, whose Vaishnavism influenced many important leaders including Pal, Ashwini Kumar Dutt, Satis Chandra Chatterjee and Manoranjan Guhathakurta. It may also be remarked that Chittaranjan Das was a Brahmo before turning to Vaishnavism.

Vaishnavism has a latent anti-caste component that offers the potentiality of translating reformist imperatives into popular belief. Bhattacharya used this potentiality. He was a Vaishnav who reformulated the basic tenets of his religion, so that reform spoke from its heart. It was this achievement which, among other things, accounted for his popularity amongst urban intellectuals. He opened up a possibility which promised to dispense with the schismatic character of reformism. There was no need for renunciation of belief, an act that could not escape the taint of division. There was only addition and reorientation.

Yet his ideas did not find lasting acceptance. Possibly he went too far. By engaging in actual reformist intervention, Bhattacharya transgressed the limits of upper-caste activism. However, the main area of Bhattacharya's reform activism, like that of Vivekananda's, remained the production of texts. This followed from Vivekananda's privileging of consciousness raising.[36] But Vivekananda, and later, Mukherji, wrote texts *on* the low castes; they assumed that it was primarily the upper-caste elite who needed to reform its attitudes. On the other hand, Bhattacharya wrote texts *for* the low castes. According to *Banger Digindranarayan*,[37] a biography authored by Manindranath Mandal, a low-caste leader, Bhattacharya had penned twenty books. Mandal claims that these texts had inspired the low castes to demand their rights.

Bhattacharya not only broadcast the Vedas in a popular form, but also provided necessary scriptural information to enable low castes to officiate as *purohits* (priests) for their neighbours.[38] At the same time he wrote origin myths for different castes, a textual procedure that was an essential ideological resource for castes

---

came with Debendranath Tagore. He was fully supportive of this development, seeing it as fundamental to the growth of nationalism. B.C. Pal, 'Shekaler Hindu Bhav O Swadeshikata', *Nabajuger Bangla*, Calcutta, 1964.

[36] Vivekananda, *The Complete Works*, vol. III, p. 214.

[37] Manindranath Mandal, *Banger Digindranarayan*, Calcutta, 1333[1926].

[38] Digindranarayan Bhattacharya, *Shudrer Puja O Vedadhikar*, Serajgunj, 1331[1924], f.pub. 1915, was written to educate the Shudras about the Vedas.

seeking to improve their status. Unlike Mukherji, Bhattacharya stimulated low-caste initiatives. Mukherji's investment in Brahmanical leadership was so strong that when Mandal, who was forming a platform of low-caste organizations called Bangiya Jana Sangha [hereafter BJS], approached U.N. Mukherji for help, the latter refused.[39] In contrast, Bhattacharya had no inhibitions in helping out when he was approached.

Mandal was a low-caste leader who subscribed to the key tenets of Vivekananda's Hindu integrationism. He belonged to the Pods, a caste which, although numerous, was not as organized as the Mahishyas and Namasudras. This probably attracted them more to the idea of a low-caste bloc in the first place.[40] The fact that he opts for Vivekananda's prescriptions points to a strategy of preemptive resistance against possible domination by any single group that would naturally arise in any organized low-caste bloc. Only an ideology which was not identifiable with any particular caste could operate as a common reference point, being equidistant from all low castes.

Nevertheless, anti-upper-caste attitudes remained too powerful to allow easy integration into Vivekananda's schema. Consequently, Mandal was left addressing two sets of readers. Writing in the *Nabyabharat*, he invokes Vivekananda, appeals to upper-caste conscience while reassuring them that low castes wanted neither separation nor a jettisoning of merit as a criteria for employment (which remains a powerful appeal by upper castes against reservations, even today). In *Namasudra Hitaishi* he stretches Vivekananda's assertions to a point where they become unrecognizable. For instance, he demands that low castes should be *given immediate* recognition as Brahmins, whereas Vivekananda had proposed that the inferior low castes needed to 'develop' themselves to earn Brahminhood. Sometimes Mandal becomes threatening when, for instance, he talks of emulating the Muslim League.

Bhattacharya's approach allowed too much latitude to the objects of his reform to serve the purpose of Hindu integrationism.

---

[39]Mandal informs us that he initiated a meeting of representatives of Namasudras, Rajbanasis, Poundra Khattriyas, Jhalla Mallas (Khattriya), Sahas and Malis among others, at Calcutta in February 1922. It was decided to start an umbrella organization of the low castes. Mandal dedicated his pamphlet to the latter. *Bangiya . . .* , p. 2.

[40] I owe this point to Sumit Sarkar.

Consequently he attracted intense criticism — a possibility that Vivekananda had continuously warned against. The virulence of orthodox reaction can be gauged from the fact that a pupil of Bhattacharya was ready to flout the norms of reverence due to a Guru in order to publicly criticise him.[41] Consequently, after the initial accolades, he remained at the margins of the HMS leadership, not hesitating to express his dissent at many points.

Although Bhattacharya privileged reform over integrationism, he did not completely exclude the latter imperative. Its importance was acknowledged through a remarkably influential suggestion. We may recall the significance Mukherji attached to the institutionalization of certain privileged spots of space and time (such as the waz) for sameness. Bhattacharya offered a more credible institutional suggestion. 'Everyone should become a part of a single life, a common mind. Let the sweet sounds of *harikirtan* enhance villages each evening', exhorts Bhattacharya. What he proposed was the Gaudiya Vaishnav institution of the *Kirtan*, which involved a daily congregation built around music. Kirtan provides a rooting in popular, rustic culture as well as opportunities for routinely overcoming caste barriers for a limited period. The implications of this suggestion seem even more profound when we consider that the identification of Hinduism with music later became an imperative condition for the proclamation of Hindu communal rights.

To return to a concern struck earlier, Bhattacharya's marginalization also problematizes the evident meanings of variety and sameness. Although he acknowledged the importance of variety, he was overwhelmingly preoccupied with caste egalitarianism. Yet, paradoxically, despite the singleness of focus, he inspired a much greater variety of thought among his admirers. This was in sharp and ironic contrast to both Vivekananda and Mukherji, both of whom valorized variety. They indicate the possibility that the invocation of pluralism and variety could be used to suppress the question of social asymmetries. It was not a coincidence that their versions of pluralism did not embrace the idea of internal contestation. There was no avenue left open by Vivekananda and Mukherji which could compromise their control, and allow the autonomy of a process dictated by the unmappable logic of contestation to take

---

[41] Mandal, *Bangiya* . . . , Bhattacharya also faced a regular campaign against him by the Brahman Sabha.

over. The variety principle could, without a specification of a structure of power, mask an updated conservatism.

IX

Despite its later potency in communal mobilization, the suggestion on kirtan occupies a fairly marginal position in *Jatibhed*. In any case it is not allied to antagonism against the Muslim. In fact, to the extent there is an antagonistic Other in *Jatibhed*, it is located in Christian missionaries. But the latter does not play a role analogous to the Muslim in ADR. Above all, Bhattacharya is concerned with internal reform. Thus, when he refers to Muslim invasions, he holds them to be a consequence of the sins committed on low castes by Hindus. Moreover, although Bhattacharya's Vaishnavism leads him to oppose cow-killing in his pamphlet *Go-Korbani*, he adopts the 'liberal' strategy of citing exclusively Muslim authorities to argue his case.[42]

The lack of communal intensity increases the significance of Bhattacharya's deployment of the census table, which flags off the argument. In order to understand this irony, I need to elaborate an argument made earlier regarding the increasing autonomy of the census. The process of transmutation was started by Mukherji himself. At the very beginning of its exposition, ADR asks whether Hindus were faced with an absolute or relative decline. Mukherji's figures indicate that it is a question of comparative fall. But somehow this question is never discussed. Instead, the weight of the argument reiterates the assertion made about the dying Hindu in the title, conflating the relative with the absolute. The surreptitious conversion of the statistical into the purely tropological, enormously expanded the range of concerns to which traces of ADR can be attached.

Mukherji spares no effort in dramatizing the centrality of the census. The first page of *Hindu Samaj* is adorned with a simple statistical table, showing the numbers of Hindus and Muslims since 1872 in Bengal, with a two-line statement below, stating the relative extent of Hindu decrease. This little introduction expresses the author's confidence that his concerns had become common

---

[42] Digindranarayan Bhattacharya (collected and edited), *Gokorbani ba Atmabali*, Serajgunj, Pabna, 1923.

sense; it no longer needed further explanation. The census became analogous to our Disaster Clock that measures the proximity of our planet to destruction every day.

The effectiveness of this structure is evident in *Jatibhed* which uses the invocation of the 'dying Hindu' like a musical coda to repeatedly drive home the necessity of implementing what it recommends. These references are all governed by the meaning of Mukherji's census table that is given at the beginning of *Jatibhed*. The design of this table indentures the decline and impending doom of the Hindus to antagonism with the Muslim Other. The point that Hindus are dying can only be made if their growth rates are compared to that of the Muslims'.

This tabular trope refuses to allow a comprehensive reinscription of itself. Its communal structure of antagonistic comparison remains stubbornly encoded, even when a different chain of significations is attached to it. The triumph of this sign, as seen in its inclusion within *Jatibhed*, is that it seduces through the rhetorical potential it offers for reformist mobilization. Its very use by the latter naturalizes communal attitudes. An even more vivid instance of the way this trope could introduce a surreptitious crack within a different line of enquiry, can be found in Tagore's novel, *Gora*.[43] The hero who bears the same name, believes in neo-Brahminism with missionary zeal. The discovery that he is actually an English orphan brought up by Brahmin parents punctures his assumptions, and with it, radically destabilizes all notions of identity based on the Self-Other polarity. But tucked away into an innocuous corner of the story, yet occupying a strategic place in the plot, is a more familiar tale. Pareshbabu, who is committed to a universalist notion of identity, is confronted by Sucharita, his doting ward. She seeks his advice on her desire (largely produced under Gora's influence) to convert to Hinduism. As he begins to remove the intellectual grounds from her impulse, she bursts out to say that the superiority of Hinduism lay in the fact of its survival. In reply, Pareshbabu states that Hindus were disappearing and soon it would become impossible to call the country Hindustan, since Muslims would become the majority. Not only does Sucharita retract here, but this point marks the reversal of the

---

[43] Rabindranath Tagore, *Gora*, *Rabindra Rachanabali*, vol. IX, f.pub. 1908, rpt. Calcutta, 1961.

Hindu influence in the story. After this point, Gora also begins his journey of self-realization when he starts to live in a village, encountering the self-divisive problems of casteism among Hindus, with a converse experience of Muslim unity. In sum, a picture that recalls Mukherji.

Gora was first published in the same year as ADR, and there is no way of knowing whether this passage was inspired by the latter. The point is that the common sense of the dying Hindu plays a decisive role in a text that is aligned to a different path of enquiry. While this trope is used to question the narrowness of identities, its internal constitution remains unaffected. In fact, the contrast with the Muslims is crucial to hammer in the pressure of impending doom.

What we have here is something akin to a free signifier, allowing itself to be redirected, without however surrendering its inflexible communal code. The consequence is that it accommodates itself to a variety of approaches, insinuating itself into non-identical, even contrary discourses, splitting and problematizing them, without overtly casting ripples. The net result is the production of a common sense that comes close to what Gramsci defined as the fragmented, contradictory character of popular consciousness which amalgamated traces of disparate world-views into itself. This definition does not however account for the entirety of the phenomenon which we are seeing here. For the common sense of the 'dying Hindu', contrary to Gramsci's understanding of it as something spontaneous, not only lent itself to use by organized interventions but, as a consequence, did something that Gramsci had not foreseen. It changed in tandem with a different matrix of political forces.

X

Two major changes mark the course of Hindu communalism in the twenties. The first concerns the low castes. In the first two decades of this century, prompted by the census and their self-activity, the low castes provided a major source of anxiety for their caste superiors. To a great extent, the antagonism against the Muslims was shaped by the fear that the low castes would sever themselves from the rubric of Hinduism. However, this apprehension began to recede in the twenties. The low castes remained badly splintered, but there appeared new, friendly initiatives amongst them. For instance, there was a move — which I will discuss later — amongst the Rajbansis to launch a communal campaign.

For its part, Hindu communalism began to distance itself from caste reform programmes. Divisions between the two extreme poles of the Hindu Mahasabha [hereafter HMS], the Arya Samajis and the orthodox Sanatanists, had intensified during the previous decade when the Intercaste Marriage Bill had come up for consideration in the Imperial Legislative Council. Under the moderate pro-Orthodox leadership of Malaviya, the HMS turned conservative, which led Swami Shraddhanand to resign in disgust, shortly before his assassination.[44] Malaviya sought to replace reform by sympathy. After firing a round of acrimony against Muslims in his address to the Benares conference of the HMS in 1923, Malaviya burst into tears when talking of the plight of the untouchables.[45] Clearly, the low-caste threat was seen to be so remote that their problem could be dismissed by pity.

Fears regarding the low castes did not disappear overnight. In 1924, Piyush Ghosh's act of founding the Bengal Provincial Hindu Sabha (hereafter BPHS), the regional branch of the HMS, was motivated by the news that 5000 Namasudras were contemplating conversion to Christianity. Ghosh later recalled that it was this occasion that had made him realise the importance of organizing Hindus to prevent their depletion. This imperative was intensified by continuing low-caste intransigence. While the Provincial conference of the Hindu Sabha at Faridpur was proceeding in 1925, a meeting of 2000 Namasudras was held nearby to decide on conversion to Christianity. Ghosh, who had given a speech on the low-caste problem in the Sabha gathering, was not even allowed into the Namasudra meeting when he tried to intervene there.[46]

The anxiety about the 'dying Hindu' remained, but increasingly stemmed, not from apprehensions of low-caste secession, but from the influence of non-Hindu organizations over them. This change reinforced the move to restrict the scope of internal reform — even of the minimal kind carefully overdetermined by integrationist priorities — as suggested by Vivekananda and

[44] Jordens, *Shraddhanand*, pp. 154–7.
[45] *Indian Annual Register, 1924, Vol. V*, H.N. Mitra (ed.), Calcutta, 1924.
[46] *Amrita Bazar Patrika*, 3 May 1925.

Mukherji. On the other hand, the focus was placed on the fear of an external Other. Although, in this specific instance, it was the fear of Christian conversions that impelled this, it did not take long to translate itself into antagonism against the Muslims. Here, another revealing incident needs to be mentioned. Ghosh's suggestion to form a branch of the Hindu Sabha met with a great deal of opposition from local Hindus. They feared the fate of Saharanpur, where Suddhi activities had produced communal violence. It was only after some local Muslim gentlemen were persuaded to attend the Sabha meeting that it could be held at all.[47]

It was not surprising that Suddhi activities were seen as provocative. The 'reclamation' of the Malkana Rajputs had marked the successful emergence of a proselytizing Hinduism; the interpretation of their syncretic customs as evidence of Hindu roots also allowed Suddi activists to define conversion as 'reclamation'. This notion threatened to exploit the distinction between unreformed and orthodox Islam, in order to draw out the former from the Islamic fold altogether.[48] It thereby posed a constant internal anxiety for Islamic ideologues. This accounts for the profound effect of the propaganda launched against syncretic Muslims by newly communalized leaders like Abu Bakr, a campaign that was, in fact, quite disproportionate to the actual number of converts in Bengal. In later chapters we will see how this provoked a spiralling intensity of Hindu counter-communal response. At any rate, the process helped to de-emphasize the caste question.

The second and possibly more consequential factor that moulded the twenties was the emergence of the HMS as the mass organization of Hindu communalism in the country. This changed the form and preoccupations of the common sense around the census. The HMS had been inactive during the greater part of the Non-Cooperation/Khilafat movement (hereafter N/K), being revived by Malaviya in 1922.[49] Its swift assumption of a mass,

[47] Ibid., 26 April 1924.
[48] Since Hinduism is a religion to which one cannot convert, Arya Samaji proselytizers justified the conversions by arguing that the non-Islamic practices of the Malkanas proved their original Hinduness. Thus the Samajis could claim that they were only involved in an exercise of restoration, rather than of conversion. In our times, the VHP has even claimed that the whole world was originally Hindu.
[49] Richard Gordon, 'The Hindu Mahasabha and the Indian National

all-India character at the very point when the N/K was subsiding, expresses the deeply felt anxieties that the spectacle of mass mobilization of both Hindus and Muslims raised in the communalists. The change from the communal unity of that period was marked by Swami Shraddhanand, whose speech in the Jama Masjid of Delhi had become a talisman of the possibilities of joint mobilization against the British. In August 1922, however, he announced his suspicion of a Muslim takeover of the country.[50]

What is interesting is the shared responses of Bengal and Punjab. Led by the Arya Samajis,[51] Hindu intellectuals in Punjab were preoccupied with the census from the 1880's, a period that coincided with intense communalization over the go-korbani and Hindi-Urdu controversies. The preoccupation acquired a definitive shape in Lala Lalchand's article, 'Self-Abnegation in Politics', which argued that the decline in Hindu numbers was an index of Hindu weakness and corresponding Muslim strength. The essay went on to propagate the formation of a new party devoted exclusively to Hindu interests.[52] Published the same year as ADR, 'Self-Abnegation' . . . carried a similar, if not more practical, argument. But there was also a less intellectual aspect to the complementary relationship. Punjab and Bengal provided two of the heaviest centres of rioting in the twenties. The initial wave of major riots took place in Punjab, starting in Multan and Amritsar. While the frenzy of rioting gripped Bengal a little later, Calcutta hosted, what was, till then, the biggest riot to occur in the history of the subcontinent.

The rhetoric of Muslim danger struck fertile roots in Bengal. It could tap the anxieties produced by the mass presence of Muslims in the N/K. In contrast, Muslims had been simply treated as outsiders in the Swadeshi movement, and identified as a secondary threat only when riots broke out in Jamalpur. This had made it difficult to portray Muslims as a mass political threat: even

---

Congress, 1915 to 1926', *MAS*, vol. IX, no. 2, 1975.
[50] Jordens, *Shraddhanand*, p. 127.
[51] In the 1880's, the census was used to demonstrate the extent of conversions to Christianity. It was followed by discussions on the alleged problem of declining Hindu numbers in Jammu and Kashmir in the 1890's. During 1890–1, the Arya Samaj carried out a campaign to get Hindus to describe themselves as Aryas in the 1891 Census. Jones, 'Religious Identity', pp. 86–8.
[52] Ibid., p. 90..

Mukherji's fear arose from what the colonial administration could do on the basis of representation by elite Muslim leaders. However, the period of the N/K also saw the entry of Muslims into the reformed local institutions of governance; in 1920 most of the local and district boards were manned by Muslim representatives. It was now clear that, in contrast to the low castes, Muslims had a more generalizable identity and, with it, much larger resources in terms of both education and wealth, with the help of which they could take better advantage of whatever reforms the government proposed.

What integrated Bengal into the communal map of the subcontinent was the HMS. Its imprint is visible in the pamphlets I will study. Two of these pamphlets, Saileshnath Sharma Bisi's *Hindu Samajer Bartaman Samashya* (The Contemporary Problems of Hindu Society), and Sir P.C. Ray's pamphlet are reprints of speeches, delivered as President of the Serajgunj Provincial Hindu Mahasammilani (Great Conference) in 1923, and as President of the Faridpur Provincial Hindu Sabha in 1925, respectively. The third pamphlet, entitled *Bangla Hindu Jatir Khoy O Pratikar* (The Decay of Hindu Society and its Remedy), is a purely mobilizing tract, brought out under the direct authorship of the Tangail Samaj Sangrakshini (Preserver of Hindu Society in Tangail), in 1924.[53] Together, they indicate the presence of organized power in promoting the concern with Hindu numbers, propelling its articulation in three different places in three successive years. Incidentally, this development holds out methodological consequences. Being now faced with a network around the 'Census', it would be appropriate to treat these texts as a composite, even if loosely affiliated group, while exploring their individual accents. The latter imperative should not be lost sight of, both because of the nature of Bisi's intervention, and because of the exceptional nature of *Hindu Musalman Samashya*, written by Nalini Kanta Gupta, a follower of Sri Aurobindo.

[53] Citations from these three texts are drawn from Saileshnath Sharma Bisi, *Hindusamajer Bartaman Samashya: Address of the Reception Committee at Serajgunj Provincial Hindu Mahasammilani*; Sir P.C. Ray, *Faridpur Pradeshik Hindu Sabha* 2 May 1925 and *Bangla Hindu Jatir Khoy O Tahar Pratikar*, Tangail, 1924, which was written and circulated by Tangail Hindu Samaj Sangrakshini.

XI

The projection of Muslims as the antagonistic Other did not simplify the making of a Hindu community. This difficulty led to a series of interrelated explorations. A definitive meaning of modern Hinduism, as we have seen, was the paradox of variety and sameness. Yet, the relationship between the two poles that constituted this paradox was an unstable one. It occasioned several individualized resolutions, evident in Vivekananda for instance. These testified to the problem of resolvability itself; at times, the poles were turned against one another almost within the same time and consciousness, as we have seen happening in the case of U.N. Mukherji; or, as in the case of Bhattacharya, one marginalized the other. In the twenties, some degree of stability was provided by organizational form. The HMS was structured on the premise that Hinduism was a composite of all religions, with the exception of Christianity and Islam (and minor ones in the Indian context, like Judaism). But this catholicity was provided with an implicit singularity of mobilization and preoccupation by the organizational shape that constituted the HMS. Interestingly, the inspiration behind this shape was none other than the constellated structure of the Congress, of which the HMS remained a subsidiary till the thirties. But 'Hindu' was not the same as 'Congress', and new tension spots arose to challenge the organized paradox.

Bengal's Hindu communalism suffered from two kinds of unresolvable tensions. The first of these concerned the relationship with Vaishnavism. It may be recalled that while Mukherji had marked the extreme phase of Hindu reform when Hinduism was treated purely as a mode of social organization (culled and abstracted from the conglomerate of practices and beliefs that went under the rubric of Hinduism), Bhattacharya's Vaishnavism had reintroduced the importance of religious belief. In the twenties we can see a move towards a synthesis of these two positions. But the move to give Vaishnavism a crucial position in the definition of a Hindu community in Bengal was, at the same time, one that denuded it of doctrinal beliefs. An indication of this phenomenon can be gleaned from P.C. Ray's denunciation of 'Swamijis' and 'Babajis' as a sign of the degeneration of the times, while hailing Chaitanya as a major source of inspiration.[54]

[54] *Amrita Bazar Patrika*, 4 May 1925.

Vaishnavism was straightforwardly harnessed to exclusively organizational objectives by Piyush Ghosh who was both the editor of *Amrita Bazar Patrika* and a leading organizer of the BPHS. In his essay, 'The Best Way to Organise the Hindus',[55] he depicts Chaitanya as engaged in producing a 'common basis viz., the cultural unity of Hinduism'. At the same time, he jettisons the anger against upper-caste discrimination which, in both Vivekananda and Bhattacharya, accompanied warnings against low-caste breakaway. It is this religion of mobilization that Ghosh seeks to reinduct when he invokes fears of the Muslim. He locates the ideal in dying for Hindu 'religion and home and hearth', which was a common newspaper phrase that invariably implied a physical Muslim threat.

Bangla Hindu Jatir Khoy O Pratikar (hereafter *Jatir Pratikar*) develops Bhattacharya's heritage when it refers to the importance of 'sankirtan' and 'mahasabhas' introduced by Chaitanya to introduce equality. By far the most important suggestion it provides is one that develops Mukherji's idealization of the waz. It concerns the proposal to create village-level 'Dharmasabhas' drawn from Vaishnav traditions, where Hindus of each village would be obliged to meet weekly.[56] The *Jatir Pratikar* proposal envisions a comprehensive scheme that, besides the waz, draws also on Church services. For it also specifies an itinerary: the proceedings would begin with a collective prayer followed by kirtan, and then by some advice from a preacher.

To grasp the full implications of these suggestions, it is necessary to refer to Vivekananda again. Nineteenth-century reform movements, epitomized by the Brahmo Samaj, attempted to produce 'Societies', collectives which would have their own rituals, interactions, values and culture. The Brahmo Samaj attempted to produce a society within a larger society. The problem with this organizational form was that it rapidly got marginalized as a sect. On the other hand, Vivekananda named his activist organization, the Ramakrishna Mission. The preference for 'Mission' reveals the degree to which Vivekananda altered the reformist agenda to limit its ambition of providing a full-fledged alternative to existing

---

[55] Ibid., 10 and 11 April 1925.
[56] Earlier, Malaviya had called for establishing 'Harisabhas' at the village level which would meet every month. Address to the All India Hindu Mahasabha at Gaya, 1922, *Indian Annual Register, vol. IV.*

Hindu 'society'. Although it drew on the institution of Sannyasi orders, the structuring influence was that of the Jesuits. Like the latter, it emphasized its ideality and distance from quotidian life by its coherent organization and ideological purity, in order to ultimately emerge as a model for common folk. Paradoxically, it is precisely this ideality which inhibits the Ramakrishna Mission from acquiring norms of everyday interactions, thereby preventing it from acquiring the contours of a sect.

But this built-in marginalization had to be changed for the purposes of accelerated mass mobilization. The *Jatir Pratikar* shows how this was sought to be achieved. It takes Vivekananda's notion of an ideal institution but locates it within existing Hindu 'society'. But this would not be an emulative model. It would simply provide a sphere in which equal social interaction, mimicked by spatial proximity and affective/rhythmic sharing of musical devotional experience, would be attained in order to be privileged as a source of common subjectivity. This would not upset social hierarchy. The *Jatir Pratikar* speaks of Chaitanya's reforms as based on a relaxation of caste rules which did not threaten the 'respectable' position of the upper castes. Clearly, among all the pamphlets we have seen, the *Jatir Pratikar* is also the most clear-headed about subsuming the notion of egalitarianism by sameness.

The technicist view of religious institutions is premised on an expectation, that the propagation of religious identity without the encumbrance of religious beliefs would allow it to sideline the problem of internal dissensions of beliefs. But this did not happen. The burden of associations, developed around rituals, nomenclatures and institutions, could not be suddenly detached. And this created problems for Hindu integration at the all-India level. For instance, Gaudiya Vaishnavism was strongly associated with Bengali Hindu regional identity. The problem this created was signalled by Bhattacharya in the Benares session of the HMS. He expressed anger and humiliation at the fact that Chaitanya did not figure as an iconic reference point of Hinduism, although Ram, Buddha and Krishna were invoked.[57] In *Biplabi Sri Gouranga* (Revolutionary Chaitanya), Bhattacharya writes emphatically that Chaitanya could not be ignored because his religion was prevalent in Manipur, Bengal, Orissa and Vrindaban.

[57] Digindranarayan Bhattacharya, *Biplabi Sri Gouranga*, Srinabadwip Sri Gouranga Mission, 1360 [1953].

The intensified territorialization of Vaishnavism must be understood in relationship to the hardening of Bengali sub-nationalism following the transfer of the capital to Delhi in 1912. The proliferation of Marwari wealth from the inter-war period together with the indisputable centering of the nationalist movement in the upper regions of the country with Gandhi's assumption of leadership, intensified the sense of Bengali distinctiveness. This had serious consequences for the HMS. Much of the vital energies that had gone into its making was drawn from the communalization of the Hindi-Urdu controversy, the living heritage of which was evident in the fact that the proceedings of the HMS in Calcutta, 1925, were conducted in Hindi. Its effect on the composition of the conference was so transparent that it inspired the normally sympathetic *Amrita Bazar Patrika* to comment dryly that 'it looked as if the meeting was being held not in Bengal but elsewhere, the number of Bengalee delegates [being] rather few ... '.[58]

A quick glance at the life of Sir P.C. Ray will indicate the complex effects produced by this situation. In his status as a major scientist, entrepreneur (he founded Bengal Chemicals) and ideologue against the 'invasion' of upcountrymen, he summarized regional pride in his person. In 1923 he had delivered a sympathetic lecture on Islam.[59] In the phase he got close to the HMS however, he came out in favour of the Marwaris, certifying them as Bengalis.[60] However, by 1932, when his autobiography was released, he had become critical of 'Hindu Sabhas and Sangathans' for not practising the catholicity that they preached.[61] This turn coincided with a renewed criticism of the 'economic conquest of Bengal by the Marwaris'[62] and combined with an affectionate recollection of the Islamic influence imbibed by his father. Significantly, his days with the HMS were not mentioned.

[58] 12 April 1925. This 'upcountry' image was sought to be utilized (opportunistically) by anti-communalists such as the journal *Hindu Musalman* (3 August 1926, p. 37) and Mrs Naidu in her tour of Bengal as President of the Congress in the same year.
[59] Convocation Address at the Aligarh National Muslim University on 7 February 1923. *Acharya (Sir, Dr) P.C. Ray's Three Convocation Addresses*, Compiled by R-K-B-K Acharya Prafulla Chandra Sammilanee, Calcutta, 1989.
[60] *Amrita Bazar Patrika*, 12 April 1925.
[61] Acharya P.C. Ray, *Life and Experiences of a Bengali Chemist*, Calcutta, 1932, p. 529.
[62] Ibid., p. 20.

Clearly, the paradox of Variety and Sameness verged on a contradiction. The nature of such identity formations required the privileging of singularity. After all, it was the need to construct a single structure of Hinduism that marked the historically novel aspect of the modern thinker-activists of Hinduism. Given the importance of centering, it was apposite that this centre would be defined by those who organizationally and discursively wielded greater access to its definition and control.

This revealed another phenomenon. Bhattacharya's and Ray's experiences underlined the fact that identities were neither self-enclosed nor fully appropriable. While identities could be mutually reinforcing, they could not dispense with their specific histories and associations. Centering the Hindu identity could, as we have seen in Bhattacharya, provoke the provincial affiliation into an insurrectory proclamation of itself. Further, Ray's provincial pride pointed to the disturbing implications this alteration held for Hindu communalism; it could lead to a new ideological direction in which the Muslim and Marwari upcountryman began to change places.

The general problem was exacerbated by political opposition. Since the HMS was theoretically open to Hindus of all persuasions, it allowed the Swarajists an opportunity to attempt a takeover of the HMS. Saileshnath Bisi's speech at Serajgunj (given in *Bartaman Samashya*), was delivered in the context of the Bengal Pact (whose crucial effects I will elaborate later) that marked the most ambitious attempt — made by the Swarajists under the leadership of C.R. Das — at providing an institutional foundation to communal unity. Bisi attempted to reorient some of the key issues raised by the HMS, from a Swarajist perspective. He blamed the illiberalism of Hindus for the conflict on go-korbani, while recalling the days when Hindus and Muslims would listen to music together (which implicitly criticized Muslim objections to the playing of music before mosques). In effect, he skilfully deployed the traditions of reformist self-critique in order to neutralize communal antagonism, while invoking the liberal traditions of both religions. This perspective prepared the grounds for him to call for support to C.R. Das. A year after Bisi's speech, an attempt was made by J.M. Dasgupta in the Bangiya Hindu Sabha conference to float a new Executive Committee that included C.R. Das. He was virulently opposed by other members and Bisi, who sided with him, was also dropped from the Committee.⁶³ It was clear the HMS had severe limits to its tolerance.

The problematic character of unifying Hinduism meant that the quest to stabilize this paradox had to carry on. It was, in fact, given a decisive turn by Nalini Gupta in Bengal during the mid-twenties, through the notion of Hindutva. Hindutva referred basically to the cultural essence of the country, constituted by the historical process of assimilation of different religions and cultures. Involved here was a nomenclatural shift from Hindu to Hindutva, which combined two things. As a well-used derivative of Hindu, it implicitly defined its parent as the inspiration for the country's ethos; on the other hand, by erecting Hindutva as a cultural idea underpinning nationalism, it sought to bypass the problematic variety embedded in 'Hindu', constituting its singularity in an ideological essence which was anterior to and included the variety of the country. In other words, Variety started functioning as a species of sameness. Drawing on an analogy with Hindusthani classical music, Gupta talked lyrically of Hindutva as the basic musical phrase, while the rest were simply peripherals like *alaap*, *gamak*, etc.

It was V.D. Savarkar, the revolutionary terrorist from Maharashtra, who provided the most successful definition of Hindutva. His view, published two years previously, provided a concrete definition of the Hindu (of Hindutva) as one whose birthplace coincided with the place of origin of his religion. It also fleshed out this explanation by providing Hindus with a history of shared geographical associations and cultural ideals. He was also clear about the importance of an unremitting enemy. 'Nothing', he proclaimed, 'could weld people into a nation and nations into a State as the pressure of a common enemy.'⁶⁴ This, needless to add, could be best supplied for Hindu communalism by Muslims.

Gupta lacked this pragmatic focus. He tended to define Hindutva too broadly. Consequently, he even attempted to include the Muslim in Hindutva's fold. Nor did Gupta recommend any corresponding institutional initiatives. He talked instead of a unity based on controlling characteriological excesses — the Muslim of his *tamas* (implicitly defined here as the quality of aggressiveness and preoccupation with temporal achievement), and the

---

⁶³ *Amrita Bazar Patrika*, 8 June 1924.
⁶⁴ V.D. Savarkar, *Hindutva: Who is a Hindu?*, Pune, 1923, p. 34.

Hindu of his *satva* (the quality of other-worldliness) — in order to achieve an equilibrium. However, by raising the need for Hindus to become more aggressive, Gupta, in effect, reaffirmed Hindu communal propaganda that had called for the same sort of transference, gesturing at the inherent biases in the notion of Hindutva that even its well-intentioned users could not but use as a reflex.

XII

As we have seen, the structure of the sameness/variety paradox was highly vulnerable to the pounding of circumstance. The category of variety had to include not only a multitude of religions/denominations and castes, but also, in the context of changing mass politics, rival political views and regional identities, all of which kept altering according to the logic of shifting political correlations. This was obviously a tall order for the principle of sameness to absorb and, consequently, Hindu communalism needed a commensurately malleable discursivity. In effect, it required the discursivity of common sense, one which was fluid, could permeate different formations of power while lending itself to the requirements of popular mobilization towards a single objective, whether organized or spontaneous. The flexibility of the census common sense provides the key to its importance. Two developments took place in its 'life' in the twenties. Firstly, in tandem with the general tendency we had seen, the census was detached from the problem of low-caste reform and aligned to the question of widow-remarriage. This took place against a background in which gender started occupying the most important place among Hindu communal concerns. Secondly, the very character of the census changed, becoming more portable while expanding its range of significations.

The new temper was indicated by Bisi's speech. The explanation he offered for declining Hindu numbers had nothing to do with caste; on the contrary, it led him to a consideration of the ban on widow-remarriage. The forefronting of gender involved a shift away from the problem of untouchability, which Bisi discussed separately — suggesting a certain move towards its marginalization. In contrast, the importance of widow-remarriage was underlined by reiterating its necessity in the conclusion. The census was even more straightforwardly deployed for its new object by P.C. Ray. Beginning his speech by invoking the census, he asserted that the drop in Hindu numbers was caused by the ban on widow-remarriage. He deviated thereafter into Mukherji's analysis of peasants (the Hindu lacking initiative, the Muslim possessing it), but came back to offer widow-remarriage as the first item on his list of solutions. He also included a table which showed that the number of Hindu widows outstripped that of Muslim widows in the 15 to 30 years age group. In the process he set the seal on the new direction given to the census.

The figure of the widow corresponded to three of the major objects of Hindu communal reform. The first was apparent in Gupta. Citing the census and drawing upon Vitalist ideas, he observed that the imbalance in population growth rates was due to the lack of sufficient reserves of Life Force in the Hindus; he went on to locate this energy in the reproductive powers of women. Within such readings, remarriage was motivated by resource utilization. This attitude related to widows in the same manner as newspaper articles of this time did to cows, both posing the problem of efficient breeding.

But there was also a negative, threatening imperative. Both *Jatir Pratikar* and *Bisi* looked upon the widow as a potential source of moral contamination in the household. In the transference of sexual exploitation on to the widow, they followed Vidyasagar, whose humanitarian appeal for widow-remarriage had been laced with apprehensions of corruption by sexually deprived and (hence) vulnerable widows. In this typification, one can see correspondences with a figure that is antagonistic to the cow, that is, the Muslim. For both widow and Muslim were yoked together by the fear of their sexual excess. There was, in fact, a structural encouragement of complicity with the Muslim. The widow's position in the household was located at its extreme margins, a site of vulnerability that was exacerbated by Muslim perceptions. Apropos of allegations of women abductions in the Mymensingh riots of 1907, the district magistrate stated that these emanated from 'merely threats' since the status of Hindu widows was 'the subject of comment among Mahomedan neighbours'.[65] Located outside the protection that

[65] Political: Confidential, no. 514 of 1907, Govt. of E. Bengal and Assam. WBSA.

the domestic identity of female chastity provided, the Hindu widow was both an invitation and a threat.

But the marginal position of the widow in the Hindu household possessed another analogue. It corresponded to the borderline position of the low castes. And both posed the threat of breakaway. There was, however, a significant attempt at displacement here. This was prompted by the growing ban on widow-remarriage among the low castes themselves. Thus, *Jatir Pratikar* asserted that the decline in Hindus was due to the low castes. But instead of discussing inter-caste relations like the earlier generation, it blamed their marriage practices, and recommended widow-remarriage. The latter would not only multiply Hindu children, but also dispense with the dowry system. In effect, the extension of the preoccupation with widow remarriage among the low castes, created a channel through which the anxieties centred on the widow, the brittle battle between resource maximization and sexual excess/ social loss, the cow and the Muslim, was sought to be stretched into the preoccupations of the low castes. A double resolution was attempted. The fear of low-caste breakaway was assuaged by the possibility of an inter-caste concern with gender, which could fill in the space left by the receding significance of reform.

All said and done, however, the widow-centred preoccupation revealed the underlying methods and trends of Hindu communalism rather than supplying its central concern. There were severe problems with this issue. First, there was the question of guilt springing from the humanitarian origins of this discourse in Vidyasagar. In a liberal mood, this could explain the widow's vulnerability to Muslim 'seduction' by their deprivation within Hindu households. This argument was explicitly provided by Ray. Coupled with the way this discourse could thin out the conviction in confronting the Muslims, there was an organizational problem. The ban on widow-remarriage was not a uniform feature of caste mobility. In fact, differences on this issue contributed to the breakup of Namasudra unity in 1922. In this context, promoting this preoccupation would mean involvement in intra-low-caste struggles. Thus it was not surprising that the preoccupation with the widow tended to give way to an issue with a stronger and less complicated emotional charge. The power of this other preoccupation was nowhere more evident than in the ruminations of Ray and Bisi.

After offering widow-remarriage as a remedy, Ray transited to a new concern: 'All the wives of our kin, who are being abducted, and whom, because of our weakness and cowardice, we cannot rescue from the hands of the depraved — we should save them and give them a place in the bosom of society'. Likewise, while talking of widow-remarriage, Bisi suddenly elaborated upon the heartlessness of Hindu males who refused to accept their abducted wives. The sudden transition to the abducted wife theme in both cases, took place while discussing widows. The instance of Ray, in particular, indicates that the jump was occasioned by an irresistible power of association. Significantly, these passionate lines were not repeated; it was as if they appeared in spite of Ray's intentions.

The issue of abductions is sufficiently important for me to devote a full chapter to it later. I will confine myself to two observations here. The first is that it served the purpose of unity with low castes on a common platform more successfully than that of widow-remarriage. Secondly, the election of woman as signifier and index of direct and unmediated Muslim 'oppression' made the very presence of the former a source of constant communal anxiety. The figure of the woman now emphasized the wife as the potential site of outrage, carrying the fear of the Muslim into every home. This provided a compelling imperative for mobilization.

XIII

The trope of the census gained flexibility over time, allowing it to be used in an additive capacity (Bhattacharya) as well as permitting its order of explication to be altered (as in the twenties). Finally, we have seen how the common terrain of gender permitted it to signal the concern with abductions. New bits were thereby attached to an old motif, bringing to it their separate significance. Alongside this, the census trope also began to take on the task of dramatizing an immediate fear.

Before exploring this new area, it is important to recognize the structural changes that take place within the trope of the census. The reorientation of the census in the twenties, meant that it became less of an object of explication in itself, than a signifier of other preoccupations. This dramatically enlarged its flexibility.

But it required a corresponding formal alteration for it to signify different yet related things at the same time.

The census, especially in its presence in Mukherji's writings, carried a heavy baggage of statistics and elaborate explications. This restricted its use. But in the twenties, when mass politics had entrenched itself (being not confined to 'high' moments like the Swadeshi), political messages demanded an immediate accessibility. The 'census' did not wither away in these circumstances. It adapted itself.

Interestingly, it was Mukherji who provided direction again. This lay in the invention of the phrase, 'the dying Hindu'. This phrase 'packages' the fears and anxieties of Mukherji's argument while pruning away the elaborateness of explication. It could be used like a slogan. At two important points, Shraddhanand wrote books with titles that proclaimed the need for 'saving' the 'dying race'.[66] Further, the retention of the emotional at the cost of the mathematical (partially accomplished in the changeover from relative to absolute decline), allowed the numerical aspects of the concern to be used freely and with greater dramatic effect. Piyush Ghosh, for instance, claimed that it would take 400 years for Hindus to disappear;[67] in Faridpur, Ray identified the limit as 200–250 years, while, at a HMS meeting at Nasik, Jagatguru Shankaracharya warned that it would take a mere century for the process of extinction to be completed.[68]

However, the census insinuated itself much more easily into related interests. At a public meeting held at a rice mill in Ultadinghee, an industrial suburb of Calcutta, Pandit Devratan Sarma, Secretary, HMS, asserted that Hindus had physically and numerically degenerated. He then referred to a spate of riots to proclaim: 'So when calamities like that of Kohat, Sharanpur, Malabar and Ajmere befell them, they [the Hindus] were defenceless . . . '.[69] The census gathered a new, unstated implication here; the Hindus were decreasing because of physical liquidation by Muslims. We

[66] Ten days after he established the Bharatiya Hindu Suddhi Sabha in 1923, Shraddhanand issued an appeal entitled, 'Save the Dying Race'. The second occasion occurred when he wrote *Hindu Sangathan, Saviour of the Dying Race* in 1924 after his retirement from Mahasabha activities. It was published in 1926. Jordens, *Shraddhanand*, pp. 151–7.
[67] 'The Best Way', *Amrita Bazar Patrika*, 10 April 1925
[68] *Amrita Bazar Patrika*, 1 December 1925.
[69] Ibid., 7 April 1925.

come as close as we can possibly get, to the use of the census as a battle-cry.

It is the notion of the threatened male body that permits this unmediated connection between Hindu numbers and riots. This recalls the sub-text of Mukherji's preoccupations, although it is necessary to remind ourselves that when he talked of the need for training, he was referring to the structure of morals and motivations. The twenties see a preoccupation with the trained male body as an object in itself. After witnessing a display of physical exercises in a club, Piyush Ghosh declared: 'Bengalees as a nation were degenerating and were a dying race. Physical culture was the only remedy to this race-degeneracy.'[70] His newspaper regularly carried articles that preached the virtues of physical fitness. The possibility of violence contained in this concern, was expressed by Lajpat Rai, when he exhorted his audience to be like Arjuna when he faced his beloved enemy, Bhisma.[71]

The defenceless female body was counterpointed by the necessity for a physically trained male body; both were integrally linked to the anxiety of Hindu numbers, which were related to fears of breakaway by low castes and women. The census began to refer to a differentiated field of significations which expanded the ideological boundaries of Hindu communalism. And this permitted displacements to be used freely, without anything being ultimately repressed. The position and nature of each theme was qualified by the addition of others, being drawn from different points of time and gathered together in the twenties. It produced a gigantic network that was as much an ideology as a call to physically inflict one's anxieties on an enemy, that was needed for the Self to be created in the first place.

[70] Ibid., 28 April 1925.
[71] Ibid., 8 April 1925.

2

Muslim Peasant Improvement, Pir Abu Bakr and the Formation of Communalized Islam

I

Interestingly, the idealized figure of the enterprising Muslim, that had provided the cornerstone of Mukherji's arguments in ADR, recurred in the twenties. There is a sense of despondence in Bibhutibhushan Bandopadhyay's comparison of Muslim peasant prosperity with the plight of the absentee rural Hindu upper class in his travel record of 1929.[1] Hindu and Muslim societies had featured in a comparable manner in Sarat Chandra Chattopadhyaya's social romance *Palli Samaj* (1923). In this novel, only Muslim peasants support the progressive agenda of social reform and economic improvement, which the hero Romesh attempts to initiate in a largely unwilling caste society.[2]

In Mukherji's period, it was still possible for the bhadralok to imagine that rural Hindus could compete with the enterprising Muslim. But by the twenties (no doubt aided by the censoring of efforts at caste improvement), that prospect seemed to be disappearing. Bandopadhyaya's despair or Chattopadhyaya's wish-fulfilling romance of Hindu improvement indicates the bhadralok's increasing diffidence in his ability to mobilize rural Hindus to catch up with their ideal Muslim. A significant development may help us to understand this loss of self-confidence. It concerns not simply the economic well-being of the Muslim peasant (through jute) which was not new, but the emergence of an intelligentsia catering to an economically and morally improving Muslim peasantry. The

---

[1] Bibhutibhushan Bandopadhyaya, *Diner Pare Din*, Calcutta, 1394[1986], pp. 5–15.
[2] Sarat Chandra Chatterjee, *Palli Samaj*, Calcutta, 1364[1957].

consciousness of the idea of Improvement among Muslim peasants underlined the corresponding 'backwardness' of the Hindu peasant world-view.

Although there is a greater number of texts committed to orthodox Islamic concerns in the National Library catalogue, I have chosen Improvement texts as a point of entry into the formation of Muslim identity in the twenties. This is because the latter defines the change in Muslim identity more sharply. And, as a corollary, these texts place more importance on the relationship with the Hindu other. Equally important is the fact that they reveal multiple possibilities of identity formation. There are at least three major identities that Improvement tracts attempt to negotiate.

Finally, these Improvement tracts provide a fuller explanation of why the Muslim identity could become communal. Existing narratives of this turn, normally tend to dwell on the competition regarding the number of seats to be reserved for members of each 'community' in educational institutions and government employment. These concerns formed the stuff of negotiations between the top level players of politics in the twentieth century, pioneered by urban Muslim ideologues such as Sir Sayyid Ahmad and Ameer Ali.[3]

This explanation leaves the countryside out of consideration and, consequently, cannot explain the support or passive acceptance extended by rural Muslims to the reservations question. Although there were existing linkages between city and country among the Muslim activist intelligentsia,[4] the activity of individual leaders cannot explain such a large question with so much, and so many, interests involved. At the same time, when the rural sources of an exclusivist Muslim identity are considered, they are

---

[3] Sir Sayyid stated (1883) that in India, where there was 'no fusion of the various races', electoral representation would lead to the domination of the 'larger community' over the 'interests of the smaller community'. Cited in Peter Hardy, *The Muslims of British India*, Cambridge, 1972, p. 137. The memorial to Morley inspired by Ameer Ali in 1906, advanced an almost identical argument. Syed Amir Ali, *Memoirs and Other Writings of Syed Ameer Ali*, Syed Razi Wasti (ed.), Lahore, 1968, p. 83.

[4] Keramat Ali, for instance, gave his celebrated *fatwa* declaring British India to be a *dar ul Islam* in a meeting of Abdul Latif's Muhammadan Literary Society of Calcutta on 23 November 1870, held at the latter's house. Cited in Hardy, *The Muslims* . . . , p. 111.

approached simply as a consequence of the economic structure of the countryside. Two kinds of approaches have been employed here. The older kind has been the simple conversion of class into community, proceeding from the observation that the majority of Muslims were peasants and the majority of Hindus were landlords. A sophisticated reformulation of this method has been to treat Muslim peasants as a homogeneous economic unit, and then see it as coincident with a single community.[5] Besides conflating 'community' identities with communal ones, these analyses do not explain the ideological and discursive conditions that could have transformed the 'peasant' into the communal Muslim.

II

I wish to preface my analysis of the Improvement texts by briefly exploring the conditions of publication. This would provide us with some understanding of the character of the Improvement intelligentsia and their networks.

The National Library catalogue shows that while publications on Islam had started proliferating by the end of the nineteenth century, it was in the early twentieth century, especially in its second decade, that tracts on Improvement began to be produced in large numbers. The most striking feature of these tracts (which range from twelve to eighty pages), is that a vast number of them are written by authors who proclaim themselves to be residents of villages or of places that fall under a post office or police station. There was a veritable explosion of texts written by these authors. Sponsorship was extended by landlords, the traditional patrons of *punthis* (hand-written manuscripts), by important members of the newly formed district/local boards, and most significantly, by religious establishments, especially that of Pir Abu Bakr.

A substantial number of texts were published by the authors themselves. This phenomenon was assisted by the rapid switch to the publication of Bengali texts. This probably filled in a demand

---

[5] See Chatterjee, *Bengal 1920–1947*, Bose's argument in *Agrarian Bengal*, overlooks the campaigns against moneylending and economic relations with Hindus, which predate the depression by decades. It also ignores the Pabna riots and the anti-moneylender campaigns in Dhaka and Kishoreganj (he considers only the Kishoreganj riots of 1930, which falls within his period).

that had already been created by Urdu texts written by nineteenth-century reformers.[6] Further, the assurance of a readership in Bengali and the facilities of communications stimulated entrepreneurial ambitions. Besides, writing and publishing, as Digindranarayan Bhattacharya's instance suggests, could become something like a cause, especially when it was directed at subjects such as social reform.[7] Incidentally, an enormous expansion in Muslim controlled newspapers began to take place from the days of the Swadeshi movement.[8] Clearly, the printed word fulfilled a need for social activism in a period that was marked by the exclusion of Muslims from a major mass movement.

These Improvement texts stress everyday, practical activity. There is an intense concentration on everyday life and habits. Smoking, cleanliness, bathing practices of women, clothing habits are some of the details with which these texts attempt to 'place' their readers into a community. The notion of a community then, emerges as one which is more familiar and embedded than those projected in Hindu texts. Simultaneously, these Improvement texts almost spontaneously provide pragmatic, organizational suggestions. These include social funding, giving financial aid (including *baitemul, zakat* funds, central village *tahabil* [depository], etc.) and Rayat Sabhas. *Sahitya Sangrakshan*, a text that identifies the encouragement of a specifically Islamic literature as the key to the material improvement of Muslims, devises a novel way to build village libraries. The author recommends the presentation of books at weddings, which could then be collected to form a library.[9] These authors not only give advice on the everyday; they attempt to make their literature part of the everyday itself.

[6] An observer in Calcutta in 1832 listed seven reformist books written in Urdu and printed locally, that were available in the bazars of the city. Barbara Daly Metcalfe, *Islamic Revival in British India: Deoband, 1860–1900*, Princeton, 1982, p. 69. Keramat Ali too had penned forty-six books. Ibid., p. 70.

[7] Leading Muslim intellectual activists were also editors of newspapers. For instance, Mujibur Rahaman was editor of *The Mussalman*, Akram Khan that of the *Mohammadi*, while Maniruzzaman Islamabadi edited *Islam Darshan* and later *Dainik Soltan*.

[8] Mustafa Nurul Islam, *Muslim Public Opinion as Reflected in the Bengali Press, 1901–1930*, Dhaka, 1973, p. 1.

[9] Mohammed Ali, *Sahitya Sangrakshan: Bangiya Musalmaner Sahitya Raksher Upay* (Defending Literature: Ways to Preserve Muslim Literature), Dhaka, 1927, pp. 29–34.

The privileging of the quotidian clearly distinguishes these texts from the grand schemes of reorganizing Hinduism. There is another point of difference. Unlike the linear, argumentative structure of both the upper- and low-caste texts we have studied, the ones on Muslim improvement deploy a large variety of genres, including essays, stories and poems.[10] Their literary efflorescence has a practical relevance. In order to become part of the cultural universe of rural Muslims, these texts had to insert themselves into a leisure time that was traditionally devoted to punthi reading, which was, for the rural Muslims, a distinctively Muslim form of cultural activity.[11]

The 'local' and 'everyday' became, paradoxically, through the circulation of these texts, part of a province-wide concern. This was, in great part, due to the close linkage between such texts and newspapers. Some of these texts were authored by newspapermen; *Sahitya Sangrakshan* for example, was written by an ex-editor of *Banga Nur*. More common was the practice of writing articles in newspapers, which were later incorporated into books. Moreover rural and urban print spaces interpenetrated. Mansur Ahmad recalled how proud his whole village felt when his work was published in a Calcutta journal.[12] On the other hand, the limited readership for newspapers edited by Muslims (since Hindus did not read them), made the mofussil readership a more important component of Muslim newspapers than for Hindu newspapers. Consequently, print was an area in which the countryside could aspire to intellectual recognition, if not parity, with urban cultural life.

---

[10] The consequence is a rich polymorphic phenomenon. These tracts include long poems arranged as couplets to lend themselves to oral transmission as in punthis, simple narratives that have a typicalized plot and protagonist, discursive prose including polemical tracts and ethical advice. Sometimes many of these are deployed within a single text.

[11] Punthis were long manuscripts written in verse. They incorporated a great deal of Hindustani and Persian words, and dealt with a wide range of subjects from religious reform to engrossing stories. Rafiuddin Ahmad, 'Conflict and Contradictions in Bengal Islam: Problems of Change and Adjustment', *Shari'at and Ambiguity in South Asian Islam*, Katherine P. Ewing (ed.), Delhi, 1988, pp. 116–18. They were sometimes read through the whole night, as a counterpoint to Hindu festivities.

[12] Mansur Ahmad *Atmakatha*, Dhaka, 1974. All references to Ahmad's life, except where otherwise mentioned, are drawn from this text.

III

The Improvement tracts were shaped by a major change in the history of Muslim exclusivist identity. Following the defeats of the Wahabis and Faraizis, their schismatic energy was replaced by schemes of Muslim identity that were gradualist and aimed at an extensive constituency. Keramat Ali was a key figure in effecting this change. For forty years he travelled the length of the interiors of East Bengal in a boat that carried a college. Equally important was his association with the urban Muslim intelligentsia which supported colonial pedagogy. For instance, he issued his celebrated fatwa declaring British India *dar ul Islam* [land of peace] in 1870, at a meeting of Abdul Latif's Muhammadan Literary Society in Calcutta,[13] thereby reversing its Wahabi characterization as *dar ul harb*. The full significance of this emerges when we examine the ambitions of the administration.

The British administration's attitude to Islamic pedagogy was dictated by the need to avoid another reformist rebellion. W.W. Hunter, who was set the task of altering the policy towards Muslims,[14] produced a subtle solution. He proposed the insertion of profitable subjects in the existing syllabi. Colonial intervention could reorient the structure of Islamic pedagogy, even as it was absorbed by the latter. In general, Islamic education had a 'liberal' orientation. Deoband, for instance, taught little vocational education, and that too, badly.[15] But there was a potential space for its expansion. In addition to knowing the basic religious texts (*manqulat*), Islamic pedagogy had emphasized 'rational' subjects (*maqulat*) which studied the knowledge produced by human beings.[16]

---

[13] Hardy, *The Muslims*, p. 111.

[14] The immediate reason was the 'Rebel Colony' founded by Sayyid Ahmad Barelvi, against whom a massive war was fought by the British in 1863, at great cost to the latter. A large number of his followers had been recruited from Bengal. W.W. Hunter, *The Indian Musslamans: Are They Bound in Conscience to Rebel Against the Queen?*, Lahore, 1968, f.pub. 1871.

[15] Two vocational courses were offered – calligraphy and *tibb* (a medicinal system derived mainly from Greeks). Tibb was however opposed by Rasid Ahmad Ganghoi, a leading *ulema* of Deoband, and was introduced only at the end of the century. Metcalfe, *Islamic Revival*, p. 103.

[16] According to Metcalfe, maqulat subjects 'ranged from Arabic grammar and rhetoric to logic, mathematics, philosophy and theology, to above all books of legal commentaries and jurisprudence'. *Islamic Revival*, p. 19. The

The new, profitable subjects recommended by Hunter could be 'naturalized' by the maqulat slot. This would not disturb the preoccupation with religious learning, but alter the internal balance of subjects.[17] This recommendation was compounded by the Government's Resolution of 1871,[18] and further consolidated in 1904 when *maktab* education was standardized.

It is this structural stimulus we need to keep in mind, when we consider the kind of education recommended by Improvement texts. The main attraction imparted to education was that of providing knowhow for accumulating wealth. The frontispiece in *Adarsha Krishak* features a farmer with a plough in one hand and a book in the other.[19] The transformative powers of education acquires magical proportions in *Krishaker Unnati*, which suggests ways by which peasants can acquire wealth. The author, Mohammed Hamidi, claims that the *bimal* (pure) light of education would dispel the sin of ignorance along with 'the peasants' misfortunes'. This invocation is immediately tied to a practical recommendation: Hamidi explains how education could allow peasants to balance expenditure with income.[20]

The reference to purity has obvious religious connotations. This is made explicit in Garib Sayer's assertion that '*ilm*' (the root word of ulema) education would restore Islam's past glories.[21] The alliance between the spiritual and practical is extended by *Adarsha Krishak*. Garib Sayer had also talked of the need for vocational training, such as, sowing multiple crops and cultivating commercial crops. Bhayali's *Adarsh Krishak* makes this alliance into a characteriological necessity. It features a model self-educated peasant

---

dars-i nizami syllabus, devised by the Firangi Mahallis in the eighteenth century, greatly expanded the number of maqulat subjects. Ibid, p. 31.

[17] Hunter declared that, 'we should render that religion perhaps less sincere, but certainly less fanatical', Hunter, *The Indian Mussalmans*, p. 183.

[18] Sufia Ahmed, *Muslim Community in Bengal 1884–1912*, Dhaka, 1974, p. 11.

[19] A.F.M. Abdul Hayy Bhayali, *Adarsha Krishak*, Mymensingh, 1328 [1921].

[20] Khademul Islam Mohammed Moazzuddin Hamidi, *Krishaker Unnati O Dukha Durdasher Pratikar* (Peasants' Improvement and Remedies for their Sorrows and Misfortunes), Khulna, 1929, pp. 12–13. Citations are drawn from this edition.

[21] Garib Sayer, *Krishak Bandhu*, Calcutta, 1317[1910]. rpt. 1332 [1921], pp. 23–6. Citations are drawn from this edition.

called Usman, who diligently reads religious works and books on agriculture in equal measure.[22]

This combination of the spiritual and the practical formed a grid on which lived subjectivities were sought to be typified. Munshi Mohammed Jaynal Abedin's autobiography projects his career as an exemplary one. Thrown out of his house by his foster-mother, he travelled from village to village, doing odd jobs, and encountered a succession of *maulvis* and *pirs*. Despite his perambulations he acquired literacy. This enabled him to set up a maktab which turned out to be a profitable venture. Running the maktab also gave him the confidence to start purificatory campaigns against unislamic practices. All these achievements pave the way for the narrative climax which was his marriage to a rich man's daughter. He then started a shop and wrote his autobiography.[23]

Wealth becomes so important, that it is made into the most important feature of Islam itself. Already in the *fin de siecle* years, Delawar Hosaen Meerza wrote: 'The progress of a people is evidenced by the increase and spread of wealth and knowledge.'[24] The chairman of the Chittagong Islamia Conference (1925), proclaimed wealth to be the 'twin' of religion, and went on to give it a decisive role: 'The race whose material or temporal situation is not good, will also have the bonds of its religion weakened.'[25] Of course, as we will see, the spiritual/moral imperative remains a key component, but what happens is a redistribution of emphasis given to the economic and spiritual, respectively. The economic sphere of the peasants' life becomes the crucial area of concern. Additionally, his material experience becomes the source of pedagogical instructions, while scriptural directives are employed in a supportive capacity.

The specific target for criticism and reform in the Improvement texts, is extravagance. The sources of extravagance pertain mainly to festivities. Expenditure on children's wedding (including bride price), is criticized as the product of Hindu influence. In *Krishaker*

---

[22] Bhayali, *Adarsh Krishak*, p. 14.
[23] Munshi Mohammed Jaynal Abedin, *Atmakahini*, Dinajpur, 1333[1926].
[24] 'The Economical Condition of Mohammedans, 1869–1876', *Muslim Modernism in Bengal: Selected Writings of Delawar Hosaen Ahmed Meerza 1840–1913*, Sultan Jahan Salik (ed.), Dhaka, 1980, p. 53. However his pioneering recommendations were not influential.
[25] *Speech of the Chairman of the Reception Committee, Chittagong Islamia Conference*, Chittagong, 1925, p. 3.

Unnati, Hamidi argues that for Hindus, dowry is a substitute for the daughter's share of inheritance, but is irrelevant for Muslims, whose daughters are given a share of their parents' property. Besides invoking scriptural injuctions, he narrates the story of Fatima who was given only two bangles for her wedding by Muhammad. He finally quotes reports from the *Muhammadi* and *Hanafi* newspapers, which showed how people were ruined by moneylenders from whom they were forced to borrow in order to pay dowry. Rashid, a resident of Mymensingh, tells us of a Karimullah Sheikh who borrowed from Kanai Poddar to observe *fatihah* for his father's soul, and compounded it by taking more loans on account of his son's marriage. He had to ultimately surrender his land to Poddar.[26]

Other items of reform include cutting expenditure on clothes worn to fairs. This practice is defined by Hamidi as a Hindu custom, and is associated with prostitutes. In *Mussalmaner Arthasanket*, Rashid criticizes social competition between Muslims, which leads to wasteful expenditure such as buying racing cows and horses, which results in indebtedness to the moneylender. Expenditure on litigation — a major preoccupation with newspapers since at least 1904[27] is also condemned. Hamidi traces litigation to a fall in religiosity, but suggests that if a lawyer had to be employed, it ought to be a Muslim.

The discourse on Muslim peasant extravagance was already established by nineteenth-century British administrators, who identified 'utter improvidence' and 'fondness for litigation' as causes for indebtedness.[28] What was new in the Improvement texts was an implicit reformulation of popular Islam, that emerged from the combination of the practical with the ethical. A contrast with Samuel Smiles' *Self-Help*, which was the original mover of

---

[26] Mohammed Abdur Rashid, *Mussalmaner Arthasanket O Tahar Pratikar* (The Economic Problems of Muslims and their Remedies), Calcutta, 1928, rpt. 1938, pp. 33–5.

[27] 'The *Naba Nur* stated that year: 'Very few Hindus ruin themselves in litigations the way Muslims do.' Islam, *Muslim Public Opinion*, pp. 199–200. Incidentally, the setting up of arbitration boards had been one of the big successes of the Khilafat movement. There were 15 such arbitration boards in February 1921, which jumped to 866 by April 1922. File No. 395, Serial Nos. 1–3, 1924. 'History of the Non-Cooperation And Khilafat Movements in Bengal', GOB: POLITICAL. WBSA.

[28] Bose, *Agrarian Bengal*, p. 98.

Improvement as a social ideology, will define the novelties of this formation. Written in mid-Victorian England, the focus of *Self-Help* — behind which one can read the spectre of Chartism — was on individuals, who, through common qualities of character (such as effort), managed to overcome social barriers of class. In the discourse on Bengali rural Muslim improvement however, the practical–moral grid ensures that each act of economic progress, is accompanied by a corresponding contribution to the Islamic community.[29] As early as 1910, M.I. Ali Ahmadi, who wrote *Unnati Sopan*, stated that while other communities were 'busy finding out the means for their own improvement', the 'Muslim community . . . is silently bearing the torture of insult, hunger and indebtedness, and is losing respect for their own religion'.[30] The Improvement texts imbricate the commitment to community imperatives within the very act of material improvement. Usman, the model farmer in *Adarsha Krishak*, calls out the *azan* when he goes to work in his fields, and so regular is he in doing both, that mothers know when to wake their infants up by his cry! Usman's work activates the collective, everyday life cycle of his society, by a simultaneous dedication to profession and religion.

IV

But this amalgam of individual profit with collective betterment, imposes its limits. Obviously too much improvement can make social mobility rupture the community. One of the forms this anxiety took, was a concern with the division between an Islam based education and the more socially profitable pedagogy of *pathshalas*. For instance, as the eldest son of an employee of an English shipping company, Waliullah, the author of *Yuga Bichitra*, was sent to the pathshala to acquire an English education. In order to counterbalance family opposition, his father earmarked the second son for Arabic and Persian education, the traditional

---

[29] Islam already offered a strong tradition of moral exemplars, the culminating point of which was the life of Mohammed. In this period, the tradition was also used to celebrate socially concerned individuals. For instance, Hamed Ali says, apropos his subject, Hajji Mohsin, that, 'without imitating their [that is, the 'great' Muslims] bright characters and the ideal life of the noble men of our community, there is but faint hope of the recovery of this degraded society'. Ahmed, *Muslim Community*, p. 353.

[30] Ibid., p. 350.

subjects for religious learning.[31] The familial form of this division is important, for, as I will later show, it indicates linkages between the rural and urban wings of the Bengali Muslim intelligentsia.

Despite their approval of social mobility, the Improvement writers differed from the Aligarh school, which geared its pedagogy towards acquiring white-collar jobs.[32] The former were not enthusiastic about higher education. Garib Sayer sees it as socially disruptive: '*bak hoye hansa madhya kare bicharan*' (it makes one a stork amongst swans). The rationale of this warning becomes clear, when he advises his readers to forsake their *chakri* (urban clerical professions) and take to farming[33] Hamidi associates higher education with Hindu babus and western influence. The use of 'babu' and 'chakri' is important, for they were popularly regarded as the binary obverse of the peasant and his manual labour. Clearly, Improvement texts saw the peasant as inseparable from Islam.

Paradoxically, while the Improvement ethos militated against excessive mobility, it was also an ideology which corresponded to the need for self-legitimation by the relatively prosperous peasantry. The new class of prosperous Muslim peasantry (that had benefited from jute) had acted in a collective and organized manner. The *Anjumans* that mushroomed during the turn of the century, were generally formed by rich peasants, and their activities included the social and economic improvement of rural Muslims. Rafiuddin Ahmad cites the remarkable story of Maazuddin Ahmed, who formed an Anjuman which ran on voluntary subscriptions and spent all its money on social improvement.[34] Some even set up co-operative banks.[35] These objectives interacted fruitfully

---

[31] Mohammed Waliullah, *Yuga Bichitra*, Dhaka, 1967, pp. 2–3. That this was not an exceptional tale, is indicated by Mansur Ahmad's family which, though Wahabi, slotted two boys to study in the *diniline* (religious stream) and one to join the pathshala started by a local magnate and family friend. His parents did not permit him to learn English.

[32] I owe this observation to Sumit Sarkar.

[33] He also attacks western education by claiming terrorism (Sayer is a loyalist) to be its product. Sayer, pp. 31–41.

[34] It also received donations and grain from *zakat* contributions. It spent all that money on establishing maktabs and *madrassas*, maintaining the local mosque, and providing loans to poor cultivators and traders. Rafiuddin Ahmed, *The Bengal Muslims 1871–1906: A Quest for Identity*, Delhi, 1981, p. 168. These organizations settled disputes and set up co-operative banks.

[35] For instance, one set up in Serajgunj, Pabna. Rajat Kanta Ray, *Social Conflict and Political Unrest in Bengal 1857–1927*) p. 77.

with the Khilafat movement, which had drawn a great deal of its energies from the socially constructive orientation of the Non Cooperation programme.[36]

More pertinently, such attempts at pooling in capital were necessary, because of the large credit requirements of jute production. To this was added the uncertainties of jute prices,[37] whose moorings in international price fluctuations[38] made its character seem even more alien. The effects of this instability left its mark on the nature of recommendations itself.[39] While Garib Sayer — writing in 1912, that is during the long boom in jute — envisages only ways of acquiring wealth, the less 'innocent' texts of the twenties focus on its conservation. The imperative of collectivity with its implications for the cooperative mobilization of capital, would become even more necessary in this situation.

While recognizing the power of the Improvement world-view to generalize itself through organized, collective, even mass, action, it should not be forgotten that vertical cleavages had been growing steadily from the nineteenth century, during the beginnings of the jute boom. This was commented upon by district magistrates, and produced much anxiety within the peasant intelligentsia. Caste discrimination — as seen from *Mussalmaner Jatibhed* which was written against it — was growing.[40] Rashid's anger against the indifference of the rich towards poor peasant co-religionists, assumes that the rich were a necessary source of

---

[36] The more temporally oriented activities of the 'swaraj' campaign were extended into the interiors in 1921. This involved a programme for the establishment of primary national schools, co-operative societies, cottage industries, arbitration boards. A.Y.S. Alam, *Khilafat Movement and the Muslims of Bengal*, M. Phil Thesis, Jawaharlal Nehru University, 1979, pp. 152–6. By January 1921, these preoccupations became so popular that Khilafat demands were made an adjunct of the demand for swaraj. Ibid.

[37] Two periods of booms had occurred between roughly 1905–1913, and 1922–1925. The biggest boom took place between 1907–13, being cut short in 1914 with the outbreak of war, when prices fell by nearly 40 per cent of its 1913 level. Prices recovered in 1919, only to slump in the 1920–22 period. From 1925 there was a fall, which accelerated with the Depression. Bose, *Agrarian Bengal*, p. 79.

[38] Ibid, p. 32.

[39] Tanika Sarkar, *Bengal, 1928–1934: The Politics of Protest*, Delhi, 1987, pp. 19–20, Bose, *Agrarian Bengal*, p. 80, Abedali Mian, *Kalir Chakra*, Rangpur, 1333[1926].

[40] Mohammed Yakub Ali, *Mussalmaner Jatibhed* (Caste Divisions amongst Muslims), Hooghly, 1334[1927].

76 Carving Blocs

charity and patronage. This was a belief that accounted for a great deal of the influence of people like Pir Abu Bakr. However, the intensity of Rashid's anger resists an easy or full recuperation, indicating a degree of intractibility about the problem.

It is here that the location of the Hindu other in these Improvement texts becomes significant. It may be recalled that the Hindu was overwhelmingly embodied in the figure of the moneylender. The structure of these tales requires the Hindu other to tempt the Muslim peasant and entrap them in debts. Thus the Hindu is both the origin and the beneficiary of Muslim economic misery. Interestingly, the texts do not envisage the Hindu as an other who is made distant by the sheer volume of resources at his command. On the contrary, the Hindu is seen as a contaminating presence in the self. What this structure achieves is to avert the question of social differentiation. Making the Hindu a sign of internal moral transgression legitimizes the accumulation of wealth. If improvement is a moral act that yields palpable acts of piety for Muslims, then what prevents the achievement of this ideal is the failure to reform one's desires. The problem of social differentiation is not simply suppressed. It is preempted.

By internally locating the Hindu, these texts insert their recommendations within the Wahabi and Faraizi traditions of purification. The Wahabis and Faraizis may have become marginalized in the twentieth century,[41] but their campaign for purification still enjoyed considerable prestige.[42] Improvement texts radically reoriented their tradition. Hindu influence, in the nineteenth century, was attacked on theological grounds for violating the transcendental Oneness of Allah and his message, through *shirk* (associationism) and *bedat* (unholy innovation),[43] not for being economically ruinous.

---

[41] Hunter reports that many Wahabi preachers had started to emphasize the message of purification at the cost of jettisoning the call to rebellion. On the other hand, the traditional mulla establishment were reasserting their authority by citing the Wahabi ransacking of the Holy cities as an instance of their anti-Islamic orientation. Hunter, pp. 57–9.

[42] Mansur Ahmad's grand-uncle, the *ghazi* returned from his frontier wars to launch a campaign against music as anti-Islamic. Although he was a Wahabi and not treated as part of the majority community of Hanafis, and despite the general resentment he acquired (resulting in secret attacks on his person), he nevertheless got his way. *Atmakatha*, pp. 30–3.

[43] For instance, the Wahabis objected to the fatihah (prayers for the dead)

The persistence of purification in our period, suggests an important psychological problem related to subordination. It may be recalled that the major area of reformist concern was that of festivities. Participation in Hindu festivals by Muslims had been a major source of the syncretic culture of rural Bengal. An important aspect of Hindu festivals was their elaborate pomp and pageantry, enabled by the support of rich, parvenu landowners. On the other hand, orthodox Muslim festivals were fairly sparse affairs.[44] This allowed the appeal of Hindu festivals to cut across religious divides, especially through forms such as *jatras* which rooted dramatic spectacle in poetry and story.[45]

Tamizuddin Khan, who spent his boyhood in Faridpur, recollects: 'As against the plethora of Hindu festivals Muslim festivals were few and far between. Muslim festivals were generally of an austere character devoid of frivolous merry-making.'[46] Desire — embodied by the excess in Hindu festivities — lies at the heart of this fairly conventional structure of opposition with stern moralism. Less expressive, but more important socially, is the power of austerity. Its importance stems from its enabling function in countering social asymmetries that were legitimized by those festivities.

It is well known how distinctions in language and space marked the relationship between the upper castes and Muslims. Occasions like jatras played a great part in legitimizing these hierarchies since they attached desire to the proclamation of power by the upper castes. Mansur bitterly recalls how the majority of the audience at jatras in Dhanikhola were Muslims who attended, despite the ignominy of being made to stand in segregated enclosures.[47] An

---

for not only resembling the *shraddh* ceremony of Hindus, but also because it was thought that the worship of dead mortals, amounted to associating them with God in the realm of worship and was thus a form of shirk. Abhijit Dutta, *Muslim Society in Transition: Titu Meer's Revolt (1831)*, Calcutta, 1986, p. 32. Here, of course, such transgression are viewed as primarily economic.

[44] I owe this insight to Tanika Sarkar. See the elaboration of this point in Gustav von Grunebaum, *Muhammadan Festivals*, London, 1951, rpt. 1981, pp. 3–4.

[45] Tamizuddin Khan recalls that the only dramatic performance he ever saw outside those held in school, was a jatra hosted by a Saha landlord. *The Test of Time: My Life and Days*, Dhaka, 1989, p. 31.

[46] Ibid., pp. 37–8.

[47] Waliullah also recalls the many attractions of Durga puja, when Muslim

attack on this kind of participation had to confront the desire itself. This was achieved by identifying the desire with Hindu hegemony, thereby converting its meaning into one of entrapment. Conversely, the equation gave to Improvement a sub-text of social liberation and community bonding. Being well-off becomes evidence of freedom from the entrapment in Hinduized desires and correspondingly, the ability to help Muslims.

But the figure of the Hindu does more than this. Earlier I had discussed the social responsibilities enjoined by Improvement. The invocation of the Hindu Other makes this more concrete. By embodying in him the horrors of a non-Islamic life, he becomes a constant reminder of Islamic duties. A story about A.K. Ghuznavi, a landlord of Tangail (Mymensingh) who was to become a co-leader of the generally disliked, loyalist ministry with Byomkesh Chakravarty, illuminates this. In 1926, while leading the campaign against the playing of music before mosques, he had, it was reported, allowed music to be played at his daughter's marriage. In a period when the very playing of music was deemed unislamic, Ghaznavi had to make amends. Summoning a meeting of his tenants at Dilduar, he began his speech with a long prayer to Allah, then dwelt on the fallen state of Islam, and finally announced economic and religious concessions.[48] Vulnerability to Hinduness could only be offset by religio-economic concessions, making them a palliative alternative to the former.

IV

Till now I have dealt with what I have extrapolated from Improvement literature as its dominant theme. This concerns the production of a new Muslim identity grounded in religio-economic power. The othering of the Hindu provides a rallying point for both

---

labourers would get *bakshis*; equally important was that 'the music would make them forget the remembrance of the day's hard labour'. *Yuga*, p. 62.

[48] Among the five concessions announced by Ghaznavi, four concerned scholarships, permission to dig/possess tanks, *kutcha* walls, trees and hold 1/5 of land as rent free (following a Mughal law); one allowed freedom to construct mosques. Past and Present Condition of Muslims, Mass Meeting of the Muslims of the District of Mymensingh, held at Dilduar (Tangail), Hindu-Muslim Unity — Appeal for Mutual Toleration: Sunday, the fourth of July, 1926, Presidential Address by Hadji Mr A.K. Ghaznavi, enclosed in File No. 179/1/1926, NAI, Home Poll.

economic empowerment and ritual purity. But the discourse of Improvement is not co-terminus with this ideological framework. It also relates to other identity formations although these are located at its margins. But their implications are far from marginal, since they challenge the very structure of Hindu-Muslim separation.

I have already indicated the problems of trying to translate class into Muslim community. Garib Sayer's instance further illuminates the problems attendant on such attempts. While denouncing landlord oppression, he insinuates the fact that most of the zamindars were Hindus. Somehow the very language of majoritarianism allows Sayer to use this equation in an absolute sense. All Muslims, by extension, are given a victim status, thereby effacing the presence of Muslim landlords. Sayer's attempt, however, is less than successful since there is a residue of Namasudra peasants who cannot be fitted into any category. He dismisses the problem by referring to their exclusion by upper castes, while remaining silent on their relationship with the 'Muslim'.

If, in this specific case, the figure of the Namasudra needed censoring to equate Muslim with peasant, there were other discursive situations in which the symmetrical opposition between Muslim/peasant and Hindu/landlord/moneylender broke down completely. For instance, Badiazzaman indicts the zamindari system in an insurrectionary poem 'Praja O Zamindar': 'Society has awakened again/ broken its chains, raised its head'.[49] Lines such as these bear the imprint of Nazrul Islam's poem *Bidrohi* (1922). Badiazzaman's second poem images zamindars as huge stomachs fattened on peasant's blood. It recalls Nazrul even more forcefully by imagining lightning playing around the *praja's* head like the *kalbaisakhi* storm, while bloated zamindars roll on the ground.[50]

Although elements in Badiazzaman's poetry suggest that his commitment to class antagonism may not have been consistently radical, the point is that when he resorts to revolutionary rhetoric, there is no attempt to locate problems and solutions within the internal moral area of peasant habits. A similar pattern is evident in and more powerfully articulated by Hamidi's *Krishaker Unnati*, which was written in 1928 during a period of consolidation of the

---

[49] Khondakar Mohammed Badiazzaman, 'Praja O Zamindar; Ekta Kabita', *Banger Zamindar*, Mijangunje, Ullapara, Pabna, 1332[1925], pp. 2–3.
[50] 'Bhunrir Bhabishyat: Arekti Kabita' (Fate of the Paunch: Another Poem), ibid, pp. 4–5.

Krishak Praja Party. Hamidi elaborates a great deal on inner reforms. But towards the end, another voice articulates class contradictions. This critique is a systemic one. Citing the provisions of the Tenancy Act against *abwabs* in order to acquaint his audience with their rights, he simultaneously expresses scepticism about the value of the effort itself, since 'the *latsahib's* (the grand lord, i.e. the British), representatives (referring to members of the Legislative Council), are zamindars, nearly all the Honorary Magistrates are zamindars who dismiss Muslim peasants as 'dirty ryots'. This opposition leads him to invoke a new force: 'Therefore the praja's have awakened, empowered'.

He recommends the formation of Ryot Sabhas and advises social boycott of the zamindars. Further, he emphasizes the importance of negating communal identities in the fight against the zamindari oppression, and expands the category of the *ryot* to include all rural occupations: 'The Brahmin ryot should not act as his *purohit*, the maulvis and mollas must not be present at his *fatua [fatihah]* — Kamar, Kular, Chutar, Sahis, Mashrit, Krishan, Kamla, Dhuli, Teli, Jela, Mudi . . . all of them are ryots. Ryots will look after their own rights, whether they belong to this area or another, this district or that — Hindu, Muslim, Christian, all of them are ryots.'

This line of thinking in Hamidi marks the furthest extremities of the possibilities present in the peasant identity. But even in reformist tracts based on class identities, the presence of communal antagonism is absent. *Zamidarer Bajeaday Ba Abwab* (The Zamindar's Illegal Exactions or Abwabs) and *Chirasthayi Bandobast O Bangiya Rayat* (The Permanent Settlement and the Bengali Peasant) are two pamphlets written by Syed Mahabub Ali, a propeasant barrister.[51] These were circulated to mobilize support for his organization, the Bengal Central Rayat Association. Although clearly reformist,[52] the stress on class categories produced a self-conscious emphasis on the combined interests of Hindu and Muslims. On the communally explosive issue of abwabs for instance, he states that they were extracted for the construction of both

---

[51] Syed Mahabub Ali, *Zamindarer Bajeaday Ba Abwab*, Calcutta, 1924, *Chirasthayi Bandobast O Bangiya Rayat*, Calcutta, 1924.

[52] This organization dedicated itself to establishing 'friendly relations between the zamindar and rayat, to defend the rights of rayats . . . and to pass legislations favouring them . . . ', Ali, *Zamindare Bajeaday*, p. 1.

masjids and *mandirs*. This approach is reinforced by describing a corresponding history which establishes a continuity between Hindu and Muslim rule. He states that it was really the British who had legitimized zamindari malpractices during the anarchic conditions following the breakup of the Mughal empire.

Class identity opened up possibilities that were difficult to contain within Muslim exclusivism. Class struggles, involving members of both religions, had been evident in several significant rural upsurges in British India.[53] For our purposes, class-based identity made the composite notion of the Muslim peasant, a less than stable one. 'Muslim' and 'Peasant' could at best co-exist, without merging into a single, indissoluble unit. Beyond a point, the two constituent identities led to separate directions. Consequently, the transition from one to the other, is often made through abrupt discursive switches. After inveighing against zamindars, Hamidi suddenly turns to the subject of child-care. Regarding this, he refers only to Muslim practices, clearly assuming an exclusively Muslim readership.

But this also indicates the pull of the community identity. In this period class affiliations did not provide the impulse for recreating subjective behaviour. It was not allied to any project for a social reform of habits and desires. Among other things, it was this sphere of subjective reform that allowed Islamic exclusivism to dominate. Thus, the same Hamidi who provides a splendid rhetoric of communal unity through struggle, turns to the structure of Hindu Muslim separation, when he argues against 'immoral' practices such as dowry. In order to illustrate his contention that dowry is a product of Hindu influence, Hamidi states that fifteen to sixteen Muslim zamindars had been ruined by this practice. This argument reverses the general trend of illustrating negative peasant precedents to give a (negatively) exemplary status to Muslim zamindars. Class affiliations then seem to be limited to the context of resistance to zamindari oppression alone; once the attention shifts to the province of habits, the frame of reference becomes a religious collectivity.

---

[53] See Rajat Kanta Ray, 'Colonial Penetration and the Initial Resistance: The Mughal Ruling Class, the English East India Company and the Struggle for Bengal 1756–1800', *The Indian Historical Review*, vol. XII, nos. 1–2. July 1985–January 1986, K.K. Sengupta, 'The Agrarian League of Pabna, 1873', *Indian Economic and Social History Review*, vol. VII, no. 2, 1970, pp. 260–2.

We have here a terrain of shifting, coalescing possibilities. In general, this pattern characterizes identity formation amongst Muslims in this period, especially the early twenties. Similar tendencies are evident in the organizational sphere. Parallel to the Anjuman movement, without being antagonistic to it, was the growth of *Krishak Samitis* (peasant associations) that started sprouting from 1915 in the context of war scarcities.[54] Their lineage could be traced to the Bengal Tenancy Act of 1885 when some of them, such as the Tippera Samiti, were formed to campaign for further changes in the Act.[55] Ryot Sabhas mushroomed in the mid-twenties when the Government proposed amendments in the Tenancy Act. The Anjumans and Krishak/Ryot Sabhas did not exclude one another, since both dealt in different measures with the economic and the religious. But the fact that mobilization was done under separate rubrics, indicates separation on the basis of dominant imperatives — in one case that of exclusivism, in the other that of class — which dramatizes separate possibilities, something that is confirmed, as we shall see later, by the Krishak Praja Party (hereafter KPP).

KPP combined class mobilization with another, less explicit, allegiance — the provincial. If the peasant could slide into the Muslim, it could just as easily ally with the Bengali. In *Krishaker Unnati*, Hamidi prefaces his affirmation of class solidarity by addressing Bengali peasants. He talks of the Bengali peasants' problems in terms of the effects of the Permanent Settlement. Shared history encouraged the provincialization of the peasantry. But the Bengali identity possessed other implications as well. Explaining Huq's popularity, Waliullah says that 'he did not easily understand anything that was not about Bengal or Bengalis.'[56] This near chauvinistic emphasis on Bengaliness by Waliullah is illuminating. Although the later importance of Bengali identity is not so visible in the period under study, clearly its possibilities were already unfolding. Amongst these was the emphasis on a Bengali nationalism that superseded the Hindu-Muslim division. Akram Khan asserted in his speech as President of the Bengal Mussalman

---

[54] Sugata Bose, 'Class, Nation and Religion in Peasant Politics: East Bengal from Non-Cooperation to Partition', *Bengal Past and Present*, vol. CIII, parts I–II, Nos. 196–7, January–December 1984, Calcutta, p. 17.

[55] Ibid, pp. 17–18.

[56] Waliullah, *Yuga*, p. 46.

Sahitya Samiti in 1919: 'The Muslims of Bengal since the very beginning have accepted Bengal as their motherland and Bengali has been their mother tongue . . . Hindu and Muslim are the twin children of mother Bengal and today they are politically united . . . The good day will come when through their literature Hindu and Muslim will recognize each other as real brothers.'[57]

Two things need to be noted. First, it was only the Bengali identity that permitted a nationalism which superseded Hindu and Muslim identities, while rooting both in a common affectivity. The Khilafat movement had played a major role in producing a self-assertive political identity for Bengali Muslims since it threw up a new mofussil-based, Bengali leadership. The latter were tied together by common adherence to the Bengal Provincial Khilafat Committee. This gave them a coherence which enabled them to resist the pressures of the Central Khilafat Committee that represented the non-Bengali leadership under Azad. This preoccupation with the superordinate status of the Bengali identity also involved a comment on the regional divides within sub-continental Islam. Bengal had been negatively characterized in the Islamic world from the Mughal times.[58] Further, the very *dobhasi* language, with its limited though necessary relationship to the sacred language of Arabic, confirmed for the Sharif, who traced their ancestry from outside the province, the corrupted character of Bengali Muslims.[59]

Consequently, the Bengali Muslim intelligentsia kept its distance from an exclusivist, pan-Indian Muslim identity. However they were also excluded from the more Sanskrit based Bengali of Hindu intellectuals. Their practices prevented Muslim intellectuals from unequivocally affirming a common cause with Hindus. Mansur Ahmad, for instance, had incessant wrangles with Hindu intellectual administrators who kept censoring words with Arabic and Persian origins which made Ahmad turn increasingly to a segregated literature of the Muslims.

[57] Alam, *Khilafat Movement*, p. 212.
[58] Richard M. Eaton, *The Rise of Islam and the Bengal Frontier, 1204–1760*, Delhi, 1994, see especially pp. 167–71.
[59] In his 'Note on Muhammadan Education in Bengal'(1903), N.A.K. Yusufzai claimed, ' . . . the Musalmans, fond as they were of their own national languages, such as Arabic, Persian and Urdu, could hardly bring themselves to swallow Bengali, which they considered a Hindu language, and which in fact they looked down on for ages as a tongue of a subject race'. Cited in Sufia Ahmed, *Muslim Community*, p. 9.

Unfortunately, the stress on provincial identity also opened up a channel for inferiorizing Muslims by Hindu litterateurs. Literature had played a formative role in creating a Bengali Muslim intelligentsia. Some of the pioneering institutions of Muslim mobilization in the nineteenth century were Literary organizations. Literature was widely seen as the source of distinction for any language, which made it a crucial component for any language based identity. The Bengal Renaissance had already revealed the creative possibilities of Bengali literature. For the nascent Bengali Muslim intelligentsia, these held out the prospect of anchoring provincial distinctiveness in literary achievement.

The natural tendency of this aspiration was towards affirming communal unity through a common language. In the twenties, two figures stand out in this endeavour. The first is Nazrul Islam who, despite his radical politics, was widely revered as the first modern Muslim poet who was equal to the best Hindu poets. Nazrul unembarrassedly used the resources of both Muslim and Hindu themes and images. His reach can be partly explained by his connections with the lingering traces of a rural syncretic culture, as well as with the more contemporary experience of schooling. Many first generation Muslim litterateurs like Mansur Ahmad, developed their love for literature through Hindu teachers and their familiarity with works of the Bengal Renaissance. Reinforcing this turn to a sense of sharing through literature, was the replacement of the literary sovereignty of Bankim Chattopadhyaya by that of Rabindranath Tagore, who, from 1907 onwards, became uncompromisingly hostile towards Hindu communalism.[60] Additionally, his universalist notion of creativity proved to be crucial in motivating influential Muslim authors, notably Abdul Wadud.

---

[60] Commenting upon the problems of the Swadeshi movement, Tagore asserted in 1908 that, 'They (Hindus) have never thought for a moment that we have never given proof of our real interest in the welfare of the Musslamans or of the common people of our country.' See Gordon, *The Nationalist Movement*, p. 93. In the twenties he located communal antagonism in religious orientation. The Hindus were liberal in their beliefs, but exclusivist in their casteist customs; the Muslims were open in their customs, but illiberal in their ideas. Tagore felt — a little desperately perhaps — that unity could only be achieved through education and *sadhana* (devotion). 'Hindu Mussalman', written to Kalidas Das, *Rabindra Rachanabali, vol. xiii: Prose*, Calcutta, 1368 [1961], pp. 355–8. He offered a more profound insight into communalism, when he traced it to the growth in religious pride.

Analysing the histories of the two cultures, Wadud tried to locate Hindu-Muslim unity in the overlapping and negotiable spaces between them.[61]

However, if literature provided exceptional resistances to communalism, it also revealed intense vacillations. Sarat Chandra Chattopadhyaya's instance is illuminating. His short story *Mahesh* depicted the tragic love of a Muslim peasant for his cow towards which the Hindu zamindar exhibited cruel indifference.[62] This was published in 1923, that is, at the point of the collapse of the Non-cooperation/Khilafat, and the beginnings of communal mobilization. By 1926, Chattopadhyaya was unable to resist the pressures of mass communalism, and he publicly denounced the Muslims as a community.[63] Nevertheless, his very vacillation betokened the possibility of further revisions. This prospect was fulfilled in his 1935 speech, when, referring to the inclusion of part of his novel, *Ramer Sumati* in a syllabus, he declared that this might help Ram, but the problem was that there were also Rahims in the country![64]

That a self-conscious attitude towards communal unity appeared in the literary sphere only in the twenties, is a comment on its ambiguous heritage. Both the anti-communalism as well as the oscillations contrasted with the indifference, if not unwarranted antagonism, of nineteenth-century Hindu writers towards Muslim. This produced a self-division in the Bengali Muslim between the exemplary achievements of the Renaissance and a resentment of its procedures of inferiorization. The dilemma was exemplified in the response to Bankim Chattopadhyaya's work, which, in many ways, was responsible for much of the complications in the first place. It evoked a response of intimate resentment associated with the feeling of betrayal. For it is only betrayal that can characterize Mansur Ahmad's response. Despite knowledge

---

[61] Kazi Abdul Wadud, *Hindu-Musalmaner Birodh*, Shantiniketan, 1935.

[62] A campaign was launched against it by Hindu communalists. Chatterjee recalled in his address to the 10th meeting of the Muslim Sahitya Samaj in 1936, that it was removed from the Matriculation syllabus on the grounds that it would be hurtful to Hindu students, since it featured cow-killing! 'Mussalman Sahitya Sadhana', *Saratsahityasamagra*, Sukumar Sen (ed.), Calcutta, 1392[1985], p. 2170.

[63] Sarat Chandra Chattopadhyaya, 'Bartaman Hindu-Mussalman Samashya, *Hindu Sangha*, Ashwin 19, 1333[1926], ibid.

[64] 'Mussalman Sahitya', pp. 2169–70.

of the communal implications of Bankim's works, he nonetheless started reading them. His reservations were confirmed, when he went through *Durgeshnandini* and *Rajsingha*. Yet he was so moved by Bankim's language, that he had memorized the whole of *Durgeshnandini*! Even less complicated responses betray a deep knowledge of the literature that inferiorized Muslims. In the *Islam Pracharak*, Siraji criticized a whole range of Hindu writers, including Iswar Gupta, Rangalal Bandopadhyaya, Bankimchandra and Nabinchandra Sen for not hesitating 'to abuse the whole Muslim race'.[65]

This deep resentment was related to the importance of literary stereotypes. While stereotypes were most obviously manifested in literary works, they carried with them a long history. Important struggles by the socially disadvantaged groups from the latter half of the nineteenth century, were directed against degrading definitions of the Self by the socially dominant Other. The most important site of such struggles was that of language. This can be seen in the acts of renaming collectivities (such as the conversion of Chandals to Namasudra), — which was a standard feature of caste movements — in order to rid oneself of upper-caste nomenclatures carrying negative associations. A major cause of the growing resentment of linguistic inferiorization was the rise of a geographically mobile print based intelligentsia. While their native places had naturalized verbal inferiorization by enforcing spatial distinctions (such as the ones we had noted in jatra performances) travelling to new places involved a process of defamiliarization. The self-confidence wrought from geographical (and social) mobility necessarily clashed with established practices of inferiorization. In these new situations, stereotypes became a major source of resentment. Newspapers were filled with complaints against reflexive attitudes displayed by ordinary Hindus: 'Their sweetest endearment for Muslims is *nere* . . . . When a number of Muslims board a train or steamer . . . Hindus say 'Good gracious, a flock of *neres* have got on . . . '[66]

The potential for communal unity within the literary sphere was further eroded by the positions of the liberals and the actions of the orthodox. Literary production had been opposed by the

---

[65] Islam, *Muslim Public Opinion*, pp. 142–3.
[66] Ahmad Ali in *Falgun*, 1918. *Muslim Public Opinion*, pp. 114–15.

latter. This increased in volume as the numbers of influential literary works began to grow in this period. *Islam Darshan* (1921) described novels as 'pitchers of poison', while *Al Islam* delicately suggested that they debilitated the youth.[67] Nazrul Islam's poetry, especially its syncretic imagery, attracted extreme but complicated feelings of rejection.[68] Unremitting opposition resulted in the alienation of the literary intelligentsia from the orthodox; the influential group of intellectuals clustered around the *Saogat*, for instance, were firmly antagonistic towards *mollas*. On the other hand, their alienation from Hindu litterateurs, resulted in their embracing an exclusivist identity. But this, at the same time, weakened their position regarding those who claimed to be the bearers of a pure Islam.

Their vulnerability was exacerbated by the rooting of a section of the orthodox in provincial identity. In order to counter Christian missionary propaganda, Munshi Meherulla's Sudhakar group began using a 'pure' Bengali, in order to preach an aggressive, anti-Hindu, Islam.[69] They influenced people like Syed Ismail Hossain Siraji of Serajgunj, who, according to Q.M. Hossain, wrote 'some fiery literature with the object of praising Islam and its heroes at the expense of Hindus and their culture' in his later life.[70] A person who was involved with this group from its inception in late nineteenth century, was Pir Abu Bakr. More than just a gifted charismatic leader, he represented an influential all-Bengal establishment and an ideological formation that tried to reorient the serrated terrain of Improvement in an unambiguously communal direction. It is a consideration of his influence to which I will turn next.

[67] Chandiprasad Sarkar, 'Bengali Muslim Politics, Society and Culture During the Khilafat-Noncooperation Movement', *Bengal Past and Present*, vol. CIII, parts I–II, nos 196–197, January–December 1984, pp. 8–10.

[68] *Soltan* summed up this complex response, when it commented that 'Bidrohi' was, 'Inspired by Hindu ideals', which was 'especially distressing to us, because no other poet has been born in Bengali Muslim society with talent such as his', Syed Emdad Ali, *Banga Bhasay Mochlem Prabhab*, February 1924, See, *Muslim Public Opinion*, p. 151.

[69] This group had consistently opposed Swadeshi, unlike Siraji and the *Soltan* that had initially supported the movement. I owe this observation to Sumit Sarkar. Their main aim was to prevent conversions to Christianity, and their campaign was 'communal' in character. Sufia Ahmed, *Muslim Community*, pp. 309–11.

[70] Ibid., pp. 316–17.

V

Bakr claimed to be the Pir of Assam and Bengal, wielding control over fifty-two *zillas*. The seat of his establishment was located in the relatively inaccessible village of Furfura in Hooghly. Above all, he used the key sources of mass power of the period, that is, of deploying organizations together with the printed word. Associated with no less than eighteen organizations throughout his life, they included both province-level organizations which he chaired, such as the Anjumane Waizine Hanafiya and Anjumane Ulemaye Bangla, and local-level associations such as Anjumane Islamia (Faridpur) and Anjumane Tablighe Islam (Rangpur). The publications brought out by his establishment numbered an awesome 2000, many of them like the tracts I have discussed. He was associated in different ways with twenty newspapers.[71] One of these was the Pabna based *Raoshan Hedayet*, whose editor, Munshi Jamiruddin (Vidyabinode), headed the Hadal Madrassa — a place we will encounter again.

What gave him a province wide influence however, was his extensive organization. His preachers were scattered over different districts, writing texts and preaching. Maulana Ruhul Amin, his chief lieutenant, wrote one hundred and thirty-three texts, while Pir Nasiruddin of Barisal penned a comparable number. Bakr's personal presence was impressive; audiences of 30,000 would sometimes gather to hear him speak. Waliullah recollects that while accompanying Bakr on *hajj*, 2000 of his followers stayed on the pavements of Calcutta till he was ready to move.[72] Bakr carried out a number of religious campaigns in Calcutta itself,[73] and commanded great influence there.[74] The focal point of his activities was the *Isal i Soab*, a festival of offering prayers for the dead. Marginal to conventional Islamic practice and opposed by

---

[71] Both figures of texts and newspapers are drawn from *Furfurar Hazrat*, compiled by Allahma Saifuddin Siddiki, (P.O. and Village: Ankuni, Hooghly, 1993, f.pub. 1988), p. 62 and p. 68 respectively. All citations and evidence regarding Bakr's establishment are drawn from this edition, except where otherwise mentioned. Written by a successor Pir of Furfura Sharif, this is a comprehensive biography.

[72] Waliullah, *Yuga*, p. 105

[73] In 1916 he carried out a major drive for Islamic purification in Khidirpur, Sealdah and Chandnichowk.

[74] Waliullah, *Yuga*, p. 104.

the orthodox, it was started by Bakr in the nineteenth century, and became central to his spiritual empire. Spanning three days, it was attended by over a lakh of people everyday, including followers from Calcutta.[75] Sometime it was used for political purposes. In 1924, for instance, it passed resolutions opposing any form of Swaraj that would not be governed by Islamic laws.[76] But it served, as we will see, an even more fundamental purpose.

The Improvement ethos occupied a crucial place among his concerns. The objectives of the Islam Pracharak Samiti, of which Bakr was the President (A.K. Ghaznavi and the Imam of the Nakhoda Masjid of Calcutta were the other office bearers) included the removal of extravagant habits, illiteracy and mutual wrangles. In 1921, the Anjumane Waizine Hanafiya Bangla — an organization dedicated to establishing the regulative role of the Koran and the Hadis — hosted the annual meeting of the Hadal Khilafat Committee, the report of which outlined objectives that included teaching contemporary farming techniques and undertaking religious education of the peasantry.[77] Bakr also started educational institutions, the most important of which was the Hadal Jatiya Islamia Madrassa, which offered the Old as well as the more temporally oriented New Course.

Above all, he produced a tangible, living community of Improvement through the *Isal i Soab*. We are fortunate in possessing a record of this festival in 1923 written by Abdul Bari, a liberal Islamic intellectual.[78] Prompted by the growing reputation of Bakr in his native district of Noakhali, Bari went to Furfura with a curious but open mind. By the end of the festival he became a follower of Bakr convinced by the size of the crowd — estimated by Bari to lie between one to one and a half lakhs. So many people, he thought, could not be wrong.

Central to this story of conversion is the experience of an active Muslim community organized around piety, which confirms some of the major objectives of Improvement. The festive community

[75] Abdul Bari, *Isal i Soab Darshan*, P.O. Rajgunje, Noakhali, 1924, p. 5
[76] *The Mussalman*, 14 March 1924.
[77] *Hadal Khilafat Committee: Sabhapatir Abhbhashan* (Chairman's Address), *Anjuman Waizine Hanafiya Banglar Tritiya Barshik Calcutta Adhibeshane Pathite (Read in the Third Annual Session in Calcutta [of the organization])*, Calcutta, 1328[1921], p. 17. IOL.
[78] Bari, *Isal*, p. 2.

is lyrically described: everyone eats the same food, hospitality is abundantly offered, and even nature is in full bloom, The participants are generally rich with some beggars conveniently visible to allow demonstrations of acts of charity. Pir Abu Bakr himself is easily accessible and indefatigably involved in the monetary details of organization. In contrast to the traditional pomp of important Pirs, he is simple in everything: attire, habitation, even in the way his children play like ordinary children. The financial burden of this festival is mainly borne by Bakr. The Pir is rich, but displays his wealth by producing an Islamic community. Like the ethos of Improvement, the material and the pious come together in a mutually self-confirmatory relationship.[79] Besides the implicit motifs of Improvement, which include social equality, simplicity, abundance, work, wealth and charity, Improvement objectives were overtly structured into the festival programme. The crucial, second day of the proceedings was climaxed by numerous waz (sermons on more worldly affairs) delivered by many famous speakers, the theme of which was the necessity of Improvement in the present age of competition.[80]

But Bakr's relationship with Improvement was not simply a corroborative one. He was, after all, a religious leader, involved in the production of a more theologically oriented Muslim identity. Ironically, it was Bakr's theological talents which allowed him to extend Improvement in a communal direction.

We have noted how Improvement reformers tried to bypass the sectarian inheritance of the nineteenth-century reformers, even as they manoeuvred to appropriate some of its key emphases. Bakr provided this structure with a theological direction and boundary by associating it with Hanafi law which was followed by the Sunni mainstream. In contrast to the nineteenth-century reformers who formed minority sects, Bakr's drives were directed against dissenters from the mainstream. These groups included both itinerant *besharia* pirs as well as more organized groups such as the Bauls, the Wahabi remnants, the Jaunpuris (descendants of Keramat Ali), the Ahl i Hadis and the Shi'is. His sectarian campaigns could not be seen as schismatic because they represented the interests of the majority.

---

[79] All details are taken from Bari, ibid.
[80] Ibid., p. 25.

Bakr buttressed his appeal to Hanafi Sunni majoritarianism by skillfully deploying his status as a pir. His rooting in orthodoxy and privileging of the Law allowed him to project his status as a Sharia Pir, that is, one who, instead of acting as direct mediator with Allah, disseminated the true Law according to which he regulated his own behaviour. Bakr claimed Naqshbandiya lineages and attacked Wujudiya doctrines.[81] Even as he campaigned against the Wahabis, he claimed lineage from both them and Keramat Ali.[82]

At the same time, he did not completely relinquish the popular expectations surrounding a pir. His practices were designed to recall those of the less legally-based tradition of pirism, evident in the proximity of the *Isal i Soab* to the *urs* (festivities observed on the death anniversary of a saint). Moreover, by claiming to be the *Mujaddid Zaman*, that is the authoritative interpreter of the law for his epoch, he fused the absolute status of the Law, with the individual charisma popularly attributed to pirs. According to his opponents, Bakr's followers even included his name in the kalimah. This was a profound act of arrogance, since the kalimah was the primary article of belief for Islam because it affirmed the Oneness of Allah and Mohammed as his messenger.[83]

By crafting a majoritarian Islamic bloc which was popular as well as orthodox, Bakr gave both tangibility and theological certitude to the Improvement ethos. He also rooted it unambiguously in Islamic identity. His actual theological flexibility and capaciousness, allowed him to tap the sources of Bengali affiliations which, under different circumstances, could have had a disruptive effect on the affirmation of Muslimness.

His prodigious production of Bengali texts, dramatically extended the efforts of Munshi Meherulla and the Sudhakar group.

---

[81] The *Wahdat 'l Wujudiya* doctrines of the Sufis held that all Creation partakes of the essence of God. Bakr's anti Wujudiya conviction is stated in *Furfurar*, pp. 92–3. More specifically, Hazrat Jamalauddin Ahmad, from whom he received his training in the Hadis, was taught by a pupil of Sayyid Ahmad, while Bakr's grandfather fought with Sayyid Ahmad himself. Ibid, pp. 5–9.

[82] His official biography traces his intellectual lineage from Sirhindi through Waliullah, Sayyid Ahmad and Keramat Ali.

[83] The kalimah was the first of the five foundations or pillars of practice. Bakr's kalimah persisted for three editions in a text penned by Nasiruddin of Barisal. Fakir Mohammed Hossain Bikrampuri, *Kalimah Samashya*, Dhaka, 1924, p. 7.

This had larger implications than simply using the Bengali language for Islamic propaganda. Forefronting his Bengali identity allowed him to attempt a reversal of the accepted terms of the spiritual relationship between Bengal and North India. Calcutta residents attended his *Isal i Soab*, and these included many wealthy non-Bengalis, who were normally snobbish about the Islamic credentials of the Bengalis. Moreover, he had disciples in places as far away as Bokhara, acquired respectful audiences in Arabia, and even led a purification campaign in Ajmere Shariff, the pride of the spiritual empire of the Chistiyahs. At the same time, Bakr's ancestry was traced to the first Abu Bakr, the companion of Mohammed and the first Khaliph. The fact that he did not relinquish his exalted non-Bengali origins, made him a living testament of the equality of Bengal's Islam to those of other places.

I have tried to show Bakr's profound reworking of Islamic orthodoxy that opened it up to Improvement, as well as his attempt to produce a popular, Hanafi majoritarianism. His orientation interlocks positively with two (the Muslim and Bengali) of the three identities which formed the composite spectrum of affiliations that inhered in the Improvement ethos. But focusing on this aspect also draws attention to Bakr's relative lack of concern with peasant interests. This question becomes very important because Bakr was himself a landlord, and its discussion will help us to understand the nature of the Muslim peasant affiliation, and its vulnerabilities to a communal cause, a little better.

We have seen how A.K. Ghaznavi had, in a trade-off against allegations of personal compromise on the music question, incorporated many of the provisions of the Tenancy Amendment Bill. In contrast to their Hindu counterparts, Muslim landlords were more willing to concede some of their privileges to the peasantry. Ghaznavi's case shows that this was probably motivated by the prospect of a corresponding increase in political support from the peasantry. The history of the family of Abdul Karim Khan, author of *Taraf Gourangir Itihas*, shows how small independent landholders were, by the turn of the century, turning to Improvement objectives, peasant organizations and larger political prospects.[84] Ghaznavi's actions thus appear to be part of a larger culture, shared across the spectrum of landholders.[85]

[84] Abdul Karim Khan, *Taraf Gourangir Itihas*, Mymensingh, 1935.
[85] Interestingly, both Ghaznavi and Bakr were loyalists, although Bakr

Neither Bakr nor his organizations highlighted the question of peasant's rights.[86] On the other hand, his status as a landlord was emphasized. His financial support of the *Isal i Soab* acted as an example of how a Muslim landlord could fruitfully use his wealth to create a community among otherwise disparate Muslims. His Islamic credentials were further reinforced by his strong opposition to moneylending.[87] Unlike a range of other Muslim spokespersons, Bakr propagated an unconditional ban on this practice. The fact that he was himself the member of a class that traditionally combined moneylending operations with landlordism indicated the importance of Islam which could be seen to have a regulative power over landlords themselves. Bakr's example provided a belief in the social benefits of Islam, even as it helped to perpetuate the silence on peasant rights.

There were also other conditions that helped him to deflect attention away from potentially negative images of the landlord. A suggestive story needs to be narrated here. A year before the outbreak of the Pabna riots in 1926, a Congress Enquiry Committee reported that an incident of conflict between Muslim bargadars and Hindu jotedars had been given a communal colouring by a local Anjuman meeting.[88] The latter had remained silent on the issue of bargadari rights. Significantly, Bakr was very influential in Hadal (Pabna district), the place where it had occurred. He had established the well-known Hadal Madrassa there; he was also closely associated with the Hadal based newspaper

---

sometimes deviated into the opposition. See Sattar, *Imamul Mocchelmein Hazrat Mohammed Abu Bakr Siddiki (Ro:) Pir Kablar Jiban-Charit*, Calcutta, 1929, p. 86. Ghaznavi was also Joint Chairman of the Anjuman Waizine Bangla, and the chief Patron of the Islam Pracharak Samiti. *Furfurar*, pp. 45–52. Along with Bakr, he took a leading role in objecting to music before mosques. Neither of them dealt with peasant rights.

[86] The Anjuman Waizine took up the question of the Tenancy Bill in 1929, when it was difficult to ignore it, but vaguely confined itself to a criticism of it as anti-tenant. The next resolution, which was more specific, called for a freeze on the confiscation of peasant's lands by zamindars or moneylenders. It is symptomatic that these resolutions occupy the sixth and seventh places in the charter of demands.

[87] *Al Islam*, the organ of the Anjuman Ulema i Bangla, supported the institution of Muslim moneylending, while opposing interest. The liberal *Shikha* even sanctioned the charging of interest. Islam, *Muslim Public Opinion*, p. 208.

[88] *The Mussalman*, 23 May 1924.

Raoshan Hedayet, whose editor was known for his anti-Hindu views.[89]

These details provide some interesting indicators. The crucial one concerns the implications of the likely involvement of the Bakr establishment in this conflict. While its communal mobilization could not obviously help the jotedars in this case, the very fact of privileging communal over class imperatives would help peasants beleaguered by bargadar demands — when the peasant happened to be Muslim. In other words, the Hadal incident suggests potential situations for an entente between landlords and peasants, in which the latter would not be averse to moderating the importance they attached to questions of land rights.

In Chapter 5 we will see how such situations did indeed occur. However one should not overstress their importance. The study of the Bakr establishment also gives us an opportunity to examine convictions that motivated desires and antagonisms which, even while being stimulated by class interests, exceeded their compass. These convictions can only be understood by the seeing the antagonistic otherness of Hindus as an essential part of Bakr's ideological formation.

VI

Bakr's projection of the Hindu as antagonist was mediated through certain internal campaigns Bakr carried out against rival Muslim sects or syncretic groups, located at the fringes of Muslim society. I will begin by elaborating his antagonism toward Akram Khan, for which a brief preface is necessary.

Till the founding of the KPP, the Muslim political scene in the first three decades of this century was dominated less by organizations, than by individuals who had organizations attached to them. This was an unstable structure in which leaders with religious following could flourish. This meant that theological differences could be rapidly translated into political ones. In the twenties the primary mode of translating the theological into the political was through rival views and interpretations of the relationship with the Hindus. It was this dynamic that moulded the relationship between Bakr and Khan.

[89] *Muslim Public Opinion*, p. 303.

Interestingly, their two careers ran parallel to each other. Both were educated in religious literature, came from rural backgrounds and were committed to a unified Islamic identity. Akram Khan enthusiastically joined Bakr in leading the Anjuman Ulemaya i Bangla, which was formed in 1913, immediately after the revocation of the Partition of Bengal. While Bakr was the Chairman when it was founded, by the time the consolidated report of its performance came out three years later, Akram Khan (along with Maniruzzaman Islamabadi, who turned against both Hindus and Akram Khan in the mid-twenties), was playing the leading role.[90] However, while Bakr combined Islamic catholicism with schismatic intolerance, Khan was committed to the paradox of a liberal fundamentalism. This was a serious difference.

It is not generally known that Akram Khan was the leader of the Ahl i Hadis sect, which insisted on regulating Islam by the Koran and Hadis.[91] This affiliation put him into an unfriendly relationship with the Hanafi catholicism of Bakr; the Mohammadis (that was their popular appellation, hence the name of Akram Khan's newspaper) for instance, were thoroughly opposed to both the *Isal i Soab*, as well as *Tawwasuf*, the Sufi metaphysical knowledge which Bakr claimed to possess. There were several important *bahas* engaged between the two sects, the reports of which were circulated in printed tracts.[92] At the same time, the emphasis on individual interpretation of the Koran and Hadis, seems to have paradoxically allowed Akram Khan a liberal social and political world-view antagonistic to Bakr's orthodoxy. This concerned not only his views on women, but also on Hindu–Muslim unity.

I have referred to Khan's emergence as leader of the Anjuman Ulemaya. This was not surprising because, far more than Bakr, Khan was committed to anti-colonialism. It was precisely in this direction that Muslim politics was turning, after the revocation of the partition (1916 was the year the Lucknow Pact was signed). Significantly, his commitment to communal unity to confront the

---

[90] *Anjuman i Ulemaye Report 1913–1916*, Calcutta, 1918.
[91] Metcalfe, *Islamic Revival*, p. 270. The Ahl i Hadis objected not simply to the unorthodox practices of Sufism, but to Sufism itself. Ibid, p. 274.
[92] See for instance, Mohammed Baccher Biswas, *Lakshmipurer Hanifa O Mohammader Bahas*, (Shibnagar, P.O. Kothchandpur, Jessore, 1328 [1921]. *Furfurar* claims that about 20 such tracts were written against the Mohammadis.

British, sprang less from an all-India perspective, than from an intense commitment to Bengali nationalism, the superordinate character of which is revealed in the citation made above.

This leads us to the commonly known aspect of his life, which concerns him as the most important Muslim supporter of C.R. Das and co-architect of the Bengal Pact. But his Swarajism also created major problems. It was as a member of the Swarajists that he got Das to lead a campaign on the peasant question, which was quickly aborted by the landlords who supported the Swarajists.[93] The unsuccessful mobilization of peasants was probably suicidal for Akram Khan. He lost the opportunity to mobilize against Bakr on an issue in which the latter was vulnerable. Khan also led a brave, unflinching campaign on the 'music before mosque' question, arguing that Islam was critical of music in only particular circumstances, and that it was not absolutely *haram* as Bakr asserted.[94] His lack of success on this question — not least because of Hindu intransigence — compounded the failure of his political bloc.

It was possibly the Noncooperation/Khilafat movement that crystallized the difference between the two leaders. Their perspectives on the movement diverged, which accounts for their choice of mutually antagonistic political paths after the movement. Bakr's support for the Khilafat excluded endorsement of the 'Swaraj' component. Bakr steadfastly expressed suspicion of Hindus, and carried out a campaign against the symbols of religious federationism that the movement produced. He objected to raising slogans in praise of Gandhi on the grounds that only Allah was capable of receiving such honour, while carrying out a campaign against the practice of tying *rakhi*,[95] which was an intensely charged physical symbol of communal unity.

To insist upon Muslim exclusivism in the course of a joint struggle like the N/K, was to obviously define the difference with

---

[93] Kenneth McPherson, *The Muslim Microcosm: Calcutta, 1918 to 1935*, Weisbaden, 1974, p. 86.

[94] He argued that music was haram only when it was played for sinful purposes, and not because music was itself sinful. Mohammed Akram Khan, *Samamshya O Samadhan*, (Calcutta, 1930), pp. 63–4. Contrary to the stereotypes of Islamic fundamentalists today, his reliance on the Koran and Hadis alone appeared to have given him a liberalism that his less fundamentalist antagonist lacked.

[95] Sattar, *Imamul Mocchelmein*, pp. 86–7.

Hindus as unbridgeable. It implied, that for the Muslims, the difference between the British and the Hindu lay in the purely contingent sphere of immediate tactical objectives. Moreover, many of Bakr's injunctions carried a sub-text of antagonism, and, because of this, allowed Hindu communalists to raise questions about the depth and nature of Muslim commitment to joint struggle. That Bakr's venture was less than innocent, is also suggested by his post-N/K policy. While desisting from challenging the popular Bengal Pact, he nevertheless partnered his son-in-law, Fazlul Huq, in holding meetings that called for Muslim exclusivism and incited suspicion of Hindus.[96] More importantly, he seized upon the first conflict that broke out in Faridpur over 'the music before mosque' issue in the post-N/K period, and enlarged its significance by issuing a *fatwa* on the question.[97]

Such conflicts had profound consequences. They superseded theological niceties and could become a source of religious self-definition itself. Thus Bakr claimed that go-korbani was a basic feature of *jatiya gaurab* (racial pride), while other communal ideologues asserted that dissenting on the question of eating beef, was the sign of a *kaffir*.[98] This particular logic could be extended to arrive at non-negotiable declarations of Muslim supremacism![99]

The imbrication of communal antagonism into Muslim identity was extended by transposing it to sectarian campaigns. Sectarian and communal battles were joined together. Equally significant was the extension of both into a less visible battle within the Muslim household itself. This complex process will become apparent in the terms in which the Bauls were attacked.

The campaign against the Bauls became widely known, because they took their detractors to court for publishing a pamphlet called *Baul Dhangsha Fatwa*, (Fatwa for the Destruction of Bauls), the contents of which incited Muslims to do what its title

---

[96] The first was held in Faridpur on May 3, 1925, followed by one held in Murshidabad on the 25th of the same month. *Amrita Bazar Patrika*.
[97] May, First Half, *Fortnightly Reports*, No. 25 of 1924, NAI. This was foreshadowed by his fatwa prohibiting the playing of music in worship in 1920, which had been directed at besharia pirs.
[98] Fazlur Rahman, *Go Korbani*, (Porbaha, Nadia, The Author, 1924), p. 17.
[99] Thus one pamphleter claims that not only would Muslims lose their religion if they forsook go-korbani, but it would also make them cowards like Hindus. Khondkar Ain al-Islam, *Garu O Hindu-Mussalman*, Calcutta, 1317 [1910], p. 12.

proclaimed.[100] Maulvi Reazuddin, the author of this pamphlet, was a close associate of Bakr. It was part of a larger campaign against besharia fakirs, which can be dated to articles written in the *Islam Pracharak* in 1905. Besharia pirs tended to be unlearned, but they cited the canonical texts of Islamic to authorise unorthodox ideas. Significantly, campaigns against them occasioned the formation of entire syndicates of maulvis. The author of *Kalir Phakirer Khela*, a pamphlet which incites physical attacks on a besharia fakir, was sponsored by a host of local maulvis.[101] The Anjuman Ulema i Bangla had started this trend. They had initiated the campaign against the Bauls of Rangpur in 1915–16.[102] Battle lines here took the contours of a united front of all the learned against unlearned religious authorities. As such, it was bound to appeal to the pedagogically minded Improving intelligentsia. Incidentally, the *Islam Pracharak*, which was also edited by Maulvi Reazuddin, was supported mainly by landlords.[103] The campaign against the besharia fakirs also signified another point of possible entente between the new peasant intelligentsia and the landlords.

In the second decade of this century, the campaign against the Bauls co-existed with the anti-colonial, pro-religious unity phase of Muslim politics. It was the Bakr establishment, led by Reazuddin, who gave it its unregenerate anti-Hindu character. The campaign by the *Dhangsha Fatua* organization (they even possessed an office, named after their pamphlet) alleged that the Bauls were secret agents of the Suddhi movement.[104] According to their detractors, the Bauls claimed they possessed and practised the secret knowledge of excised parts of the Koran. Their secrecy made it easy for Reazuddin to portray them as conspirators. An analogue to purification was thereby created: the Bauls, who represented Hindu theological influence, were internal to Islam and could therefore mislead Muslims. As such they complemented the zone of Hindu influence within Muslim peasant habits.

100 *Amrita Bazar Patrika*, 14 January 1925.
101 Abbasali Nazir, *Kalir Fakirer Khela: Alimganer Nasihat*, Dhaka, 1920, p. 20. Maulvis of four villages (including one located in Tippera) supported him.
102 *Anjumane*, p. 40.
103 Islam, *Muslim Public Opinion*, p. 294.
104 Maulvi Reazuddin Ahmed, *Phakiri Dhoka Rod*, (Bangalipur, P.S. Sayyidpur, Rangpur, 1333[1926], p. 40.

The anti-Baul campaign drew on the fears created by the conversion of the syncretic Malkana Rajputs. The Suddhi movement cited the Hindu elements in Malkana practice to argue that they had not really converted to Islam, and that what the Suddhi was doing, was to merely 'reclaim' them to the fold of Hinduism. It thereby did not violate the basic orientation of Hinduism, which, according to them, did not convert others. These campaigns and arguments, naturally lent themselves to communally fruitful anxieties about the syncretic Bauls. It became easy to inspire the suspicion that they were agents of conversion to Hinduism lodged in the bosoms of Muslim society. Reazuddin claimed that there were one crore Muslims whose customs were close to that of the Hindus, and there was, therefore, good reason for them to join the Arya Samaj through the Bauls.[105]

Bakr's campaign for purification went deeper than this, for it was tied to an internal imperative of reconstituting the Muslim household. A third element was joined to the combine of syncretic sect with Hindu malevolence. This was provided by women, and the specific drive that Bakr aimed at, was their segregation. This campaign was organically related to the other two, through the terms in which the Bauls and Fakirs were castigated. A major element of the propaganda against them, was that they allowed the free intermingling of the sexes. *Kalir Phakirer Khela* obsessively dwells on this theme; the main activity of the besharia fakir which is attacked here, was apparently that of organizing orgiastic dances and impregnating the wives of his followers when they went to seek his counsel. At the end, the fakir is revealed to be a Brahmin in disguise.[106] A similar campaign is launched against the Bauls, even if the pornographic element is given a more theological orientation. Capitalizing on the presence of plebian Vaishnab elements in their doctrine, many of which involve sexo-yogic exercises and concepts, the involvement of women in their worship was seen as a way of seducing followers of Islam into Hindu ways.[107]

The campaign against the Bauls, I suggest, was a crucial element in the campaign for the public segregation of women, which was something that was structured into the very notion of Improvement. Garib Sayer for instance, recommends measures on how to

---

[105] Ahmed, *Phakiri Dhoka*, p. 41.
[106] Ibid, p. 15.
[107] *Baul Dhangsha*, pp. 155–6.

prevent womenfolk from coming back from the village pond after their bath, in an enticingly wet state. *Adarsha Krishak*, on the other hand, shows how natural vegetation can be grown to provide a natural purdah.[108] Such drives toward segregation is premised on the nullification of the women's consent, and it is not surprising that some texts go to the extent of providing instructions for the husband on how to regulate the different aspects of his wife's life.[109] Bakr obviously catered to these predilictions by refusing to meet women followers. Nor were there women to be found during his *Soab* festivities.

However Bakr devised a more imaginative campaign than the crude one of simple confinement alone.[110] He was compelled to do so. For part of the ideological challenge that he faced from Akram Khan, was on the question of gender. Khan advocated the liberalization of purdah for women. Taken in conjunction with his advocacy of women's education, it implied creating opportunities for a greater public role for women. The two leaders differed correspondingly on the question of womens' participation in Id, with Bakr opposing the proposal and Akram supporting it. Similar demands for liberalizing the condition of women's exclusion had begun to be articulated from the beginning of the twentieth century, and reached its apogee in the twenties in the work of the Shikha group and in journals such as the *Saogat*. It should be mentioned here that this movement was becoming a general one. We shall see in a later chapter how radical demands were being made by Muslim women themselves.

Two instances will indicate the general drift of Bakr's understanding on this question. In order to compensate for the lack of guidance from himself, his female followers were allowed to receive counsel from his wives. This no doubt increased the authority of women within the sphere of orthodoxy itself, with the attendant benefit of allowing easier and more consequential

---

108 *Adarsha Krishak*.
109 See for instance Abdul Auyiyal Marhum, *Mahila Bandhab*, (originally entitled *Aonratka Khayer Kha*), translated by Mohammed Amjad Ali Shilani, Dhamrai, Dhaka, 1331[1924]. See also Moulvi Abdul Aziz, *Najat*, (Noakhali, 1925 and Maulvi Hakim Masheer Rahman Qureshi, *Narir Pahitrata ba Purdah Raksha* [Womens Purity or Defending Purdah], Calcutta, 1925.
110 Nevertheless a follower of Bakr advised the hard disciplinarian method of divorcing unruly wives. Mohammed Emdad Ali, *Milan Jug Ba Niti Rahashya*, Bhandariya, P.O. Bhandariya, Barisal, 1329 [1922], p. 35.

concourse between women, who could lose inhibitions produced by segregation of gender spaces itself, and talk more freely about their problems as women. It should be remarked here, that consciousness of the ritual sphere as a woman's domain of autonomy, was part of popular common sense; Mansur Ahmad's wife, for instance, resisted the intrusion of his liberal ideas into her ritual life, on these grounds.[111] An even more interesting contribution that Bakr made, was that he gave the right of divorce to women — although only on the condition that they were wives of followers of besharia religious authorities. In a brilliant paradoxical move, which could appear to only the theologically gifted, Bakr enlarged the orthodox limits of womens' consent, only to produce their segregation from public life. Sexual subordination was reaffirmed not by denying women their capacities for choice, but by acquiring their consent to their own segregation. The act of sexual segregation was represented as a way of removing the besharia threat, thereby defending Islam from Hindu machinations. Bakr's purdah was also designed as the woman's contribution to the cause of a communalized Islam.

To sum up, the communal other for Bakr signified more than a single presence. The figure of the Hindu provided the looming, unifying sub-text of his sectarian campaigns. It became both an antagonistic, monolithic other, as well as a unifying thread of these various schismatic campaigns. Otherness was a composite entity, produced by mutual referentiality. It implied a circuit of others, and operated not on the principle of suppressions alone, but involved a process in which the others interpenetrated, thereby orchestrating a whole range of antagonistic and mutually reinforcing boundaries. If the campaign against besharia pirs put Bakr on the same side as Khan, the insertion of it into a larger campaign for communal separation consolidated a Hanafi majoritarianism that defined itself against the latter. Simultaneously, by linking both with the campaign for female segregation, Bakr could make all three offensives, essential parts of the process of reproducing communal antagonism. Equally significant was the way Bakr fastened this constellation of others to the widely dispersed ideas of Improvement. This intervention involved not so much a direct reorientation of Improvement preoccupation — although that was

---

[111] This, despite the fact that she became a Congress worker.

surely involved — as much as an interlocking with them through theological concerns. In the process he attempted to go beyond the limits of theological preoccupations, in order to cater to the new needs, desires and ideas of an upthrusting Muslim peasantry, imparting to them a decidedly communal turn.

VII

From what I have said so far, it is clear that I have privileged rural Bengal as the decisive site for the formation of a Muslim identity and all that it involved. Before concluding the chapter, I wish to briefly consider the analogous and confirmatory experience from urban centres which contributed to a province-wide spread of communalization. This involves an examination of palpable connections between the rural and urban experiences of communal relations, transmitted through agencies located in the latter. The whole question involves far too large an area of study for my purposes here; what I do wish to focus upon, is a particular social segment that ties the rural to the urban. It consists of those who come from villages to pursue their education in urban areas.

Let me add as a preface, that this was an extremely influential section. They flourished in urban settings, becoming lawyers, journalists, political leaders and spanned a large range of personalities such as Fazlul Huq, Mujibur Rahman, Mansur Ahmad and Akram Khan. It should be added here that their influence was most pronounced on the question of reservations, which was the dominant preoccupation of the Bengal Pact. The latter had, as we will see in the next chapter, become a symbol of a political process in which both Hindus and Muslims could participate together in the post-N/K period. It was these students who stood to gain the most from reservations. In its basic features, the migration of this group followed the course of Hindu emigration to the city that had started from the nineteenth century. But this comparison also defines some distinctive characteristics of this first generation of Muslim migrants. These are important, for they will help us to understand the continuing proximity of these once rural intellectuals to their native people.

I have already mentioned an enabling condition that concerned the division, in better-off rural households, between the purely religious and the more vocational pedagogies. This produced —

in the same move that it created internal divisions within the family — a potentiality for those pursuing urban careers to retain links with rural homes through the family. In a context of growing self-consciousness about a peasant community, it neutralized much of their possible marginalization from rural society. The phenomenon was reinforced at the discursive level. The link between education and Improvement allowed the possibility of the urban centred to address rural concerns. For instance, it is more than a simple oddity that a student of Dhaka University wrote a tract on ways in which to form non-interest-based co-operative credit societies in villages.[112] An even more indicative instance is provided by the Chittagong Islamia Society Chairman's speech. In large part directed towards mobilizing the professionals of the town, it attacked Hindu newspapers and spokespersons for opposing reservations for Muslims. But the speech also concentrated on classic improvement objectives, like curbing expenditure on litigation and marriages.[113]

What should also be understood here is the specific experience of communal relations in the city, which gave to the notion of segregation — that provided a social and ideological charge to the issue of reservations — a terribly potent appeal. What I wish to explore here, are some of the enabling conditions for the symbolic ramifications of reservations. An important one among these was the fact that students from the interiors stayed in segregated areas. Those who could afford it, stayed in special hostels for Muslims: Shamsuddin remembers that he stayed in Curzon Hall in Dhaka, the middle section of which was occupied by only Muslim students, and was called the Secretariat Muslim Hostel.[114] In times of rioting, these hostels could become points of mobilization.[115] Those who could not afford hostels, lived as *jaigirs* (house guests, a custom of urban Muslim notables who practised it to help Muslim students), or in rooms attached to mosques.

It ought to be remarked here that a significant section of these students already carried a background of resentment, if not a record of active challenge, to socially discriminatory practices

---

[112] Mohammed Ansur Ali, *Shud Nibaran Samiti*, Mymensingh, 1926.
[113] Ibid., p. 3.
[114] Abul Kalam Shamsuddin, *Atit Diner Smriti*, Dhaka, 1968, p. 12.
[115] Abul Fazl, *Rekha Chitra*, Chittagong, 1968, pp. 105–6.

inflicted by upper-caste, village bhadralok. A new spirit hung in the village air. Mansur Ahmad recalls how he woke up to the fact of discrimination, upon hearing Hindu zamindari functionaries addressing his elders by the familiar 'tui', while they used the respectful address of 'apni' for the indigent astrologer just because he was a Brahmin. This led Mansur to confront the functionaries when they came fishing one day. As soon as they used 'tui' with Mansur, he replied in kind. His elders beat him up for this transgression, but had no answer when Mansur raised the question of injustice.[116] Instances such as these abound in histories of this period, and are well-known. What is of interest here is the fact that, a similar context was encountered in urban centres. The explosive possibilities of such situations were unfolded in schools.

By the end of the nineteenth century, education had become an area of communal controversy, although the differences were produced mainly on questions of syllabi, with senior Muslim spokespersons such as Maulvi Abdul Karim, the Inspector of Schools,[117] playing the leading role. What was new in the period I am studying, were conflicts between schoolboys, or between students and teachers, over everyday modalities of social exchange. The importance of these can be guaged from *Atmakatha*, where the description of Mansur Ahmad's pedagogical life in urban centres is marked by incessant communal conflict. In one of his schools in Mymensingh town, he found that Hindu and Muslim boys sat separately, with the front bench (meant for the 'good', intelligent boys) monopolized by Hindu students. This arrangement was accepted by other Muslim students. When Ahmad sat in the front, they were prepared to apologize on his behalf. However, Ahmad, who was also confident of his considerable academic talents, would have nothing of it and sat in the front. Ahmad committed a double transgression, since this state

[116] *Amar Dekha*, pp. 14–16.
[117] In his report to the Deputy Inspector of Education, Karim had objected to the Hindu bias of pedagogy. He opined: 'As soon as a Muhammadan boy enters school he has to commit to memory names such as Ram, Sham, Jadav and Madhav; Hindu mythological names such as Lakshmi, Saraswati, Kali and Durga, names of Hindu reformers . . . are well known to Muhammadan pupils attending vernacular schools'. The Indian Education Committee accepted this point of view. Cited in Mozammel Haque, 'Impediments which delayed Muslim Progress in Education 1900–1911: An Analysis, *Studies in Islam*, vol. XVIII, nos. 3–4, July– October, 1981, p. 172.

of affairs had been supported by the Hindu teachers, who dominated that profession. Consequently, Ahmad had another fight on his hands, when, in an echo of his childhood, one of his teachers gave vent to his sarcasm about Ahmad's act of sitting in the front bench, using various figures of contempt for Muslims.

As with other things, it was the sphere of ritual conflict that provided a province-wide focus and rallying point of all such conflicts. This struggle took place over the holding of Saraswati puja in school premises. The main strife of this type took place in 1925 in the Latiff Seminary in Barisal town. The customary holding of Saraswati puja in school premises, was now contested by Muslims. They demanded permission to perform go-korbani,[118] clearly suggesting thereby, that they held the puja to be a symbol of Hindu hegemony over the schooling system.

Such conflicts were not new; Mansur Ahmad tells us how he led a move to hold *maulid sheriff* (observance of the Prophet's birthday), as a counter to Saraswati puja in his school. What was novel was the insertion of these conflicts into the province-wide process of communal mobilization that was going on in the twenties. This could be witnessed in a variety of local incidents; for instance, a school master from Bhola town (Barisal), decided to show his solidarity for Satin Sen's satyagraha against Muslim objections to playing music before mosques, by leading a whole troop of schoolboys who marched into Patuakhali.[119] Such conflicts became widespread in 1927 (the year that followed a series of terrible riots in Bengal), occurring in Bankura, Chinsura, Dhaka, Faridpur, Feni (Noakhali dist.), Mymensingh, Krishnanagar, in addition to Patuakhali.[120] This new sphere had already provided, by the time of the Barisal dispute, opportunities for intervention by adult communal campaigners like Bakr's compatriot, Nasiruddin. By calling for the insistence on go-korbani by Muslim students if Saraswati puja were not suspended,[121] Nasiruddin made this practice into a neat campaign formula. It also

---

118 'Situation in Patuakhali in the District of Bakarganj: Diary of Events', File no. 500, Serial nos. 1–16, GOB: Political Dept: Police: Confidential. WBSA.
119 Ibid.
120 *Fortnightly Reports*, January–February, File no. 32/1927, NAI.
121 See Mohammed Emdad Ali Shah, *Koo Riti Barjan* [written according to the advice of Shah Sufi Hajj Nasiruddin Ahmad of Barisal], 1922.

contributed to changing the minds of adults like Satin Sen, who, before the conflict in Latiff Seminary, had led joint struggles of Hindu and Muslim peasants. He subsequently campaigned for the right to play music before mosques.[122]

For Muslim students, the social asymmetries revealed in such controversies were framed by other relations of discrimination. They faced these in both their future prospects, as well as in the expression of everyday desires. Muslim spokespersons dwelt at length on how it was nearly impossible for them to get jobs, since the Hindu Babus would employ only their relatives. Similar problems faced Muslims in intellectual fields: Mansur recalls how his contract with a publisher was unfairly cancelled, when he had refused to publish a glossary on the Muslim words that he had used in his book (since a similar procedure was not adopted for sanskritized Bengali written by Hindus). On the other hand, the everyday was bounded by the imposition of disabilities on Muslims. Torn between desire and self-respect, Mansur and his friends would stand in front of Hindu sweet shops which they could not enter because of untouchability rules. The point of this story is not the fact that they could not get what they wanted, but that the anonymity of the city allowed them the possibility to assume another identity in order to satisfy their desire. Sometimes they would eat sweets by pretending they were Hindu. A similar story concerns certain sex workers of Calcutta who did not entertain Muslims. Mansur's friends told him that the only way to gain admittance to their company was to dress as a Hindu.

I wish to look a little more at the effects of this anonymity provided by the city. It leads to paradoxical consequences. The fact that it permits changeability, does not seem to solve the problem of identity. On the contrary, the possibility of changing one's affiliations appears to make it even more important. In this way it contributes to the privileging of the outward signs of the body, thus providing the only marks of identification in conditions of anonymity. The intensification of the significance bestowed on the semiotic of the body, leads to it becoming a necessary accompaniment of ideological choices. Each shift of Mansur's opinions — and there are several — was accompanied by a change in the

---

[122] *Fortnightly Reports*, March first half. In retaliation, a dead cow was placed within the Seminary campus. Later the Seminary itself was burnt. 'Situation at Patuakhali'.

way he looked. For instance, when he joined the League Against Mollaism, he altered the colour of his beard and wore the more Bengali looking *punjabi* rather than *kurtas*. This preoccupation with outward appearance was the most interesting point in a speech given by a contemporary intellectual, Maulana Malihabadi who, according to Mansur's report, argued that the Prophet had recommended the folding of beards, so that Islam could attract others by embodying the values of civilization.

At this point it ought to be stated that the power of this concern derived not only from urban pressures, but had roots in nineteenth-century conflicts within Islam. The beard occupied a special place; Titu Meers' revolt began when a beard tax was levied on his followers by the local zamindar who was encouraged by his Hanafi peasants.[123] By the twenties of this century, the beard had become a general issue; fatwas were passed. One of these were issued by a maulvi from B.M. College of Barisal town, which had been heavily influenced by the ongoing communal controversies in that district.[124] In other words, the increasing preoccupation with the way Muslims looked had the potentiality of linking up with the concerns of rural Islam; both can, in fact, be seen as part of the same history. By the same token, the body semiotic once charged with communal meaning, provided a conduit for the spread of communal antagonism.

The sense of pride in Islam figured in the body semiotic, could easily slide into a proclamation of supremacism. This can be seen in *Milan Jug*, a pamphlet ostensibly written for the purpose of communal unity. It addresses upper-castes practices connected mainly to untouchability. It talks of the importance of beards for Muslims, but also goes on to say that it makes them superior to Hindus, because its absence signifies a lack of manliness.[125] On

[123] Dutta, *Muslim Society*, p. 23.
[124] Mohammed A. Rahman, *Dari Kata Fatua Arthat Ja Parimane Dari Kata Sharanushare Haram O Ja Parimane Dari Chhata Jayez Tahar Bibaran*, (Fatwa for the Shaving of Beards or to what extent is it haram and to what extent is it permissible), Barisal 1925. In 1926, a communal controversy had been sparked off in B.M. College, when Muslim students performed go-korbani. Satin Sen led a procession to demand the right to celebrate Saraswati puja in the College in retaliation. Shantisudha Ghosh, *Bir Sangrami Satindranath Sen*, Calcutta, 1978, pp. 55-6.
[125] Mohammed Emdad Ali Shah, *Milan Jug ba Niti Rahasya*, P.O. Bhandaruiya, Bairsal, 1327[1921], p. 10. See also Mohammed Ibrahim, *Nafaol Mocchelmein ba Mashayal Tattva*, Calcutta, 1925, p. 28.

the other hand, the speech of the chairman of the Chittagong Islamia Conference indicates a powerful metaphoric use. He asserts that by wearing the same clothes and body signs, Muslims become part of a single body. This recalls U.N. Mukherji's aims for Hindu society, and is indicative of common grounds shared by the two communal formations. The chairman's ambition is distinguished by a closer proximity to violence. He claims that by producing this body, a reservoir of common feeling would also be produced, so that 'they [the Muslims] find it difficult to tolerate any hurt to their religion'. Although he exhorted this in the context of Ibn Saud's anti-shrine offensive in Arabia, the event that framed the entirety of the speech was the local offensive against reservation for Muslims by Hindu newspapers and spokespersons, which included the Hindu Mahasabha.[126]

In the next chapter we will see how the preoccupation with religious 'feeling' became a reference point for the production of a violent Islam which had violent implications. And, even later in the thesis, I will show how the body semiotic became, in the process of rioting, an important sign of antagonistic communal divide.

---

[126] Chairman's speech, Chittagong conference, pp. 20–4.

3

Burial of a Fakir, Calcutta 1924: Towards Communal Rupture

I

Communal mobilization has often widened the implications of a local conflict so that it gathers a general symbolic and institutional significance. In contemporary India, this process has underpinned a country-wide campaign. The controversy over the Ram Janambhumi was a local one for over a century, until it was metamorphosed into a symbol of Hindu–Muslim antagonism and made to dramatize the necessity of altering the very constitution of the country. While this agitation has the structure of a campaign formula, the controversy that I will examine in this chapter — the burial of a Fakir in the New Market of Calcutta — shows us the pre-history of such campaigns when its uses were being discovered.

To be sure, quarrels over sacred space were not new. In 1897, a contemporary, Hemendraprasad Ghosh remarked on the novelty of communal tension in Calcutta, and traced it to the attempts of some poor Muslims to resist the demolition of a mosque — constructed in the land of a Hindu bhadralok at Tala — by the police.[1] Fifteen years later, the proposed demolition of a mosque by the civic authorities in Kanpur resulted in severe rioting.[2] In the twenties there were several quarrels over temples in Calcutta.

---

[1] 'Diary of Hemenprasad Ghosh', Pratul Chandra Gupta (ed.), *Bengal Past and Present*, vol. CIII, parts I–II, nos 196–7, January–December 1984, p. 65.
[2] Sandria Frietag, 'The Roots of Muslim Separatism in South Asia: Personal Practice and Public Structures in Kanpur and Bombay', *Islam, Politics and Social Movements*, Edmund Burke III and Ira Lapidus (eds), London, 1988, pp. 119–22. The riots became a rallying point for all shades of Muslim opinion in Bengal. Abu Yusuf Alam, *Khilafat Movement and the Muslims of Bengal*, M.Phil thesis, Jawaharlal Nehru University, 1979, pp. 81–93.

The character of such contentions began to change after the onset of the dispute I will be talking of. Broadly speaking, the change was marked by the intervention of provincial-level leaders and institutions in what had earlier been confined to local passions and solutions.[3]

Unlike the conflicts related above, the burial controversy did not involve actual violence, even if violence was threatened. On the other hand, it spawned a debate which raised questions about the very basis of the governance of public space (which carried implications for the character of the governance of the country). This led to a communalization of political forces in the city, and culminated in the restructuring of an emerging mass public sphere. I will describe this process by exploring the involvement of the three concerned camps, that is, the Europeans, Muslims and Hindus.

The crucial period of this controversy spanned from mid-October 1924 to December 1925. This provided an interregnum between the N/K movement, on the one hand, and a spate of terrible riots that afflicted Calcutta between April and May, 1926, on the other hand. The contrast between the two phases could not be greater, for the N/K marked the last anti-colonial movement in which Hindus and Muslims mobilized together. The controversy over the burial of the fakir both expressed and shaped this transition, which is why the involvement of three parties, representing three broad political orientations, is important.

The controversy arose when a fakir was buried by his followers next to one of the main gates of the New Market where he had sat for fifteen odd years. Objections were made by European residents who were the main patrons of this market, and their representatives attempted to pass a resolution for the exhumation of the body. The Swarajists who formed the majority in the Corporation and whose leader, C.R. Das, was the mayor, adopted an equivocating stance, trying to sideline the issue by postponing it. There was, however, vociferous support for exhumation from a growing number of Hindu Swarajist councillors. This became the dominant trend after the demise of Das. Correspondingly, the issue mutated into simple antagonism between Hindu and Muslim.

---

[3] For instance, in 1924 there was a controversy over part demolition of a temple by the Royal Turf Club authorities in Barrackpur; this was however quickly settled locally. *Amrita Bazar Patrika*, 31 January 1924.

II

The fakir did not spawn a coherent community around himself in his lifetime, possibly because he did not speak and only communicated through very rudimentary gestures. Consequently, he had no doctrines and required no ritual. In fact, even his Muslimness was a function of his reputation. 'As a majority of people say he was a Mahomedan saint, it may be assumed that he was one', declared a letter to *The Statesman*.[4] But there were also contrary opinions on the matter, which indicated that the religious identity of the fakir had probably not mattered very much during his lifetime. For instance, a letter appeared in *The Statesman* from one Q. Ahmed, which claimed that his enquiries had shown the fakir to be a disreputable 'Madrassi' Christian. He withdrew his charges a few days later in another letter,[5] but they were substantially reaffirmed by investigations conducted by a special committee formed later in the year by the Corporation, and reiterated by a series of letters, articles and editorials. Moreover, there were many letters written by Muslims to *The Statesman*, which questioned the whole affair from an orthodox standpoint.[6]

In the absence of any overarching religious affiliation, it would be appropriate to say that there were various collectivities that made up his followers. A group of gamblers surrounded him physically. They betted on horse races and looked on the fakir as a magical source of tips on winning horses. Although socially marginal, their presence throws light on an important feature of the fakir's worship, which I will elaborate later. The socially and economically powerful groups were the butchers[7] and Peshwari fruit-sellers of the market. They sought the fakir for his benediction, the nature of which is indicated by the fact that the fruit-sellers eagerly awaited the fakir's act of snatching food from their

---

[4] Letter from Amjad Hussain, 26 October 1924, *The Statesman*.

[5] His first letter appeared in the 18 October 1924 issue; his rebuttal came the next day!

[6] A letter from 'Not a Grave Worshipper' stated that although he had respect for saints, 'as a true Mahomedan' he was against grave-worship, 22 October 1924, *The Statesman*.

[7] The butchers appear to have kept their distance from the gamblers. One of them, Shaukat Ali, who was in his teens during the controversy, told me and a friend that the fakir was surrounded by *ganja* smokers. Interview with Shaukat Ali, June 1990.

stalls. They interpreted this as a sign that their business would prosper on that day. The market was flourishing,[8] and both groups catered to a steadily increasing European clientele. These two professional groups were, in a way, crucial to the basic rationale of the market, for the New Market (which was its popular appellation; it was actually named after Sir Stuart Hogg, chairman of the Municipal Body of Justices) had been established in 1874 to supply food in hygienic conditions to Europeans.

It was in 1990, while searching for the burial spot of the fakir, that a friend and I encountered Shaukat Ali. He claimed that his butcher's shop had been in the possession of his family for over a hundred years.[9] Along with the fruit-sellers, they were renowned enough to be recommended as an important 'sight' by travel guides to Calcutta of that period.[10] The sense of pride accruing from the recognition of being an integral part of the most famous market in the city was complemented by the security of tenure that was ensured by the nature of municipal contracts. The other group, the fruit sellers, consisted of Pathans. Intrepid travellers, their trade derived from their monopoly over dry fruits which they brought all the way from Afghanistan. Regarded as belonging to the third rank of Calcutta Muslim society (of a total of four) by members of the *haute ashraf* such as Syed Ameer Ali,[11] they were seen more generally — at least according to the findings of Siddiqi[12] — as dominant amongst the 'foreigners' of Calcutta

---

[8] If one reads back a trend, then the wealth of the market can be assessed from the fact that even in the 1970's, New Market accounted for about half of the total income the Corporation derived from all its markets. Sivaprasad Sammadar, *Calcutta Is*, Calcutta, 1978, p. 43. Between 1914 and 1923–4, the revenue had doubled. *The Statesman*, 18 March 1926.

[9] The butchers' stalls were erected in 1907. Samaddar, *Calcutta Is*, p. 43.

[10] One wrote 'it is quite one of the noteworthy institutions of the city' H.E.A. Cotton, *Calcutta Old and New*, Calcutta, 1907, p. 948. Another specified, 'It is best visited early, as the fruits, vegetables, fish and meat stalls are seen to fullest advantage.' Col. H.A. Newell, *Calcutta the First Capital of British India: An Illustrated Guide to Places of Interest with a Map*, (pub. details absent).

[11] Ameer Ali says they were amongst the earliest settlers, but ranks them after the Syeds and Mughals. 'Racial Characteristics of Northern India and Bengal', *Memoirs*, p. 293.

[12] M.K.A. Siddiqi, 'Caste among Muslims of Calcutta', in Imtiaz Ahmed (ed.), *Caste and Social Stratification among the Muslims*, Delhi, 1973, p. 141. They were also fiercely nationalist. Gulam Jilani Khan, the solitary Pathan councillor, spoke only in Pushtu during Corporation debates.

Muslims. They were also involved in the leather trade and their shops were prominent in the Nakhoda Masjid compound. These establishments also dealt with moneylending, a trade with which Pathans were identified.[13]

Despite the substantial, middling status of these two groups, they belonged to a section which operated from open stalls in the market. These encouraged rough-and-ready business transactions. In contrast, shopkeepers engaged in more elaborate exchanges with their patrons in the privacy of shop interiors, possessed an air of superior social standing. On the other hand, operating from open stalls meant that while their competition to attract customers would be more vociferous, outside peak business hours, the butchers and fruit-sellers could more freely converse with one another, thereby entering into a more sustained face to face relationship than shopkeepers serving within their own little shops. The affiliation to the fakir on the part of these two groups was then, also a marker of their socially distinctive sphere.[14] The fourth group was composed of women, and there is too little evidence to indicate their identities and motivations in visiting the fakir,[15] although it was claimed that many were Hindus and even included non-Indians — which provides more evidence to suggest the initially non-denominational character of the fakir.

Not all followers of the fakir were necessarily part of a collective identity and, certainly, there was no single identity that bound them. But what can be deduced are facets of a socially common experience, that did not, however, yield a socially consolidated group. This was the experience of migrancy that was common to most of the natives who populated Fenwick Bazar, the Corporation ward in which the market was located.[16] At the most elementary

[13] Mcpherson, *The Muslim Microcosm*, p. 16.

[14] The fact that they were not Bengali speaking, would have added to their sense of foreignness, as large numbers of shopkeepers were Bengali Muslim. H.H. Chowdhury, *Memoirs*, Dhaka, 1988, p. 30.

[15] One reason was probably the medicinal powers attributed to fakirs. In a city which had a pitiable one thousand registered medical practitioners in a population that was around ten lakhs, this was but natural (*Census of India, Calcutta*, vols 1 and 2, 1931).

[16] This ward had a total of 15,114 immigrants (of a total of 30,975 persons). 491 out of every 1000 were born in Bengal, and 509 per 1000, outside Bengal. It should be observed that the first category included those who had been permanently settled due to previous migration from other provinces. *Census, 1931*, p. 15.

level, the presence of gamblers (who could presumably accepts bets on behalf of the traders), together with reports of the lottery-like way the fakir's *baraka* worked for the shopkeepers, points to the significance of money for migrants. After all, in a fundamental sense, the migrants' life was a gamble, for it was based on a trade-off between the certitude of a home, and the unknown vicissitudes of a new life in which the main feature was to make money. And access to quick money could shorten one's exile. Stories of fakirs who defrauded gullible migrant workers of large sums in exchange for the prospect of quick returns, were not uncommon.[17] For the more prosperous migrant traders, especially the Peshawaris whose economy rested on migrancy as a social system, gambling could be attractive not only from a desire to increase their wealth, but to play with the tumultuous and uncontrollable force of money, the demands of which they had to obey rigorously in the sphere of their livelihood. In short, gambling was an integrative institution which was posited on the need to emotionally master the vicissitudes of a money economy. In a market that was linked closely to international price fluctuations through its European clientele, money behaviour would be even more unknowable. On the other hand, it should be added, that the specific form of gambling involved — that is, of horse racing — could be especially significant for the shopkeepers. It provided one of the few areas where the operations of fortune ensured a certain equality with their European customers who had introduced these races in the first place.

III

The conversion of a dead person into a Pir in order to tap the sources of his attributed *keramat* was not unknown. For instance, Mohammed Waliullah, a contemporary observer, recollected how Fazlul Huq's grave in Dacca became, for some time, a dargah for gamblers on the races.[18] What set apart the New Market fakir from such instances was the fact that he also possessed a popular hagiography, which, even if rudimentary, was remarkable in its implications. The most significant element concerns a couple of stories which tell of the supernatural powers of the fakir, the

---

[17] See *The Forward*, 13 November 1924.
[18] *Yuga Bichitra*, p. 46.

conventional testament of baraka (divine powers/grace). Stories of his power were widely circulated in print. This can be seen in both a pamphlet called *Fakirer Keramat* (hereafter FK) that was written to mobilize support for his burial,[19] and in newspapers. These stories are still retold by butchers and Peshwari fruit-sellers in the market today. The first tale is about the time he used to sit in the southern gate which was used by the Europeans and their acquaintances. A sergeant came one day and ordered him out. That same night a huge fire broke out, destroying a corner of the market.[20] After that no one disturbed him in his new home in the eastern gate, an area that was regarded as a native quarter. The second story concerns the fakir's pet dogs, who were a nuisance to passers by. They were poisoned anonymously, and would have died, had not the fakir come and revived them. Although the second story is not directly connected to any action by the authorities, it clearly belongs to the same genre as the first. Both stories contain the motif of civic propriety; they have to do with the civic question of the 'right of way'. This was an issue that was to be repeatedly raised later by the Europeans, who objected to a *mazaar* (a pir's grave which is worshipped) being built over the fakir's body.[21] It was, thus, not surprising that the persons we interviewed in the market, telescoped the two incidents. They claimed that the authorities first poisoned the dogs and then evicted the fakir.[22]

The fakir enabled his followers to appeal to a law that was superior to that of the administration which controlled their working space. The need for such an appeal gestures at a set of surrounding tensions, which need to be unravelled in order to understand the possible extensions of the meaning of these stories.

[19] S. Rahman, *Fakirer Keramat: Darbesher Ascharya Jibon Katha*, 1924 (pub. details absent). This was sold for a paltry sum of three paise, and did well enough to go into a second print run.
[20] *FK*, p. 4. The Corporation incurred a loss of 3 lakh rupees, ibid. Shaukat Ali, our interviewee, claimed that the sergeant went to the lake located near Esplanade, and pleaded with the fakir to come back.
[21] The prospect of a shrine created the apprehension that, 'The passage in question will : . . . eventually develop into a sacred spot, and crowds are bound to assemble, interfering with the right of way.' Letter from Dorothea D., 22 October 1924, *The Statesman*.
[22] While Shaukat Ali claimed that the Market Superintendent had done the deed, Mohammed Maksud Ali, who was one of the owners of the shop under which the body of the fakir now lies, stated that the sergeant had poisoned them. Interview with M.M. Ali, June 1990.

These can best be understood by examining what the fakir's cause was up against, that is, by looking at the matter from the European point of view. This gives a better idea of the burden of anxieties that the migrants raised among the people who still mattered most in the running of the city, and hence, by implication, indicates the extent of pressure put on the natives by the authorities. What was becoming painfully clear to the Europeans in this period was that their spacious enclaves in Calcutta — which stood out from the rest of the city by the luxurious presence of open spaces — were becoming increasingly vulnerable to the general city-wide tendency of overpopulation due to the inflow of migrant workers.[23] Correspondingly, the geography of their prized enclaves was also changing. For European Calcutta was acquiring the look that was to inspire that peculiar combination of affliction and warmth which it imbibes today. It was beginning to look like the old, Indian Calcutta, where shops festered on pavements, and the city presented a continuum of shops, houses, crowds and traffic. The two places of European pride, the Park Street and Chowringhee, were falling victim to this pattern. Innumerable letters and articles in newspapers expressed concern, pointing to the march of unstoppable causes. In addition to migrants, land prices were going up and rooms on the ground floor were rented out to shopkeepers.

The pressure of population was undermining the principle of segregation from Indians, which was a fundamental premise of European life in India. This was reinforced by other racist tribulations connected to the locality in which the market was situated.

The New Market was located in Ward No. 13, also called Fenwick Bazar. Here, the European society of Calcutta mingled with the Indian. South of it lay the European wards such as Kalinga and Park Street, in which were situated places dear to the Europeans, such as Park Street, the classy avenue of Calcutta. In contrast, to the north of it stretched, from east to west, the

[23] The population of Fenwick Bazar, that is the ward in which the market was located, increased by twenty per cent between 1921 and 1931, which amounted to over 5000 persons. Fenwick Bazar had an average of 161 persons per acre (which would increase if the market area was taken into account). The European population increased by eleven per cent, although the rise in real terms meant that their numbers only went up from 1498 to 1670. *Census of India, 1931.*

Puddapukur, Bowbazar and Waterloo Street wards which were thickly settled by Indians. The majority of Indians with whom the Europeans came into contact in Fenwick Bazar, were Muslims.[24] Here, in Ward 13, could be seen the general pattern of the communal geography of Calcutta, described by Nirad Chaudhury as one in which Muslim and Eurasian concentrations were sandwiched between European and Hindu areas.[25] The significance of the Muslims can be better appreciated if we keep in mind that this area contained many Eurasian residents. Racism as an ideological attitude involves notions of characteriological superiority based on biological difference. The Eurasians complicated the neat binarization which racism involved. Not only biologically, but also culturally. The high density of population, coupled with the increase in the number of Eurasians in Fenwick Bazar, meant that then (as now), Muslims and Eurasians must have very often lived together in the same building, their mutual lifestyles becoming familiar to each other, at least through their children who tend to play across community lines. In fact the fakir's followers, who included European and Eurasian women, provide evidence of cultural sharing.[26]

The New Market epitomized this proximity, for it was a market where the sellers were nearly all Indian, and their customers generally European. In some cases, as with tailors, the closeness could sometimes become too intimate, producing sexual anxieties.[27] However, the more unspectacular but closer proximity was ensured by normal market exchange. Within a colonial dispensation, contact between Europeans and Indians of lower classes could only have taken place through highly formal and hierarchized protocols. In the New Market, on the other hand, they met on terms of greater equality. They related as owners of commodities, an association that was reinforced by the fact that exchange would

[24] There were 4,054 Hindus per 10,000 persons in Fenwick Bazar, while the proportion of Muslims was 4,399 per 10,000 in 1931. *Census of India, 1931.*
[25] Nirad C. Chaudhuri, *The Autobiography of an Unknown Indian*, London, 1951, p. 263.
[26] 'The curious sight of an European lady kneeling before him [the fakir] and begging for a favour was noticed one day. She went away happy. It was no uncommon sight to see, even, Anglo-Indians of both sexes bringing this strange and weird-looking saint offerings of money, food and fruit'. *The Forward*, 17 October 1924.
[27] *Yuga*, p. 209..

take the form of a contest of wits: bargaining there, says Newell, was the norm![28]

The burial of the fakir appears to have intensified these latent anxieties to a frighteningly ridiculous extent. Pent-up European anger crafted a vicarious animosity against those associated with the fakir. Campaigns were carried out to evict the recalcitrant poor.[29] The focus was on beggars and stray dogs. 'In shops and streets given up to the selling of food the first element of attraction is cleanliness, but a walk through these quarters of our chief market is an ordeal', lamented *The Statesman*, going on to specify their target as 'filthy and diseased' beggars who 'loaf about among the food'. It recommended their ejection 'because they are a menace to health and because they are a nuisance to shoppers and vendors alike'.[30] Six gurkhas were specially requisitioned to remove beggars. Consequently, the numbers of beggars and vagrants fell from 3,522 males and 6,264 females in 1921 to 2,169 males and 1,0924 females in 1931.[31] For the dogs, a 'lethal chamber' was erected at the cost of Rs 2000.[32] Twenty-six dogs were killed in the first flush, and there were regrets that the lack of sufficient jurisdictional powers prevented the Corporation from dispensing with more of those hapless beings.[33]

The citation made above, regarding the proximity of beggars to food stalls, indicates how the burial issue could supply an adequate trope to embody European anxieties. The entombment of the fakir at a site that was close to the main supply of food for Europeans, made the issue of racial intermixing a question of their very physical constitution. It dramatized, through metonymic extension, the insidious proximities of the native that could not be shut out by doors of cars, houses and offices. The consequence had to be borne by beggars and dogs. Being the most vulnerable parts of the increasing heterogeneity of Calcutta's street culture

[28] 'Fixed prices are the exception. Bargaining is the rule.' Newell, p. 7.
[29] A letter to *The Statesman* from a resident of the posh Bishop Lefroy Road, proudly related a successful campaign to evict a fakir, with the help of the Chief Executive Officer of the Corporation, 27 October 1925.
[30] *The Statesman*, 16 August 1925.
[31] Part of the reason for the drastic fall in the numbers of females was because prostitutes were declassified from this list in 1931. *Census of India, 1931*.
[32] *The Statesman*, 29 August 1925.
[33] *The Statesman*, 27 October 1925.

made them ideal targets for the rabid animosity that was politely encoded in the appeal to the 'right of way'.

IV

This battle between the indigent population and an administration sensitive to racist anxieties, had been waged for a long time. The fakir's life is the best testimony to its persistent and intense character. It reveals a pattern of incessant evictions. The biography of the fakir was compiled by one who wrote a letter to *The Statesman* and it was substantially ratified by the findings of a committee appointed by the Corporation to enquire into the question.[34] He was a coolie from Madras (although this could well be a popular euphemism for the whole of South India). He was implicated in a murder charge, and was deported to the Andamans. Fortunately for him, as part of the celebrations for George V's accession, the government ordered amnesty for all the imprisoned. Thereafter, he found his way into Calcutta where he was remembered as one who had settled in front of a 'Madrassi' Church in Market Street from where he was eventually evicted.[35] The vagrant left and settled in front of the main gate of the market, collecting alms, but not talking to anyone. He was evicted again, and removed himself to the eastern gate, which was least used by the Europeans and the Indian upper class. He was adopted here by the shopkeepers, and it was here that he found his final niche.

This small story, which would probably have been even more representative if it had been completely lost, is one in which identity is so completely **stripped** that it becomes a blank sheet. Eviction was a prospect that was too intimate to repress; like

---

[34] As often happens in such cases, peoples' lives get to be known from hearsay, especially when they are dead. I draw attention to the information given by Q. Ahmed's first letter to *The Statesman*, which was substantially borne out by the committee report. Of course, this does not mean that the report itself was completely accurate. Its findings were contested by A. Razzak, a Corporation Councillor. He claimed that the evidence was based on the testimony of a Christian. *The Forward*, 15 August 1925. Nevertheless, the fact that it was accepted by most, suggests that the story was seen to be a probable one for such a man in the city. Ahmed said that he had acquired his information from the shopkeepers of the market.

[35] *The Forward*, 17 October 1924.

Sitaladebi, the small pox goddess, it could only be appeased. Uncertainty of settlement was not confined to the utterly destitute alone. Much the same experience could be had as a consequence of bureaucratic decisions carried out by the Corporation. For instance, in the months preceding the fakir's burial, there had been a large scale eviction of butchers from their homes in Karaya, a locality that was not far from the New Market. Many of the butchers of the market had lost their homes in this drive.[36] Despite their relative prosperity, the butchers had to undergo the same sort of experience of powerlessness over their home in the city as the poor migrants. Their living condition was equally vulnerable to municipality decisions. The vagrant then formed the frightening, intimate Other of even relatively prosperous, but socially disempowered migrant groups.

Being the sacred personage that he was, the fakir did not simply live a life of victimhood alone. Let us look back at the story. The major transition which structures it is the transformation from victimhood to retaliation. The interesting point is that the two facets of the fakir's divinity — his victimhood and his magical powers of retaliation — are seen as successive states. It is only after shifting to the New Market that his status as a vagrant is complemented and overshadowed by his magical violence. This defines the fakir's powers as not simply the product of a personal attribute, but of a symbiotic relationship with the New Market. In this connection, it may be recalled that the active intervention of the shopkeepers gave the fakir security of settlement in his new abode near the eastern gate. As such, the fakir's story indicates a sub-text of pride in the followers' consciousness of being active contributors to his powers. And if we remember the tale of the fakir's eviction by the sergeant, then the possibility of the extension of this consciousness of collective contribution to the fakir's powers into the articulation of an anti-colonial sentiment can be visualized. I suggest there were enough indications in the state of the New Market to motivate this extension.

An interesting fact needs to be noted here. According to the *Fakirer Keramat*, the fire incident took place in 1914. This was,

---

[36] According to Q. Ahmed's letter (cited above), the butchers of the market had been very discontented 'on account of the wholesale acquisition of their hearth and home at Karaya [a neighbourhood locality] by the Calcutta Improvement Trust'.

following the revocation of the partition of Bengal in 1912, a period that saw widespread pan-Islamic stirrings in Calcutta. It was in this context that a series of agitations took place in the Kidderpore Docks area amongst Muslims. The problem arose because some mosques needed to be demolished in order to implement a project for the extension of the Docks. An agitation against this was started in the same year as the fire broke out, climaxing in anti-administration meetings among Muslim residents of those localities in the following year.[37] In a sense, the fakir's life in the market can be said to have been created in the first stirrings of an Islamic anti-colonialism.

The fakir himself was believed to have had scant respect for the normally patronizing Europeans, a facet that was cherished by his followers. The initial report in *The Forward*, which was based on the follower's version of the fakir, observed that the fakir 'was not popular with Europeans, for he was no respective [sic] of persons, dirty in appearance and often rude to them. Many is the time that he has ignored the white man talking to him and he has thrown their gifts after them'.[38] It is also significant that the *Fakirer Keramat* prefaced the stories of the fakir by relating a tale of the *'pir bhai'* (literally, Pir brother) of his alleged mentor. Apparently Tajuddin Baba of Nagpur, the 'pir bhai' was locked up by the government for insanity. This did not trouble him, however, for he magically appeared in the streets one night.[39] Obviously the story derives its ironic significance from the double meaning of madness.[40] More importantly, the representation of the British as jailers who try to imprison the sources of the power of the fakir which they cannot comprehend, signals an opposition to colonial hegemony. It was, in fact, an apt story for the prevailing mood of

---

[37] 'Agitation in connection with Kidderpore Mosque', File no. 449, Serial nos 1–2, 1917. *GOB: Political: Confidential*, WBSA. The Kidderpore Docks were not far from the New Market; it was also in the neighbourhood of the race course, all of which suggests the impact of events there on the market. It should also be noted that the background to this agitation had been prepared for by anti-British riots over the Kanpur mosque incident in 1912.
[38] 17 October 1924.
[39] Rehman, *Fakirer Keramat*, p. 5.
[40] *Pagal* or *Khepa* signified divine inspiration. It was popularly used by popular cults such as the Bauls, often serving as suffixes to some of the names of their singers. The other meaning denoted human madness, as is commonly used.

Calcutta's markets, for these, including the New Market, had played an active role in political activities especially *hartals* (general strikes) held in the city.[41] A possible reason was the domination of Muslim politics in Calcutta by merchants. Of the ten Muslim councillors elected with the help of the Swarajists in 1924, five were merchants.[42] On the other hand, the local Anjumans were dominated by the petty merchants,[43] indicating a political nexus that extended across the social scale. Their business ensured intimate links with shopkeepers, and the domination of the Swarajists in Calcutta's politics meant that the New Market amongst others, continued to play an important role in demonstrating the mobilizing power of nationalists.

Such a self-conscious anti-colonialism was bound to manifest itself within the everyday sphere of market transactions. This was felt very palpably by the Europeans, for it appeared to have transformed the basic joys of shopping there. Besides the satisfaction of everyday needs, the New Market had been designed to provide a comfortable European niche to experience native culture. While the compulsions of marketing necessarily brought Europeans into proximity with Indians, the experience was held in check and neutralized by the sense of spectacle that the New Market offered. Like the Parisian arcades in which Walter Benjamin visualized Baudelaire, the covered area of the New Market allowed a vision of crowds that blended oriental colour with continental glamour. Here, both people and objects could be displayed without any great risk of intimacy. In fact, this human spectacle featured among the charms of the market listed by travel writers.[44]

By the twenties, however, instead of being the people who gazed at the passers by, the Europeans found themselves to be the object of the latters' gaze. Letters talked of the way the market was getting crowded by people who seemed to have no work, except

[41] When Gandhi announced his fast on the occasion of the All Party Unity Conference at Delhi (held in the same month that the burial took place), Calcutta and its suburbs observed a hartal; shops along the whole stretch from Shyambazar in the north to Hogg Market were either closed or half-open. *The Mussalman*, 3 October 1924.
[42] Mcpherson, p. 80.
[43] Ibid., p. 24.
[44] 'The motley throng, which surges along the numerous passages, is fully as interesting, and even more characteristic than the wares offered for sale . . . .' Newell, p. 7.

to look at Europeans.[45] Correspondingly, the other joys of marketing seemed to be diminishing. The indulgent attitude to bargaining, as seen in the reference to it by Newell, was now replaced by gripe. Letters poured into *The Statesman* after the burial, complaining of the rude behaviour of shopkeepers. The psychological distance provided by the authority surrounding the image of the Coloniser Patron was breaking down. The resulting impatience and anger of the latter was charged with fears associated with N/K and its contemporary, everyday traces. An editorial in *The Statesman* explained the 'importunate and truculent' behaviour of shopkeepers and pointed accusingly at the N/K: 'if offended by anyone in control they [the shopkeepers] run little hartals of their own until they get their own way — for which sort of behaviour they might plead distinguished precedent'.[46] What the Europeans appeared to recognize in the N/K was more than simple disorder. The judicial language of the citation made above reflects the European awareness of the legitimation that the N/K provided to popular, public activity. We have seen earlier that the main source of anxiety of the Europeans was the lack of a segregated space. On the other hand, the migrants needed to create a secure space for themselves in urban conditions. The heritage of the N/K was implicitly recognized by both as the source of the migrant's claim to security of space.

V

According to what can be culled from the depositions of the deputy mayor, the market superintendent and the chief executive officer (all of which were given before the committee appointed by the Corporation), the crowd initially approached Mr Baker, the market superintendent, for permission to bury the body where it lay. Baker refused, and they went away to look for an alternate burial spot. One was found and purchased. However, while they were gathered around the body, someone said that the fakir's body could not be moved from where it lay. Interpreting it as the wish of the fakir to be buried where he was, the followers now decided to go

---

[45] An editorial in *The Statesman* wrote of 'the crowds of undesirable people who haunt the New Market for no ostensible purpose except to stare at respectable buyers and make remarks about them'. 25 October 1924.
[46] 18 March 1926.

ahead with their earlier resolve, regardless of the consequences. By now news had travelled to disturb Corporation bigwigs, and both the chief executive officer, the deputy mayor and Shamsul Huq, a councillor, reached the place. In the parleys that followed, Subhash Bose, the C.E.O, approached Fazlul Huq who okayed the burial as part of orthodox Islamic practice. The next day the whole action was given public sanction by the newspapers, including *The Statesman*, which reported that the Corporation had given its approval.

The story is an index of the new kind of power that the fakir represented. Studies of the relationship between religion and mass national level movements have typically shown how religious motifs, especially that of symbolism, were deployed to gather popular support. The fakir's case shows that this was not a one-way process, for, in the process of interaction, the religious sphere became imbricated with the institutions and desires of mass struggle. On the one hand, we have seen how the traditional charisma of the fakir was drawn from the inverted relationship with the migrants' lack of control over urban space as well as the desire to momentarily overcome the power of an opaque money economy that demanded close subservience to its logic. This was now joined to a positive belief in popular movements that asserted itself against the wishes of European administrative personnel. It must be observed here that the N/K movement had seen the involvement of renowned pirs such as Abu Bakr of Hooghly and Badshah Mian of Faridpur,[47] which provided legitimacy and confidence to the movement. There was also a more informal sort of pirism, which resulted from the importance given to the leaders of the N/K. For instance, Mansur Ahmad recalls how his speeches were so compelling, that he started being regarded as a pir.[48] The New Market fakir was, however, different. He derived not only his pirship, but the whole range of his meanings, from his followers.[49] The most significant of these was produced by the

[47] When Pir Badshah Mian was arrested, he was accompanied by thousands of his followers to Calcutta all the way from Faridpur. Alam, Khilafat Movement, p. 178.

[48] *Atmakatha*, pp. 195–9.

[49] I have used fakir and pir interchangeably; as a matter of fact, this very elasticity of usage is a result of the way the fakir's followers wrought his meaning. His pre-eastern gate life can be said to resemble that of a fakir's, in the sense that a fakir is distinguished above all, by his ceaseless travel. A pir,

attempts of the followers to legitimize their beliefs through public institutions.

As is well known, a mazaar is normally cared for by the heirs of the pir, with powers being concentrated in the hands of the *sajjada nashin* (the guardian of the shrine). There were some local instances in Barasat and Hooghly, of mazaars being maintained by the followers of the pir.[50] In contrast to the latter, the New Market offered a new phenomenon. In the course of the negotiations with Corporation officials, a Mazaar Committee was established. Now, the institution of a committee with its notion of accountability to its constituency, was already familiar to the Islamic world in Bengal: both the Anjuman e Ulema i Bangla and its Jamaite counterpart, had operated with such institutions in order to justify both their use of public subscriptions, as well as demonstrate the accountability of those institutions to all strands of Islamic thought, since their avowed aim was to unite all schools of Ulemas without creating an order of domination for any. To a heterogeneous lot such as the followers of the fakir, both the imperative of accountability to different persuasions, in addition to financial responsibility (Rs 3000 was collected on the first day after the burial)[51] were important. But, given the public character of the space in which the fakir was buried, it was also imperative to acquire authoritative public legitimation. And this was made possible by the idea of a committee, for it allowed the incorporation of persons who were vested with public authority. The Mazhaar Committee included three important members of the new Corporation.[52]

---

on the other hand, is a charismatic figure who is settled in a particular locality, with an institutional structure that could outlive him. Clearly, the fact that the market fakir was given a settled place, and above all by the attempts to create an institution in his memory, he could be said to have attained the status of a pir. I may add here that the regular rituals that are associated with his shrine, which is still worshipped today (although furtively), has all the trappings of a devotion to a pir, with incense sticks, flowers, money and finally, according to some of present day followers, an urs. I have normally used the designation of fakir to refer to him in order to avoid coining a new, awkward appellation.

[50] Dr Girindra Nath Das, *Bangla Pir-Sahityer Katha*, (Barasat,24 Parganas: 1383[1976]), pp. 112, 201.

[51] *The Forward*, 17 October 1924.

[52] Suhrawardy was made president, while out of the three vice-presidents, two — Shamsul Huq and Abdur Rauff — were well-known Councillors. *FK*, p. 15.

Of course, all this depended on the confidence of the shopkeepers to accomplish what they regarded as the fakir's last wish to be buried where he had lived and died. And, in turn, this was determined by the changed character of the Corporation after the N/K. The popular significance of the Corporation lay in the fact that it was seen by Nationalists as a microcosm, or rather, a local test case for self-governance. It thus exceeded its constitutional brief, which, by making it accountable only to rate-payers, had given it a narrow social base.[53] In the reception given to him and Lajpat Rai by the Corporation in 1925, Madan Mohan Malaviya proclaimed that 'The work of Self-Government of the Empire will be judged by the work of the Self-Government in this city, in the most important city of the Indian Empire and the measure of unity and harmony that prevails in the administration of the Corporation of Calcutta . . . '.[54]

The habit of seeing the reformed Corporation as symbolic of the independence that was to come, was started by Surendranath Banerjea, whose Moderate ministry took credit for initiating its reform in 1918. He pompously announced that it had created 'a veritable *swaraj* in the government of the second city of the Empire'.[55] But this symbolism was naturally recast by 1924 when it was actually provided with a field for political forces that had crystallized within Indian society. In the post-N/K period, this meant responsibility to mass demands. Since Swaraj was promised to be a state of governance by the people of the country, it followed that the Corporation could become a site of lobbying for those not otherwise enfranchised to vote for it.

An institution responsive to popular demands removed the compulsion to take recourse to open agitation with its attendant losses and sacrifices. It was ideally suited to the needs of small shopkeepers who could not afford to openly defy the predilections of their customers or the administration. The fakir's followers enthusiastically witnessed the proceedings in the Corporation which lay adjacent to the market. The first meeting on the 22nd was attended

---

[53] In the March 1924 elections, held under the new Act, there were 70,523 voters. The total number of votes cast amounted to 49.6 per cent of the electorate. *Report on the Administration of Bengal*, p. 50.
[54] *Amrita Bazar Patrika*, 17 April 1925.
[55] See, *Report on the Working of the Reformed Constitution in Bengal, 1921–1927*, Calcutta, 1928, p. 62.

by few Councillors.⁵⁶ No doubt, like the parliamentarians of today, they did not expect their application to everyday business to be witnessed. At any rate, they appear to have been comfortable with the inherited elitism of the Corporation's functioning. In contrast, the visitors galleries were full and the crowd spilled into the corridors, while the press table had no less than fourteen reporters in attendance.⁵⁷ This mass attendance had a salutary effect on the interest of the Councillors who were subsequently punctual and regular.

VI

What I have been exploring so far is the way the various tensions structuring Calcutta's urban space in the twenties related to an institution of public authority. The whole relationship became problematic because the latter had emerged as a popular institution that drew its representativeness from the energies of a mass movement. At the heart of the problems posed by this change, was the character of the entity that mediated between urban space and the revised public authority, that is, the newly emergent mass public sphere. In order to appreciate this complication I will begin with a quick recapitulation of the Public.

The idea of a religious Public, whether Hindu or Muslim, was already extant in the nineteenth century. But it had then pertained to the sphere of personal laws alone. And these were premised on a segregation of religious communities. The idea of a 'Public' in these cases did not operate as a general notion, applicable to all collective identities. Superficially, the governing notion of an Islamic Public involved in the New Market burial may seem continuous with this heritage. But the context of its occurrence gave it a very different meaning. For what was apparent in the years immediately following the N/K, was the emergence of a mass public that could institutionally consolidate the Hindu Muslim federative mutuality left by the N/K.

At the moment of its conception, the particularism of the 'Islamic' component did not create a problem. The Swarajya Party was premised on a federation of Hindu and Muslim collectivities,

⁵⁶ *The Forward*, 24 October 1924.
⁵⁷ *The Statesman*, 24 October 1924.

which had been underwritten by the Bengal Pact. Passed in December 1923, the Pact promised a larger share of appointments to Muslims in the Corporation, as well as the voluntary banning of the playing of music before mosques and the freedom to perform go-korbani. Its most important feature was the promise of a majority share of jobs to Muslims after the attainment of Swaraj The seriousness of these commitments were validated by Subhash Bose's appointment of twenty-five Muslims to the Corporation, a few months before the burial. Given this supportive atmosphere, the burial was celebrated as a sign of the cultural mutuality that could accompany the federative arrangements which the Swarajya party embodied. Initially, there was, at every step, a sense of joint effort. The very process of negotiations became emblematic of governance by communal unity, for the final consent came from none other than the new darling of the bhadralok, Subhash Bose, who, moreover, proceeded on the advice of the chief Muslim antagonist of the Swarajists, Fazlul Huq. Further, the sense of unity was consolidated by the newspapers which dwelt on the syncretic implications of the fakir. *The Forward*, the main newspaper of the Swarajists proclaimed explicitly, 'All — whatever it was, men respected him, and claimed by Moslem, Hindu and Christian, he becomes a symbol of unity, which his grave in the market will emphasise'.[58] The *Dainik Basumati*, a leading vernacular newspaper that was also in the forefront of the Hindu communal challenge, approvingly dwelt on the notion of renunciation as embodied in the fakir, no doubt to appeal to the proclivities of its Hindu readers.[59] Even the initial report in *The Statesman*, written possibly by a junior reporter, referred to the many Hindu women who came to visit the shrine, and portrayed the event with a degree of reverence.[60]

What was involved here was a new, inclusive notion of the public sphere as a circuit that connected ordinary working people

[58] 17 October 1924.
[59] 31 Ashwin, 1331[1924]. Cited in *FK*, p. 4.
[60] 16 October 1924. The deep sympathy with which the reporter witnessed the proceedings is palpable in his description: 'For over fifteen years Data Sahib sat in the passage, a lonely figure speaking to no one and begging from none', his 'few wants' being supplied by Muslim tradesmen. The report concluded: 'All day yesterday there was a never ceasing flow of visitors to the scene, the crowd completely blocking the lane [which bordered the market, called Kora Bardar Lane] as well as the passage.'

and their commitments to popular representative institutions and the press. Unfortunately, the very terms of its grounding contained its vulnerability. The problem with this public was that it did not have enough time to devise its own norms, its internal mechanisms of common appeal that goes by the name of 'public good'. On the contrary, this new mass public was a non-formal, ad hoc extension, whose real source of legitimacy was a mass movement that had failed. Its overwhelming dependence on political processes alone meant that this new notion of the public could not absorb a reconstitution of the political sphere. Such a configuration did take place, and it came through an unexpected route.

On 16 October 1924, together with the largely favourable report in *The Statesman*, appeared another item which reported the objections to the fakir's burial by Colonel Crawford, Secretary of the European Association. He obviously represented powerful interests, since the very next day the lead editorial in the same newspaper criticized the burial. A week later the campaign was joined in the Corporation by the European councillors, spearheaded by D.J. Cohen.[61] The main objection was on grounds of hygiene. Their argument appeared to be fairly strong, for, as mentioned earlier, the New Market had been founded on this basis. As the first municipal market in the city, it could attribute its existence to the recommendations of a Fever Hospital Committee which had been perturbed by the dangers of epidemics posed by existing markets.[62]

The European campaign appeared to represent an exemplary intervention in the public sphere, being carried out in newspapers and consolidated in the appropriate public body. It should be noted here, that the Provincial Government did not intervene in the affair as part of its policy.[63] On the other hand, the campaign in

[61] *The Forward*, 24 October 1924, reported that D.J. Cohen had moved a resolution in the council, wanting the body to be exhumed. He was supported by Campbell Forrester, who demanded an immediate discussion on the Cohen resolution.
[62] Samaddar, *Calcutta Is*, p. 43. According to Cotton, there was 'an old bazar called Fenwick's Bazar, with . . . filthy lanes and bustee surroundings' which the New Market replaced. *Calcutta*, p. 948.
[63] This was part of a general policy. According to the Government's official declaration, while the administration retained powers of control in appointments, contracts, loans, audits, in the making of bye laws etc. in the

the newspapers was carried out mainly by individuals who wrote letters to them: in this sense, it was truly a public sphere that was being produced through orderly debate, and even if there were some abusive letters, these remained unpublished. The bridgehead of the attack was, of course, vested in the European Councillors, who kept up a steady pressure. When there seemed to be a danger of the issue being forgotten, as happened during a short interregnum after Christmas, 1924, it was Miss Lloyd, another European Councillor, who raised it again.[64]

Further, the grounds of their appeal, that is, of sanitation and hygiene, were themselves of fundamental public importance. It has been shown in other contexts that these notions were ideologically loaded. But what ought to be stressed is that they belonged to an order of ideological forms which were generalized by demonstrating striking practical effects: for instance, it was no coincidence that the concentration of municipal resources in looking after the sanitation of the European quarters, had some relationship with the fact that an immensely larger number of persons died from cholera in the overcrowded and badly serviced native quarters.[65] Consequently, the debate over sanitation normally took the form of unequal access to it, which obviously reinforced its position as a public question of general concern. The fact that the shopkeepers asked for permission from the Corporation indicates that they were cognizant of the general framework in which the market operated.

Yet, sanitation failed to provide a common ground for discussion. In retrospect, this may not be surprising, given the nature of intensities involved. The invocation of sanitation in this context was employed in a transparently *malafide* and exclusively ideological manner. The sheer facts of the question militated against its acceptance. In its very first editorial, *The Statesman* declared that the burial did not constitute a danger to hygiene since the burial

---

Corporation, it kept its interference to a minimum. *Report on the Working of the Reformed Constitution*, p. 69.

[64] *Amrita Bazar Patrika*, 5 February 1925.

[65] Amiya Bagchi provides eloquent testimony from an earlier period. Out of 697 deaths that occurred from cholera during the fourth quarter of 1882, 540 occurred in wards located in the north of the town [where the native concentrations were most evident], as against 157 in the nine southern wards, while only two deaths had occurred in the Park Street and four in the Waterloo wards. 'Wealth and Work in Calcutta, 1860–1920', *Calcutta: The Living City, vol. 1, The Past*, Sukanta Chaudhuri (ed.), Delhi, 1990, p. 214.

spot was located twenty feet from the nearest food stalls. Later it did a complete turnabout on the same issue.[66] On the other hand, what was clear was the character of European objections in the 'Letters to the Editor' column — many of which were censored for their explicit racist invective.[67] More than anything else, to elaborate a point made earlier, what became apparent was the political character of the European objections. That the fakir's burial raised terrible anxieties about governance was explicitly referred to by *The Statesman* when it criticised the Corporation's consent to the burial on the grounds that it was 'undoubtedly a legacy from the disastrous policy of the Noncooperation movement'.[68] What was being indicated here, was the new responsiveness of the Corporation to the mass constituency of nationalists. By the time it had mutated into a Hindu–Muslim issue, *The Statesman* provided an even more frank appreciation of the political implications of the European position, when it stated that the controversy had demonstrated the untenability of Hindu–Muslim unity itself.[69]

As stated, it was ultimately the Hindu councillors who attracted the ire of the fakir's followers. No doubt this was occasioned by a displacement of resentment, but this transference was itself determined by the significance of the support that Hindu councillors extended to their European counterparts. There would, of course, be a sense of betrayal on the procedural level. After all the only European involved in the action had made his position clear at the outset; European opposition and the bad faith, which had motivated it, was not entirely unexpected. On the other hand, it

---

[66] By August of the following year it ranted: 'If a popularly elected Corporation was to survive in Calcutta it was bound to meet the challenge at once to *public health*, to common decency and to its own rights given by the burial of the *pir* in the principal food market of the city.' [italics added]. 16 August 1925.

[67] It is not surprising that *The Statesman* was flooded with letters immediately after the event, which were probably so racist that they could not be published. The editorial politely mentions that they were too 'angry' to be published, but makes their import clear, when it carries on to advise the Europeans that it 'would be indecorous to treat the question on racial lines . . .'. 17 October 1924.

[68] Ibid.

[69] It proclaimed that the burial controversy 'blows away pretence and lays bare reality. The Hindu–Muslim Pact was an unnatural bond . . .'. 16 August 1925.

was Subhash Bose who had given his consent. This was the backdrop to the spectacle of collaboration of some Hindu Councillors with Europeans that confronted the crowds assembled to witness the Corporation debate on 22 October. Cohen's resolution was seconded by B.C. Das on that day.[70] The other Hindu Councillors remained silent. In the following months the same pattern continued, except that more Hindu Councillors joined Das, including important Swarajist members such as Sarat Chandra Bose, the brother of Subhash Bose.

By increasingly treating the issue as one that concerned Muslims alone, the Hindu Councillors seemed complicit with the philosophy of reserved constituencies. What was worse was the humour they expended on the fakir's followers. The tone was set by *The Statesman* in its first editorial on the subject. After patronizingly suggesting that their readers ought to understand the psyche of the 'ignorant' masses, it could not resist ridiculing their beliefs: ' It appears that this remarkable man was really a Madrassi Christian, and acquired a thoroughly deserved reputation for wisdom for not uttering a word for 15 years ... '.[71] Such *bon mots* flourished publicly, but what was less forgivable was when Hindu Councillors also started guffawing. Thus C.C. Biswas in February 1927 stated that if the C.E.O. did not implement the resolution on exhumation, it would prove the truth of the definition of sainthood which he then proceeded to recite: 'One whose breath/The air doth taint/ Before his death/A bundle of bones/That fools adore/When life is o'er.'[72] There was not only irresponsibility involved in these forays into jocularity, but it was also a flaunting of the limits of their representativeness, revealing the fact that they did not see themselves as accountable to the Muslims of their constituency.

Given the backdrop of the N/K on which so much of the meanings of this period were plotted, the alienation would amount to more than a simple disenchantment with Corporation procedures. A sense of betrayal that follows close on the heels of a newly formulated trust, is more bitter than if there had been no affirmation of mutuality at all. What helped in preparing the preconditions for the bitter communalization of this issue was the attempt to question the burial by controverting the religious identity of

[70] *The Mussalman*, 24 October 1924.
[71] 17 October 1924.
[72] *The Forward*, 10 February 1927.

the fakir. As we have seen, the fakir's religion was not regarded as equivalent — if it was at all relevant in the first instance — to a single religious identity. On the other hand, not only individual Councillors, but even the Corporation's enquiry committee spent much of its attention on proving the fakir was a Christian. Two things were involved here. The first was that while the Committee confined itself to recommending the walling up of the shrine, the question of the fakir's identity was used to create the popular climate (through constant reiteration in debates as well as newspaper columns) in which the Corporation resolution on the exhumation of the body could be passed. Given the thrust of the hagiographical stories, exhumation would withdraw the fakir's baraka, and replace it by his wrath. Conversely, the maintenance of the status quo meant that his spirit would come to visit the place where he had finally acquired uninterrupted occupation.

Secondly, even as this was being sought to be done, the very basis of the beliefs of the fakir's followers was being questioned: they were being told that their belief in the fakir amounted to nothing. The followers did not possess a vocabulary to declare their beliefs; their convictions could neither draw on orthodox Islam, nor could they express themselves in a language of self-conscious syncreticism. At best, their faith could be defined as a manifestation of popular Islam, the strength of which lay in its intimate and inverted relationship with everyday life, a frame of reference which made religious identity a not particularly important factor for the purpose of worship. What they did possess, however, was a claim on their leadership, which was an inheritance of the N/K movement. And the power of this claim became increasingly apparent as Muslim councillors became progressively isolated. It was in this situation that the logic of events took over.

VII

Till the death of C.R. Das in June 1925, it was still possible to disaggregate the Hindu response. But Hindu communalism, driven by a growing paranoia in the Hindu middle class about the provisions of the Bengal Pact, was growing in terms of ideas, dispositions and organization. It had been Das' personal charisma, skills and non communal reputation that had prevented a wholesale attack on the Pact. His death signalled a reversal of the situation.

The trouble began immediately afterwards, with Gandhi at its centre. Gandhi had opposed the Bengal Pact at the Cocanada Congress, thereby strengthening the anti-Pact campaign with the addition of influential groups like the Marwaris, bhadralok spokespersons like Surendranath Banerjea and newspapers such as the *Amrita Bazar Patrika*.[73] This was the background to Gandhi's controversial declaration that he wanted J.M. Sengupta to succeed Das as mayor since he could not find an eligible Muslim candidate (which naturally included the deputy mayor, Huseyn Suhrawardy) for the post.[74] In accordance with his wishes, Sengupta was elected mayor in the middle of the month. But less than a week before that happened yet another complicating circumstance arose. Dr Abdullah Suhrawardy, a respected Muslim leader who had established the Pan Islamic Society as early as 1905 in London, was put up by the Swarajist Party as their Presidential candidate for the Bengal Legislative Assembly. This was possibly a preemptive move to correct the communal balance, given the impending election of the new Hindu mayor. It backfired. Suhrawardy was defeated by an independent candidate, Kumar Shibsekhar Roy. A few days later, Abdulla Suhrawardy resigned from the Swarajist Party in protest against Gandhi's declaration on the mayorial question, accentuating the question mark that hung over the alignment of Muslim Councillors to the Swaraj party — and not least because he was also the brother of the deputy mayor.

Meanwhile, as if this was not enough, matters on the burial question continued to get more tangled in the post-Das days. Rai Ramratan Bannerji (who was to become a front-ranking Swarajist leader in the Corporation), ably reinforced by two European Councillors, passed a resolution to adopt the recommendations of the committee that had suggested exhumation. When the matter was insisted upon, all the Muslim Councillors except two (which included the deputy mayor), walked out. However, business carried on as usual inside the meeting, and a period of two months was

---

[73] Mcpherson, pp. 78–9.

[74] Gandhi declared: 'Indeed if the Moulana Sahib's [i.e. Azad] suggestion had not come to me, I would have continued to prosecute Mr Suhrawardy's claims as I have come to know something of his ability, and I was entitled to presume his honesty from his occupation of the chair of the Deputy Mayor.' *Amrita Bazar Patrika*, 31 July 1925. Gandhi's certification of Suhrawardy seemed too close to irony, for it to be complementary at all.

given to Muslims (on the grounds that they were most interested in the question) to exhume the fakir, failing which, the chief executive officer would undertake the task. Five days later, in his first major public announcement, Sengupta admitted that nine Muslim members had resigned from the Congress Municipal Party. Ironically, the organization had been founded by C.R. Das in coordination with Huseyn Suhrawardy and other Muslim members.

Possibly the last nail in this coffin was hammered in by *The Forward*. Five months after the death of Das, in the context of the Corporation decision to give two months time for the exhumation of the fakir, *The Forward* brought out an editorial that declared:

Having regard to this fact [that the fakir was Christian] as also to the admission by some of them that the burial of the 'Pir' was an encroachment on the rights of the Corporation, the Mohammedans of Calcutta ought not to raise their voice of dissent against the decision of the Corporation. They have fought and lost. Their defeat ought not to leave any sore behind.[75]

The syncretism it had proclaimed a year earlier, was now repudiated by the rhetoric of battle. Indeed, there was a sense in which it could be seen to crow over the defeat of an antagonist. This attitude offered little scope for Muslim initiative at compromise.

By that time, of course, Muslim communalism had also begun to influence the movement, which made the tone of Swarajist Councillors like Razzak, who had sedulously pursued the matter, come close to pleading.[76] With the death of Das, the breakup of the Swarajists and the increasing aggressiveness of the Hindu Councillors, Swarajist Muslims were becoming isolated. Suhrawardy himself made a last-ditch effort, declaring that the Muslims were prepared to accept any agreement short of exhumation; nor would they object to the way the Corporation decided to use that space thus released. Ironically, the proposals that were floated by him came very close to what was finally agreed upon,[77] which, as

[75] 18 August 1925.

[76] In a meeting in September, he 'implored' the Corporation not to disturb the grave, saying that Muslims did not claim this as a matter of right, 'but they hoped the Councillors out of their reverence, if they had any for the Mahomedan religion and community, would refrain from the exhumation'. *The Statesman*, 16 September 1925.

[77] One of the proposals was to construct a bridge over the burial spot, the other was to erect new walls which would only enclose the space of the grave,

Maksood Ali related in an interview, was to have two shops located on top of the burial spot, one owned by a Muslim and the other, by a Hindu.

Yet, when the proposals were circulated and when chances still existed for an agreement, Hindu Councillors, preceded by newspaper campaigns, resisted an accord. Their justification was that their constituencies (which would probably contribute only a handful to the clientele of the New Market) had given them a mandate against agreements that did not enforce exhumation![78] The logic of the dominant Hindu position of this period continued to unfold itself, and when the issue was raised after the murder of Swami Shraddhanand in 1927, it was clear that the discourse of civic rights was being left behind. During the course of the debate as to whether the Corporation should acknowledge Swami Shraddhand's demise as a national loss, B.K. Bose intervened to insist on the burial issue being taken up as a retaliation against certain remarks made against the dead leader.

By then much blood had been washed up by the Hooghly. But even before the year of the great riots in 1926, the 'fakir controversy' had taken a decisive turn towards communal antagonism. In fact, the burial controversy was a shaping influence on the outbreak of the riots. The wholesale communalization of the controversy was effected by the entry of Pir Abu Bakr. His intervention involved more than a simple shift. It raised a series of new questions on the character of Muslim communalism.

VIII

Two important questions crop up immediately. Why did the followers of the fakir allow Bakr to communalize their cause? Secondly, how did Bakr manage to circumvent his orthodox commitment to stamping out besharia practices, of which the cult of the market fakir was surely a glaring instance?

The groups which formed the backbone of the fakir's burial campaign were the Peshwaris and the butchers. Despite their

---

allowing the area, released on both sides of the grave, to be used for shops. *The Statesman*, 22 October 1925. The difference with the ultimate solution was that the shops were located on top of the grave.

[78] Of course the majority of European Councillors, too, felt that it was not a matter for compromise. *The Statesman*, 29 October 1925.

considerable political clout, the Peshwaris were surrounded by a host of negative stereotypes,[79] mainly because of their moneylending operations. These circulated among both Hindus and Muslims and were powerful enough for an anti-Sikh riot — participated in mainly by Muslims during June 1924 — to include Peshwaris amongst their targets.[80] The riots had occurred in Kidderpore and Karaya, both of which, were connected to the market. In his recollections, Abdul Jabbar pictures them as hanging in groups around factory gates, waiting like hawks for their debtors to emerge.[81] An article in *The Statesman* showed them as an urban analogue of the moneylender of rural Bengal: they preyed on poor folk, extorted an inordinate rate of interest and used physical intimidation.[82] So fearsome was their reputation for bullying that even judgements in court were based on this stereotype alone.[83] Clearly, for many Peshwaris, Muslim communal identity could seem like a sanctuary, which, among other things, would preempt the possibility of rioting directed exclusively against them.

The butchers, on the other hand, had become the privileged objects of Hindu communal attention. The annual session of the All India Hindu Mahasabha, held at Calcutta in April 1925, targeted butchers in their bid to recreate Hindu festivals. To celebrate Janmashtami in 1925, the Hindu Mahasabha circulated a list of dos and donts: a specific clause was devoted to abandoning economic ties with those who slaughtered cows.[84] Possibly through their association with cow killing, the butchers centred on themselves some of the worst stereotypes of Muslim violence. In July 1926,

---

[79] Although a major exception ought to be mentioned here, which is the story 'Kabuliwala', by Rabindranath Tagore. The plot revolves around the friendship between an itinerant Pathan trader and a Bengali Hindu child.

[80] Commissioner of Police Report to Chief Secretary, Bengal on rioting against Sikhs. File no. 243/1924 NAI.

[81] Jabbar, 'Kabuliwala', *Banglar Chalachitra*, p. 167.

[82] It said that the authors' sweeper had to pay two rupees eight as interest per month, on a principal amount of Rs 20 which he had borrowed fifteen years earlier. 5 May 1927.

[83] B.H. Keays, the Addl. Chief Presidency Magistrate of Jorabagan acquitted a Bengali lad of walking into a house occupied by Kabulis without permission. He thought that the latter's accusation was stranger than the story 'of a lamb walking into a Lion's Den'. *The Forward*, 14 November 1924.

[84] The actual resolution read: 'They [the Hindus] should also take a vow on the day to stop all monetary dealings with men who kill cows', *Amrita Bazar Patrika*, 4 August 1925.

Swami Biswananda, a freewheeling sannyasi-cum-trade unionist turned Hindu crusader, claimed to have gone incognito into a violent Mohurrum procession that had tried to start a riot. He circulated a report on it in which the group he held to be the most aggressive were the butchers.[85] Not surprisingly, a permanent legacy of the 1926 riots is a cluster of butchers' shops, started in the course of the riots by Hindus, which announced their religious identity through signboards (sometimes stating they were 'Bengali' which meant Hindu): these shops can be seen even today.[86] It is not difficult to imagine that the burden of these stereotypes would facilitate the communalization of the butchers, for whom a communalized Islam would not only offer the security of a larger collectivity, but also guarantee them a privileged position within it.

More than anything else, the very logic of conflict appears to have made the fakir's burial into a cause that transcended their everyday concerns. The European customers began a move to boycott the market as a retaliation against the burial,[87] and it was successful enough to the force shopkeepers' associations to plead with them. But it was a measure of the still extant solidarity between all the shopkeepers of the market, that their memorials did not refer to the burial at all, and, consequently, offered no concessions on that score.[88]

The fakir, whose benediction in his lifetime consisted largely of the bestowal of monetary grace, was, after his death, now transformed into a symbol for whom monetary sacrifice was made. The fakir now became a conventionally pure and absolute symbol of transcendence. This was an important development since the absolute status of the fakir could provide an alternate court of appeal

---

[85] Biswananda substantiated his observation by reporting that at a point when other Muslims had fled, the butchers took out their hidden daggers. *Amrita Bazar Patrika*, 23 July 1926.

[86] I owe this observation to Sumit Sarkar.

[87] A letter from 'Tweedsider' claimed that attendance at the market had fallen by fifty per cent. *Amrita Bazar Patrika*, 28 October 1924.

[88] A letter from Abdul Ghani on behalf of the Hogg Market Traders Association, stated that the body was constituted by stall-holders, and its 'fundamental aims and objects are to ensure a constant observance of polite etiquette, attention, and civility towards their European counterparts'. It went on to blame the shop assistants for the misbehaviour their customers may have experienced. *The Statesman*, 2 November 1924. The Secretary of this organization bore a Bengali Hindu name, D.C. Bose.

to the fragmented N/K heritage. It prepared the grounds for the fakir's appeal to seem higher than that of a shared, mass public and gave to the fakir a status that was homologous to Islam itself. Once the process of questioning the Muslimness of the fakir began, it was but a small move to slide the fakir into the transcendental status of Islam itself, for which lives could be offered.

But if the followers of the fakir were ready for Bakr's intervention, what allowed the latter to suspend his problems with unreformed Islam? Bakr's reformist zeal was not unknown in Calcutta. In 1916 he embarked on a campaign against besharia Islam in Kidderpore, Sealdah, Karaya and Chandnichowk, locations that formed a crescent around Ward 13. These campaigns were apparently very popular, attracting audiences of twelve thousand strong.[89] In an even more ferocious effort, as part of his campaign against grave worship, he demolished 24 *dargahs* in Calcutta on a single day.[90]

I have posed this question in terms of Bakr's theological preferences alone. But it has a more general bearing on the nature of Calcutta's Islam. In contrast to rural Bengal, where the nineteenth-century reform movements were associated with the more plebeian (at any rate, non-upper-class) Muslims, in Calcutta it was the *haute ashraf* and the new rural migrants who represented the orthodox sections. Waliullah, a member of the new rural middle-class migrants, observes that Calcutta's Islam was structured by an opposition between upper-class reformed sections on the one hand, and a mass of unreformed followers, on the other hand.[91]

In ordinary circumstances, the two spheres could have carried on, unmindful of each other's theological predilections. But the same process that made the followers stand up to European opposition, also informed their relationship with their upper-class ashraf brethren. As I have been implying, by giving the lower order a confidence in their collective strength and making the leadership responsive to that power, the N/K brought into close proximity different social groups with their respective beliefs. The burial was a dramatization of this phenomenon, for it publicly

---

[89] *Furfurar Hazrat*, p. 87.
[90] Ibid., p. 137.
[91] Waliullah states that he did not see any religious sabhas or debates in Calcutta, while religious life was inundated with the worship of pirs and graves. *Yuga Bichitra*, pp. 103–5.

asserted the importance of what would be seen as unreformed Islam, into the intimate sphere of gastronomic and personal consumption by the *haute* ashraf. Not surprisingly, the reaction of the latter was a swift one.

Muslim condemnations of the burial appeared in the 'Letters to the Editor' column of *The Statesman*, a newspaper that was read by Europeans and upper-class Indians. In fact, this was the same constituency which patronized the New Market.[92] Consequently, it is not surprising that Muslim objectors not only mobilized orthodox arguments, but attached them to invocations of the privileges of the ratepayers. For instance, a letter from one Salahuddin Ahmad expressed surprise at the burial, and attributed it to 'the illiteracy of persons who knew nothing of their religion and are the easy prey of self-styled saints'.[93] Another letter writer, claiming to express an orthodox view, commented on the 'religious susceptibilities of the masses' who were 'mostly moved by rumours rather than by conscientious and rational considerations', and called on the Public to ask the authorities to remove the grave, and boycott the market pending that event.[94] The idea of the Muslim Public had been monopolized by the *haute* ashraf who read and ran newspapers and were nominated to important public bodies. It was the class underpinnings of this Public that came to the fore, when an intimate sphere of their lives was being affected.

The lack of a unified Muslim Public and, consequently, the difficulty in using it as a rallying cry, also made it imperative to appeal to something that *could* unify, and this was very important for the leaders who had supported the burial. It should be added here that the former included people with impeccable orthodox credentials: not only was the Imam of Nakhoda Masjid, the premier mosque of Calcutta, present during the burial, but the three vice-presidents of the Mazhar Committee were all maulvis.[95] These leaders were related to the ashraf — whether directly, as in the case of the barrister, Huseyn Suhrawardy, or via orthodoxy, as the Imam's case implies.

---

[92] According to *The Statesman*, the market was 'traditionally supported mainly by Europeans and the most prosperous among Indians', 18 March 1926.
[93] *The Statesman*, 31 October 1924.
[94] Letter from 'A Moslem Citizen', *The Statesman*, 22 October 1924.
[95] *FK*, pp. 4–7.

I have stated earlier that it was the notion of accountability to mass imperatives which made the top-level Muslim leadership and their institutions responsive to the pleas of the fakir's followers. This idea was a new feature, since the closest notion to it in traditional Islam, that of the *ummah*, designated a community that was governed by Islamic laws. In this case, the idea of a mass collective possessed an appeal that was more autonomous of strict Islamic regulations. But this only increased the problems of the leadership who had to balance the orthodox proclivities of the upper class with the commitments of the fakir followers. This problem was intensified by the fact that Islamic Law did not favour the followers. It quickly became apparent that not only had the burial been wrong, but proceeding from that fact, that exhumation was permissible.[96] The response of the leadership to this predicament revealed an internally divided approach.

A.K. Azad, who was highly respected as an Islamic leader and theologian, formulated the importance of the mass imperative, albeit in an embarrassed manner. Attempting to find a common ground with the Europeans, he invoked the importance of segregation as essential to orthodoxy. 'Islam enjoined that the graves should be at secluded quarters, where no worldly transactions took place, where no one's rights were interfered with', he proclaimed. At the same time, when faced with the question of exhumation, he admitted that it was permissible, according to Islamic law, but suddenly changed track to state that 'these technical points were unknown and unintelligible to the masses', who had buried the fakir in the understanding that they had got permission from the relevant officer.[97] It is interesting that this peculiarly disjunct way in which the importance of mass imperative was sought to be absorbed by the more orthodox, became in the case of Huseyn Suhrawardy, a schism. He was possibly the most active supporter of the followers of the fakir. However, in his speech to the Corporation he played a different tune. While justifying his act of

---

[96] Azad, quite forthrightly declared that the burial was not justified by Islam. A letter from 'A Lawyer' quoted from Bailie's *Digest of Mahomedan Law*, which stipulated: 'When a body has been buried in the ground . . . it cannot be exhumed without some excuse. But it may be lawfully exhumed when it appears that the land was usurped, or another is entitled to it under a right of pre-emption.' *The Statesman*, 26 October 1924.

[97] *The Forward*, 30 May 1925.

permitting the burial, he delivered a homily. 'I tell you frankly', he said, 'that we, the Mohammedans are deteriorating gradually in moral fibre, and becoming more and more superstitious so that, until people are properly educated, you are likely to get such incidents.'[98]

It was through bypassing this schism that Bakr stole a march over the others. To begin with, he took the same stand in essentials as Azad, except that he was more aggressive about it. He criticised the burial, but proclaimed his opposition to exhumation on grounds that did not apologize for itself as Azad's did. He reiterated the responsibility of the Corporation in giving permission for the burial.[99] However, his conspicuous commitment to the *Sharia*, also made it imperative for him to invoke something that would have nothing to do with Islamic legality, and yet retain the force of an imperative. He discovered this in the appeal to 'sentiment' and 'feeling'. His newspaper, the *Hanafi* opined, not quite making clear the distinction between civic and Islamic legitimacy, that: 'It has been argued that those who ordered the burial had no power to do so.' It went on to assert nonetheless, that while this 'may be true . . . that is no justification for wounding the feelings of the whole Muslim community'.[100] Obviously, the claim of 'feelings' here allowed the pronouncement to shift the grounds of appeal from legality altogether. In a letter issued by Bakr and the old Khilafatist, Abdur Rauf on the burial issue, an appeal was made to the 'sentiments of the people'. But, it then went on to proclaim, that if they were violated then 'it is feared that it will no longer be possible to keep under control the already excited mob, and the consequence would be . . . sure bloodshed amongst the Muslims'.[101]

The appeal to community feelings and sentiments was not confined to the Bakr establishment. Its spread is evident in the appeal made by the Mohammadi to the effect that, 'When the actual harm has been allowed to be done, the removal of the body at this stage will mean dishonour to the departed soul and an

[98] *Amrita Bazar Patrika*, 23 May 1925.
[99] Although criticizing the burial of the fakir as the action of some 'misguided Muslims' in his public meeting of August, he denounced the exhumation as unjust since Corporation officials had granted permission. *The Statesman*, 25 August 1925. A month later, he focussed exclusively on the exhumation in his circular. *The Statesman*, 26 September.
[100] 21 August, *Hanafi RNP* no. 35 of 1925.
[101] *Amrita Bazar Patrika*, 3 October 1925.

affront to Muslim sentiments.'[102] These categories could spawn and legitimize a united front, bypassing sectarian and class cleavages as well as legal problems. However, the problem with such appeals was that their conceptual amorphousness needed to possess the definitiveness of an imperative. And this could only be acquired through violence. We have already seen how easily the invocation of feelings in Bakr's letter slid into a threat of violence. It is no less revealing that the two newspapers I have cited located their idea of feeling in close proximity to communal violence in the passages cited above. While the *Hanafi* warned that the Muslims would not 'witness the removal peacefully', the *Mohammadi* alerted that it would 'needlessly enkindle communal animosities'.

IX

To understand the political circumstances in which Bakr entered the scene is important, for it points to the critical phase in which the whole political structure of communal relations was suspended in an uncertain balance. Bakr's intervention was a crucial factor in helping to tilt it. Already, before the death of Das, Bakr had lent support to his son-in-law, Fazlul Huq. The latter had turned to a Muslim exclusivist programme, after being forced to resign as Minister of Education by the Swarajists who, as part of their campaign of disrupting the reforms, voted against sanctioning the grant for minister's salaries.[103] From the beginning of 1925 he had started on a campaign tour of the mofussil in which he propagated a pro-Tanzeem line.[104] Of significance was the fact that his meetings were hopelessly unsuccessful until Bakr joined forces with

[102] 28 August 1925, *Hanafi RNP* no. 36 of 1925, NAI.

[103] Huq initiated a meeting of Muslim leaders in October itself. Together with Abul Kasem, his old colleague from the days in which they collaborated together with C.R. Das, he published a notice in December, announcing that the October meeting had decided to convene a meeting of Muslims from various parts of the province to form an all Bengal Muslim organization for the protection of 'political and 'other interests'. *The Forward*, 2 December 1924.

[104] In his Presidential address at the Moslem Conference at Behrampur, he stated that he would be carrying out a census of masjids in Bengal to make them 'the units of my organization in every district'. *Amrita Bazar Patrika*, 24 May 1925. He aggressively declared that he was a Muslim first and an Indian afterwards, knowing fully well the communal furore such a statement had caused when Mohammed Ali had declared it. Ibid., 5 June 1925.

him.[105] Bakr intervened in the fakir controversy only after the death of Das, and, as if to make clear the reason for his timing, issued a statement which exploited the insecurities that the death had left. In the letter written with Rauf cited above, he prefaced his appeal to Muslim sentiments by asserting that after the death of Das, it was useless to expect anything from the Swarajists. His intervention came immediately after the resignation of the Muslim Councillors from the once-united Congress Municipal Party.

Bakr promptly tried to take the issue to the streets. The Bengal Provincial Jamiat-ul-Ulema flagged off the campaign by castigating the Corporation decision as 'the most intolerable encroachment on the religion of Islam'.[106] A few days later, Abu Bakr announced a meeting to be held at Halliday Park. There is evidence of serious mobilization since Mohammed Daud, the leader of the Seaman's Union, held a meeting on the burial question at the same time with his union constituency. The meeting was only partially successful since it did not attract a huge crowd. But it included a galaxy of distinguished leaders, composed not only of expected names like Fazlul Huq, but others such as Wahed Hosein and Nurul Huq Chaudhury MLC, whose attendance occasioned much surprise in the editorial columns of the *Patrika*.

Violence was already present in the air. The year had started in the shadow of the Kohat riots in the North West Frontier Province, in which Hindus had been evicted by their Muslim neighbours. This started a nation-wide controversy on the rehabilitation of the exiled. A few months before the controversy, there had been riots in Kidderpore, while on the very day that Bakr had his meeting, there were riots among mill workers over the playing of music before mosques in Titagarh, located close to Calcutta. It was thus not surprising that Bakr's call for violence inspired similar calls for retaliation from the more communalized sections of the Hindu press, led by the *Dainik Basumati* and *Viswamitra*.

[105] The series began discouragingly in Serajgunj. Only fifteen delegates attended. Initially there were only forty people in the audience! No one understood his speech since it was in English, and before the translation could be read out, the audience had departed. *Amrita Bazar Patrika*, 1 February 1925. In May of the same year, however, the Muslim Conference at Faridpur was successful. Ibid., 4 May. In Murshidabad, later that month, he got an audience of eight thousand people! Ibid., 26 May. It was in the last two meetings, that Bakr's presence was evident.

[106] *Amrita Bazar Patrika*, 19 August 1924.

The latter proclaimed: 'This attitude of the Muhammadans is intolerable, and we would be the first batch of martyrs if they threaten violence or attempt to disobey the national decision.'[107] For the first time, public representatives of the two communities were openly threatening violence. And it was happening in a situation when the Swarajist Party, a key institutional dyke against the wave of communal consolidation, was, because of the pressures of the burial issue, breaking up on communal lines. The limits to dialogue seemed dangerously close.

Thankfully, the only violence that occurred on this issue was confined to print. However it is interesting that when the issue was recalled by participants, it was seen as something that directly led to the riots of April 1926 in Calcutta. Not only was this narrative circulated in the autobiography of a contemporary,[108] but this was also the version given to us by Mohammed Maksud Ali.[109] Such confusions are understandable, given the fact that the April 1926 riots followed so closely in the tracks of the controversy. The burial clearly produced the preconditions for riots, but their mutual relationship also extended to establishing institutional links between different levels of Muslim leadership. The fulcrum of this was the relationship established between Huseyn Suhrawardy and Mina Peshwari. Mina was not only a wealthy trader, but also a renowned criminal in Calcutta. He is said to have sworn his loyalty to Suhrawardy, for having staved off the Hindu attack on the burial at his own cost.[110] Suhrawardy reciprocated his friend's favours, when he personally released Mina from a police station where he had been confined for alleged participation in the April riots. It is a measure of the popularity of the two, especially of the sturdy following that Suhrawardy had personally created for himself,[111]

---

[107] 7 October 1925, RNP no. 40 of 1925, NAI.

[108] Chowdhury, *Memoirs*, p. 46.

[109] Both versions claim that the riot occurred because Hindus and Muslims wanted the fakir to be theirs. According to Ali, the Hindus wanted to build a temple, while the Muslims insisted on a mosque, leading finally to '*maramari* [a fracas]'. The British then intervened to block up the site with cement. Chowdhury tells a similar tale, reporting that the Hindus desired to cremate him. Ibid., pp. 45–6.

[110] Waliullah, *Yuga*, p. 231.

[111] The burial controversy gave Suhrawardy a mass constituency for the first time. He was popularly known as 'barrister' among the residents of *bastis*. His hold over grassroots politics is suggested by the fact that he regularly

that a proposal to enquire into Suhrawardy's conduct was met with a day's hartal by many of Calcutta's markets.[112]

Unfortunately, it was not only the narrative of communal violence to which the fakir's controversy contributed, but also to the questioning of the notion of Swaraj. It did so easily, given the Corporation's symbolic implications. But what should also be reckoned with, besides the symbolic relationship between the Corporation and Swaraj, was the importance of the Bengal Pact. While the Pact dealt in the main with reservations, it also attempted to devise ways to adjudicate ritual differences and introduce, in a limited way, the idea that Hindu and Muslim laws could be subject to the views of the majority of elected representatives of each community.[113] No doubt, there were many problems with this ambition of giving an overarching prominence to religious identities and helping to stabilize them through a framework of religious federation. Although the heritage of the N/K, as I will show later, went beyond this federated notion, the Pact nevertheless represented — especially because it was underwritten by a joint struggle which involved more than religious demands — a crucial symbol as well as a future institutional framework of Swaraj. In other words, the character and workings of the Corporation (which was imbricated in the struggle for Swaraj), the Bengal Pact and Swaraj formed a circuit of political symbolism that, in the mid-twenties of Bengal, had an inter-dependent character. It was all three things that were implicated in Bakr's Halliday Park speech, where, according to *The Statesman*, he stated:

---

held court in his office. He would listen silently to the tales of the *Mohalla sirdars*. Waliullah, *Yuga*, pp. 265–7.

112 *The Mussalman*, 8 June 1926.

113 The Preface to the provisions states that the ambition of the Pact was 'to establish the real foundation of Self-Government in this Province . . . '. It agreed that the representation in the Legislative Council would 'be on the population basis with separate electorates'; representation to local bodies to be in the proportion of 60 (for the majority) – 40 (for the minority) in each district; and fifty-five per cent government posts to be reserved for Muslims. In the section entitled 'Religious Toleration', it stated that no resolution or enactment affecting any religion would be passed, without securing the consent of seventy-five per cent of the elected representatives of that community. Music before mosques would be banned, with no interference with gokorbani. Further there should be arbitration committees set up in each sub-division. 'Hindu–Muslim Pact', *The Indian Annual Quarterly Register*, vol. I, no. 1, January–March 1924, H.N. Mitra (ed.), Calcutta, pp. 63–4.

Hindu Swarajists, owing to their innate bigotry, had proved their unfitness to approach any Muslim religious question in a spirit of catholicity; they wanted to control Muslim religion by means of voting.

He concluded that this was only a foretaste of swaraj.[114]

As I have said, all three notions were important, but for a provincial-level leader like Bakr it was the Bengal Pact that was the lynchpin of the problem. It constituted the real force which underpinned Muslim support for the Swarajists across the province. In his antagonism towards the Pact, Bakr was not alone. The Pact appears to have become increasingly unpopular with influential sections of the Hindu middle class. When Das died, none of the obituaries and only a few messages of condolences, mentioned his contribution in initiating the Pact. Instead, they dwelt on the safe and acceptable subject of his personal sacrifices. Bakr's assertions can be seen as an act of extreme rhetorical aggression designed to break the Swarajist alliance. And it certainly had a desired effect in the relevant quarters. The *Ananda Bazar Patrika* proclaimed: 'The very mentality to make such an unjust demand [that is, of exhumation] and willingness to accede to it through fear prove our unfitness for Swaraj'.[115] In the course of appealing to Swaraj as a reference point, communal discourses begin to invert some of the key values of Swaraj itself. For Hindu communalist discourse, this process reached its denouement in late 1925, when Bhai Parmanand counterposed the striving for Swaraj against the 'protection of Hindus'[116] as the new objective.

Without considering the full scope of the Hindu communal offensive against the Pact, one cannot understand the intensity and implications of Muslim responses, nor the abrogation of the Pact itself. The next chapter will examine the campaign that made the self-protection motif invoked by Parmanand, into an obsession with Hindu communalist circles of the period.

---

114 25 August 1925.
115 7 October 1925. RNP no. 41 of 1925.
116 *Amrita Bazar Patrika*, 1 November 1925.

4

'Abductions' and the Constellation of a Hindu Communal Bloc

Part I

I.i

From roughly the second half of 1923, that is, in the immediate wake of the N/K, stories — disseminated mainly by newspapers — began to circulate about the oppression of Hindu women by Muslim goondas, located principally in Eastern Bengal.[1] It did not take long for these reports to become a commonsensical point of reference for Hindu communalists. Especially because, as a response to the reports, some of the most prominent members of Bengali Hindu society got together in early 1924 to form the

[1] I am indebted to Indrani Chatterji, whose paper on the same subject (later written up as part of her M.Phil dissertation for the Jawaharlal Nehru University, New Delhi) stimulated my thinking on the topic. Her argument, best summed up in her own words, claims that the Women's Protection League (WPL) campaign was 'connected with violence within household structures [thus also reinterpreting] the Mussalman spokesmen claims about these women being 'immoral widows'. Personal communication to me. Samita Sen's 'Honour and Resistance: Gender, Community and Class in Bengal, 1920–40', *Bengal, Communities, Development and States*, Sekhar Bandopadhyaya, Abhijit Dasgupta, Willem van Schendel (eds), New Delhi, 1994, is a perceptive traversal of grounds shared with the present chapter. A major difference I have with her article is that instead of placing the communalized preoccupation with abductions in the late 1920's, I position it in the middle of the decade. This is not a matter of chronological nitpicking, but accounts for a large difference in the meanings of this preoccupation itself. While Sen sees the abductions theme as a response to the Sarda Bill, I argue that it has a far more ambitious range of significations which can only be understood if it is located in its right context. Urvashi Butalia, Kamla Bhasin, Ritu Menon, Veena Das and lately Gyan Pandey, have been working on the same subject, but in the context of the Partition riots. I also take this opportunity to thank Dr. Kanai Chattopadhyaya for allowing me access to his collection of Women's Protection League literature.

Women's Protection League that was designed to protect Hindu women from abductions by Muslim criminals. The formative years of this preoccupation (it was to last in its organized form for over two decades), coincided with the height of the fakir burial controversy and interlocked with its effects to intensify the campaign against the Bengal Pact.

The nature of the concern with abductions was shaped by a paradox. On the one hand, the campaign did not possess a powerful organizational centre: at the height of its popularity in 1925, a press release on the organization stated that it had a mere forty-eight volunteers — of which ten had been expelled for reasons that were not specified.[2] Nor did it throw up any remarkable instances of mobilization. The climactic point of its career in this regard occurred in 1929, when fiery speeches were delivered and physical confrontation threatened, in a meeting held at Albert Hall, Calcutta. However, it was attended by about a thousand persons only.[3] On the other hand, the magnitude of its effects seemed to exist in inverse proportion to this unimpressive record. For instance, it stimulated a large number of autonomous initiatives from correspondents of mofussil areas to report instances of abductions they had gathered from hearsay, to metropolitan newspapers. A contemporary like Waliullah held this campaign to be the most important factor in spreading communal ill-will in the mofussil.[4]

The asymmetry between organization and spread can only be explained by the power of orchestrated common sense, which we have encountered in another form in the first chapter. Along with the 'dying Hindu', the abductions theme created a web-like structure of communal cognition that highlighted different points of antagonism with the Muslims. At the level of stereotypes, the figure of the Muslim abductor tapped the same source as the concern with the 'dying Hindu', which was that of the sexual hyperactivity of the Muslims.[5] However, the preoccupation with

---

[2] *Amrita Bazar Patrika*, 9 August 1925.

[3] 'Abduction of Hindu Women: Press comments and resolutions of the Albert Hall meeting on the subject', 535/29, Serial Nos 1-2, GOB: Political, 1930, WBSA.

[4] Waliullah, *Yuga₁*, p. 211.

[5] See Sen's comprehensive survey of literary stereotyping on these lines in Bengal Hindu literature. 'Honour', pp. 216-20. See also P. Aggarwal's

abductions did not involve the production of an extensive worldview that reinterpreted the stereotype, for the simple reason that, unlike the preoccupation with the census, abductions did not possess a theoretician like U.N. Mukherji, nor did it spin out any theories. Its discursive field was limited and repetitive, the variety being provided by the differences between the events that concerned abduction. Its power really emanated from two sources. The first stemmed from the complementary influence of newspapers and legal institutions, both of which propagated this concern. While one of the (two) founders of the Women's Protection League was S.R. Das, the advocate general, the other was K.K. Mitra, the editor of the prestigious *Sanjibani*.

Both lawyers and journalists, it should be added here, were highly vulnerable to communal influence in this period. The mofussil lawyers, who were a prime target for mobilization by the Women's Protection League, were remembered by Shantimoy Roy as being a particularly communalized body in the pre-independence period.[6] The lawyers were related to the zamindars (who would in any case form their more valued clientele),[7] the class most threatened by the self-assertions of Muslim ryots. It was not surprising, therefore, that the lawyers of Rangpur provided the first group of people who clustered around the Women's Protection League. The first major rallying together around the abduction question — apart from acts of founding Women's Protection League units — occurred in a Rangpur court, which had met to decide the guilt of those who had abducted Suhasini, the sixteen-year-old daughter of a pleader of

---

discussion on the Padmini–Alauddin legend that constitutes a paradigmatic communal romance of (attempted) abduction. 'Surat, Savarkar and Draupadi: Legitimizing Rape as a Political Weapon', *Women and the Hindu Right*, T. Sarkar and U. Butalia (eds), New Delhi, 1995.

[6] Interview, 4 April 1988. Corroborative evidence is provided by O.M. Martin, a district official of those times. He testifies that 'the dominant group of pleaders and *vakils* were bitterly anti-Muslim'. Martin Papers, p. 186, CSASC.

[7] Mansur Ahmed, *Atmakatha*, p. 419. According to Tanika Sarkar's findings, 89.13 per cent of the lawyers of Bengal were Hindus; apparently an overwhelming number of them supported the Zamindari system before the Floud Commission. *National Movement and Popular Protest in Bengal 1928–1934*, Ph.D Thesis, Department of History, Delhi University, September 1980.

Rangpur. The court was filled with pleaders, *muktears* and local dignitaries. But it was not only the dramatic potential of abductions that was tapped by the lawyers. They also played a crucial role in relaying the concern. Roy recalls that the *kacchari* was a place where rural litigants would pick up news and ideas and disseminate them in their villages. Print was used to extend this reach. The pleaders of Rangpur were persuaded to publish copies of judgements passed in the Sessions Court as a book.[8]

If law provided the stage where this preoccupation could be made palpable to the public, newspapers elaborated its compass and generalized it into an everyday concern. Atul Sur and his friends would scan the legal columns of newspapers for stories of Hindu girls abducted by Muslims.[9] Many stories of abductions published in *Amrita Bazar Patrika*, were culled from court proceedings.[10] The general precondition for this intense interest was the increasing communalization of newspapers — a tendency that prompted a diplomatic warning by the Congress Working Committee.[11] It was thus not fortuitous that the run-up to the founding of the Women's Protection League was a meeting of the Indian Journalists Association, presided over by K.K. Mitra; speakers included P.K. Sarkar of the newly established *Ananda Bazar Patrika*, and tributes were paid to that paper as well as *Amrita Bazar Patrika* and *Basumati* for assisting in the campaign against abductions.[12]

Involved here was the monopoly of newspapers over the representation of the everyday. This pertained to the selection of news, the display of those items, and the terms of reportage. The most effective way they privileged a given preoccupation was through headlines. By repeating its theme day after day, headlines provided a continuity between different instances of abduction, blanketing differences between cases of abductions and their heterogeneous

[8] *Amrita Bazar Patrika*, 24 May 1924.
[9] Atul Sur, *Satabdir Pratiddhani*, p. 159. Sur was a journalist who wrote a history of the Stock Exchange.
[10] Newspapers were also read by rich peasants. Ahmed says that his Dadaji regularly read *Mihir O Sudhakar*, while his uncle subscribed to *Bangabasi* and *Hitbadi*. His school teacher made him subscribe to *Prabashi*. *Atmakatha*, pp. 244–6.
[11] *Amrita Bazar Patrika*, 29 November 1923.
[12] *Amrita Bazar Patrika*, 30 April 1924.

details. Consequently headlines acquired a power with which they could override even judicial pronouncements. For instance, an item that dealt with the acquittal of a Muslim for abduction, was headlined, 'WOEFUL STORY OF A GIRL'.[13]

Besides the combined effect of lawyers and journalists, the second source of the massive impact of abductions lay in the particular structure of the preoccupation. Above all, the massive impact of abductions stemmed from its particular structure. The narrative of the oppression of Hindu women by Muslim goondas in the eastern parts of Bengal compacted into itself, elements that were imbricated in diverse social narratives. The fact that the narrative managed to constellate this diversity within itself allowed it, in turn, to assert the comprehensiveness of Hindu-Muslim antagonism. The 'dying Hindu' too did this. But whereas its power was generated by its detachability from the original narrative and by its conversion into a sign for diverse preoccupations, the common sense about abductions was structured by a specific chain of referents that composed its master story. Abductions in the twenties, orchestrates a simultaneous range of anxieties and projects. While featuring the question of gender at its fulcrum, it interlocks with problems of caste, class, political institutions and movements. Moreover, the theme of abductions relates in a variety of ways with these concerns: in some cases it displaces them and at times it works as a mobilizing force. In general, the multiple operations of the abductions theme shows once more how the banality of communal common sense conceals the process of problematizing and recreating an awesome range of social relations. Correspondingly, this requires a method that elaborates the uses of this theme in their specifically different, yet interlocking contexts. I will begin with the immediate provocation for this concern.

---

[13] *Amrita Bazar Patrika*, 24 August 1929. Waliullah blames a great deal of the communal antagonism on newspapers, with their headlines given in bold superscript which were often belied by the main report. These incited communal antagonism. *Yuga Bichitra*, p. 208. *Hindu Musalman*, a journal promoting communal unity, remarked sarcastically that just as kirtan could not be sung without mentioning Krishna, newspapers could not communicate their news without using headlines that would fuel communal antagonism. 25 August 1926.

I.ii

The preoccupation with abductions had originated in a protest against the sexual harassment of women workers by British tea planters in the 1880s. Ironically,[14] K.K. Mitra had been a moving spirit of this campaign.[15] Nearer to our period, an anti-colonial offensive had been launched in 1923 against the alleged rape of women of Charminair village in Faridpur district by policemen. The campaign had emblematized the common oppression of Hindus and Muslims by the administration, since women of both religious persuasions had been affected.[16]

By communalizing the issue, the Women's Protection League removed the anti-colonial implications of this concern.[17] A small qualification is needed here. The Women's Protection League blamed only the Muslim 'goondas' and not the whole Muslim community. The shifting of the noun to an adjective served a more subtle communalism. While it stigmatized the Muslims as a community that produced, and, what was worse, tolerated

---

[14] Mitra emerged as one of the leading campaigners against the Pact. He suddenly discovered that Muslims lacked patriotism. *The Statesman*, 6 January 1924. Mitra's Anti-Circular Society was one of the few Samitis created by the Swadeshi movement which had Muslim activists; it had also kept away from the Shivaji *Utsav* with its communal undertones. Sumit Sarkar, *Swadeshi Movement*, p. 304. His alteration is a testament to the intense fear of a Muslim dominated administration. Sir P.C. Ray also began to attack the Pact after the Cocanada resolution.

[15] It was in the context of the Sadharan Brahmo Samaj campaign in the tea gardens in the late nineteenth century, that one of their missionaries by the name of Ramkumar Vidyaratna took up the case of a married coolie woman who had died as a consequence of sexual assault by a white man in 1884. The Calcutta based *Sanjibani*, of which K.K. Mitra was a co-founder, took up the case. Kanai Chattopadhyaya, *'Parishista'* [Afterword], Krishna Kumar Mitra, *Atmacharit*, Calcutta: 1386(1979), p. 297.

[16] *Fortnightly Reports*, 25 and K.W, June second half and July second half, 1923, NAI. The campaign had been led by journalists, although it had been conducted under the influence of Congress mobilization, the axis of which had been provided by its enquiry committee headed by P.C. Guha Roy.

[17] It is interesting that in the same period, working-class mobilization around the affiliated issue of molestation was directed against European factory bosses. Samita Sen, 'Honour', pp. 230-2. This suggests an attempt to steer clear of the communal mobilization, although the involvement of leaders like Santosh Kumari Gupta in both the Trade Union front as well as the BPHS (see below) on this question, suggests an attempt at a reorientation of the issue, rather than supplying a contestatory variant of the discourse.

'budmashes', the allegation simultaneously limited the sphere of the Women's Protection League's substantial activities to Law. In fact, the Women's Protection League merely[18] asked for the reintroduction of whipping as a punishment. It was one of the few concessions they got from the administration. This limited legalism defined the limits of the League's anti-colonialism.[19]

This strategy bears the imprint of S.R. Das' presence. He had become advocate general in 1922. Firmly committed to the view that Hindus and Muslims would fly 'at each others' throats' without the 'restraining hand of a [British] Government',[20] Das was a frank collaborationist. It was his initiative that seems to have shaped acts of collaboration by mofussil lawyers. The report on the Suhasini trial, referred to above, begins by relating the fact that members of the local bar (mentioned by name) and three muktears represented the Crown. They had volunteered their services free.[21]

All this, however, begs a question. Why was a separate organization set up for the abductions issue when the HMS could have taken it up? Outside the province the HMS had no inhibitions in this regard. In the Benares session of the HMS in 1923, Malaviya had included the defence of women as a pressing imperative for Hindus, and referred to increasing cases of abduction reported

---

[18] It did not raise questions of what constituted evidence, or the arbitrary nature of punishments. For instance, an alleged rapist was fined only Rs 60 for abduction, but was acquitted for rape because there were no witnesses; of that amount, an insultingly paltry sum of Rs 25 was given to the complainant. *Amrita Bazar Patrika*, 3 February 1925.

[19] This was not a foolproof strategy. The involvement of policemen in abducting women resurrected anti-colonial sentiments. Taken beyond a point, this could lead to the reiteration of an anti-British united front. The alleged molestation of a Hindu girl by the Superintendent of Police, Malda, led to the following call by the local *Gour Dut*, 'We request both the Hindus and Muslims of Bengal to unite together and remedy this wrong done to them.' 19 October 1925, RNP no. 43 of 1925, NAI.

[20] S.R. Das, 'A Letter to my Son on Indian Politics', *The Modern Review*, vol. XXXVI, nos 1–6, July–December 1924, pp. 397–8. A cousin and political rival of C.R. Das, he ended his career as Law member of the Viceroy's Executive Council. Obituary, *Amrita Bazar Patrika*, 28 October 1928. He had been an unsuccessful candidate for election to the Legislative Council in 1923 and along with Surendranath Bannerjea, was singled out by the Swarajists as a candidate whose defeat was of the highest priority.

[21] *Amrita Bazar Patrika*, 27 May 1924.

from Eastern Bengal. In contrast, the Serajgunj meeting of the BPHS made hardly anything of abductions: Santosh Kumari Gupta simply moved a resolution stating that abducted women ought to be taken back,[22] while Lajpat Rai's presidential speech at the All India Hindu Mahasabha Conference in Calcutta the following year, did not bring up the subject.[23] Even the Hindu Sabha of Rangpur, a district that pioneered this concern,[24] kept silent.

We had noted in Chapter I, that in Bengal the HMS was plagued by its 'upcountry' image. The impact of this extended beyond organizational problems. Its importance was also related to the fact that, with the initiation of the Bengal Pact, regional identity emerged as a political platform. The rejection of the Pact by the Coconada Congress firmly confined it to Bengal. C.R. Das sought to offset this circumscription by appealing to regional sentiments. He told Congress members that they had insulted Bengal by voting against the Pact.[25] Regional appeal was consolidated in the campaign that followed. In a mass pro-Pact meeting, C.R. Das defined Bengali identity as posited on and transcending, a federative principle : 'Bengal is the common home of the Bengalees — be he a Hindu, be he a Musalman.'[26] The notion of a shared place was extended in the course of the campaign. An article by Motilal Roy defended the Pact by stating that it expressed the 'forwardness' of Bengal. The latter had 'developed a distinct consciousness . . . which . . . [was] far ahead of the other provinces of India'. Bengalis, he also claimed, were not Aryans.[27]

This discourse could not be fought from the HMS platform. Given this, the constant emphasis on the Bengaliness of the problem of abductions, despite its emergence as an issue elsewhere

---

[22] *Amrita Bazar Patrika*, 5 June 1924.
[23] This was surprising since Rai dwelt on other gender-related issues, such as the problems of purdah, child-marriage and widows. *Amrita Bazar Patrika*, 12 April 1925.
[24] The Secretary, Rangpur District Hindu Sabha in 'An Appeal to Bengali Hindus', talked about saving the 'once great but now dying Hindu race', dwelling on malaria, Hindu poverty, and the problems of the caste system, but omitting references to abductions. *Amrita Bazar Patrika*, 9 April 1924.
[25] Letter from T. Mukherjee, *The Statesman*, 4 January 1924.
[26] *Amrita Bazar Patrika*, 13 January 1924.
[27] 'The Lessons of the Pact: Provincial Individuality versus All-India Consciousness', *Amrita Bazar Patrika*, 6 January 1924.

in the country, becomes significant. In appealing for the defence of Bengali women appropos the Baroda Sundari case, Chittaranjan Guhathakurta stated that, 'the tears of those victims would be prejudicial to the welfare of Bengal . . . '.[28] The leaders of the Women's Protection League were all Bengali; only in 1926 was the Marwari leader Padamraj Jain temporarily activated on this issue. Moreover, the Bengali identity of the abducted women was always kept in the forefront. This was reinforced by the specification of the abductions-prone regions — initially the North Bengal districts, which, by 1929, spread to five Eastern Bengal districts.[29]

The emphasis on the Bengali character of abductions undermined the rationale of the Pact. It tore asunder the transcendental claims of Bengali identity that the Swarajists had sought to impart. In the Legislative Council, Sanat Raychowdhury pointedly asked for clarification on the extent of involvement of Muslims and Hindus. He enquired whether it was increasing 'specifically in the East Bengal districts . . . .?' and if it was 'assuming the proportions of a class war?'. The connection insinuated between Muslim majority areas (and hence power in those districts), and the growth of communalism could not have been clearer.[30] Simultaneously, the charge against Muslim goondas — in a natural metonymic extension — began to cover all Muslims. In his 1926 speech, Sarat Chattopadhyaya alleged that Islamic culture was supportive of abductions, and observed that those Muslims who did not express the desire to abduct Hindu women, merely lacked the courage to do so.[31] The ferocity of this attack underlined, more than anything else, the paranoia of the prospect of Swaraj which allowed for a Muslim dominated administration.

The relationship of apartness-in-proximity between the Women's Protection League and the HMS was bridged in the late twenties.[32] The enactment of the Bengal Tenancy Amendment

[28] *Amrita Bazar Patrika*, 25 April 1925.
[29] A centre page advertisement in the *Patrika*, for a meeting on the abductions issue in 1929, read in big letters, 'ABDUCTION IN BENGAL: MEETING AT ALBERT HALL'. 20 August 1929. It was at this meeting that the five districts were specified.
[30] *Amrita Bazar Patrika*, 20 August 1929.
[31] 'Bartaman Hindu–Mussalman Samashya'.
[32] In 1929, the Women's Protection League demanded that the Government should institute a Committee of Enquiry, composed, significantly

Bill in 1928, the provisions of which strengthened raiyati rights at the expense of the landlords',[33] made the sense of threat experienced by the bhadralok, too strong for it to maintain feelings of regional discriminations. But this happened much after the revocation of the Pact. Incidentally, this move corresponded to a similar relationship between the issues of conversions (which, as we have seen, had been led by the HMS in Bengal) and abductions. It was only in 1929 that the thematic complementarity between the two was spelt out by Kelkar in his Presidential address to the BPHS (Bengal Provincial Hindu Sabha).[34]

In general, as I have argued in Chapter I, the shift to gender related issues in the twenties indicates a general turn within Hindu communalism. The latter no longer located the Muslim threat as an avenue to mobilize low castes. The emergence of Muslims in mass political struggles during the N/K made them into a direct and exclusive preoccupation. This change was inversely related to the weaknesses of low castes in either launching big mass movements, or of producing unity among themselves. A less evident cause was provided by the abductions issue itself. It was something that was generated from within the low castes themselves, specifically from a sizeable segment called the Rajbansis, who were located in Rangpur district of North Bengal. This facilitated a serendipitous conjuncture of caste and abductions for Hindu communalism just during the declaration of the Bengal Pact and the outbreak of communal antagonism in the rest of the country.

---

enough, with five members each from the Women's Protection League and the HMS. *Amrita Bazar Patrika*, 23 October 1929. A week later, it was demanded that the non-government component should consist of five Hindu Sabha representatives, and only two from the Women's Protection League. Ibid., 30 October 1929.

[33] The Bill made basically two kinds of provisions. Tenants were given transferability rights subject to a fixed fee to be paid to the landlord as well as the landlord's right to preemption. Underaiyats who paid a fixed quantity of the produce would be classified as tenants, and those who had a homestead on their land and held them for over twenty years could not be evicted.

[34] After stating that conversions were deviously carried out, he immediately switched to asserting that he could provide instances of kidnapping of Hindu women: Muslim success at conversions was evident in their population gains. *Amrita Bazar Patrika*, 27 August 1929.

I.iii

'We find that lawlessness is becoming the order of the day at Rangpur, where oppression on helpless women is very often being perpetuated without there being a remedy',[35] declaimed the *Ananda Bazar Patrika*. Although abduction cases were reported from places other than Rangpur, the Women's Protection League concentrated its attention there. The reason was that this district provided the locale for effecting a network between low-caste organizations and the Hindu reformists/communalists which had been unsuccesfully attempted in 1922 by the Bangiya Jana Sangha (hereafter BJS. The low-caste organization involved here was the Kshatriya Samiti. It represented the Rajbanasis, who were treated as *antyaj* (those prohibited from entering the kitchen or a temple of the high castes). Its campaign against abductions proved a very significant witness to the power — and corresponding weakness — of the Hindu communal movement in Bengal.

It may be recalled that Manindranath Mandal managed to rope in an enthusiastic Panchanan Barma, the leader of the Kshatriya (which was what the Rajbansis redesignated themselves as) movement, into the BJS. Mandal provided Barma the opportunity to network with Hindu leaders. But for the most part, the BJS remained a Calcutta based organization on paper consisting of top-level caste leaders alone. In contrast, the Kshatriya Samiti represented an important mass force in the districts of Dinajpur, Jalpaiguri, Rangpur as well as the princely state of Cooch Behar. The Samiti reached down into villages, where it developed a substantial number of basic units called *mandalis*.[36] What gave it spectacular significance was that, after the Namasudras, the Rajbansis formed the most populous caste in Bengal.[37]

The mention of Namasudras raises a question. From about the second decade of this century, the Namasudras had engaged in

[35] 26 December 1925, RNP, Bengal, no. 1 of 1925, NAI.

[36] The Kshatriya Samiti organized *mandal samitis* in villages which would function as village governments, spread education, preach ritual reform and function as co-operatives. By 1926, there were three hundred such *mandalis*. Sekhar Bandhopadhyaya, p. 228.

[37] The total population of Namasudras in 1921 amounted to 2,004,911 persons, while the Rajbansis consisted of 1,663,948 persons. *Census of India*, cited in Swaraj Basu, *The Rajbansis of North Bengal: A Study of a Caste Movement 1910–1947*, Ph.D Thesis, Calcutta University, 1992.

fairly regular riots with Muslims. And yet, despite the best efforts of Hindu communalism, the Namasudras never really made a joint cause with them. Possibly the most spectacular entente between the two was struck in 1929. But this did not involve Muslims. The Hindu Sabha — led in this instance by Swami Satyanand — only extended assistance to Namasudras in their drive to enter a Kali temple in Dhaka.[38] On the other hand, there was no commensurate history of communal violence between the Kshatriyas and the Muslims. According to the District Gazetteer, 'Hindus and Muhammadans of the cultivating classes regard each other with the most complete toleration.'[39] Which brings us to the question: why then, did the Kshatriya Rajbansis turn to communal mobilization?

I wish to answer this through a little detour. Rangpur had already been associated with abductions in the upper-caste imagination. The highly popular romance of *Debi Chaudhurani* written by Bankim Chandra Chattopadhyaya features an abduction at a decisive point in the story. Debi Chaudhurani's low-caste companion participates in the abduction of Debi for the benefit of her lecherous upper-caste lover. The abduction fails, while Debi acquires the friendship of a powerful dacoit who makes her the leader of his gang. Even earlier, an origin myth of Rangpur made an association with — not abduction — but what is implicitly affiliated in Bankim's story, that is the idea of 'loose' moral standards among lower castes.[40] Possibly the most subtle testimony of this

---

[38] The immediate context for this agitation was the resolution initiated by Swami Satyanand in the Bengal Provincial Hindu Conference to permit everyone to enter temples. At the same time, a Namasudra had entered a Kali temple in Dhaka (where the Conference was being held) and asked for the water with which the Goddesses' feet had been washed. Now tension between the Namasudras and Brahmins had been brewing for some time in that city, and it was only logical that the impertinent Namasudra was beaten up. In response, Satyanand led a satyagraha for temple entry, fully supported by the HMS. The police forced them back, and there was violence. After this, the movement died suddenly. Behind this rapid demise was the fact that no Namasudra leader or organization had supported this satyagraha, possibly because they were preparing for a confrontationist position against the upper castes, which was expressed through their opposition to the Civil Disobedience movement and the possibility of Dominion status the following year. Sekhar Bandopadhyaya, pp. 523-7.

[39] J.A. Vas, *Eastern Bengal and Assam District Gazetteers: Rangpur*, Allahabad, 1911, p. 48.

[40] A story of how Rangpur derived its name, related it to *rang* (jest). The

composite bias of abductions and (im)morality is provided by Piyush Ghosh. He wrote insinuatingly, 'We have also to see whether the outrages in the Mofussil are due to low morality among the masses or they are due to the hatred of the Mahomedans towards the Hindus or vice versa.'[41]

Much of the visceral revulsion[42] was possibly the consequence of the marital customs of Rajbansis. These have been detailed by Swaraj Basu. Bride price was customary, and the initiative for a match had to come from the groom's side. There were four basic kinds of marriages. The two 'regular' ones were called 'phulbibaha' in which the marriage of a boy to a virgin was solemnized formally by a priest or his equivalent in authority, and 'Ghor-dzia Biha' in which an orphan or poor boy who could not pay the bride price, was kept in the bride's house for a probationary period, after which he was married in a permanent form. The less formal ones included 'panichita' in which a poor male unable to pay the bride price approached the girls elders to sprinkle some water with mango twigs on the heads of the to-be couple, and 'chotrodani' which involved the marriage of a married woman even when her husband was alive. Widow remarriage was called 'ga-goch', while, if a widow got the consent of a man to live with her as protector, it was called 'dangua'. Divorce was a simple matter and no maintenance allowance was required.[43]

---

piece of humour was contained in the reply of a Prince of that area to the King of Benares, describing his land in a sanskrit *sloka*, well-known to Brahmin pandits of North Bengal. It said, 'I come from a land in which widow and wife/In popular view are but one and the same;/Where no garment is worn save the *mekhola* gown/Which is bare above breast and bare below knee'. Ibid., p. 2. The dress referred to, was worn by Rajbansi women, a fact which socially defines the ambiguous morals of the place alluded to in the first two lines.

[41] The article was entitled 'The Bengal Provincial Conference', and was an attempt to influence its agenda for the Serajgunj conference. *Amrita Bazar Patrika*, 30 April 1924.

[42] Vas comments that Muslims resorted to abductions becuse of 'the low standard of morality among the mass of Muhammmadans, the prevalence of polygamy and the numerical inferiority of females among them,' *Gazetteers*, p. 123. It is a testament to the exclusivism of these elite representational systems that they could locate similar characteristics in two neighbouring social systems, without perceiving their complementarity. At another point in his Gazette, however, he observes that the sexual customs of the low castes and the Muslims were similar, as was the phenomenon of abductions.

[43] Swaraj Basu, pp. 51–2. It can be argued of course that while the marital

In keeping with the general pattern of sanskritization, the Rajbansis sought to remove the flexibility of their marital customs. The upwardly mobile Rajbansi jotedars sought to privilege 'phulbibaha' as the only valid form of marriage, no doubt because it most closely approximated the upper-caste ideal of chastity.[44] A reason for this shift to enforced monogamy for women is the preoccupation with genealogical purity, the creation of a pure, unalloyed past, which finds its other expression in the preoccupation with the writing of histories that seek to trace caste ancestry to the high texts of Brahmanical Hinduism.[45] In this connection, it is significant that the Rajbansis repudiated all connection with their tribal past as Koches; when their Muslim neighbours wished to insult them, they would address them by that tribal name.[46] The change in identity sought through the process of sanskritization involved the identification of women as physical repositories of liminality, who, in their person, dramatized the thinness — and thus the profound importance — of boundaries that lay between the purity and contamination of descent.

A consequence was to remove women from the common social spaces that could allow this liminality any possibility of expression. The 'Chandals' prohibited their women from visiting the market place, even before they redesignated themselves as Namasudras.[47] Another manifestation of this urge to make women subservient to genealogical determination, was the attempt to stop widow remarriage. Chadreswar Ray, a publicist of the Rajbansis, passed strictures against their women from visiting the market as well as against widow remarriage.[48] The widow remarriage question was

---

customs of the Rajbansis show a decided preference for polyandry, the Muslims tended towards polygamy. However, Basu also states that Rajbansi males married more than one woman, p. 4. On the other hand, the explanation that Vas offers for the difficulties of tracking down abduction cases amongst Muslims, puts the onus on the women, since they entered into multiple relationships — clearly indicating that polyandrous practices were not uncommon among Muslims. Vas, *Gazetteers*, p. 123.

[44] Swaraj Basu, p. 62.

[45] Basu characterizes the primary aim of the journal, *Kshatriya*, as the invention and propogation of imagined caste history, p. 112.

[46] Vas, *Gazetteers*, p. 40.

[47] Sekhar Bandopadhyaya, p. 131. The other demand was to urge the Government to discontinue the practice of employing chandal convicts as scavengers in jails.

[48] Swaraj Basu, p. 100.

so important for the Namasudras that it contributed to a split amongst them in 1922.[49]

The Namasudra experience again recalls problems regarding the Rajbansis. Swaraj Basu sensibly observes that the Rajbansi spectre of Muslims abducting their women was inspired by their strategy of confining women. Taking the Namasudra experience into account however, this raises the problem as to why the Muslim was required for this purpose in the first place. The question of inter-communal sexual relations had created tension between low castes and Muslims. In 1924, a riot nearly erupted between Pods and Muslims, when a Muslim married a Pod widow and claimed her property. Accused of theft, he was forced to parade through the village with the head of a dead pig hung from his neck.[50] Similarly, in 1929, the abduction of a Namasudra widow by a Muslim nearly led to a riot in some villages in Barisal.[51] Yet, in contrast to the Rajbansis, neither instance produced communal mobilization.

We have returned to our initial question concerning the reason for communalization of the Rajbansis, albeit with greater knowledge and a more manageable focus. One could attempt an answer through a comparison with the Namasudras. The Namasudra movement started in the nineteenth century, before the Census of 1901 began to stimulate claims to upward mobility from low castes. It evolved as, and remained, a popular protest against upper-caste arrogance.[52] On the other hand, the Kshatriya Samiti was founded in 1910, in the aftermath of the Gait Circular. The latter had brought together many upper-caste activists and platforms which were shared by U.N. Mukherji, Surendranath Banerjea and K.K. Mitra's *Sanjibani*.[53] In other words, the Kshatriya

---

[49] At the Bengal Namasudra conference held at Perozepur in June of that year, the other issue of debate was whether to join the Boycott movement. Sekhar Bandopadhyaya, p. 481.

[50] The Muslims retaliated by smearing the face of a Hindu with the blood of a bullock! *Fortnightly Reports*, May first half, 1924. NAI, Home Poll, File no. 25.

[51] *Amrita Bazar Patrika*, 20 August 1929.

[52] The 'Chandal' movement of 1872–3 in Faridpur and Bakarganj included social boycott of upper castes as protest against their refusal (led by the Kayasthas) to dine in the house of a Namasudra headman. Sekhar Bandopadhyaya, p. 131.

[53] The *Sanjibani* declared, 'a reduction in the number of Hindus by

movement originated at a point when the upper castes were making a special effort to woo their lower orders. This neutralized much of the controversy that the Namasudras had aroused. Moreover, Guruchand, the Namasudra leader, was an organic intellectual, belonging to the village where he started his movement (and maintained as his headquarters). In contrast, Panchanan Barma, the leader of the Kshatriya movement, was an outsider to Rangpur, the centre of movement. The talented son of a rich farmer in Cooch Behar, he made his way to Calcutta where, in addition to a degree in Law, he also acquired one in Sanskrit — an early pointer to his inclinations towards High Hinduism. He settled in Rangpur because he could not find a job in his native district.[54] Barma was the first Rajbansi lawyer, a fact which betokens a necessary social and professional dependence on upper-caste members of the Bar: a story which we will come to later.

It is, therefore, not surprising that we find him networking with U.N. Mukherji and Digindranarayan Bhattacharya, while playing an inspirational role in the founding of the BJS. But what is a little unexpected is the language in which Barma supported the BJS. In contrast to other caste leaders who referred to their frustrating experiences as low-caste organizers, Barma gave unqualified praise for a venture in a way that effaced its distinctive low-caste character. He declared that it was imperative to bring about unity of different sections of Hindus, and benefit the nation.[55] Barma represented the right wing of the BJS. As such, he can be easily fitted into the straightjacket of a camp follower of the upper castes. Except for at least two reasons. One was the fact that the Rajbansis, amongst others, petitioned the government for communal representation in local and self-governing bodies in 1918;[56] the other is that the Kshatriya Samiti supported the Non-Cooperation movement in 1921 to express their disappointment at not being enumerated in the Census according to their wishes.[57]

---

excluding the Depressed Classes from it will tell very severely on their political status in their country'. Cited in Papia Chakravarty, p. 46.

[54] Swaraj Basu, p. 138.
[55] Manindranath Mandal, p. 25.
[56] Swaraj Basu, p. 150.
[57] Swaraj Basu, p. 199. Only a year earlier, *Kshatriya*, the journal of the Kshatriya Samiti wrote appropos of the Raj; 'God has dispensed even handed justice by placing the Indians for their proper education in the hands of a

Obviously, the failure of the Non-Cooperation movement contributed to the turn to Hindu Mahasabha. There was already a supportive context for this alliance. Sitanath Goswami, a functionary of the Hindu Sabha movement, appears to have been present in Rangpur from around 1922. He was introduced in the founding session of the Women's Protection League as a kind of a native informant on Rangpur abductions: he had, apparently, worked for fourteen months in villages there.[58] However, the decisive year for this coalition was 1923 when the HMS started charting a separate political course from the Congress, hardening its Hindu appeal and adopting a more cooperative stance towards the Government. Alliance with the HMS at this stage could give the Kshatriya movement access to the Government, while also keeping alive the possibilities of securing a recognition of their sanskritized status from an upper-caste, national party.[59] But there is another fact that is more significant for the point I am making about the independence of Rajbansi motivations.

The Kshatriya Samiti campaign against abductions predated the Women's Protection League's efforts. It was Panchanan Barma who first publicized the issue by raising it in the Legislative Council. By 1924, the pages of the *Kshatriya* were filled with reports of abductions:[60] even in the latter half of 1925, Panchanan Barma continued to report abductions by Muslims, which were translated and published by the *Patrika*.[61] In fact, the HMS trailed the Kshatriya Samiti on this question. It was on the grounds of this pre-existing campaign that Malaviya was able to link up cases of violations of women that were associated with riots, located mainly in the Punjab, with those of abductions in East Bengal.[62] The local campaign by the Rajbansis was thereby nationalized.

---

noble nation from far-off Britain', rendering impossible the 'jealous rule of the Rajas'. Sekhar Bandopadhyaya, p. 238.

[58] *Amrita Bazar Patrika*, 1 May 1924.

[59] Bandopadhyaya suggests that a section of Sahas attempted to secure a superior status by participating in the upper-caste-led Swadeshi movement. Bandopadhyaya, p. 238.

[60] Swaraj Basu, p. 17.

[61] See 20 September 1925.

[62] In the Benares conference of the HMS in 1924, Malaviya talked about the critical condition in East Bengal, where a few Muslim rowdies openly insulted Hindu ladies, who had to hide in tanks to save their honour. Apparently these rowdies would stand in front of bathing ghats to insult ladies.

It is this effect of simultaneity — which is actually the consequence of the weaving of separate sets of events into a single narrative by a national-level organization — that deflects attention from the separateness of local motivations. The segregation of narratives provides an opportunity to explore the internal tensions that prompted the Rajbansi's designation of Muslims as abductors of their women. A minor fact about the Non-Cooperation movement might give us a clue to begin with. It concerns incidents of protests against *hat-tola* (levy charged on sellers by the owners of hats) that appeared to have erupted without the consent of any authoritative organization in Rangpur.[63] The hat-tola would be specially unpopular with the *adhiars* whose sole resource was the share of the crop they received as sharecroppers, and who would be disproportionately dependent on the profits they made in the hats. Incidentally, the anti-hat-tola campaign was a crucial mobilizing point of the Tebhaga movement in Rangpur, which broke out less than two decades later.[64] If one reads back from the Tebhaga agitation, then it is significant that the Rajbansi middle-class jotedar (the backbone of the Kshatriya Samiti) joined with the big zamindars at that point, in opposing the adhiars. A fact, which, when placed against the important role that zamindars (which I will elaborate later) played in the abduction issue, raises the suspicion whether the Kshatriya Samiti leadership was not uninfluenced by similar assertions of adhiar initiative.[65]

Retrospectively, the Tebhaga points to the narrative of class identity. In fact, as early as 1908, a Rajbansi tract warned of internal class divisions.[66] This schism resisted comprehensive hegemonization by a Kshatriya identity. There was, of course, the particularity

---

Amrita Bazar Patrika, 25 August 1923, cited in 'Newspaper Extracts regarding Hindu Mahasabha Proceedings', NAI, Home Poll, Progs. No.198, 1924. Clearly elements of the abduction narrative of Jamalpur, 1907, when bathing Hindu ladies were allegedly dishonoured, entered into this report, which was implied to be relevant for a later period.

63 Swaraj Basu refers to poor raiyats who, without outside help, 'sporadically' protested by refusing to pay rent, chaukidari tax, and hat-tola. Basu p. 199.

64 Ibid, p. 213.

65 Vas refers to an existing tradition of independent protest action by raiyats in Rangpur, *Gazetteers*, p. 83.

66 Harakishore Adhikari, *Rajbansi Kulpradip*, Calcutta, 1908. I owe this reference to Sumit Sarkar.

of the conjuncture, in which the authorization of protest by the momentum of Non-Cooperation combined with a down-swing in jute prices between 1920–2.[67] But this only emphasized the economic and cultural gulf within the Rajabansis. In contrast, the issues dividing the Namasudras in 1922 were less traceable to internal, class-like divisions.

To a great extent, the difference was a matter of location. The Namasudras inhabited the heartland of East Bengal, which, following Sugata Bose's characterization, was dominated by the small peasant economy, in contrast to the jotedar-adhiar divide in the Northern districts, which included Rangpur. The jotes were of different sizes, but what united them was the contractual power the jotedars wielded over their undertenants. In many cases this reduced the status of adhiars to nearly that of serfs.[68]

By itself, this may not have mattered much; rents were still comparatively low, the land-man ratio not too unfavourable, and the zamindars still mindful of paternalist functions.[69] Unfortunately for the Rajbansi elite, the very nature of their marital customs could be resistant to the suddenness of changes required by their drive for a better self-image. The ideal of chastity which they sought to impose on their poorer brethren had to reckon with stubborn difficulties. The first was that the existing scheme of marriages was flexible in economic terms, catering as it did to a variety of social and economic eventualities. Secondly, it would be equally difficult to restrain women from the market-place. While Rangpur had the lowest proportion of women working in the fields, they provided about two-fifths of the total number of

[67] See *Agrarian Bengal*, p. 79. Prices picked up again to hit a minor boom in 1925.
[68] According to Sugata Bose, the smallest jotedars worked as adhiars. However, this did not mean that there was no tangible difference between the two categories. Normally adhiars were men with plough, cattle and possibly a little land with raiyati rights. But they were regarded more as servants of jotedars, the latter financing them in lean months, in addition to taking the decisions regarding production. In this situation, the poorer adhiars were not much better than serfs. Ibid., pp. 1–13.
[69] Vas claims that most cultivators were 'eminently prosperous' (p. 83), and that the rise in rents had not overtaken increase in prices of agricultural goods; nor was population in excess of cultivated land. Written rent receipts were given throughout the district, and in 1874 as well as in 1908–9, both periods of scarcity, the zamindars had donated liberally, *Gazetteers*, pp. 84, 116.

traders.⁷⁰ Obviously, household economies would be correspondingly dependent on such earnings. Nor was there much opportunity for the economic improvement of the lower orders which could have produced a supportive section amongst them.

It may be observed that cultural distancing can lead to a schism within castes, as it did with the Kaibarttas after the growth of an educated class amongst them.⁷¹ The Rajbansi elite's new lifestyle was not part of a collective programme as it had been with the Namasudras in 1872-73. Nor did they, as the Namasudra movement had done through the *Matua* cult, evolve an ideology that could provide them a shared commitment to their distinctiveness.

Such efforts had also to reckon with the objects of reform, the women. Bride price may not, by itself, be indicative of the ability of women to consent or refuse prospective offers, although a comparison with the institution of dowry suggests greater freedom for women to choose their partners. What provides more conclusive evidence is that widows were both permitted to remarry and approach men they trusted, as well as the even more remarkable custom of allowing married women to marry again. Women were also allowed a greater level of social mobility than conventional upper-caste women, together with more freedom to choose their public 'vices', such as smoking!⁷² Possibly the most significant comment on the relative freedom of women, is the fact that so many played a prominent role in the Tebhaga movement.⁷³ And this, it goes without saying, was, equally, evidence of their success in resisting the definitions involved in the 'abducted woman'.

In effect, the Kshatriya Samiti offered its authority and resources to mount a drive for repression within households. It offered a vision of male equality, an opportunity to stamp out growing class

---

[70] Amongst the Rajbansis in the four important administrative units in 1911, there were 3,009 male, and 1,863 female traders. In contrast while there were 414,812 males in cultivation, there were only 9,110 females similarly engaged. *Census of India 1911*, cited in Swaraj Basu, p. 77a. These figures should be treated as indicators only, since Census statistics on these subjects tended to be unreliable due to the problem of categorization.

[71] The Chasi Kaibarttas who had one in three males literate, divorced themselves from the Jelia Kaibarttas. Sekhar Bandopadhyaya, p. 182.

[72] Swaraj Basu, p. 51.

[73] According to Nikhil Chakravarty, then reporting the movement, in Dinajpur, Rajbansi women fought the police and rescued their men from them. Swaraj Basu, p. 224.

differences by ganging up against an entity who was present in all classes. In turn, this would ensure that the past could be wiped out, and the Rajbansi elite could rise immaculate in the image of high texts. However, the invocation of the sexually threatening Muslim male by the Kshatriya Samiti expressed a lack of confidence in accomplishing this project by caste appeal alone. The vehemence of the campaign betrays an uncertainty. This comes out even in translation. The floridity of Panchanan Barma's verse counterposed Muslim lust against idealized figures of women, in order to incite male pride:

> Shame, shame, the dead men, shame.
> The hooligans are taking away your mother and sisters,
>   still you remain cool?
> Look at our women, they are great.
> Let the lumpen *neres* [Muslims] come, we will teach them
>   a lesson.
> We will save our religion, we will protect the pride of
>   our father and brothers.[74]

If there were negative, internal reasons for the invocation of Muslim lust, it also opened up an expansive prospect. While allowing them to become internal to a broad nation-wide movement, the nomenclature 'Hindu' also permitted the Kshatriya Samiti to appeal to socially inferior groups. The Kshatriya Samiti reports on abductions which it sent to the Press in 1924, indicate a large number of cases concerning poorer and socially inferior castes, mainly the Bairagis. In a political environment which privileged numbers, the Rajbansis formed about two-thirds of the Hindu population of the district.[75] As a proportion of the total population this was not very much,[76] but it certainly counted for more if politics was to be communally consolidated. In such an eventuality, the Kshatriya Samiti's hegemonization of subordinate groups would reinforce its authority within the more general category of 'Hindu'.

In effect, the Rajbansi elite was acting as a relay of the method of domination that belonged properly to the upper castes. 'Properly', because the Rajbansi elite could not aspire to general

[74] Cited and translated by Swaraj Basu. pp. 117–18.
[75] Vas, p. 38.
[76] In 1921 there were 791,143 Hindus, and 1,706,177 Muslims. *Rangpur District Gazetteer: B Volume, Rangpur District Statistics, 1911–12 to 1920–21*, (Calcutta: The Bengal Secretariat Book Depot, 1923).

social domination. They suffered both from internal vulnerabilities and from their success. Their two major sources of mobilization were an effective reportage network linked to their newspaper, the *Kshatriya*, and court cases, such as the one conducted in Kurigram in 1924, concerning a Rajbansi woman.[77] In short, it was the same sort of mobilization that was sought by the Women's Protection League. And this meant that there could not be room for two such organizations.

As the day for founding the Women's Protection League approached, the Kshatriya Samiti reports grew less frequent in metropolitan newspapers. Subsequently, the reportage was dominated by the Sishusahay Matrimangal Samiti, a Calcutta based organization (whose secretary B.K. Mukherji, was upper caste) which rapidly concentrated its resources in Rangpur.[78] The more decisive contribution was made by *Amrita Bazar Patrika* correspondents themselves. This was a prelude to the effacement of the Kshatriya Samiti's role by the Women's Protection League. Immediately after the founding of the Women's Protection League in April 1924, K.K. Mitra undertook a successful tour of Rangpur. Undoubtedly aided by cases of abductions that took place even while he was there, he established branches of the Women's Protection League in Rangpur towns of Gaibanda, Kurigram and Kakina within a fortnight.[79]

What was remarkable was the enthusiasm he inspired. Much of it was due to the abduction of Suhasini, the daughter of a Brahmin muktear of Gaibanda who was also a Raychaudhury, a title, whose possession indicated proximity to the Raychaudhurys who formed a substantial section of the powerful landlords of the district. The case — which was among the first which the Women's Protection League took up, and in which their lawyers offered their services to the Government — attracted swarms of people to the court.[80] The Women's Protection League's swiftness in establishing itself as the centre of attention suggested a favourable reception amongst the mofussil bhadralok. This process would be obviously facilitated by upper-caste domination of the legal profession. The Women's

[77] *Amrita Bazar Patrika*, 2 May 1924.
[78] See *Amrita Bazar Patrika*, 9 May 1924. Its report was given prominence in the inaugural meeting of the WPL. Ibid., 1 May 1924.
[79] *Amrita Bazar Patrika*, 10–17 May 1924.
[80] *Amrita Bazar Patrika*, 27 May 1924.

Protection League was also better connected, being led by not only a reputed editor with a host of journalistic contacts, but also supported by the advocate general, backed up by powerful leaders and organizations. Not surprisingly, it was dominated by prominent upper-caste figures: the president of the Rangpur Bar Association himself presided over the founding of a Women's Protection League branch.[81]

Abductions provided a lucky break for Rangpur's upper castes. While there had been an old stock of Brahmins who traced their ancestry to the thirteenth century, a more significant phenomenon was the wave of upper-caste migrants who came to dominate the professions in Rangpur from the late nineteenth century.[82] They were obviously upstarts in a Rajbansi dominated area. Nor could the prospect of upwardly mobile Rajbansis dominating Hindu mobilization have added to the comfort of these new migrants.

Clearly, the entente could not last. In 1926 it broke. Two things happened. The first was Panchanan Barma's defeat in the Legislative Council elections that year at the hands of a Brahmin candidate, which indicated the importance that property based franchise gave to the upper castes (which may have, ironically, contributed in the earlier election, to Barma's Hindu turn). More decisive was the formation of the Depressed Classes Association and Federation which effectively realized Mandal's ambition of bringing low-caste organizations together. It was in this context that the Rajbansis petitioned the authorities, to provide them with the same facilities that had been extended to Muslims. The fact that these events took place in the year 1926 is ironic since it saw the most successful effort at communal mobilization.

It was also difficult to remain segregated from the Muslims. After all, they shared too many common customs, even gods, that could not be suddenly swept away by the surge of communal mobilization.[83] The strength of these connections made its presence felt in the communalized discourse, producing fissures within

[81] *Amrita Bazar Patrika*, 10 May 1924.

[82] The early Brahmin settlers came from Mithilia, Kannauj, Oudh from between the thirteenth to the sixteenth centuries. The new upper-caste migration started from the late nineteenth century, and they quickly occupied employment in government and kutchery, railway and commercial jobs, as well as dominated the liberal professions. Vas, pp. 45–6.

[83] Vas, *Gazetteers*, pp. 40–4; Swaraj Basu, p. 176.

the latter. In one of his writings, Panchanan Barma stated that Muslims and Rajbansis hailed from the same stock. Conversely, upper-caste non-acceptance also had its effects. The hierarchical distance between castes in Rangpur was extraordinarily great, since the gap between the Brahmins and Shudras was only filled in by a shrinking number of Kayasths.[84] Resentment of upper castes was sharp. Panchanan Barma never forgot the way his colleague's cap, which he had mistakenly worn, was thrown away by its owner because it had been contaminated by a low caste.[85]

Nevertheless, the campaign against the Muslims left its bitter legacies. It stimulated corresponding activity from Muslim communal groups. We have seen the Bakr establishment's communal campaign against the syncretist Bauls in Rangpur.[86] The broad appeal of this campaign among Muslims is understood better in light of the embattled psychological state of the Muslims produced by the anti-abductions movement. This intensified suspicion of Baul syncretism. Maulvi Reazuddin blamed them for a Hindu–Muslim confrontation in which 50–60,000 persons were involved.[87] The Kshatriya Samiti reported that Muslims felt that the Bauls had been inspired by the Rajbansis.[88]

If nothing else, the legacy of communal suspicion made it impossible for the Rajbansi elite to ever unite with the Muslims as Kshatriya Hindus. When inter-communal unity did take place in the Tebhaga movement, it was on the basis of a different identity altogether.

I.iv

While Rangpur provided the locus of abductions, the discourse often included the whole of rural Bengal in its sweep. The *Dainik*

[84] The number of Kayasths was 8,500 and decreasing, while the Brahmins amounted to 11,000. Vas, *Gazetteers*, p. 47.

[85] Swaraj Basu, pp. 88–90.

[86] In this period, the campaign was centred in a subdivision called Nilphamari, a highly prosperous, densely populated area, which contained three of the six towns that Rangpur possessed. There was a large population of Bauls, who were vegetarian and cited Islamic texts to campaign against cow-slaughter. *Amrita Bazar Patrika*, 14 January 1925.

[87] Maulvi Reazudin Ahmed, *Phakiri Dhoka Rod*, (Bangalipur, P.O. Sayyidpur, Rangpur: 1333[1926]), pp. 1–3.

[88] This is what was reported by the Kshatriya Samiti in its 1927 conference. Swaraj Basu, p. 177.

Basumati declared, 'At several places in Bengal it has become well-nigh impossible to live in villages on account of the . . . systematic outrage of Hindu women practised by them [i.e. 'a goonda class of Muslims'] . . . '.[89]

The regional extension of the discourse indicates its relevance to a larger spectrum of social processes than the network between bhadralok professionals and Rajbansis. Already, the challenge to zamindari interests thrown up by the Pabna riots of 1873 (a riot that was basically economic in character) was represented by newspaper reports of rape of Hindu women.[90] Later, a sensational element in the newspaper reportage of the Jamalpur riots in 1907, was provided by the alleged abduction of Hindu women by Muslims. It was then that the figures of the vulnerable, rural Hindu female and her powerless male counterpart, spread as a common shame. Nirad Chaudhury's father sent away his family after the Jamalpur riots, declaring that he did not wish to emulate rural Hindu folk who, when Muslims threatened, deserted their womenfolk and children.[91] Images circulated by metropolitan newspapers created a sense of insufficiency among mofussil males. The purpose of underlining this lack was not simply to create a general feeling of inferiority. It also granted importance to a group which was becoming discursively disadvantaged. This was the zamindars.

Motivated by the Jamalpur riots, Maharaja Suryakanta Acharya Chaudhury, the powerful zamindar of Muktagacha (Mymensingh), apparently floated the idea of starting a volunteer's organization. The volunteer's association aimed at organizing Hindus and providing legal aid for volunteers. The latter objective was crucial since the general aim of the enterprise soon developed into one of retaliation by burning Muslim villages and abducting their women![92] He got immediate support from the Anushilan Samiti, a

[89] *Dainik Basumati*, 25 December 1925.

[90] Newspapers such as *The Hindu Patriot* claimed it was an uprising of Muslims against Hindus, and along with *Amrita Bazar Patrika* carried reports of plunder, arson and rape. They were exaggerated. K.K. Sengupta, 'The Agrarian League of Pabna, 1873', p. 262. No doubt the purpose was to dramatize the evil that attended the threat to zamindari order.

[91] Chaudhury, *Autobiography*, p. 235.

[92] He started looking around for Namasudras to do the dirty job, and when they refused to be tempted, Das and his associates even toyed with the idea of hiring Muslims, till the Maharaja insisted that only Hindus could do

revolutionary terrorist group whose guru, P. Mitra, instructed Pulin Das, one of its leaders, to obey the zamindar because he was the only one with courage and resources to lead Bengal. Incidentally, the revolutionary terrorists, as I will show later, were to play a very important role in this concern.

While Acharya Chaudhury's initiatives represented what was really a local aspiration, by the 1920s the image of the zamindars as Hindu guardians against Muslims, became a province-wide discourse. In a Women's Protection League meeting held in the shadow of Suhasini's abduction, Shyamlal Goswami called upon zamindars to return to their villages and protect poor and helpless tenants.[93] While this was a tall order for absentee zamindars, its real significance lay in the discursive importance given to them. The rescue party for Baroda Sundari was got together with the support of the zamindar of Amlagachi village, and, accordingly, he received a special mention along with Sitanath Goswami (a local representative of Hindu Sabha), in the newspapers.[94] The zamindar came to embody the heart of Hindu defence against Muslim depredation.

The scaffolding for this guardian image was derived from the zamindars' traditional access to resources of violence. Significantly, the zamindar was represented as rescuing women in his capacity as commander of a private army and not as an individual. The report of Suhasini's rescue highlighted the zamindar's arrival with sixty *lathials*, in a way that made the team (of presumably policemen) sent by the authorities seem like a mere additional force.[95] The legitimization of traditional zamindari control over local resources of violence and compulsion, created new possibilities for extending the zamindars' status. By the time we come to our survey of the Mymensingh riots in 1930, we will see that this relationship of the zamindar with all Hindus was contracted into the person of the zamindar, so that he came to typify the rural Hindu condition itself.

---

the job! Pulin Bihari Das, *Amar Jiban Kahini*, Amalendu De (ed.), Calcutta, 1987, pp. 158–9.

[93] *Amrita Bazar Patrika*, 28 July 1925.

[94] *Amrita Bazar Patrika*, 25 April 1925.

[95] Bejoy Kumar Roy Chaudhury, the zamindar of Tulsighat and also a prominent Congressman of Gaibanda subdivision, took sixty lathials in order to rescue Suhasisni. *Amrita Bazar Patrika*, 20 April 1924.

It should be reiterated that this discourse not only refurbished the zamindar's image but, as the Jamalpur riots indicate, it also mobilized rural Hindu professionals. In the twenties, the relationship between, on the one hand, the mofussil gentry with zamindars, and the abductions preoccupation on the other, arose in the context of two specific threats. The first was provided by the lengthening shadows of the Bengal Tenancy Amendment Bill, although, as we will see, in the mid-twenties there still appeared to be non-communal ways of mobilizing against it. Stronger apprehensions were stirred by the organs of local self-government. An understanding of this twin phenomena will both provide clues to the shaping anxieties of the abductions discourse, as well as show the social relations it was trying to mould. I will begin with the debate on the Tenancy Amendment proposals.

In many ways, the mobilization around the Tenancy Bill seems less communally implicated than what, judging from its consequences retrospectively, should have been due to it. Possibly, too many hands were too full of more pressing concerns such as the Pact. While the Kerr Committee introduced some of the salient issues in 1923, the Bill was introduced in the Council in 1925.[96] It spawned much discussion at the end of 1925; many ryot meetings were held and some exploratory attempts made at countering its provisions. Attempts were made to acquire a province-wide platform by involving leaders like Fazlul Huq.[97] Besides, the alliance between the economic and religious identities which we had encountered in the context of the Improvement tracts, was also apparent in meetings such as the one held in Mymensingh by ulemas and ryots.[98] However, unlike the situation in 1928, when

[96] The proposals of 1925 were designed to provide transferability rights to tenants, while giving under-raiyats a more stable occupancy right. The latter provision did not meet the approval of the majority of the Select Committee, *Amrita Bazar Patrika*, 12 July 1926. In 1928, all references to bargadars (sharecroppers) were dropped. Chatterjee, *Bengal*, pp. 1–5.

[97] At a meeting held in Salimpur, Mymensingh, attended by no less than 15,000 persons, which was presided over by Ismail Hossain Seraji and addressed by Ashrafuddin Ahmed, Secretary, Bengal Provincial Jamiat-ul-ulema, it was resolved to send a deputation headed by Fazlul Huq to the Government. *The Mussalman*, 7 January 1925. Similarly in Ghiur, Dhaka, a rayat conference was presided over by Huq, and was attended by provincial-level leaders like Emdadul Huq and Maulvi Naziruddin, the editor of *Kangal*. *The Mussalman*, 30 January 1925.

[98] It was held in Gaffargaon, Mymensingh under the auspices of Bhowal

Hindu and Muslim legislators split on communal lines while voting on the Bill, commitments were still undecided in the mid-twenties.

In general, over the decade, Hindu-dominated parties tended to produce no answers commensurate with the scope of the political and economic challenges. Some amount of radical rhetoric was churned up by the terrorist organ *Atmashakti*.[99] The Swarajist campaign for agrarian reforms had come to nought. Significantly, in this period, even the HMS was attempting some sort of economic initiative for the rural hinterland. Krishak O Rayat Sabha (KORS), for instance, appears to have been close to the Hindu Mahasabha.[100] Reportedly, a 'large meeting' was held under its auspices in a Hooghly village, where the speaker, a manufacturer of agricultural implements, called for the creation of cooperatives and reform of Hindu society; the report ends with the line that the Babus assured them of all support.[101] Its class and identity orientation was evident.

Although this organization had started early, nothing much came of its efforts.[102] This was not surprising, given the frankness of zamindari opposition to all rural reform. The Hindu landowners learned nothing from the populism of their Muslim counterparts like A.K. Ghuznavi. There was, for instance, a touch of crudeness in the response of Maharaja Sashi Kanta Acharya Chaudhury, whose family history of involvement with Hindu communalism went rather deep (he was the son of Surya Kanta Chaudhury whom we have encountered earlier), and who was himself active in the

---

Anjumani Islamia, probably a local body, and had Emdadul Huq and Tyabuddin Ahmed, both MLC's, attending. *The Mussalman*, 7 January 1925.

[99] *Atmashakti* apocalyptically declared that if 'unequal, unnatural and unjustifiable' relations between the zamindar and raiyats were not removed, 'the fire of revolution which is at present burning secretly in the hearts of the raiyats will, if allowed to remain in that state, inevitably burst forth some time or the other, reducing to ashes all oppressions and injustice', 6 February RNP No. 7 of 1925.

[100] A newspaper announcement of a meeting of the KORS stated that it would be held alongside a Hindu Sabha conference at Dasghara, Hooghly. U.N. Mukherji had been asked to preside, and invitees included Swami Biswananda as well as 'leading pundits'. *Amrita Bazar Patrika*, 17 April 1924.

[101] *Amrita Bazar Patrika*, 5 April 1925.

[102] An announcement for one of its later meetings on the Bill, stated itself to be in favour of raiyats, but gave equal prominence to issues not exactly germane to the Bill, such as irrigation and the price of agricultural products. *Amrita Bazar Patrika*, 23 October 1925.

Hindu Sabha movement. He presided over a meeting of the Mymensingh Landholders Association that included leading zamindars and talukdars, in which it was decided to raise funds to start propaganda work against the Tenancy Bill.[103]

The general failure of Hindu landlords and their representatives to evolve any satisfactory answer to the impending economic challenge gave greater significance to 'abductions'. An indicator of the way it communalized the Tenancy Amendment debate in the late twenties can be seen from the extension of the discourse. It was after the Tenancy Bill was passed in 1928, that the Women's Protection League meeting of 1929 replaced the generalized reference to the mofussil and/or Rangpur, by a specification of five districts in East Bengal.

This was to come later. And herein lies a paradox. If the Tenancy Bill became communalized only in the late twenties, then this was the result of a general communalization that followed the 1919 reforms. The institution of elected representatives to local bodies guaranteed by the latter, meant that the numerically preponderant Muslims would acquire a larger share of rural power. The degree of the political challenge to the Hindu bhadralok corresponds to the intense and general communal anxieties generated by the abductions theme. Above all, the conjunction of 'abductions' with the changing character of local bodies created a popular communal frame for viewing the issues of the Tenancy Bill. And this was the consequence of the fact that the controversies spawned by the local bodies were more extensive in their social implications.

Much of the significations of the 'mofussil' element in the abductions preoccupation is not visible because of the kind of histories of the local and district boards. These are dominated by the more dramatic, and emphatically nationalist, preoccupation with the anti-Union Board agitations that spanned the twenties.[104] On the other hand, Gallagher's analysis of the workings of local

---

[103] It appears to have been a new organization, no doubt established to counter the Bill: this was only its second general meeting. *Amrita Bazar Patrika*, 8 April 1926.

[104] These began with the agitation in Midnapur that propelled Birendranath Sasmal into becoming a contestant for leadership of the Bengal Swarajists; this was succeeded by the Laukati agitation in Bakarganj, led by Satin Sen and concluded in this decade with the agitation in Bankura. Needless to add, all these were directed against the government.

and district boards has presumed too much. His essay regards Muslims as a monolithic entity that is simply provided avenues of expression by a colonial administration that appears to be benignly working towards a linking up of the provincial and local level of politics.[105] Consequently, Gallagher reveals nothing of the controversies generated by these bodies, or the way they were being linked to collective aspirations. In fact, he provides no indication of what could have been leading them in a communal direction.

The obvious, though crucial, point made by Gallagher is that these boards progressively acquired larger Muslim representation.[106] More specifically, F.O.Bell recollects that while Union Boards in Tangail were 'usually controlled by the richer and shrewder Muslim peasants', the district boards drew in the 'better educated members' among the Muslims.[107] These bodies provided avenues of power and control to those who exemplified the virtues of Improvement. Since these were public bodies, it can be deduced that they strengthened the hold of the Improvement discourse by demonstrating that the individual motivation of a Muslim to excel — embodied in those who controlled these bodies — was one which was not divorced from societal commitment.

Not surprisingly, powerful Muslims increased their influence within this new dispensation. It may be recalled that the author of *Taraf Gourangir Itihas* was a member of the local board of Tangail (incidentally the area in which Bell had also served), and of the Mymensingh District Board, in addition to being member of a variety of committees attached to Masjids, Tanzeem, Anjuman Islamia, dispensary and co-operative banks; he also served on the boards of two madrassas and one school.[108] This range of influence is unsurprising given the patronage that was available to these institutions. For instance, the total receipts of the Rangpur District

---

[105] John Gallagher, 'Congress in Decline 1930–39', *Locality, Province and Nation*, Gallagher, Johnson and Seal (eds.), Cambridge, 1973.

[106] In 1920–1 Muslims controlled more than half the local boards in six of the fifteen districts of Rajshahi, Dhaka, Chittagong Divisions; by 1934–5, that many in twelve districts. There were more Hindus in district boards, since there was provision for nominated members. Nevertheless, the number of Muslims who dominated district boards rose from two each in Rajshahi, Dhaka and Chittagong Divisions in 1920–1 to nine in 1934–5.

[107] 'Record of Life in the Indian Civil Service, F.O. Bell, 1930–47', F.O. Bell Papers, MSS.EUR.F.180/8–16, IOL.

[108] Khan, *Taraf Gourangir*, p. 55.

Board in 1920–1 amounted to Rs 657,672; out of a total of 2,136 educational institutions in that district, no less than 1,682 were aided by the authorities.[109] This new logistical terrain could also mean that, unlike the discursive area of Improvement, the battle with the Hindu Other did not need to be waged only within the Self, but could also be directed externally, that is, against Hindu claims to unfair traditional privileges. Parenthetically, it may be noted that the Muslim zamindar would be offered an opportunity to acquire an influential position in this new constellation of Muslim power. This would help in subsuming class divides within communal ones.[110]

Contrary to Gallagher's assertions, it was the Swarajists who first made an organized link between the provincial and local levels of politics. But their monopoly produced its own problems. As we have seen in the case of Abu Bakr, they faced communal opposition. This gained popularity because of the resistance to giving Muslims the size of representation proportionate to their population. In Pabna, local Swarajist Muslim leaders demanded about fifty to sixty per cent of the nominees for the district board elections of 1925. The Pabna Congress Committee leadership refused. Consequently, the elections were fought on communal lines and Muslims won a majority of seats. But Hindu candidates instituted a number of court cases which resulted in the invalidation of elections in Pabna town and an injunction on nine successful candidates from Serajgunj sub-division.[111] However, these nine disregarded the injunction and held a meeting of the board. When the judge sentenced them for this violation, a hartal was declared in Serajgunj. Later, a massive welcome was given in Ullapara to the jailed candidates who had been released on bail.[112] According to both the *Amrita Bazar Patrika* and official analyses of the Pabna riots that broke out in mid-1926,[113] this controversy

---

[109] *Rangpur District Gazetteer, B. Volume*, The powers of the district boards included the appointment of petty officials, control of road building and water supply, power in the administration of vernacular education and to levy cess. Gallagher et al., *Locality, Province*, p. 281.

[110] I owe this insight to Sumit Sarkar.

[111] *Amrita Bazar Patrika*, 10 July 1926.

[112] *Amrita Bazar Patrika*, 29 December 1925.

[113] 'Report and Judgement passed in connection with communal riot at Pabna', Home Poll, 11/XI/1926, NAI.

provided the most important cause of communal estrangement in the district preceding the riots.

The case that generated the strongest province-wide ripples involved the Noakhali District Board's policy towards education. In March 1925, the district board proposed that the education budget be allotted according to the population ratio between Hindus and Muslims (which meant a 77:23 ratio of distribution in favour of Muslims). The Hindu vice-chairman resigned and Hindu members walked out, while the proposal was pushed through by the Muslim chairman without voting. The proposal was passed despite the opposition of the inspector of schools, who argued that reformed madrassas were getting large grants from provincial revenues.[114] This communal onslaught needs to be understood in relation to Swarajist influence. Earlier, in the course of a local board election, a Muslim communal group headed by an ex-official had procured a favourable order on electoral proceedings from the administration. The case was taken to court and, significantly, the plaintiff was supported by both Swarajists and Khilafatists,[115] clearly indicating a lack of communal polarization. In contrast, during the election of the chairman and vice-chairman that took place at the end of 1925, the Swarajists and the Muslim communal opposition tied, and it was only the casting vote of the president supervising the poll, that accounted for the latter's victory.[116]

For the bhadralok, whose distinctive identity was culled from their monopoly over education,[117] such moves could not but test

114 *Amrita Bazar Patrika*, 3 August 1925.

115 Among the irregularities pointed out by the court, was the specification by the D.M. that polling would be suspended for an hour for Jumma prayer. The Munsiff felt this was wrong since it provided an opportunity for whipping up communal feeling by openly exhorting the congregation to cast votes for the defendants. *Amrita Bazar Patrika*, 27 June 1925. It is a measure of the opposition to the communalists that, in 1923, the non-cooperators won a majority in both the local and district boards in Noakhali. *Fortnightly Reports*, January second half, no. 25 of 1923, NAI.

116 *Amrita Bazar Patrika*, 6 December 1925.

117 Official reports gleefully observed that the 'protestations of an earnest desire for the extension of primary education and for the improvement of the condition of the lower classes, accompanied by declarations that the country is too poor to bear enhanced taxation and that the Reserved Departments swallow up an undue share of the provincial resources, are not incompatible with the conviction that the restriction of education to a limited class and the

their sense of reality. Especially because Noakhali set a precedent which, as the communally biased *Dainik Basumati* quickly pointed out,[118] was followed by the Jessore District Board. The other implications were no less staggering. Like the discourse of the dying Hindu which circulated and expanded in a metonymic chain reaction, the communalization of institutions followed a similar course. Electoral wrangles led to court cases, which also got communalized in the process,[119] while education budgets were used to consolidate communal positions. The implications of this situation were staggering. The official response to the Noakhali District Board resolution stated that the application of this principle, 'to roads, dispensaries, water supply and drainage etc. is the threatening logical extreme.'[120] We shall have occasion later, when looking at riots, to appreciate the deep incisions of reality that this apparent caricature contained.

However, it is important to warn against the idea of a necessitarian evolution to communal polarization in the sphere of local self-government that this narrative could suggest. In a letter to his mother, a district official described a district board meeting in Faridpur as being held in a room the size of their dining room 'back home', filled with fifty odd persons, 'each shouting at the top of their voice to make himself heard above the general pandemonium'.[121] Even after discounting the spectacle of oriental chaos, there is an evidential aspect that is borne out by the fact that the district boards were widely regarded as centres of factional quarrels. This was not unnatural since the 'award of contracts was a prime source of interest' in their meetings.[122] The intense disappointment

---

continued submission of the mass of the population are in the interests of the middle class'. *Fortnightly Reports*, March first half, no. 112 of 1925, NAI.

[118] According to the *Basumati*, this Board [the elections to which had been very communalized] curtailed medical expenditure to provide funds for maktabs and madrassas. It also complained that the local Sanskrit College had been deprived of Rs 1700 out of its normal allocation of Rs 2000. *Fortnightly Reports*, April first half, no. 17 of 1929, NAI.

[119] 'The defendants in the Noakhali Local Board dispute, asked for their case to be transferred on the plea that they would not get justice from a Hindu judge since communal questions were involved: *Amrita Bazar Patrika*, 30 June 1925.

[120] *Amrita Bazar Patrika*, 3 August 1925.
[121] Baker Papers, CSAC.
[122] Bell Papers.

of the colonial administrators at the 'failure' of Muslims to unite, led them to express it officially. 'Not a Hindu has been elected', reported the district magistrate of Mymensingh, an observation regarded as sufficiently acute to be included in the *Fortnightly Reports*. It continued, 'Yet at the same time it is fair to say that never was intrigue and faction more alive in the District and Local Boards than at the present moment.'[123] Such division amongst the Muslims produced, in some cases, room for Hindus to also act as a pressure lobby, which is what happened in a dispute between two Muslim leaders in Bakarganj.[124] Of course, the most important factor that militated against an immediate, outright communalization of local politics was the Swarajist hold over these boards.

What we have here is a double movement, in which significant waves towards communal polarization tended to flounder and thin out into fragmented affiliations. However, this indecisive communal antagonism produced a disproportionate fear within the Hindu bhadralok. The discourse of abductions played a crucial role here by painting the rural condition in lurid communal colours. This portrayal strategically sought to undercut the discourse of proportionate representation itself by replacing it with the criterion of aptitude for governance. Abductions revealed a double disqualification of the Muslims — their 'sexual proclivities' as well as their 'general antagonism towards Hindus'. It sought to displace the criteria of governance from the population-based idea of power to that of ontological orientation.

This shift produced more general reverberations than those pertaining to the sphere of self-government alone. As we have seen, a corollary of this campaign was to bestow an aura of glamour on the zamindars. The latter were not, of course, a homogeneous lot since sub-infeudation created many lesser Hindu zamindars. By being mobilized as Hindus by the anti-abductions campaign, the latter were encouraged to idealize the figure of the guardian zamindar. Besides attempting to fabricate a landowning bloc, the abductions discourse implicitly addressed the threat — embodied in the Bengal Pact — to professional interests. There was already a sentimental relationship, in addition to economic ones, between landowners and urban professionals. But these connections were

---

[123] *Fortnightly Reports*, March second half, no. 32 of 1927, NAI.
[124] *Fortnightly Reports*, May second half, no. 32 of 1927, NAI.

rhetorically intensified to the point where the distinctions between the two disappeared altogether. The *Amrita Bazar Patrika* claimed 'that under the category of landlords practically the entire middle class of *Bhadralogs* of Bengal who form the backbone of our society are included'.[125] This bonding was used to help in imploding the Bengal Pact. An *Amrita Bazar Patrika* article castigated the Pact as 'infinitely worse' than the Lucknow Pact, and the first concrete instance of its 'baneful consequences' that the author offered, was the Noakhali District Board resolution.[126]

Till now, I have explored the effects of the 'abducted woman' on areas of male-dominated activity. To sum up, we have seen its ability to effect an institutional and ideological entente between different political opinions within the Hindu elite. This created a complementary source of mobilization for Hindu communalism, the effects of which contributed to a larger climate of attitudes which communalized the land question, the workings of mofussil power structures in addition to urban professional culture. More generally, it problematized the idea of a federated polity. But it was able to do all this in the first place, because the concern with the abducted woman provided a bridge to relate to low-caste preoccupations.

This brings us to the question that lies at the centre of this concern: What happens to the 'abducted woman' herself?

Part II

II.i

As mentioned earlier, the combination of newspapers with court proceedings produced a stable flow of news regarding abducted women. Many cases stretched on for years, prolonged by retrials. Two of these that played a crucial part in the foundation of the Women's Protection League, demonstrates just this. While Baroda Sundari was abducted in the middle of April 1922, her case was still being reported three years later. Suhasini's case took more than two years to settle and occupied a corresponding length of newstime. In turn, newspapers imparted a dramatic power to the proceedings

---

[125] 26 November 1925.
[126] Pramatha Nath Bose, 'Open Letter to Mahatma Gandhi', 19 July 1925.

in court and, what is more important, generated the discursive field of this preoccupation.

Newspapers did not give equal newspace to all attempts at, and allegations of, abductions. On the other hand, drawing upon the novelistic ability of giving certain narratives an emblematic status, newspapers tended to focus on a handful of cases, which, by that token, were made to typify the general phenomenon. In fact, it was these typicalized cases that tended to directly generate organizational action. K.K. Mitra declared that the motivating impulse behind the Women's Protection League was the widely publicized abduction of Baroda Sundari. I will deal with five such cases.

Keshab was the second husband of the seventeen- or eighteen-year-old widowed Baroda Sundari. It seems to have been a union of convenience, for Keshab already had an invalid wife along with two sons and one daughter by her. In her deposition to the court of the additional district and sessions judge at Rangpur, Baroda recalled that it was 10 pm on the 6th of Chaitra (around the third week of March), 1329 (1922) when the incident occurred. 'I was then preparing betels, recliningly seated on the bed-stead of our bedroom', she reported. Hari Sundari, the first wife, lay unconscious in an epileptic fit, while Keshab fulfilled the duties of a male by relaxing with his hookah. 'A lamp was burning in the room', as Baroda Sundari suddenly heard knocking on the door and then saw it being rapidly broken down. Three men rushed in and began to beat up her husband. They then turned their attention to her. They dragged her out and left, draping her over their shoulders. Their number increased from three to between fifteen and twenty men. Many of these men had made purchases at her husband's grocery shop.

They then took her to about five different houses where regular attempts were made to sexually assault her. One day she gathered that the police were on their way. Possibly sensing the end of their escapade, three of them gangraped her. 'I did', she said when asked if she had resisted, 'but I was too weak from continuous fasting [she was only given *chira* and *khai*, both byproducts of rice] and removal from place to place, to offer any resistance. Several of the accused had knives in their hands which they held close to my throat and threatened to kill me.'

After being continuously shifted, one day she heard voices

calling out her name. She managed to rush out and find a rescue party headed by the Zamindar of Amlagachi village which included her husband.

One day she received a summons from Hem Chandra Sen, the inspector of Gaibanda. After they had reached the Thana, her husband was asked to leave. The Daroga then propositioned her on behalf of the Inspector. When she refused, he caned her. At this point, the Inspector intervened, stopped the caning and ordered his two subordinates to leave. He then raped her.

The Inspector did little to arrest the gang. It was rumoured that he had been bribed by the accused. Baroda refused to heed his summons any more, declaring that even if it spoiled her case, she would not become a 'bazar woman'.[127]

Suhasini was the sixteen-year-old, married daughter of Banamali Raychaudhury, a muktear of Gaibanda. A Brahmin, he was possibly related to one of the Raychaudhurys who supplied most of the zamindars of Rangpur. As she was returning from a neighbour's house one day in Falgun, 1329 (1922), Suhasini was forcibly taken, dragged and beaten all the way to Khizruddin's house. After three failures at escape, she finally reached her father's house only to be told by him to go away to an ashram. Upon reaching the railway station she was arrested by a police party led by Kamarzama, the sub-inspector of Gaibanda. He confined her in his apartment and then turned her over to Khizruddin. Finally the SDO ordered a search,[128] and if the first report on this case is to be believed, the police were accompanied by a party of sixty lathials led by Bejoy Kumar Ray Chaudhury, the zamindar of Tulshighata. She implicated her father in the 'nefarious transaction'.[129] The judgement at the retrial also stated that her father was a co-conspirator.[130]

But her ordeal was far from over. It was to end only when she took her own life. Just before that happened, she sent a letter to the Women's Protection League expressing her gratitude. She wrote that although she had managed to come back to her own people through the League's mediation, social retribution had been swift

---

[127] All quotations from Baroda Sundari, and most of the details are taken from the 21 April 1925 issue of the *Amrita Bazar Patrika*.
[128] The details regarding Suhasini given above are taken from the 27 April 1924 issue of the *Amrita Bazar Patrika*.
[129] *Amrita Bazar Patrika*, 20 April 1924.
[130] *Amrita Bazar Patrika*, 25 February 1925.

and cruel. Her father-in-law had lost his job. She had no way of being accepted by society again. 'They [her family] . . . don't touch food from my hands . . . I have not the slightest peace in my *sansar*. Now I wish to spend the rest of my days in an ashram', she wrote, asking the Women's Protection League to help her get there, wryly observing that she did not think her husband would object to such a plan.

It is difficult to speak in the face of such horror. Yet much was written and spoken, and the anguish went to service a structure of discourse and feelings that, in turn, had specific institutional and political consequences. An analysis of this is obviously my prime interest, but before I begin, a note of methodological warning. The cases I am analysing had already been chosen by the newspapers, and their choice was obviously ideological. However, as I will elaborate later, these are close, stage by stage, representation of events. Often the course of events went against the grain of the discourse; sometimes the very terms of representation allow us to glimpse a condition outside its boundaries, and to that extent allows us to map out its appropriations. In short I will not attempt to employ a rigorous and rigid grammar of representation, precisely because the particular kind of discourse we are confronting is far too rich for that.

What stands out is the extreme brutality of these incidents. This concerns not simply the volume of male violence, but its collective character. In sharing this feature, the Baroda Sundari and Suhasini cases are not exceptional, although they mark its extremity. Bistoo Dasi, a Rajbansi cultivator, recalled her oppression as an itinerary: 'I was made over to the latter [which was a gang whose members had names like Kristo, Mangal, Haridas, Gendla] after Abdul, Mait, Tamiz, Hafez, and Kabil ravished me in a bamboo grove. The Bajra men [ie. the other group] took me to Krito's house and thence to Gendla's. . . . All of them ravished me on the way from one place to another. Next night at midnight Gendla of Bajra and Tokrai brought me back to our village and left me in the "bil" [pool of water]'.[131]

Once violated, the woman becomes common property. As such, her relationship with men is analogous to that of a 'bazar woman'. But the difference with the latter is more revealing, for it shows

[131] *Amrita Bazar Patrika*, 3 May 1924.

that sexual relations with married women were inextricable from violence. Many of the abductors were wealthy enough to give rise to allegations that they had bribed the police, or even bought over the kin; they could obviously afford sex workers. What departed from the experience with a sex worker was that the women resisted, providing the occasion for asserting male mastery. The very physical stature of the abducted was contracted. Bistoo Dasi was dragged like a sack of rice across the ground. Many years later, a widow who had been abducted by fifty men was actually discovered inside a wooden box.[132] It was as if the implied analogy with a caged curiosity was meant to demonstrate that the raison d'etre of women was to be used at will. In inverse proportion to the utter isolation and diminution of the violated woman, such acts of violence bred a male bonding, different from the individualized exchange with the prostitute. There seems a collective exhilaration involved in the manner of abduction. Baroda Sundari's abduction was so open that her abductors even stopped to rest in an open field; when some people nearby, attracted by Baroda's cries, approached, they were simply warned off. This was a general condition: as many as five hundred and twenty-two gangrapes were committed between 1926–31. While a total of 4,362 women were abducted, the total number of culprits stood at 7,547, that is, almost double the number of victims.[133]

The character of the abductions yields two diametrically different narratives. The first is, of course, the communal. The other, that traces a different path, is one I will delineate later. Collective abduction ratifies a basic stereotype of the communal condition that had been elaborated by Mukherji. It shows the collective and organized nature of Muslim society. The force of this image makes the individual complications of a communal narrative appear as insignificant exceptions. The sheer excess of Muslim activity could submerge the role played by the Hindu police officer, just as it could blank out, in the Kushtea case (which I will describe later),

---

[132] *Amrita Bazar Patrika*, 30 August 1929.

[133] *Annual Report of the Women's Protection League for the Year 1938* (in English), This aroused a general outrage in the WPL in the thirties: 'rapes and outrages on women are not probably uncommon in other parts of the world, but rape on a helpless girl by a number of scoundrels one after another till the girl becomes unconscious or is almost bled to death is a thing peculiar to the soil of Bengal'. Ibid.

the role of a Muslim in sheltering the violated women. In contrast to the corporate character of Muslim enterprise, the condition of women could act as testimony to the powerlessness of the Hindu male (without which the abduction could not have presumably occurred) and, through that route, provide an emblem of the general Hindu condition.

A crucial underpinning of the motif of Hindu powerlessness — which again recalls Mukherji — is their poverty. Although Suhasini is a bit exceptional (her father was a 'leading muktear'[134]), her case can be coupled with the poverty theme because it reveals Hindu vulnerability. In the inaugural meeting of the Women's Protection League, a speaker talked of combating conditions which 'make it impossible for poor middle class people to live in the mofussil with their families'. The majority of cases, however, pointed to a more established concern, that is, the poverty of the low castes. Baroda Sundari's husband seemed poor, given the fact that all of them were cramped into a single room at night; Jashoda Sundari, whose case I will take up later, was the wife of a day-labourer; Bistoo Dasi was herself a cultivator, while Surabala Baisnabi was a beggar, who was told by her abductor that she had been taken because her brother could no longer support her.[135] The secretary of the Sishusahay Matrimangal Samiti stated that 'the weakness and poverty of the Hindus, the majority of Mahomedans contrasted with the minority of Hindus and the extremely isolated character of the Hindu society, materially helped the occurrences of abduction'.[136]

It is a reminder of the enduring flexibility of the 'dying Hindu' that it can provide a meta-text for concerns not directly derived from it. The abduction preoccupation can refer to 'dying Hindu', even as it marginalizes what is crucial to the former, that is, the concern with caste tension. The fact that it is women who are at the centre of this discourse not only means that a bloc can be produced between the upper and lower castes, but also, that two very different kinds of vulnerabilities can be elided: the middle-class condition can be put on par with the poverty of the low castes by the simple expedient of demonstrating that the women of both are defenceless. In the first place, of course, the woman can be

[134] *Amrita Bazar Patrika*, 27 May 1924.
[135] *Amrita Bazar Patrika*, 22 April 1924.
[136] *Amrita Bazar Patrika*, 1 May 1924.

loaded with such general significations, because she is also an attribute of male honour.[137] Honour is, in fact, one of those general categories of patriarchal societies by which the oppression of women is classified as an affront to the male. Honour, however, operates through several registers, being differentiated by social position and time. For the Hindu bhadralok public, it was associated with autonomy. To recall Tanika Sarkar's argument, the home in the nineteenth-century Hindu imagination was seen as a site for asserting the freedom of male Hindu control they had lost in the public domain.[138] Not surprisingly, the 'abducted woman' became a sign of the threat to male dominion: 'The householder will not be able to live in peace with his family in his own house — how is this?' rhetorically asked the *Sanjibani*.[139]

If the structure of the 'dying Hindu' inspired communal energies indirectly (the Muslims proliferated/Hindus died, on the basis of their own social dynamics), the 'abducted women' introduced a candid, no-holds-barred antagonism between Hindus and Muslims. The latter acquired its power from the contrast between the complete powerlessness of the Hindu condition, on the one hand, and the gravity of an immediate stake (honour/autonomy/control), on the other. This particular ideological structure yielded two kinds of possibilities that were complementary, but separated in intentions. The first was a political one which lead to de-emphasizing the importance of the anti-colonial struggle. I will deal with this strand later. At this point I wish to deal with the second initiative that concerned the question of internal reform.

The 'abducted' woman paved a smoother way for Hindu reform, even if the implications of the latter were more restricted than that offered by the 'dying Hindu'. For instance, after the Kushtea outrage, Hindu zamindars allowed the lower castes entry into a Kali temple.[140] This was preceded by a campaign to reform

---

[137] Samita Sen, has an extensive discussion on honour. However, her assumption of honour as a fixed idea that can be used in various contexts without changing its inherent meaning, does not contribute to an understanding of its specificities and the malleability of the discourse.

[138] Tanika Sarkar, 'Rhetoric Against Age of Consent: Resisting Colonial Reason and the Death of a Child-Wife', *Economic and Political Weekly*, vol. XXVIII, no. 36, 4 September 1993.

[139] 3 June 1926, RNP no. 24 of 1926, NAI.

[140] The Namasudras, Helemalis and Sutradhars amongst others had demanded the right to enter the Kali temple of the Narail zamindars. On 12

the popular custom of boycotting women abducted by Muslims, in which Suhasini's tragedy played an important part. The fear, attendant on the social boycott of Suhasini and her family resulting in her suicide, was articulated succinctly by the professor of a Mymensingh college: 'What will they [the villagers] do with the so-called "purity" of their society', he queried, 'if the society itself goes out of existence?'[141] It was a fear which reinforced those associated with the 'dying Hindu'. Moreover, while Suhasini may have chosen suicide others could convert, which was, as I will show later, an ever-present possibility. Not surprisingly, letters poured in to express sympathy with Suhasini's husband and even offer him employment.[142] Earlier, the orthodox pandits of Rangpur declared that there was no bar to Suhasini taking her 'rightful place' beside her husband after performing the prescribed penances.[143] Later, the president of the *Mahasammilani* of the orthodox pandits of Bhatpara ratified the stand of his Rangpur counterparts.[144] More important still was the support given the following year by the Bangiya Brahman Sabha, which expressed orthodox Brahmin opinion; not the least important aspect of their resolution was that it simplified the *prayaschitta* (penance rituals) to a simple dip in the Ganga.[145]

However, the consensus effected by 'abductions' can be seen as an attempt to merely reform the margins of the general structure of purity-pollution, in contrast to the 'dying Hindus' which was concerned with doing away with the structure itself. Clearly, the more direct engagement with the Muslims motivated by the abductions concern, involved an attenuation of the internal imperative of reform. That a reformist component remained at all, was primarily because of the drastic actions of women like Suhasini themselves.

In fact, the question of consent and choices of women threatened

---

July, barely over two weeks after the Kushtea incidents, the Babus of Narail allowed them entry into all their temples. *Amrita Bazar Patrika*, 18 July 1926.

[141] Letter from Jnanedra Nath Chawdhury, *Amrita Bazar Patrika*, 5 March 1925.

[142] The letter of an 'esteemed gentleman' was published offering a post in the 24 Parganas District Board to Suhasini's husband, if he was an undergraduate. *Amrita Bazar Patrika*, 12 March 1925.

[143] Ibid.

[144] *Amrita Bazar Patrika*, 20 April 1925.

[145] *Amrita Bazar Patrika*, 29 July 1926.

to rip open the very structure of the abductions discourse. The characteristic strategy to confront this problem was not a reformist one. It was another kind of move that combined discursive appropriation with political mobilization.

II.ii

Jashoda Sundari belonged to a village in Police Station Fatikchari in Chittagong. The first report on the affair appeared nearly a month after her alleged abduction.[146] The case went to court and the magistrate's judgement was delivered on 14 November that year. Jashoda was between sixteen and eighteen years of age and had been married to Rajani Kanta Nath for eight or ten years. The prosecution argued that she had been taken away by a few Muslims from the side of the tank where she had gone with her husband. Eight days later, when her abductors went to the hat, she escaped. But the next morning, around fifty or sixty men came to Rajani's house and dragged Jashoda away. When the brothers went to the police, the latter refused to register the case without a bribe. This, the family could not afford. Meanwhile, the Defence claimed that Rajani was too poor to maintain her and had illtreated her. She often visited Muslim houses for meals. On two successive Fridays, it was claimed, she had visited the maulvi of the Hanafia mosque and implored him to convert her, which he did, but only after she threatened suicide. Subsequently, she lived in a few Muslim houses. Later, she appeared before the president of the Union Board to declare her conversion and the fact that her husband's folks had threatened to beat her up. She then disappeared.

The magistrate held the defence story to be 'utterly improbable', since 'one would not expect this woman' to go alone to the mosque. He dismissed the defence plea that the maulvi had informed the husband after the first time Jashoda had visited him. He found it unnatural that the husband should 'try to reason with his wife instead of employing arguments that were far more forcible'. Moreover, since Jashoda was the mother of a little boy, 'it would have been most unnatural for the mother to stay away on her own accord'.[147]

[146] *Amrita Bazar Patrika*, 3 July 1926.
[147] *Amrita Bazar Patrika*, 14 November 1926.

The basic elements of this narrative seems almost tailor-made for satisfying the belligerence of all sides to the dispute. For the Hindu communalists, besides confirming the ability of the Muslims to act collectively, it also offered the involvement of traditional Islamic authority (the maulvi) with the threateningly new (the Union Board president). For their Muslim counterparts, it drew upon a self-justificatory rhetoric — which I will examine — of the ensnaring Hindu female, and/or the triumph of the truth of Islam. This mutually confirmatory antagonism was complemented by the frank male bias of the magistrate's judgement. Being based on the crude speculations of patriarchy, it provided, for that very reason, the consensus needed to accept the judgement. These assumptions included the naturalness of utterly subjecting the female will to the demands of motherhood, the impossibility of female initiative, the public ratification of wife-beating, and, finally, an open display of the interplay of male desire and violence.[148] The only unsettling aspect of this story was the fact that Jashoda was seen in both Hindu and Muslim 'camps'. The absence of stable affiliations in this young girl was a warning signal.

Less than a month later, Jashoda submitted an application asking her husband to either convert to Islam or dissolve the marriage. A few days later, she refused to leave the jail.[149] When the case came up for hearing, Rajani Nath's counsel invoked the Queen's Proclamation for Religious Toleration, to the effect that equity should prevail 'when there is a conflict of law of the parties of different religions'. He argued that neither the Court nor Islamic law (since it was not the State religion) could override Rajani's religion (which granted him the indissolubility of marriage). The pompous patriarchialism of the judge no doubt suffered a blow by Jashoda's action, but he got his revenge. Although his judgement flowed from colonial policies, it held 'that woman' in a pincer grip. On the one hand, he ruled that if Jashoda had

---

[148] Corresponding to the act of reducing the stature of the woman by the abductors, the judge devalues Jashoda by the linguistic address of 'this/the woman', while the accompanying desire is underlined by his salivating gaze; twice, appropos of nothing germane to the weighing of evidence, he remarked, 'the woman is admittedly good-looking', and again, before he concluded, 'the parties are neighbours and the woman is decent looking'. *Amrita Bazar Patrika*, 14 November 1926.

[149] *The Mussalman*, 9–16 December 1926.

become a Muslim, then the taking away of her by co-religionists was not an offence. On the other, he satisfied the Hindu side by stating that both Hindu and Islamic laws dictated that the marital status and rights of the spouse were not affected by conversion. He prohibited the dissolution of the marriage on this ground.[150] The day this judgement was reported, another story appeared with a triumphant headline: 'Good Sense at Last! Jashoda Ready to Follow her Husband'. It said that Jashoda had decided to return to Rajani on surety provided by Rai Kamini Kumar Das Bahadur, a local, landed notable. Wearing a red sari with conch shell bangles and vermilion on her forehead, she came in a police car, followed by a big crowd.

The many conflicting positions of Jashoda testify to the sheer isolation of her condition, which made her incapable of following her desires. This was not something unique. In 1924, Surabala Boisnabi had first declared in court that she had gone willingly to her alleged abductor's place. Later, after shifting to the local zamindar's house, she withdrew her earlier statement, declaring it had been delivered under duress.[151] At every point, the woman's will was overwritten by mobilizations for 'larger' religious causes. While the orthodox clamoured about the indissolubility of Hindu marriage,[152] in Jashoda's case the *Amrita Bazar Patrika* churned out two editorials criticizing the judgement, while leaving out any consideration of her choices.[153] All the resources of Hindu communalism, seized by the paranoia of shrinking numbers, was concentrated on preventing her choice from becoming an example to other women. She stood alone. Flanking her were those whom she had regarded as her saviours, and who behaved towards her as if she were a collective possession of local Muslims. Their arguments in court, that had emphasized their own authority to determine her basic affiliations, went against the grain of what her conduct had expressed. And, at the end of it all, the court followed the position on the equal treatment of religions, and divided up her body between the two religious communities: her

[150] *Amrita Bazar Patrika*, 19 December 1926.
[151] *Amrita Bazar Patrika*, 22 April 1924.
[152] Telegram from K.K. Das to Padamraj Jain, *Amrita Bazar Patrika*, 19 December 1926.
[153] These editorials appeared in *Amrita Bazar Patrika*, 21 and 22 December 1926.

body belonged to the Muslims by virtue of her conversion, and to her husband by marriage.

Once, however, she exerted her initiative for autonomy. This was when she refused to move from jail. This was a zone where there was no husband and no stifling demands of religion. Where laws of morality did not apply, for it was the habitation of the immoral. Where there was no worry about the future, for there was no future. If the jail was used for protecting society from its misfits, then Jashoda wanted to use the jail to ward off the terrible demands of communalized society.

Conversely, Jashoda's 'return' and 'remarriage' reveals more than the attempt to reform the practice of boycotting abducted women. It also indicates an imaginative way of dealing with the problem of choice that women posed. It may be noted that the most obvious feature of Jashoda's 'remarriage' is its public character. For instance, the narrative privileges not the husband but the zamindar, who, as we have seen, occupied a special place in this mobilization. He is beheld in his multiple glories: his generosity extends to both the assistance of his wealth and hospitality, as well as to his liberality in providing social recognition to Jashoda — an evocation that reinforces his image as guardian of Hindu order. The remarriage is a ceremony of integration in which the woman is not so much married to the husband, as to the whole of Hindu society via the zamindar's agency. Involved here is a tendency towards making the relationship between the woman and Hindu society a more direct and unmediated one. It is this shift in relationship between the woman and the demands of Hindu society that provides the precondition for appropriating the woman's choices to Hindu communalism, a strategy which I will elaborate in the next section.

But Hindu communalism succeeded at a price. The second marriage is no simple restoration of Hindu male hegemony. It also bears the imprint of Jashoda's struggles. She compelled the local zamindar to underwrite her marriage by making him stand surety for her husband's good behaviour.[154] In practice, therefore, she challenged the conception of the wife as a part of the husband's being, which is so integrally structured into the rituals and justifications of Hindu marriage. Compared to the scope of her

[154] *Amrita Bazar Patrika*, 12 December 1926.

desire, this was a small space for herself that she got. The whole structure of Hindu communalism, from its defence of the indissolubility of marriage ties and paranoia about Muslim designs, to the forefronting of the zamindar, all of which her reintegration upheld, could not fulfil the freedom she demanded for her choices. Yet it is the very massiveness of this oppressive structure that, by contrast, shows the grandeur of the concession she wrought.

Moreover, the importance of Jashoda's assertion was extended by the context. The Calcutta riots had already taken place in April that year. More importantly, the after-effects of the Pabna riots that broke out a few weeks later, cast their shadow over the entire period in which Jashoda's case was fought. At no time in the previous history of Bengal had things got so comprehensively communalized. Pertinent to our subject is the fact that abductions had begun to mime key elements of riots. This was evident in the Kushtea outrage which followed the Jashoda incident. Let me recall its story.

The incidents in Kushtea occurred in the middle of 1926. A party of twenty women, seven men and four children was returning from a visit to the Selaidah Snanjatra Fair at Kushtea in the middle of 1926. As they approached the boats which would take them home, they were set upon by about ten Muslims armed with lathis. The visiting party fled, leaving three women and two men who also ran away subsequently. The visitors found shelter in Madhu Shaikh's house and, with the help of their host, formed a rescue party. In three hours, around 3.30 am in the night, they reached the place of crime. The abductors fled, leaving the three women in a distressing condition amid the paddy fields. Two had been raped, while the third had managed to keep her aggressors at bay.[155]

Like a riot, the Kushtea affair involved collective confrontation in a public circumstance. In contrast to similar cases, it could not be seen as the bullying of an isolated Hindu home under the cover of darkness. Moreover, the fact that the women were returning from a bathing fair, steeped the incident in the colours of religious violation. The Kushtea affair recalled the motifs of the Jamalpur riots of 1907, a major one of which was the alleged violation of

[155] This report draws mainly on the findings of the BPCC Enquiry Committee, *Amrita Bazar Patrika*, 9 July 1926. Some details are taken from the report of the Secretary, Hindu Relief Committee, ibid., 1 July 1926.

Hindu women after they had similarly returned from a bathing fair. The effect was to insert the Kushtea outrage into a narrative of the repetitious unavoidability of communal estrangement. Further, this outrage was also aligned to the motifs of Muslim boycott of common festivities as well as the desecration of images.[156] Both of these had, as we will see in the next chapter, become staple items of riot situations. Precisely because of this abduction-riot interface, neither the role played by Madhu Sheikh in rescuing the Kushtea victims, nor a meeting of Muslims (the Hindus had refused to participate) that condemned the incident,[157] could materially change the propaganda of Hindu communalism. On the contrary, the *Amrita Bazar Patrika* attacked those who were attempting to discount the existence of communal motivations as double-faced.[158]

Jashoda's case embarrassed this convenient intersection of abductions and riots with the question of female consent. Her actions interrogated the difference between Hindu and Muslim males, and raised the agenda of freedom in a situation where the pressures of communal violence had privileged immaculate authoritarian control. In fact, Jashoda problematized the whole edifice of communal division sustained by communal rivalry and underwritten by the 'toleration' of colonial legality. The question

---

[156] The Hindu Relief Committee report drew a continuous line between those other acts of antagonism and the Kushtea outrage. It said that the first thing that had broken the 'amicable relation' was the boycott by Muslims of two important Hindu festivals in which they had been participating 'from time immemorial', one of which was the 'Snan-Jatra festival at Khorshedpur or Selaidah as the place is variously called'. Apparently a rival fair was held on the opposite banks of the river, and according to the report, four hundred Muslims participated in lathi play. The report alleged that the Muslims who outraged the women, were drawn from these players at the rival fair. It also detailed instances of image desecration and other abductions. *Amrita Bazar Patrika*, 3 July 1926.

[157] *Amrita Bazar Patrika*, 5 July 1926.

[158] The *Patrika* expressed disappointment with the Government report for not acknowledging the presence of general communal tension (as noted in the Relief Committee report), as *the* explanatory factor. 6 July 1926. Later it published a letter from 'Truth' which stated that Shamsuddin Ahmed, a vakil who had been visibly attempting to defuse the communal antagonism arising from this incident, was the neighbour of a Muslim ex-noncooperator who had initiated the boycott campaign and that he had not raised his voice against previous anti-Hindu acts. 16 July 1926.

of female consent was to come up again in 1929, although, unlike Jashoda, the girl in this case had run away.

Sovana was the daughter of Babu Charu Chandra Ray, a pleader. They were neighbours of Maulvi Panaulla, a deputy magistrate of Barisal. 'I was on a very friendly term [sic] with Charu babu', declared the maulvi in his deposition. Mohiuddin, his wife's first cousin, who stayed with them, fell in love with Sovana. Apparently, the two guardians knew of this affair and had tried to break it up. Finally, Mohiuddin was sent away by Panaulla and a few weeks later, Sovana eloped with her lover.

This was a nice story belonging to the genre of 'Laila-Majnu-tale-in-real-life', with the guardians doing their duty and the romantic pair successfully decamping. There were no outrages, no violence, nothing to justify the headline, 'Sovana Abduction Case'. Except for the fact that it involved the profound problem of inter-communal marriage. The implications of this had made even Gandhi afraid.[159] And, according to Muzaffar Ahmed, led to the boycott of Nazrul's poetry by apparently cosmopolitan literary circles including the *Prabashi*, when he married a Hindu girl.[160]

What was remarkable in the Sovana case was the way a question of choice was converted into a situation of compulsion. This rhetorical alchemy was enabled by the issue of neighbourliness. An 'abduction' in Calcutta — which was a case of elopement — was written up as a narrative of betrayal and insidious design: 'It appears that Isshaq [the 'abductor'] rented a house at Tollygunje and the girl used to live with her father nearby. The accused having an eye on the handsome girl made himself very thick and thin [sic] as a worthy neighbour with the father'. The inclusion

---

[159] In his letter to Manilal Gandhi (dtd. 3/4/1926), he wrote, 'What you desire is contrary to *dharma*. If you stick to Hinduism and Fatima follows Islam it will be like putting two swords in one sheath; or both may lose your faith . . . . It is . . . only *adharma* if Fatima agrees to conversion just for the sake of marrying you'. He concluded his letter with some practical observations, that did not quite succeed in suppressing concern for his own reputation: 'Nor is it in the interests of our society to form this relationship. Your marriage will have a powerful impact on the Hindu-Muslim question. Inter-communal marriages is no solution to this problem. You cannot forget nor will society forget that you are my son.' Possibly Gandhi's response had something to do with the fact that it was 1926, and the paranoia that accompanies nation–wide communal upsurges, was a new experience. *Collected Works of Mahatma Gandhi*, XXX *(February–June, 1926)*, (Ahmedabad: 1968).

[160] Muzaffar Ahmed, *Kazi Nazrul Islam: Smritikatha*, Calcutta, 1965, p. 180.

of the act of hiring a house next to a Hindu-with-a-daughter within the narrative, makes it appear a part of a long, stereotypical conspiracy by the treacherous Muslim. Underlying such narratives was the notion that occupying the same social space allowed the Muslim to deploy his natural physical advantages over the Hindu. Such an unfair competition between the two sets of males made redundant the question of woman's choices: she either belonged or was abducted.

Although the Sovana case used an important riot motif, 1929 was not a year distinguished for rioting.[161] The wave of violent communal antagonism appears to have subsided by 1927. What filled the sphere of popular agitation was working-class action, while Subhash Bose's re-entry into Congress politics gave a fresh impetus to non-communal nationalism. Even reports of abductions in 1928 tended to be non-communal in nature: one case had ageist overtones, being headlined, 'Brutal Lust of a Sexagenarian. Alleged Rape on 11 Year old Girl'. Another, headlined 'Hindu Lady Attacked', related the story of a servant who attacked his mistress while robbing her.[162] Although a new space for mobilization was opened up for the Hindu Mahasabha with the landlord opposition to the Tenancy Amendment Bill, there was no mistaking the profound problems which beset Hindu communalism. The year 1929 was spent in visible preparation for the Civil Disobedience movement (launched in 1930), and to that extent deflected attention away from the communal agenda that had dominated the mid-twenties. But above all, it was the Nehru Report and Jinnah's initiative that had preceded it, that created apprehensions in the Mahasabha and its sympathizers.

Not surprisingly, the theme of abductions was stirred up to mobilize for the coming Hindu Conference in Dhaka held in August 1929. The Nehru Report was not only criticized in its nitty gritties (and rejected by the more extreme sections, such as B.S. Moonje),[163] but its very rationale was questioned through

---

161 'Although the after-effects of the communal riots of 1926 are still apparent, the year under report was generally peaceful . . . '. C.A. Tegart, *Annual Report on the Police Administration of the Town of Calcutta and its Suburbs for the Year 1929*. The corresponding report for 1928 also reported that no communal riots had taken place. Tegart Papers, Box IV, CSAC.

162 *Amrita Bazar Patrika*, 27 October 1928.

163 This, despite the concessions that the Nehru Report gave to the

abductions. After criticizing the Nehru Report at the Dhaka conference, Kelkar declared, 'Breathes there a man who will say "I will pay the price. of the honour of my wife or daughter even for purchasing Self-Government of India?"'[164] In effect, the Nehru Report was elided with abductions. More profoundly, abductions were deemed to be so important that they could be used to openly override the imperative of freedom. At the All India Hindu Mahasabha Conference held at Surat in 1929, the president of the Conference, Ramanada Chatterjee had declared, 'If I were asked which I would have, freedom from foreign domination, or security of the honour, persons and lives of our women . . . if I were compelled to choose only one of the two, I would chose the latter'.[165]

This political campaign had too much at stake in abductions to allow Sovana any freedom in choosing her life. In fact, the Sovana case was central to the campaign. That Sovana's guardian-in-law was a deputy magistrate was used as a palpable indicator of what could happen if power was shared with the Muslims. In this schema, the 'betrayal' of a shared social space functioned as a trope for the outcome of the power distribution that the Nehru Report had envisaged.

Nevertheless, despite its advantages, the blatantly blanketing character of the category of 'abductions' was nowhere more unambiguously interrogated, as it was in this case. The romance elements were too discernible, since the substance of this story, as I have hinted, was (and still is) too popularly disseminated to be symmetrically aligned to the definition of 'abduction' and the lack of women's consent that the word implied. More than any other case, that of Sovana's is an appropriate one to begin an enquiry into what the term 'abductions' implied and concealed.

II.iii

Two 'traditions' of abductions can be discerned in Bengal. The more straightforward one was related to criminal gangs.

Mahasabha, after its campaign against Jinnah's compromise plan in 1927. Sumit Sarkar, *Modern India 1885–1947*, Madras, 1992, f.pub. 1983, pp. 262–3.

[164] His basic perspective on nationalism was set out by his warning that 'National patriotism' ought not to be 'allowed to operate on our psychology like an opiate'. *Amrita Bazar Patrika*, 27 August 1929.

[165] *Prabashi Part 29, vol. 1, no. 1*, Baisakh, 1336 (1929), p. 169.

Recollecting his days as judge in the late nineteenth century, Ameer Ali talked of gang rape as a 'form of crime which happily was not then common in India had become frequent in Rajshahi'.[166] Police reports on the functioning of two criminal gangs in Midnapur stated that, 'Outrage of females was a prominent characteristic of their dacoities'.[167]

However, such open and shut cases of compulsion were not complicating. It was when abductions occurred in the context of everyday social relations that the problems arose. These centred initially on the anxieties around the widow. In an early declaration on the women's reform question, Mahesh Deb propagated widow remarriage on the grounds that their privations produced a situation where widows, 'unable to subdue nature give way to temptations which beset them on every side'.[168] This idea of the widow as a simple zone of desire,[169] was powerful enough to make her a consensual sign of sexual vulnerability. Muslim-owned newspapers and individuals defended their community on the grounds that Hindu widows initiated these 'abductions'. Ironically, Arya Samaj propaganda confirmed this impression: a pamphlet issued by them, stated that the proliferation of widows was an important reason for the degeneration of Hindus, especially because the latter could not prevent them from falling into the hands of the irreligious.[170]

[166] 'Family Traditions', *Memoirs of . . . Ameer Ali*, p. 65.

[167] 'Report on the Kapgari-Beragari Gang of Midnapore District', File No. P.3-T-18(1), and 'Declaration of Pattu Shaikh's Gang of Birpur in Midnapore as Criminal Tribe', P.3T-17(1). Progs. of the GOB in the Police Dept., Police, December 1923. IOL. Abductions were probably common in the pre-British era as well: in 1780 an abduction was carried out from near Chowringhee, by armed men. W.W. Hunter, *Annals of Rural Bengal*, rpt. Calcutta, 1965, p. 45.

[168] Mahesh Chandra Deb, 'A Sketch of The Condition of The Hindoo Women'; speech delivered at meeting of the Society for the Acquisition of General Knowledge, January 1839. *Awakening in Bengal in Early Nineteenth Century (Selected Documents)* vol. *1*, Goutam Chattopadhyaya (ed.), Calcutta, 1965, pp. 103-4.

[169] Two observations made by Dagmar Engels, *Beyond Purdah?: Women in Bengal 1890-1939*, Delhi, 1996 are pertinent here. First, that there was a long standing Bengali Hindu male fear of excessive female sexuality, pp. 100-9; second, that the proportion of Hindu widows greatly outnumbered those of the Muslims (p. 41). Both factors would intensify the communal sexual anxiety.

[170] Narayan Svami, *Arya Samaj Kahake Bale?*, Rameshchandra Bandopadhyaya (trans.), Calcutta, 1333 (1926), p. 6. Originally entitled *Arya Samaj Kya Hai?* the pamphlet was written by the all-India head of the Arya Samaj.

The anxiety around the widow was intensified by property considerations. A Wesleyan missionary complained that a widow was frightened off from conversion, because of the loss of property that it would entail.[171] We may recall the incident in which the Muslim husband of a Namasudra widow was grossly insulted when he came to claim her property.[172]

We have seen, in the instance of Arya Samaj discourse, how a fear of the consequences of a widows' desire could be resolved by translating her into a victim of Muslim lust. But there were problems with making the widow the central object of abductions. The discourse of widow reform was so firmly premised on a critique of Hindu society, that it did not allow abductions to be seen as a consequence of Muslim compulsion alone: this critique would inescapably act as a sub-text. Even more germane was the fact that most of the abducted women were not widows, but married. The pattern of abductions analysed by the *Sanjibani* showed that, out of a total of 1033 abductions, 45.2 per cent were married (of whom 70 per cent were Hindus), while only 12.7 per cent and 9.8 per cent were widows and unmarried, respectively.[173] Such cases, unlike the one concerning widows, could not be attributed to the compulsions of biological necessity. On the other hand, it was indicative of the woman's consent, precisely because her removal from marital protection clashed so completely with the accepted ideal of the subjection of the woman to her husband's being. The consternation that was hidden behind the rhetoric of abductions

---

[171] In a letter to a fellow missionary dated 12/11/19, the Bengal chairman referred to the case of 'a poor Hindu widow, who wished for baptism but was prevented by the fact that any little property she had would be entirely lost to her and her living taken away should she profess the Christian faith. How common', the correspondent concluded, 'these cases are in a missionary's experience'. Wesleyan Methodist Missionary Society (London) Archive. Correspondence. Bengal Chairman 1919–20, Box No. 848. SOAS.

[172] Interestingly enough, another 'serious fracas' occurred between Muslims and Namasudras in some villages in Barisal, on account of the abduction of a Namasudra widow. *Amrita Bazar Patrika*, 20 August 1929.

[173] Cited in *Prabashi*, Ashwin 1336 (1929), part 29, vol. 1, no. 6. The WPL in the 1938 report, which was based on more credible government figures than those supplied in the twenties, confirmed this statistical trend. It stated that 53.4 per cent of women abducted were married (with the second largest number falling under the 'unclassified' category) *Annual Report of the Women's Protection League for the Year 1938* (in English), pub. details absent. Pagination absent due to damage.

sometimes revealed itself. A *Prabashi* article declared that abductions could only cease if oppression within the household was put at an end, thereby withdrawing the 'temptation' for women to run away.[174] The necessity of blanketing all cases under the rubric of 'abduction' became much more intense, because of the larger doubts raised by married women.

Recently, Miranda Chaytor has argued that while the designation of the sexual violation of women as rape was a consequence of the shift to a concern with consent in seventeenth-century law; abduction was an earlier term that implied the theft of another's (male) belongings.[175] In modern Bengal however, as I have suggested, there was a larger space provided for the consideration of female consent. Thus the 'problem' of widows took into account — via the sexist fear of a woman's 'uncontrollable sexuality' when detached from the matrimonial safety valve — a woman's desires, and built a corresponding reformist project. In the present case, the value of the term abductions lay in not simply blanketing the question of women's consent, as it did with Barodasundari and Sovana, but equally, in allowing it to be revealed counterfactually. This it did by highlighting the multiple ways in which a woman was abused. Unlike a case of theft proper, the woman does not disappear. On the contrary, her fate is dramatized in order to underline the utter repudiation of her choices and personhood. This second, less overt, preoccupation with consent is an important one in the discourse on abductions in twentieth-century Bengal. For it is precisely this generalization of the belittling consequences of abductions, through which Hindu communalism attempts to acquire the woman's consent to its own project.

The fear of abductions does more. The invocation of the oppressive Muslim Other transposes the transcendental claims of the community and its largely patriarchal values, into a celebration of the Hindu woman's control over her body. An early indication of this move was the appeal made to the idealized role of the woman, in order to mobilize against abductions by Muslims. This can be seen in the invocation of *satitva*. The commentary provided by *Prabashi* on Suhasini's last letter, begins by exclaiming: 'Despite hitting her, binding her hands with rope and hanging her, trying

[174] 'Nariraksha', Sraban 1334[1927], part 27, vol. 1, no. 4.
[175] Miranda Chaytor, 'Husband(ry): Narratives of Rape in the Seventeenth Century', *Gender and History*, vol. 7, no. 3, November 1995.

to break her teeth, her oppressors attempted to deprive her of her satitva and purity; but with extraordinary patience, courage, mental strength and devotion to satitva, this girl saved the purity of her body, mind and soul.'[176] This is a remarkable image; the sexual violation of Suhasini is replaced completely by an incantatory rehearsal of the violence done to her, the rhythms of which appropriate the pleasurable repetitiveness of the sexual act into its own coinage. Equally significant is that the rhythm of the sentence also sensualizes, by the continuation of its repetitive, staccato structure, her act of resistance. Women's agency is given an erotic charge even as it is sublimated. It can be argued that the reference to satitva gives to Suhasini a transcendental and iconic significance. But the point of this discourse is missed if we see it as merely striving to create goddess images. On the contrary, it seeks to the make the exceptional activity of 'normal' women an exemplary phenomenon that would persuade other 'normal' women to realise their own potentialities. But if this is the point where the discourse of Hindu communalism breaches tradition, at the same time its celebration of woman's agency is done in terms that follow the contours of the male gaze. The latter gives a regulative orientation to the break.

Obviously, the normalizing role of the erotic can be fulfilled only if it works as a sub-text. Idealizing images of the assertive woman emphasized desexualized roles. But what is surprising is the appeal to the Sister in the abductions discourse. 'How can a nation hope to preserve the honour of their mothers and sisters from the hands of beastly ruffians . . . ?', asked the *Nayak* [177] after the Kushtea incident. This is a little unexpected, since the exaltation of the Mother was an established and effective symbol to represent Bengali nationhood, and, by extension, would have served the purpose of Hindu communalism equally well. Conversely, its coupling with the Sister would reduce its ideal, immaculate stature, and hence its appeal.

The addition can be explained in basically two, interrelated ways. In the numerous poems written by nationalists, especially those with extremist persuasions, the Mother was one who has already fulfilled her role through giving birth and distributing nurture.

---

[176] Translated by me. Pous, 1332 (1925), part 25, vol. II, no. 3.
[177] 7 July 1926, RNP no. 28 of 1926, NAI.

Consequently, the Mother could not but be a passive figure. And this gave supreme importance to men's (that is, the son's) agency, for it was up to them to do their duty to their motherland which had fulfilled its side of the bargain by spawning and nurturing them. The Sister, on the other hand, was one who had yet to actualize her potentialities. She still had a contribution to make. In other words, she opened up the prospect of her agency. The effect of this was reinforced by the other implication of 'Sister' which gestured at a more participatory history of relationship; there was a connotation of co-activity with the brother, which was very different from the crucible of dependencies resting on the logic of nurture and demand that specified the relationship with the Mother.

The figure of the Sister was ideally suited to a project in which the woman's choice was transferred from her personal desires to the defence of her community. In other words, a woman's public agency was privileged over her personal choices. The woman was given a new sphere of activity by Hindu communalism. Admittedly, in many respects, this reformulated the traditional web of relationships in which the woman was located. But it did so by avoiding any questioning of the basis of her relationships or expanding the area of her choices as a person. The emphasis was on action. And the new activity was the physical training of women.

As early as 1923, in the annual session of the HMS, M.M. Malaviya included women in his appeal for physical self-strengthening.[178] While the inaugural session of the Women's Protection League did not feature this as an objective, by the end of the decade, the Bengal Hindu Conference at Dhaka resolved to train, 'Hindu women . . . in the use of proper weapons.'[179] This had been preceded by a major campaign in print. *Prabashi* reprinted an exemplary story that had occurred in Budge Budge. It related how Girish Chandra Adak's wife, in his absence, defended her children and herself from dacoits and inflicted an injury that helped to

---

[178] He said: 'I have come to the only conclusion on the question of Hindu-Muslim unity. It is that each should feel the other is strong to ward off successfully an unjust attack by the other, and thus alone will [sic] harmony be maintained. I want Indian manhood and womanhood to realise its duty of defending itself.' Reported by *Servant*, Calcutta, 4.1.23, 'Newspaper Extracts regarding Hindu Mahasabha Proceedings', Home Poll., Progs. no. 198, 1924, NAI.

[179] *Amrita Bazar Patrika*, 29 August 1929.

identify one of them.[180] It also featured Shyammohini Debi's article, which, recommended making physical training a compulsory subject in women's educational institutions. She exhorted well-educated, urban women to spread this pedagogy among rural women.[181] Sometimes the drive went so far as to marginalize the role of the husband as protector.[182] The president of the Bogra Hindu Sabha presented a newly-wedded bride with a dagger, so that she could defend her honour.[183] On its part, HMS sessions provided ample encouragement. In its provincial meeting at Mymensingh in 1928, girls joined their male compatriots in exhibiting their skills at dagger play, providing a novel source of attraction and inspiration[184]

By doing this, the HMS was plugging into a parallel political circuit, that is, of the Terrorists. It was only in the twenties that some individual (and for that reason spectacular) women graduated from being supporters and ancillaries of the revolutionary terrorist movement, to becoming initiators of actions. I will elaborate the larger involvement of terrorists in communal politics later, but what is of immediate interest is the fact that, in some of the renowned cases, womens' terrorist activism was inspired by communal imperatives. One of the formative influences on Preetilata Waddadar, the first woman to lead a male group of terrorists into action, was when, as a student, communal riots broke out and 'muslim rowdies

---

[180] Kartick, 132 (1926), part 25, vol. II, no. 1.

[181] 'Nariganer Atmaraksher Upay' [Methods of self-defence for women], Bhadra, 1333 (1926), part 26, vol. I, no. 5.

[182] The importance of this can be realized by placing it against the orthodox rhetoric around the Sarda and Age of Consent Bills that were up for consideration in the twenties. Krishna Vedantachintamani, who was the most articulate and energetic representative of the orthodox Brahmanical position in this period, argued that the wife ought to be merged into the personality of the husband. Whereas the Gaur Bill would make women citizens and thereby weaken the hold of the community over her. ("The Consent Bill in the Council', *Amrita Bazar Patrika*, 6 October 1925). The persistence of such rhetoric, was a legacy of the first Consent Bill agitation. See Sarkar, 'Rhetoric Against . . . '.

[183] *Amrita Bazar Patrika*, 19 August 1926. Obviously this produced feelings of insufficiency. Waliullah recollects with some amusement, the travails of a Hindu Gandhian Congressman, who motivated his wife to get training in weights, lathis and wielding *gadas* (a traditional weapon that has a long handle and a big weight on the top), Waliullah, p. 211.

[184] *Fortnightly Reports*, April second half, File no. 1/1928, NAI.

threatened to attack Eden Hostel [of which she was a resident in Dhaka] and "loot" the resident Hindu girls', while the district magistrate refused to interfere.[185] Further, after Kushtea, a 'local ladies association' of Dhaka, called Deepali Association, turned agitational. They criticized government apathy and their leaders, and called upon women's organizations to take the initiative on the abductions issue.[186] This organization had been founded by Lila Nag, regarded as the pioneer in linking women with revolutionary activity in 1923. The *Prabashi* reported that the Deepali Association was starting a programme for training women in lathi play.[187] A significant feature was that it combined these activities with the more acceptably gendered one of social service, especially that of education.[188] This allowed the Association a more extensive impact among middle-class women.

Solidarity amongst them received an impetus via communal paranoia: One hundred and fifty women attended a Women's Protection League meeting held in the Mymensingh City School, and after a 'stirring speech' which detailed outrages on women, some became members of the organization and decided to hold a meeting themselves. Among the names of five members given, one was a doctor while the others all had graduate degrees.[189] A mofussil network of women's societies, initiated by Brahmos, was extant from the 1890's.[190] These became very active in the twenties, when they provided the foci for mobilization by the Bangiya Nari Samaj in its campaign for women's franchise.[191] A report on one of the

[185] Tirtha Mandal, *The Women Revolutionaries of Bengal, 1905–1939*, Calcutta, 1991, p. 41.
[186] *Amrita Bazar Patrika*, 21 July 1926.
[187] *Prabashi*, Magh, 1333 (1926), part 26, vol. 2, no. 4. This was possibly the same Deepali Association of Dhaka, reported in the pages of the *Patrika*, which discussed outrages on women after the Kushtea incident, calling upon women's organizations to take the initiative in stopping them. 21 July 1926.
[188] This organization established twelve primary schools, three High Schools for girls, classes to prepare girls for matriculation, industrial training centres, a female students association, and a women's hostel in Calcutta, in addition to training and physical fitness. Deepali Sangha was used for a revolutionary purpose after Nag joined the Sri Sangha, a male terrorist organization. Mandal, *Women Revolutionaries*, p. 67.
[189] *Amrita Bazar Patrika*, 27 October 1926.
[190] Barbara Southard, *The Women's Movement and Colonial Politics in Bengal: The Quest for Political Rights, Education and Social Reform Legislation, 1921–1925*, N. Delhi, 1995, p. 60
[191] Ibid., p. 83.

women's associations founded in 1925, says that it was encouraged by local pleaders and muktears:[192] a conjuncture of time and social composition that makes it not unreasonable to speculate on the motivating force of abductions. In fact, women emerged as a separate constituency for Hindu communal propaganda.[193]

The entry of women into the male preserve of physical culture would give them an attendant confidence and also ensure a sense of public participation with the male. It would mark out a new sphere of public co-activity, which would be a departure from earlier role models. The potentially reformist elements were not missed by *Prabashi*. It emphasized this with declarations to the effect that the confinement of women to domesticity was responsible for their vulnerability as Muslim targets. It also called for the banning of child-marriage (given the incidence of child wives among those abducted).[194] Proposals for reform, when they occurred, no longer needed to be regarded as defying mainstream society but, on the contrary, a confirmation of its importance. Antagonism with the other, to reiterate a theme of this thesis, removes the antagonistic edge of reformism.

At the same time there was a paradox involved here. It emerges from the fact that this male preserve of non-mechanical, body-to-body violence, is one in which the claim of male superiority was seen to possess the closest ratification from biology. The sphere of body culture was so dominated by males, that the model for it was 'manliness'. Within such a scheme, the woman could only hope to emulate the male. Or worse, like Sarala Debi, who influenced Pulin Das, the terrorist leader of the Anushilan Samiti in Dhaka, they could aspire to instigate an interest in physical culture amongst males; in order to resist everyday humiliation by the British, she recommended playing football.[195] Ultimately, the

---

192 *Amrita Bazar Patrika*, 17 August 1926.

193 Pt. Mokshada Charan Samadhaya, a Hindu Relief Committee propagandist who went on a programme of lectures on Hindu Sabhas and Sangathan, gave a special lecture for ladies in Rangpur. *Amrita Bazar Patrika*, 26 August 1926.

194 'Nariraksha' (Women's Protection), Sraban, 1334 (1927), part 27, vol. 1, no. 4.

195 Das, *Amar Jiban Kahini*, p. 46. She remained as active on the same issue in the mid-twenties. In presenting the Deshbandhu Challenge Shield at the Rajbati Football Association, she stated that the Shield, imported from England, bore the traditions of loyalty, devotion and bravery in the cause of

little 'sister' could only hope to follow in the footsteps of her brother in such matters. No doubt this added to the attractiveness of this project.

'Abductions' set the agenda for the mobilization of women in the mid-twenties. Sometime in 1926, during the frenzied aftermath of the Pabna riots, Gandhi received a letter from Mrs A. Sen and Miss P. Bose in Dhaka District, presumably eliciting advice on the question of physical training for women. His reply was embarrassed, equivocating, declining to have, 'a public discussion of a delicate question'. He justified his objection to such training on pragmatic grounds, not on moral ones: ' . . . because in the vast majority of cases such self-defence proves worse than useless and because it will take generations before our women take to the dagger or the pistol in any appreciable numbers'.[196] Gandhi's awkwardness reveals the vulnerability of the Congress to the power of abductions. This minor encounter defines the large political significance abductions could yield in making Hindu communalism a competitor to the Congress for the allegiance of women.

The extension of franchise gave women a new political significance. The reformed constitution of the Calcutta Corporation, referred to in the last chapter, allowed women to vote for the first time. In 1925, women were included in the franchise for the Legislative Council elections. Equally important was the new level of self-activity produced by the franchise question. Southard describes the 1921 campaign on the vote as 'the first political campaign in Bengal on women's issues organized by women themselves'.[197] They were emerging as a political constituency whose political choices had to be respected.[198] Hindu communalism

---

women, and declared that the football playing generation of Bengal should make the cries of dishonoured women of Bengal a thing of the past. *Amrita Bazar Patrika*, 12 September 1925.

[196] Ramananda Chatterjee had publicly questioned Gandhi's silence on this issue. The latter had written an article in *Young India* on the 29 July 1926, asking for addresses of Bengali ladies who could furnish concrete evidence of outrages in villages. The letter from these two ladies was in answer to his article. Apparently the reports given by these ladies were based on hearsay, which is why Gandhi reiterated the important questions at the end of his reply: 'Is the disease general? How many cases of real violence have happened, say, during the past six months?' Letter, dtd. 12.8.1926, *The Collected Works of Mahatma Gandhi*, XXXI.

[197] Southard, *The Women's Movement*, p. 65.

[198] The *Patrika* obviously remarked on its novelty in its coverage of the

however, had lagged behind the Congress in mobilizing women. As is well-known, women were pulled into the political arena during the non-cooperation movement, due mainly to the influence of Gandhi. In Bengal, women were mobilized for the first time during the demonstration against the visit of the Prince of Wales in Calcutta in 1921.[199] Even so, Congress mobilization extended rather than disturbed gender roles. Women were included in the procession so that they would become a potent rallying point if hurt by the police. Although this entailed costs to women that included jail sentences, public space was inscribed by gender divisions, and by becoming signs of potential violation alone, they were confirmed in their inability to participate in areas defined as male preserves.

Hindu communalism, too, accepted the basic premise of gender divisions, but went beyond the Congress in reformulating its limits. But it took back with one hand what it gave with the other. The rhetoric of the abducted woman may have instigated women into physical activity, but this venture was based — as was so much of communalism — on making the woman's body a source of fear to herself. It reinforced the traditional insecurities imposed by male dominated society. If the effect of communal mobilization was to expand the reach of women's political activity, allowing it to permeate the household itself, it was at the same time a feeling that militated against any talk of gender liberation. Fear produces obedience, not questions.

Equally, such fear tended to circumscribe the political interests of women to self-protection alone. Nationalists had mobilized women for causes other than ones that concerned themselves. This may have generated its own strategy of suppressions, but, at least, it also provided a broader vision of women's identity. Correspondingly, it delivered a more extensive base for questioning the latter, when this occurred. Nationalist mobilization had the potentiality of bringing the woman into tension with her household, and raising questions about gender oppression. On the other hand, by locating women in a tight dialectic between their sexual vulnerability and physical self-protection, communal mobilization discouraged women from situating themselves in the context of other

---

1926 elections. Although the numbers of women were not stupendous, they were not completely insignificant; in some polling stations women voters numbered more than forty. 17 November 1926.

[199] Rajat Ray, *Social Conflict*, p. 293.

political issues, or rather, from seeing themselves in relationship to roles other than their simple sexual being. Via abductions, Hindu communalism attennuated the question of gender by its obsession with sexuality.

The fact that it was able to do so, rested, of course, on the contribution made by their imagining of the Muslim. Once this disappeared, the whole structure of their mobilization around abductions appears to have folded up like a pack of cards, allowing a new range of questions to be asked. Another narrative of abductions was generated.

II.iv

As stated, since the nineteenth century there had been a strong reformist element in the relationship between Hindu communalism and the women's question. Radical elements like Swami Shraddhanand had implicitly realized the necessity of acquiring female consent in the context of resisting conversions. It led Shraddhanand to mobilize for the cause of female education and advocate both equal rights and companionability as the basis of marriage.[200] But this radical reformism was a tradition that — especially after the isolation of Shraddhanand in the twenties — was on the wane. 'Abductions' represented the new attitude of Hindu communalism. However, it did not possess a firm anchor.

In fact, the Women's Protection League was skating on thin ice. The discourse of abductions gave to the woman her body as her empire, but only as a guardian for the 'higher' demands of her religion to which that body rightfully belonged. But that demand could only exist by denying women their experience of abductions. And the possibility of recognizing that experience was ever present. The silence over the role of males in oppressing women was not an easy one to maintain. Unlike the 'go-korbani' or 'music before mosques' issues, the woman was far too meshed in with day-to-day relationships of social hierarchies to provide a stable sign of communal differentiation. Beyond a point, differentiation could not be made on communal lines because patriarchialism was far too general to allow that.

The immediate cause for the collapse of the communal structure

[200] Jordens, *Swami Shraddhanand*, pp. 25–54.

of abductions was the Women's Protection League's break with communal mobilization. Although the League report states that this took place in 1938 with a speech by Subhash Bose at one of their conferences, the turn became palpable after K.K. Mitra's demise in 1936,[201] when the League began to focus on gender questions. It thereby offered an alternate analysis of abductions, drawing on a more comprehensive range of factors with lesser suppressions. At the heart of this change was the attitude to consent. The distinctive feature of the pamphlets of the thirties lay in their unambiguous recognition of the consent of the abducted in leaving their homes. And this concern, in turn, provided the occasion for critically examining the structure of familial relations.

Traces of parental involvement had, it may be recalled, crept into the initial reporting of the Suhasini case, although these were quickly edited out.[202] Case histories of the late thirties indicate that this was not abnormal. 'Bireswar's wife Asalata Dasi was enticed away and kept concealed by her parents . . . in the month of January 1938, for immoral purposes', reads the first line of the part on case histories, in the 1938 report in English.[203] More crucial was the encouragement by those close to the family (if not a part of it) who typically prepared the girl by contrasting her present terrible state with what could be an attractive future with him. He would then persuade her to run away with him, inviting his friends meanwhile to partake of the spoils.[204]

[201] Of course one should not take public declarations at their face value. The League had proclaimed itself as non-communal earlier. What was new now was that its programme also took a corresponding turn to non-communal objectives. The invocation of Bose's speech appears to have had a purely commemorative appeal since the Report for 1935–7, which was written as a single tract after Mitra's death, seems to mark the decisive change. The 1938 Report does not depart substantially from its framework. It should be added here that what I am asserting in the following argument must be qualified by the fact that I was unable to get any WPL literature of the twenties — although all other indicators bear out my assertion.

[202] There were other stray instances of the involvement of Hindu guardians. I have already mentioned the allegation against Baroda Sundari's brother. It was reported in the Jorabagan Court, that the aunt-in-law of a minor girl in Nimtolla conspired with another woman, to deliver the girl to Fakir Mohammed. *Amrita Bazar Patrika*, 6 August 1925.

[203] *The Women's Protection League: Report of the Year 1938*

[204] *Nariraksha Samiti: 1938 Shaler Karyabibarani*, [WPL: Report for 1938], (pub. details absent), p. 4

From revealing the complicity of family authority in 'abductions' to an indictment of conjugal relations, is but a step away. When the annual report for 1938 observed that the husband could leave the wife, but that the latter had no such privilege, it defined marriage as a sphere of rights rather than as an affective relationship which Shraddhanand's reformulation had assumed. Consequently, it talked about things that were suppressed in the narratives of the twenties. Raju Bala, a fourteen-year-old wife in a Khulna village, was given over to 'Sayed and Jabbar for disposal as they liked and to this effect the accused got the signature of Sambhu [the husband] in a plain paper and one Gour became a witness to it.'[205] Equally important, case histories included those concerning marital relations; Abala Bala Majumdar was married while the first wife was lying invalid; when the latter recovered, Abala was 'tortured' and 'removed and confined from place to place' by her husband.[206] The League now gave priority to cases of abandonment. A semantic expansion was involved: 'women's oppression' which had been a euphemism for abductions, now also began to denote marital oppressions. Thus, besides dowry cases, the report talks of the abandonment of women because they lacked physical charms, or were unable to bear the sheer physical burden of domestic duties; or more simply, because they could not endure the sexual demands of the husband.[207]

Obviously, all this implied the complicity of larger social values that legitimized these actions. Interestingly, however, instead of merely appealing to the good-sense of the 'Public', the Women's Protection League put forward a programme of making the woman economically self-sufficient. It demanded: that the Daybhaga law of inheritance ought to be made applicable to all widows; a change in the laws relating to the personal property of married women; that the wife get a share of her husband's earnings in cases of marital incompatibility; the possibility of terminating marriage in case of continued oppression or abandonment by the husband, and finally, new laws for widow-remarriage.[208]

205 *The Women's Protection League: Report of the Year 1935-37*, (pub. details absent), p. 16.
206 Ibid., p. 10.
207 *Nariraksha Samiti*, p. 7. Interestingly, the Bengali report is more frank than the English equivalent; possibly the linguistic cleavage may have something to do with a perceived insider-outsider divide.
208 *Nariraksha Samiti*, p. 9.

Significantly, the forefronting of gender and economic identities seems inversely related to communal identification. A conscious effort appears to have been made in this direction. The period covered by 1937–38 was one of nationalist optimism, when preparations for elections in the course of the first experiment in self-government took place and the wings of the two communal parties, the Muslim League and the HMS, were clipped by the election results; and when, in Bengal, despite the failure of the Congress, the victory of the Krishak Praja Party ensured that a largely non-communal formation which placed a major emphasis on economic issues, would set the agenda. Equally important was the rise of the Left and Women's movements. The change was best represented in the Women's Protection League's invocation of Ameer Ali as a pioneer in the fight against abductions — despite his activity in the formative period of communalism in Bengal and involvement in an early, communalized case of abduction.[209] This was because as magistrate, he had been liberal in sentencing abductors to whipping. The election of Ali as an emblem was a sign of immense confidence, for it represented an attempt at reorienting a symbol of communalism itself. Less iconic, but possibly more effective, was the kind of statistical readings of abduction that the Women's Protection League brought out in this period, which showed that more Muslim women had been abducted between 1926–38 than Hindu, and that Hindu and Muslim males preferred to abduct women from their own religious communities, although such divisions did not prove an insuperable bar.[210]

[209] The incident was in some ways, a grisly forerunner of the Jashoda case. In 1884, a married Hindu woman had unsuccessfully tried twice to convert to Islam (in order to run away from a husband who maltreated her) and marry the Muslim man she loved. She succeeded finally, but produced communal bickerings. According to her, she took the opportunity to escape while being led to the temple by a Hindu crowd to do penance for going to a mosque. The Hindu representatives claimed she had been taken away by a big, Muslim crowd. The woman was given over to her family by the court when she changed her version again, and was consequently committed by the magistrate to the Sessions Court. According to Ali, the Hindu side, financed by moneylenders, had raised a huge amount of money to fight the case. The case became well-known throughout Punjab and Sindh. Huge delegations came to greet Ali, who had agreed to fight the case, at the railway stations that dotted his way to Karachi. In Karachi itself a crowd of ten thousand came to meet him. *Family Traditions, Memoirs,* pp. 56–8.
[210] The report of 1935–7 states that between 1926–31, the number of

'Abductions' 213

The revised League programme came close to naming patriarchialism as the real enemy. Nearly. But not quite. The personnel remained much the same as in the twenties, indicating profounder continuities.[211] It was still addressed mainly to the bhadralok even if it was not merely directed to their conscience. Further, the preoccupation with legalism implied that the agency for initiating the changes would be primarily male (because of the gender composition of the legal profession). It ruled out both the more adventurous path of realizing women's solidarity, and the more acceptable alternative of giving a separate importance, within the overall campaign, to undertaking propaganda among women. A more insidious survival was the transposition of consent into something akin to seduction. Obviously, given the fact that so many minors were involved, this generalization would be pertinent. But the danger lay in also declaring that if these abducted women were

Hindus abducted amounted to 3,499, and Muslims to 3,513 (*The Women's Protection League: Report of the Year 1935–37*, p. 10); the second table is given in the 1938 (English) Report which states that between 1934–8 the number of abducted Hindu and Muslim women amounted to 2,072 and 2,290 respectively. I have extrapolated the same trend for the intervening years for which figures have not been given. For the second part of the assertion, I have drawn from the 1935–7 report, which states:

Total number of outrages committed by Hindus on Hindu women:	1260
Total number of outrages committed by Hindus on Mahomedan women:	30
Total number of outrages committed by Mahomedans on Hindu women:	686
Total number of outrages committed by Mahomedans on Mahomedan women:	3299 (p. 10)

[211] Two important activists of the twenties were present in the panel of vice-presidents: Ramananda Chatterjee and Hirendranath Datta. The important change is marked by the appointment of a woman, Banalata Das as president. Kumudini Basu continued to play her important role, she was one of the two Jt Secretaries in 1938, but her contribution was probably greater than what her post suggests. It may also be observed that women were being inducted into local provincial-level committees: the secretary of the Bolepur branch was one Sudhamoyee Mukharji. Nevertheless, despite the growing importance of women in the organization, their roles appear to have been overwritten by their roles vis-a-vis their males. Thus the 1938 report (Bengali) introduced Banalata Das and Kumudini Basu as the widow and daughter of S.R. Das and K.K. Mitra respectively, making it appear as if they were merely surrogates; p. 2. Kumudini Basu was a poet, journalist, social and political worker, who was elected as an independent municipal councillor in 1932.

not saved, then the alternatives that faced them would be either prostitution or conversion. The classification of prostitution with conversion indicates an intense fear of the other religion. Looking back from here, we can define our discomfort with this notion of consent: it does not allow for a conscious, intellectual or emotional change to another religion, in the absence of which, the paradigm of the woman as a religious possession and her choices as based on sexual desires alone, is not quite transgressed.

Obviously I am making these points in the spirit of qualification, which, I may add, also suggests the difficulty of gender identity replacing the communal one quite completely within such a platform.

However there is another matter. This concerns a retrospective speculation that the Women's Protection League of the thirties can have on my period of study. If, as the Women's Protection League reports suggest, it was family inmates who were most likely to be abductors, then it stood to reason, that in cases where Muslims were involved, the affected 'Hindu' family would most likely be low caste. The story of a rural, upper-caste family, that of K.K. Mitra's, indicates that although there was contact between Hindu women and Muslims through popular religious practices, they were stringently separated in social life. On the other hand, the data from Rangpur suggests closer social proximity between Muslims and low castes, possibly deriving from the fact that it was mainly the low castes who had converted to Islam. Given the increase in male bonding and pride, and the emphasis on monogamous marriages as a result of sanskritization, the chances of finding more than one male partner within one's own caste would diminish. Within such a scenario, relations with a Muslim intimate could be decisive.

In general, what is clear from the male fraternity created by the dehumanizing violence on the women, is a general increase of patriarchal consciousness accompanied by a subterranean intensification of gender antagonism. This is true not only for the lower social orders of Rangpur, but also for those not directly connected with abductions, that is, Muslim women. The mobilization of Hindu communalism around the issue of Muslim abductions provided Muslim communalists an ideal opportunity to drum up popular support for appropriating the first stirrings of women's resistance to the authority vested in Muslim males. In turn, Muslim communal mobilization intensified bonding among Hindu

'Abductions' 215

women around the defence of Hinduism and the fear of Islam. It thereby helped to stabilize the 'Hindu' identity at the cost of the 'woman'.

In order to understand this process, I will briefly consider the way gender questions were tackled in the Muslim middle class response to abductions.

II.v

The abductions campaign would naturally yield immense dividends to Bakr and his ilk. The criminalization of Muslims by Hindus would reinforce and expand an exclusivist Muslim constituency. Less obvious, but possibly more profound, was the effect of 'abductions' on liberal Muslim opinion.

The group of liberal reformers included, as was the case with their Hindu counterparts, both men and women. But, whereas among Hindus gender reforms formed a subset of other religio-social concerns that were formulated and initiated by male reformers, among Muslims of Bengal it was the women who led the way. Although, they received considerable support from males, it was, above all, the activity of Begum Rokeya Hossein that sketched out the intellectual and practical horizons of the movement. While founding and running a school for girls, Rokeya dealt with ideas ranging from questions of naming and of reworking governing mythologies to property rights and the allocation of household resources. Moreover, her work defined the breadth of the movement itself, clustering around her a wide spectrum of liberal opinion. The responses to her death ranged from those who believed that she exemplified the spirit of compromise, to those who conceived her to be an insurrectionary figure.[212]

A possible reason for the initiative of women was that the Islamic reform movements of the nineteenth century, far from expanding feminine spaces, were shaped by orthodox forms of male self-empowerment. This was evident in the discursive intensification of the desire for gender segregation and control. The drive towards clear and minute regulation of women's behaviour

---

[212] See Kazi Abdul Wadud, 'Mrs Rokeya Hossein' and Mrs M. Rahman, 'Motichur' respectively. *Begum Rokeya Rachanabali*, Abdul Qadir (ed.), Dhaka, 1993, f.pub. 1973, pp. 552 and 557.

was already initiated by texts produced in North India, notably the *Behesti Zeevar*.[213] In Bengal the *Nasihat Namas* did not hesitate to mobilize ideas that were unabashedly 'impure', in order to strengthen segregation. For instance, one of them advised, 'A woman has no rest as long as she is alive. She has to serve her husband and thus worship Allah.'[214] This view of gender relations was not very different from an assumption of shirk, that is, the substitution of the object of worship. This suggests a fresh insight into the basis of the purificatory movements of the last century. A profound narcissism is at work here, which seeks to compensate the loss of intimate spiritual communities based on individual charisma. The site of charisma is transferred to the individual male. The compulsive nature of this move is highlighted by its intimate proximity to the Hindu notions of *pativrata* and satitva. As a matter of fact, both Garib Sayer and Mohammed Ibrahim (a member of the Bakr establishment), explicitly invoke the ideal of satitva for Muslim women; Ibrahim goes so far as to say it is the highest ideal for them.[215]

In the face of a syncretizing gender conservatism that was accompanied by an emphasis on segregation from, if not antagonism with, Hindus, Rokeya could not invoke an unproblematic notion of syncretism. What she offers as a response is the necessity for a critical dialogue across religions boundaries. The basis of this idea rests upon an insistence on an affinity between women and communal unity. In an essay written on the domestic tasks of women, Rokeya suddenly states that womenfolk must see to it that riots did not break out.[216] But her idea of communal unity is not syncretist. The invocation of a central Hindu idea such as satitva finds its counter-move in Rokeya's identification of the problem of gender as a universal one. Like most of those committed to communal unity in this period, Rokeya subscribes to a federative idea of religious communities. But for her, it is founded on the struggle against gender discrimination.

[213] See Barbara D. Metcalfe, 'Maulana Ashraf Ali Thanavi and Urdu Literature', *Urdu and Muslim South Asia: Studies in Honour of Ralph Russell*, Christopher Shackle (ed.), Delhi, 1991.
[214] Rafiuddin Ahmed, *The Muslims*, p. 87.
[215] *Nafaol Mocchelemin*, p. 30.
[216] 'Sugrihini', Motichur I; *Rokeya, Rachanabali*, p. 45.

Her strategy of confirming communal unity through the critique of gender relations, is shown in the way she tackles the question of abductions. It is an important intervention because the abductions issue threatened to reverse some of the key orientations of the liberal reformers. There are just two places where she refers to abductions. In an essay called '*Subeh Sadak*' where she interprets the azan as a call to women to shake away the torpor of confinement and slavishness, she refers sardonically to the growth of Nari Raksha Samitis. She characterizes them as an outgrowth of men's attitude to women as something to be guarded: like jewels or pets. Her comments here recall her essay, '*Ardhangi*', where she criticizes the continuing degradation of women in non-Muslim communities — the Parsis, Hindus and Christians — which had apparently liberated their women from purdah. Regarding the Hindus, Rokeya asserts that their paradigm of gender relations was formulated in the Ram–Sita relationship, in which Ram preserved the privileges of a husband by treating his wife as a boy treats his plaything.

While talking of the abductions issue, Rokeya does not even mention the question of communalization. Instead she reframes the whole enterprise by locating it in relationship to the social definitions of womanhood. The consequence is a silent and strong indictment of the inequities communalism seeks to perpetrate. Equally important is the federative framework that is an essential part of her critical apparatus. This is best seen in her novel, *Padmarag*. It features Tarini Bhaban, a woman's institution founded and run by a Brahmo widow. A crucial juncture of the story concerns a scene where the leading inmates gather together to tell one another about their experiences which forced them to come to the Bhaban. The group is a representative one; besides Hindus, there are Muslims and a Christian. Usha, a Brahmin girl relates her experience of abduction, focusing on the social boycott that followed upon her return. This, as we have seen, is a typical tale used by the Hindu campaigners. What makes it different is the context. It is seen here as just one of the many instances of typicalized discriminations that characterize different religions in their treatment of women. For instance, while Rafiya is suddenly given a divorce by post from her husband for whom she had been faithfully waiting for years to finish his studies in law in England, Helen cannot get a divorce from a husband who is in a jail for criminal lunatics. If abductions is just one of the many kinds of social oppression that women face, conversely, it also provides the point where an alternative is demanded. Usha's story swiftly dissolves into Rafiya's declaration of war against society. Their alternative world is present in the scene where, structured by a gender based religious federation, the women set up a common circuit of narrative exchange. Their sufferings, that have to be privately endured by virtue of the isolation they face through social discrimination, becomes mutually substitutable here. While Rafiya relates Helen's story, it is Sakina who tells us about Helen's tribulations.

This is a utopian moment when federation smudges its boundaries in a common connection. The overwhelming longing for such an existence is signalled throughout the story by the double identity of the heroine, Padmarag. The latter is both Siddika, a Muslim girl who has been made a victim of property disputes because of the segregation of women, as well as Padmarag, a person resurrected by the solidarity of womens' experiences and work exemplified in Tarini Bhaban. But this utopian moment is split again to allow the ideal to become a practical force. Padmarag elects to leave Tarini Bhaban, the place she often describes as a heaven. Risking suffering and isolation, she has to reintegrate herself back with Muslim society in order to begin the task of reforming it, that is, to affirm her solidarity with women of the larger society.

Rokeya's consideration of abductions opens out her vision of a gender based federation that is rooted in the principle of cross-cultural critique, complemented by a process of exchange through a common circuitry of feelings, ideas and work. Significantly, there is a remarkable intransigence in Rokeya's attitude to communalization. *Padmarag* was written in 1902 (although published in 1924), while '*Subeh Sadak*' was published in 1930. The continuity in her attitudes through three decades — especially its survival of the bloody twenties — is a refreshing contrast to the career of a person like Akram Khan, for whom the abductions campaign appears to have motivated a turn towards communal antagonism. There was, to some extent, a supportive context for Rokeya. Besides the anti-communal activity of women like Sarojini Naidu, there were others such as Mrs Rahman who indicted satitva in the *Sahachar* by enquiring, 'What is the value of the satitva that makes slaves of us? Why can only males marry women, why cannot women marry males?.'[217] Moreover, co-operation on women's issues extended across the lines of religion. Rokeya herself got the support of Mrs P.K. Ray and Mrs Rajkumari Das who helped her to study the structure and experiences of Bethune and Gokhale Memorial schools, in order to begin her own project of the Sakhawat Memorial Girls school.[218] Southard has shown how the excitement of reform in the twenties had outweighed the lacerations of communal antagonism.[219] A small incident vividly shows the general context. During the most intense period of communal antagonism in 1926, a three member women's delegation consisting of two Hindus and a Muslim met Smt. Bajrabhima Debi, the editor of a magazine called *Dharmadhwaj* and, on behalf of an organization called Bangiya Ramani Samaj, released a joint statement protesting against the publication of advertisements for sexual vitality.[220]

The equally nourishing, but more problematic support, came from Muslim male reformers. This liberal intelligentsia was centred in the *Saogat*, which published a steady volume of articles arguing for a many-sided reform of women's condition. Although the *Saogat* resumed publication in 1926 after a gap of five years, it quickly mobilized the left wing of the Muslim intelligentsia which went on to establish the Anti-Molla League in 1929, an organization that campaigned against the orthodoxy. The radical possibilities of this group can be seen in a collection of poems called *Nari Tirtha*, which was written by Ahmader Rahman, who was close to Nazrul Islam.[221] Following the latter, Rahman transgresses religious boundaries. His first poem, written in 1928, submerges itself in the discourse of Hindu reform. It is on the subject of child-widows, and the references to the girl's *sindur* and

---

[217] Translation mine. Cited in Chandiprosad Sarkar, 'Bengali Muslim Politics, Society and Culture During the Khilafat-Noncooperation Movement', *Bengal Past and Present, vol. CIII, parts I–II, nos 196–7*, January– December 1984, (Calcutta Historical Society, 1984).
[218] Mohtar Hossein Sufi, *Begum Rokeya: Jiban O Sahitya*, Dhaka, 1986. Mr P.K. Ray founded the Bethune Memorial Girls School.
[219] For example, women campaigners kept out of the communal imbroglio over the Education Bill in the early 1930's. Barbara Southard, *The Women's Movement*, p. 199.
[220] *Hindu-Musalman*, 1 September 1926.
[221] Ahmade Rahman, *Nari Tirtha*, Calcutta, 1931.

shakha places its firmly within the Hindu world. The poem makes a spirited indictment of patriarchal norms, rhetorically asking how long men would ignore the sorrow of women and inflict the oppression of their law. It concludes by warning men of the rebellious resources of women. From the specific and limited instance of a particular abuse, the poem goes on to indict gender oppression, which, in the same move, prevents it from making Hinduism alone seem responsible for gender tyranny.

This generalized vantage point allows the poet to directly criticise Islamic patriarchy. In the poem called *Abhishap*, he indicts the discouragement of the education of girls in pathshalas where they could learn Bengali and English.[222] The inclusion of a specifically Muslim target drives homes the hybridity of Rahman's volume. However, there is a specific syncretist strategy at work here. Rahman does not thread together plural identities into a single weave of language, but produces a double-move that recalls Rokeya. Plural identities are made to refer to the general reference point of gender oppression, producing thereby the possibility of solidarity between them. Without repudiating their differences, it opens up the possibility of exchange, collaboration, and internal change.

However, male liberalism suffered from contradictions. These contributed to the failure in generating a Muslim counter-inititative against the communal campaign on abductions. The relationship of Mansur Ahmed — a liberal reformer who was active in the Anti-Molla League — with his wife, is illuminating. Although he had no compunctions in marrying a ten-year-old girl, he opposed purdah and cherished new values in her such as 'independence', 'individuality and 'self-respect'. His father-in-law, a Mohammadi preacher, was equally self-contradictory. He preached the importance of higher education for Muslim girls, but neglected to extend its opportunities to his own offspring. Mansur's self-division is expressed by a constant guilt; he regrets having induced early conceptions in his wife, feels sorry for making her bear the burden

---

[222] An interesting aspect of this poem is that the villain of the piece is the village pir. He leads the orthodox drive against the father of a girl who allows her to study in a pathshala, By a clever sleight of hand, the poet takes up a figure who is a recognized villain of purificatory discourse, and makes him embody orthodoxy, which, by this association, is defined as irrational and impure. The connection appears credible, precisely because so many pirs like Bakr and Ruhul Amin, were actually conservative. Ibid, pp. 48–50.

of looking after the innumerable guests who frequented his house. At the same time, he records the fact that his wife started to take crucial decisions which even related to his career; later, she became a district-level Congress worker.[223]

Ahmad does not tell us what his wife felt about Hindu women, but his own view emerges as a complicated one. Hindu women provided a role model. Ahmad's first encounter with a woman outside his family occurred while attending the meetings of the Brahmo Samaj.[224] It was an event, which probably presaged support for his wife's entry into public life. His contemporary, Waliullah, felt pride in being Bengali while accompanying Congress women campaigners. According to him, they provided a lead to the rest of the country by addressing 15–20,000-strong male audiences and by doing constructive work and house-to-house campaigns.[225]

Nevertheless, while the public role of Hindu women seemed attractive for men who were against purdah, it also appears to have reinforced a pride in the chastity of Islam, whose women could not be offered for the public gaze. Even at the price of hypocrisy. Ahmad's frank catalogue of the disabilities of Muslim prostitutes may be recalled. The latter could not give the impression of being Muslim for fear of being refused lucrative locations in red-light areas. This disability gave his friends and himself the pleasure of thinking that the world would believe Muslim women were more moral than Hindu![226] Another revealing incident concerns his encounter with a woman in public. Upon treading on her foot, he immediately turned around to apologize by putting his hands together to do a *namaskar*. Later his friends laughed at him, saying she was just a prostitute.[227]

The easy recourse to pride, when faced with Hindu discrimination, in a gender conservative Islam, was clearly facilitated by internal contradictions regarding relationship with women. The spontaneous characterization of a woman in public as a Hindu, the recurrent association of Hindu women with prostitution,[228]

[223] *Atmakatha*, pp. 389–412.
[224] *Atmakatha*, p. 176.
[225] *Yuga Bichitra*, p. 160.
[226] *Atmakatha*, pp. 213–15.
[227] *Amar Dekha Rajnitir Panchas Baccher*, p. 42.
[228] This seems part of a larger understanding at a time when women were demanding rights for themselves. A major objection to granting women the vote was that only prostitutes would avail of the opportunity. Southard,

betokens a submerged desire that flowed from the Hindu woman's conceptual monopoly of female public space. Somewhere at the back of all this is the shadow of the temptress figure. This complex weave of motifs was simplified by the communal antagonism that exploded around the abductions issue, the dialectic of the temptress and the celebration of Islamic chastity came together in a single figure, that of the Hindu widow. It was the seductiveness of the Hindu widow that was widely seen to motivate the abductions of Hindu women.

Faced with insinuations of criminal lust, Muslim males pointed to the social disabilities of the Hindu widow to prove the superiority of Islam. The widow allowed Muslim communal discourse to tap an admitted weakness of Hindus.[229] So convincing was the lust of widows as an explanation for abductions, that the weekly *Hindu–Musalman*, which had been established solely for the purpose of communal unity, also advanced it as an explanation.[230] The *Dainik Soltan* insinuatingly and intelligently gloated, 'How is it that no sensation is created over the kidnapping or outraging of a Hindu girl by a Hindu male, while a hue and cry is raised whenever a Hindu widow embraces Islam out of her own accord and marries a Muhammadan male?.'[231] Widowhood also provided an explanation by its fearsome prospect. In an incident mentioned earlier, Waliullah recalled a discussion between Fazlul Huq and Khairul Aman which concluded that the reason why a particular Hindu girl had converted and married a Muslim, was that she wished to avoid widowhood.[232]

What is most painful was the way the Hindu widow provided a pretext for counter-insinuation against Hindu society amongst those who had been committed to communal co-operation. The liberal *Mohammadi* argued that abductions was nothing new in Bengal, and that Hindus had been as guilty in the matter as

---

pp. 103–4. Respectability for women was compromised by any public participation.

[229] A letter from one I.B. Roy in 1924, who described himself as a 'non-sentimental Hindu' concurred with the view that the 'abductions' were the result of Hindu widows running away. This letter was written in 1924, before the issue had become virulently communalized. *The Mussalman*, 25 April 1924.

[230] *Hindu–Musalman*, 25 August 1926.

[231] 11 August 1926, RNP no. 34 of 1926, NAI.

[232] Waliullah, *Yuga* pp. 86–8.

Muslims. 'But', it went on to add, 'since Hindu society contains a very great number of youthful and pretty widows, it is the Hindu women who are being principally kidnapped.'[233] The idea of the Hindu widow produced its own metonymic logic. In a Muslim meeting held to protest against charges of abduction, no less a figure than Akram Khan claimed that it was the women who were responsible for their abduction, the facts being misrepresented to cast a slur on Muslim youth. He combined this assertion with the issue of imposing puritanical controls on women, by stating that Hindu women were more likely to be morally corrupt since they frequented theatres and read novels![234]

I have tried to indicate the extent of the Muslim communal counter-response to the abduction campaign, by examining the failure of the reformers. What was at stake can be judged by trends that showed themselves in the middle of 1926. Abductions did not feature as a major issue during the April riots in Calcutta. It did, however, become an important motif of the Pabna riots. It was then that Muslims began to level charges of rape against Hindus for the first time. Reports came in after the riots in Pabna, that, emboldened by the prosecutions of the law which led to wide-scale desertions of villages by Muslim males fearing arrest, Hindu men were roaming the villages, threatening, if not actually molesting, Muslim women. Specific allegations were made against a party of Hindu volunteers led by S.S. Chakravarty.[235] These reports were followed by those of the Dhaka riots, which featured allegations of the physical mishandling of Muslim women by Hindu *sankharis* and police officers.[236]

A more horrible development was to occur. Possibly in response

---

[233] 4 June 1926, RNP no. 24 of 1926, NAI. Naturally this view could lead to the feeling that Muslim youths were being victimized. A letter to *The Mussalman* condemned the WPL as an organization that set out to 'punish Mussalman youths with whom Hindu girls and widows, after enormous social pinpricks and suffering, chose to elope and have illicit connection'. The display of sympathy for Hindu women however disappears in the example he gives of a Muslim youth charged with rape in Jessore. According to his version, the youth had merely accepted the favours of a Hindu woman renowned for her generosity in this respect. 27 June 1924.

[234] 'Abduction of Hindu women (Press comments and resolutions of the Albert Hall meeting on the subject)', 535/29, serial nos. 1–2, GOB: Political, 1930, WBSA.

[235] *The Mussalman*, 17 July 1926.

[236] *The Mussalman*, 23 September 1926.

to the riots first in neighbouring Pabna and then in Dhaka, as well as to the antagonism of Hindus within the town, Muslim communalists of Kushtea boycotted the immersion of Durga which they had traditionally attended. They organized a rival *mela* on the opposite bank, at the very spot 'where the female Hindu pilgrims were outraged by Mahomedan goondas a few months back'.[237] The 'outraging' of women became respectablized as a weapon of communal antagonism, and by extension, it could lend itself to the purposes of 'self-strengthening'. Muslim communalism was finally accepting the definitions of its Hindu counterparts, while the latter did not forego this invitation to display the creature they had created. It is in this perverse process that we can sense the outrage of women that was to happen two decades later in Noakhali.

Not the least saddening aspect was that sections of Muslim women also got communalized. The first annual meeting of the Muslim Mohila Samiti alleged outrages on Muslim women in Pabna.[238] Little realising that they were helping to seal the fate of so many who were yet to be sucked into the celebrations of communal hatred, as well as confirming their Hindu sisters in their Hinduness.

II.vi

Although Rokeya's intervention was a powerful one and included major practical initiatives, its full scope was unfolded at the discursive level, and often in the sphere of the imaginary. While the impact of communal divisions was resisted, the task of confronting communalism itself lacked any practical activity grounded in the solidarity of sisterhood. This absence allowed a space for the appeal to the individual sister (along with the mother) to flourish, facilitating a renovated masculinity. In turn, this provided an enabling condition for a new political bloc to be produced.

I have suggested that Hindu masculinity had a deep investment in the sister figure because the latter implicitly desexualized gender relations. This was not simply a way of respectablizing and safeguarding women's public activity by naming it in kinship terms. The desexualization also guaranteed the idea of an activist masculinity. For what the Sister supported was the celibate ideal of

[237] *Amrita Bazar Patrika*, 20 October 1926.
[238] *The Mussalman*, 24 August 1926.

Brahmacharya. As we have seen in the first chapter, the discourse around the Hindu male tended to portray him in terms of physical deprivation. Hence, it was imperative for him to husband whatever resources he possessed. While sexual excess was part of the physical prowess of the figure of the Muslim male, for Hindu males it was advisable to store their sexual energy for cultivating physical power. The 'naturalness' of this notion of sexual abstinence was easy to show, since it enjoyed immaculate Yogic lineages stretching back to the classical texts.

Brahmacharya — the stage of sexual renunciation during youth in the Brahmanical scheme of life — was the proclaimed ideal for Hindu reform from the nineteenth century, as well as the watchword for Hindu communalism. The Arya Samaj proclaimed that the absence of the practice of Brahmacharya led to the physical decay of Hindus;[239] the crucial 1923 session of the HMS not only included the ideal of Brahmacharya amongst its resolutions, but also featured a lengthy speech which even cited Herbert Spencer to argue that sex could be used as a resource to build the Self: if abstinence was observed, the power of sex was recirculated into the body to provide muscles of iron, nerves of steel and 'inestimable brains'![240] It is here that the figure of the 'sister' helps by transcending the association with the process of reproduction that the 'Mother' cannot conceal. The sister reiterates the necessity of abstinence.[241]

The preoccupation with the Brahmacharya figure suggests a corresponding lack of concern with the paranoia at falling numbers: obviously, abstinence could not help to increase Hindu fertility! What this does point to, is a preoccupation with the importance of violence and affiliated concerns. At the end of Chapter 1, I had indicated the evolution of 'dying Hindu' into a riot concern. What facilitated this transition was the idea of manliness. An editorial in the *Amrita Bazar Patrika* defined

---

[239] Svami, *Arya Samaj*, p. 5.
[240] *Amrita Bazar Patrika*, 25 August 1923; cited in Home Poll. Progs. no. 198; 1924, NAI.
[241] This is even more interesting if we remember that most of the abducted women were child-brides, and also put beside this fact the exhortation by Hindu reformers against child-marriage. As a matter of fact, the passage from the Arya Samaji pamphlet cited directly above, lists child-marriage as the other reason for physical decrepitude. Svami, Arya Samaj. By association then, the 'Sister' could in fact slide into the discourse of earlier reformist impulses.

'manliness' as 'intimately connected with physical strength'.[242] Quite naturally, the concern with the 'dying Hindu' now arose more from apprehensions of incompetence in executing violent acts. Piyush Ghosh recommended Brahmacharya and physical exercise for both boys and girls, for only then 'a Hindu will die at his post defending his religion and home'.[243] The cultivation of the body involved more than just the acquisition of strength; it also involved an attitudinal and psychological change. In his speech at the HMS session in Calcutta, Lajpat Rai declared that building gymnasiums would be the first step in rescuing his people from 'pessimism' and filling them with 'ambition with a will to win . . . '[244]

Abductions oriented manliness produced a new triumphalism. The climactic point in Pulin Das' autobiography concerns the antagonism of neighbourhood Muslims who, after having quarreled with his youthful followers, claimed they were acting under the Nawab's orders. After declaring their objective to be the abduction of the women, they attacked Das' home. After this point the battle became a hand-to-hand combat for the women-cum-home; Das was able to beat off this invasion into the inner, feminine sanctum, forcing the Muslim sardar to sue for peace.[245]

Das' 'story' is also a celebration of the turnaround of history for the Hindu hero, who is able to successfully reverse the inherited trajectory of such stories which ended with the triumphant Muslim either getting Hindu women or their ashes (the motif being a staple one in narratives of confrontation between the Mughals and Rajputs). Manliness is a project that is ultimately confirmed by the physical repudiation of the Muslim.

The popularity of the prospect of such a contest could be seen in the following account of the phenomenal response that the Jamalpur riots evoked in Dhaka: 'Branches [of the Anushilan Samiti] numbering about 500 and the total strength of members rose to some 30,000 in 1906–1908. High and low class Hindus both joined and the cause was the feeling against the Mahomedans, to which was subsequently added the hatred for the

[242] 19 April 1925.
[243] 'The Best Way to Organize the Hindus', *Amrita Bazar Patrika*, 11 April 1925.
[244] Ibid, 12 April 1925.
[245] *Amar Jiban*, pp. 161–4.

Government . . . ', wrote Hemanta Sarkar.[246] Significantly, the Jamalpur riots had occurred in 1907, a year that saw a spurt in the growth of revolutionary organizations in Bengal such as the Anushilan Samiti.[247] The spurt in organization produced a self-confidence in the metropolitan gentry, causing it to regard itself as the protector of the mofussil: everyday, according to Sarkar, Pulin Das received, 'repeated calls from the mofussil', and so famous did he become, that appeals came from as far away as Surat and Ahmedabad![248]

The preoccupation with defending one's women crystallized a long-standing psychological process, that marked an important strand of terrorism. This concerned the drive to appropriate the power of violence from its attributed site in the Muslim. A host of memories testify to the importance of Muslim instructors in imparting physical training to upper-caste Hindu acolytes, especially terrorists. Nirad Chaudhury remembered that an influential avenue through which he and his companions were inducted into the Swadeshi movement was through Physical Clubs, described as, 'institutions for giving training in patriotism, collective discipline, and the ethics of nationalism'. The main exercise consisted of lathi play and the first teachers were retainers of Muslim zamindars.[249] Pulin Das recalled how he was initiated into his career in physical exercise — the saga of which supplies the organizing principle of his autobiography — when twenty to twenty-five friends got together to form a club to learn lathi play. They appointed Abbas Sardar, a Muslim, to teach them.[250] According to Hemanta Sarkar, Das later became the favourite student of Professor Murtaza. The latter was a renowned Muslim magician-cum-lathi player, whose skills in the latter department were so highly regarded, that he was even invited by the Nawab of Dhaka to entertain Lord Curzon.[251] Incidentally, he was also hired by Sarala Debi.

[246] Hemanta K. Sarkar, *Revolutionaries of Bengal*, Calcutta: 1923, p. 48. Tegart Papers, Box II, CSAC.
[247] I owe this observation to Sumit Sarkar.
[248] Sarkar, *Revolutionaries of Bengal*, p. 48.
[249] *The Autobiography of an Unknown Indian*, p. 244.
[250] *Amar Jiban*, p. 46.
[251] Sarkar, *Revolutionaries of Bengal*, pp. 44–5. It may be more than coincidental, that Piyush Ghosh suggests the name of two Muslim wrestlers as models for emulation by the Indian team, after the miserable performance by Indians in wrestling at the Olympics. *Amrita Bazar Patrika*, 22 February 1925.

It was the zamindars who hired lathials. Broomfield states that an index of rural control was the number of lathials employed to extract debts.[252] In effect, this meant that the upper castes would not take to this profession, because it would involve encounters with the impure low-caste/Muslim flesh and bones of recalcitrant tenants. However, with the influence of public school education which stressed the pedagogical importance of physical culture,[253] and the corresponding deployment of the stereotype of the Bengali male as an effeminate being by both the British and the non-Bengalis,[254] physical culture became a necessary component of nationalist culture. Nabagopal Mitra's Hindu Melas, which tried to arouse nationalist pride by displaying various indigenously made artifacts, prominently featured physical displays. Mitra thought that it was physical power alone that had subjugated Indians.[255] These melas were organized during the decade after 1867, which partly coincided with Campbell's regime of physical culture in Bengal in the early 1870s.

Nabagopal Mitra added Western exercises (introduced by Campbell) to a set of 'Indian' exercises consisting of lathi and sword play, *gulel khela* and training in knives and guns.[256] Out of all the different weapons, it was the lathi which exercised the greatest imaginative impact. In Bankim Chattopadhyaya's *Debi Chaudhurani*, the band of Hindu nationalist bandits confront the sepoys with lathis. Chattopadhyaya breaks off from the narrative to hail the lathi as the 'national weapon of Bengal', without which, 'Bengalis had become lifeless'.[257] Its place in terrorist circles was

[252] John Broomfield, 'Peasant Mobilization in Twentieth Century Bengal', *Mostly About Bengal*, New Delhi, 1982, p. 221.

[253] According to Bepin Pal, it was Sir George Campbell, the governor of Bengal who introduced physical culture into Bengal. Pal, *Nabajuger Bangla*, p. 147.

[254] Two instances from my period will suffice. 'The Bengali could never by any stretch of the imagination be described as a fighting man', declared S.G. Tayor, a district-level officer who went on to become the I.G. of Police. 'The 49th Bengal Regiment', S.G. Taylor Papers, CSAC. Prof. Naidu delicately suggested that since Bengalis were 'intellectual and emotional by nature', they ought to be gradually introduced to physical training. *Amrita Bazar Patrika*, 30 July 1925.

[255] Bepin Chandra Pal, 'Shekaler Hindu Bhav O Swadeshikata'.

[256] Ibid, p. 146.

[257] Translation mine. *Bankim Rachanabali*, vol. 1, Jogeshchandra Bagal (ed.), Calcutta, 1397 (1990); f.pub. 1360 (1952), p. 701. Bankim's iconic

an important one. The first thing a new recruit did after receiving his *diksha* (initiation), was to watch a lathi play![258]

The privileging of the lathi had other implications. Basically, two groups supplied lathials in the countryside, the Muslims and the low castes. Pulin Das had approached the Namasudras to organize a campaign of revenge against the Muslims. The choice of Muslims as instructors of lathi-play was therefore significant; it obviously indicates the greater intensity of caste prejudice over communal biases amongst the upper castes.[259] The Muslims commanded more respect, as U.N. Mukherji's analysis showed. Moreover, for those who believed that political authority stemmed from physical power, the Muslim would be 'naturally' seen as a repository of traces left over from their former mastery over the country. Certainly, physically skilled Muslims exercised a strong fascination on terrorists. Prof. Murtaza's portrait in Das' autobiography evokes mystery. Like an ancient artisan, he is suspected of holding the keys to secret levels of skill. Das reports that he overheard Murtaza saying that he would teach those skills to only Muslims.[260] The enchantment incited a desire for appropriation. What is suggested here is a process parallel with that of appropriation through competition that we had seen in U.N. Mukherji's texts. The burden of historical mastery is placed on the Muslim, in order to be appropriated by the Hindu through the idealization of the 'lathi'.

The structure of militant male empowerment acquired a new importance in the mid-twenties. The context for terrorist nationalism changed to produce certain opportunities for interlinkage between it on the one hand, and the Women's Protection League

---

influence obviously remained palpable in the mid-twenties; the report on a demonstration of lathi play at Calcutta, stated that a large crowd had gathered to see this 'important part in the life of Bengal', adding that the authoritative picture of this had been provided by Bankim! *Amrita Bazar Patrika*, 18 September 1925.

[258] Das, *Amar Jiban*, p. 66.

[259] Nirad Chaudhury's description of the Physical Clubs reveals a great sense of social hierarchy even amongst the urban enthusiasts of Swadeshi. They were divided into two types, one for the well-educated and the other for the less-literate. *The Autobiography*, p. 245. The bias against the low castes was even more intense. Pulin Das, for instance, sees even the granting of the right to vote to the low castes, as an insult! *Amar Jiban*, p. 374.

[260] *Amar Jiban*, p. 47.

and Hindu communalism in general, on the other. After the Non-cooperation/Khilafat movement, there was a certain domestication of terrorism. The colonial administration took advantage of Gopinath Saha's attempted assassination of Sir Charles Tegart, the police commissioner, to impose emergency powers provided by Regulation III. This effectively drew out the teeth of terrorist conspiracies. However, almost as if in inverse proportion, there was an explosion in the discourses around physical culture. These included the mandatory terrorist verses extolling sacrifice to the Motherland and bemoaning the emasculation of physical energies by the state of unfreedom. More significant was another set of discourses around the relationship between physical culture and Bengali Hindu nationalism, that was specially visible in the *Amrita Bazar Patrika*. Besides highlighting news features on the subject of physical culture, the *Patrika* featured three regular columnists on the subject, which included Piyush Ghosh, whose bestselling book entitled, *The Sad Neglect of Physical Culture Among Indians*, was serialized.[261] Large numbers of suggestions and opinions on the issue were advanced in the 'Letters to the Editor' column.

As I have indicated earlier, the communal orientation to physical culture drew a great deal on a reworking of the 'dying Hindu'. The sub-text of appropriating Muslim power gained importance by statements such as the one made by Piyush Ghosh, when he declared that, 'Bengalees as a nation were degenerating and were a dying race. Physical culture was the only remedy to this race degeneracy.'[262] S.S. Goswami, who tapped Bengali pride by being billed as 'World's Champion Weight Supporter', carried a column, the title of which again recalled Mukerji, called 'Race Degeneracy and Physical Education'. In a public meeting, a certain Dr B. Ganguly attributed the failure of Bengalis in all spheres of competitive livelihood (losing trade to Marwaris, labour to tribals, etc.), to their poor health:[263] the degeneration of Bengalis began with Muslim rule and intensified under the British.[264]

Not surprisingly, the HMS played a leading role in dramatizing this concern by hosting physical culture exhibitions. The HMS conference in Calcutta in 1925 was followed by a wrestling

---

[261] It sold out in a week! *Amrita Bazar Patrika*, 11 September 1925.
[262] *Amrita Bazar Patrika*, 28 April 1925.
[263] Ibid., 4 September 1925.
[264] Ibid., 15 May 1925.

exhibition held at Halliday Park.[265] Later, in 1929, the physical culture component became so important, that the Dhaka Hindu Conference put out an advertisement for its 'Exhibition and Physical tournament':[266] it featured none other than Pulin Das, who showed off his skills with the lathi and the dagger.[267]

The campaign against abduction served to reinforce the impact of physical culture by orienting it towards a social target. The inaugural resolutions of the Women's Protection League devoted two of its six points to the formation of 'Civic guards' that would protect helpless families and 'rescue parties' which would be devoted to the victims.[268] The lathi was the major weapon in the armoury of rescue. As the HMS merged its voice with the Women's Protection League, the implications of physical culture intensified; the former gave a *carte blanche* sanction to 'all possible means' to protect 'hearth and home'.[269]

But the specification of Muslims as target was made only by implication — through the structure of interlocking concerns. Physical culture maintained a certain autonomy. By itself, the ethos of physical fitness could renew its nineteenth-century innocence of a pedagogic enterprise. The ostensible rationale of the exhibitions was to inspire and teach. This is probably what motivated Rabindranath Tagore's offer to finance some North-Indian wrestlers to exhibit their prowess in Bengal.[270] Articles authored by those who used the title of Professor added lustre to this project. When a member of the Dhaka University Court proposed that, along with drill, lathi play should be made a compulsory subject on the grounds that it was the only distinctively Bengali weapon, the resolution was passed unanimously.[271]

The pedagogic imperative really reinforced another claim. This was the idea that physical culture transcended politics. A few days before the session of the Bengal Provincial Conference held at Faridpur, Piyush Ghosh floated, in the same town, an organization called the All Bengal Health Club Association, which declared its

[265] Ibid., 19 April 1925.
[266] Ibid., 22 August 1929.
[267] Ibid., 29 August 1929.
[268] Ibid., 1 May 1924.
[269] Ibid., 30 August 1929.
[270] Ibid., 15 May 1925.
[271] Ibid., 2 December 1925.

dedication to physical culture as apolitical in nature.[272] The implication of this claim was revealed in a speech delivered at a village of the 24 Parganas where Ghosh, after claiming that physical culture was divorced from politics, went on to include the Hindu Sangathan among non-political organizations.[273] What he meant was that physical culture substituted existing political divisions by an overarching commitment to Hindu unity.

The move to project physical culture as a supra-political sphere implied less the lassitude of depoliticization, than the opportunity for physical culture to provide a consensual point of communal political mobilization. To a great extent, physical education served its purposes for it brought together the moderates and the terrorists in the mid-twenties. A distancing from anti-colonial politics combined with a belief in nationalist self-empowerment, was something that could appeal to the Moderates. Surendranath Banerjea, who penned the foreword to Ghosh's book, had inspired Ghosh to write in the first place with his belief that 'the health and physique of a nation is the first condition of national progress'.[274] On the other hand, this new physical culture acquired the support of communally minded terrorists like Pulin Das. The process of this reorientation of terrorism needs a little elaboration.

The crucial point in the entente between Hindu communalism and terrorism, was the split within the terrorists after the Non-Cooperation/Khilafat movement. The terrorists had got together in 1919 to declare their support for the coming movement, but the unfamiliar experience of mass struggle followed by its disappointments, led to some introspective moves towards secular politics. An important development was the famous series of articles by Hemchandra Kanungo, entitled 'History of the Revolutionary Movement in Bengal'. Published in the monthly *Basumati* in early 1923, they critically re-examined the communal bias of terrorism.[275] The

[272] Ibid., 30 April 1925.
[273] Ibid., 12 May 1925.
[274] *A Nation in the Making: Being the Reminiscences of 50 years of Public Life*, (Bombay, 1963, f.pub. 1925), p. 5.
[275] According to Kanungo, the terrorists appear to have calculated like accountants in their attitude to the Muslims: 'It was that if the Muslims joined in the revolution it was all to the good, because when the country became free, privileges in proportion to the extent of their help would be conferred on them. But if they did not join they would be classed as enemies.' Consequently, 'the Muslims needed no explanation to understand the plain fact that

fact that Kanungo was not exceptional is apparent from both the later trajectory of other terrorist careers as well as the fact that many terrorists were avid readers of the radical journal *Dhumketu* edited by Kazi Nazrul Islam.[276]

On the other hand, many terrorists congregated around C.R. Das, who deployed them to take over the Congress machinery.[277] They came to be known as the Karmi Sangha. Muzaffar Ahmed recalled that this group was very communal.[278] Its prejudices appear to have intensified after C.R. Das gave a speech in Faridpur (made just prior to his death in 1925) which indicted violence. The terrorists were traumatized.[279] Their growing distancing from anti-colonial politics probably received nourishment from their communal biases, the lattere no doubt being revitalized by the HMS. Consequently, they turned against the Bengal Pact.[280] This new belligerence was confirmed by their response to the career of B.N. Sasmal, a member of the backward Mahishya caste, who threatened to succeed C.R. Das. He not

---

the meaning of the salvation of India through Hindu religion, means salvation of the country on behalf of the religion of the Hindus. This meant that not only were Muslims to abstain from joining this agitation, but further, they were bound to become more bitter enemies of the Hindus than the British.' Cited in File no. P&J 3504 of 1926 available under File no. 1752 of 1925. IOL.

[276] *Kazi Nazrul Islam Smritikatha*, p. 154. Ranen Sen, a terrorist who turned to Leftism, counted Nazrul's poems as one of the influences that made him turn away from terrorism. Tanika Sarkar, *National Movement*, p. 74.

[277] See Tanika Sarkar, *National Movement*, pp. 68–9, for a discussion on the ways in which the terrorist integrated themselves with the existing machinery of the Congress, after the Non-cooperation/Khilafat movement.

[278] Ibid., p. 193.

[279] Tegart writes that 'The Faridpur pronouncement was a blow to the terrorists; they suffered financially and lost a valuable recruiting slogan by the open condemnation of their methods by C.R. Das, who was still a popular idol', 'Communal Tension', Tegart Papers II, Box II, CSAC.

[280] The Congress Karmi Sangha had a programme of establishing educational institutions and gymnasiums in addition to forming various labour and agricultural unions. It also opposed the Bengal Pact for being 'anti-national in its tendencies'. *Amrita Bazar Patrika*, 2 July 1926. Later, its stand hardened to proclaim that it would support only those candidates in the 1926 Legislative Council elections who were opposed to the Bengal Pact. Ibid., 28 July 1926. A few days later the entente with Moderates was made public, when the Karmi Sangha not only openly supported Malaviya, but did so in a meeting which was addressed amongst others, by Shyam Sundar Chakravarty. Ibid., 8 August 1926.

only raised the anti-low-caste prejudices of the terrorists, but what was worse was his strong support of the Bengal Pact. The Sangha ganged up with the upper-caste leadership of the Congress in the Krishnanagore Conference in 1926, to defeat Sasmal's challenge and abrogate the Bengal Pact. Later, the induction of Karmi Sangha members into the BPCC led to the resignation of Sasmal along with all the Muslim members of the Committee; the latter declared that the Congress had become anti-Muslim in its personnel.[281]

This reorientation of terrorism was presaged in the course of the Non-Cooperation/Khilafat movement itself. Pulin Das writes of his opposition to Gandhi's movement. This may have arisen from the prominence given to the Khilafat movement. Das joined the HMS during the N/K. At the same time he was broached for help in this period by none other than the moderate collaborationist and co-founder of the WPL, S.R. Das. A deal was struck. S.R. Das would provide him with badly needed money (terrorist marginalization had obviously cut off their supply of resources), while Pulin Das and his group would disseminate propaganda against Gandhi's movement. This decision split Pulin's group, but the latter was so convinced of the rightness of his cause that he even approvingly included a revealing incident in his autobiography, in which a police officer expressed his gladness on hearing from none other than Sir Surendranath Banerjea that Das had become a collaborator.[282] This collaboration provides retrospective support to Sasmal's criticism of the Terrorists as being in the pay of the government.[283] Significantly, Sarojini Naidu as president of the Congress in 1926, also attacked the Sangha for collaborating with the government and spreading communal virulence.[284]

No doubt the riots of 1926 — in which the terrorists played a considerable role — intensified the communal turn within the Sangha. But the Women's Protection League also contributed its bit. Incidentally, the two groups that Pulin Das says were close to

---

[281] *Amrita Bazar Patrika*, 5 September 1926.
[282] Das, *Amar Jiban*, pp. 393–7.
[283] *The Mussalman*, 25 May 1926.
[284] While shrinking from making any charge of spying against the Sangha, she implied that its members were agents of Byomkesh Chakrabarty, the famous Responsivist and Minister with Ghaznavi after the dismissal of Huq. *Amrita Bazar Patrika*, 28 July 1926.

the Anushilan Samiti, that is, the zamindars and lawyers,[285] also formed the social base of the Women's Protection League. At any rate, the terrorists would provide natural recruits for the League, since they possessed organizational experience regarding physical defence. But the Women's Protection League had its own conception of violence, proximate to, but different from the terrorist's. Firstly, in the very call for defence: violence in the Women's Protection League scheme of things was not directed at the apocalyptic call for change regularly demanded by terrorist poetry. There was merely a trace of the apocalypse in the promise of a completely new subjectivity for the Hindu male through physical exercise. But this whittled down the scope of the transformative aspects to the basically psychological. Violence for Hindu communalism was normally a threat, and a way of bargaining with its Other; it was not generally aligned to change, but used as a call for conservation. Secondly, terrorist glorification of the lathi did not preclude idealizing other, more lethal sorts of weaponry. Nirad Chaudhury describes the revolver, for instance, as the 'Alladin's lamp' of the Terrorist movement.[286] This was the obvious outflow of their antagonism with the armed might of the colonial administration. On the other hand, however problematic the Women's Protection League's relationship may have been with the colonial administration, it certainly never was confrontationist. Consequently, they never demanded anything more sophisticated than the lathi.

However, the late twenties marked a new turn. Not only were jailed terrorists being freed each month from 1928 onwards,[287] but the release of Subhash Chandra Bose signalled a new turn to political violence. Aspiring to rival the British army, Bose gave a militaristic flavour to the Congress. His volunteers attempted to

---

[285] His belief in the potential leadership of the zamindar of Muktagacha, may be recalled. Zamindars were also privileged entities in the Anushilan Samiti, and were given direct access to the inner sanctum of the Samiti. *Amar Jiban*, p. 130. Das also states that the ukils and muktears of Dhaka gave him immense support. Ibid., p. 180. Of interest is the fact that Dhaka lawyers played an important role in the riots; they would invoke the honour of women to prevent the police from searching for suspected rioters in houses. 495/1930, L/P&J/6/196 of 1930, IOL. They were also highly visible in the Dhaka Hindu Conference in 1929. *Amrita Bazar Patrika*, 5 August 1929.

[286] *The Autobiography*, p. 293.

[287] See *Fortnightly Reports*, 1928, NAI.

give the president elect of the Congress of 1928 the same imperial reception given to the Emperor and Viceroy, complete with one-hundred-and-one gun salutes and a military parade under Bose's leadership.[288] Correspondingly, he restored the anti-Imperialist thrust of violence and detached it from communal orientations.[289] Bose's impact must be assessed in the light of the fact that, after a long layoff, there was a tremendous mushrooming of physical culture clubs and associations.[290] At the same time, the terrorists became firmly integrated with Congress politics by supplying the stormtroopers of the rival groups led by Sengupta and Bose respectively. Although introducing an intense volatility and violence in Congress politics of Bengal, the ex-Terrorists did not emerge — in contrast to many of their compatriots Maharashtra[291] — as the core of a long-term ideological investment in Hindu communalism.

But on its part, the Women's Protection League managed to stir up communal controversies in the late twenties. This was evident in the anti-abductions meeting of 1929. The presence of a Muslim who objected to some of the remarks made on Islam, resulted in a fracas in which he was expelled. This triggered off a protest meeting attended by many Muslim journalists. The editors of *Hanafi* as well as the renowned Akram Khan of the *Mohammadi* proposed resolutions, one of which even threatened 'breach of peace' if Islam was insulted. According to Moberly, a member of the Governor's Council, the Muslim press had been 'intemperate': *Hanafi* and *Soltan* were warned by the government.

However, 'prominent Hindu politicians' were absent from that meeting. The prospect of another wave of nationalist agitation

[288] *Fortnightly Reports*, December second half, 1928, NAI.
[289] Terrorists almost naturally gravitated to Bose. He was described by a terrorist as a link between the Congress and the underground movement. Bose often used them in his faction fights. Ananta Singh and his men, for instance helped in ousting J.M. Sengupta from his home base; similarly Sasmal's support was also neutralized with terrorist help. Tanika Sarkar, *National Movement*, pp. 69–70.
[290] See *Fortnightly Reports*, February first half, 1929, 17/1929, NAI, through the year.
[291] I am referring to the contribution by people like V.D. Savarkar; it should be mentioned that leaders like Hedgewar were heavily influenced by Bengal terrorist culture; he was sent to Calcutta in 1910 to establish contact with Pulin Das and the Anushilan Samiti. H.V. Seshadri (ed.), *Dr. Hedgewar The Epoch Maker: A Biography*, compiled by B.V. Deshpande and S.R. Ramaswamy, Bangalore, 1981, pp. 14–16.

possibly motivated this distancing. The Hindu newspapers too cooled their passions after the Muslim meeting. But the story of abductions had a far from happy ending. There had been at least one instance, in which the alleged abduction of a Hindu girl by a Muslim actually contributed to the making of a riot. This had taken place in Titagarh in 1925.[292] But it had occurred within the working class, which was not closely integrated with the discursive universe of the English and Bengali press. Nevertheless, it was an uncomfortable portent. In 1929 a sustained campaign around abductions led to a major riot. This took place in Nischintapur village in Pakundia, Mymensingh. While *Ananda Bazar Patrika* appears to have reported two instances of abduction there, *Amrita Bazar Patrika* took the count up to five other instances that had apparently occurred since 1927. Later, a letter from the Secretary, Bengal Provincial Hindu Sabha, in 1929 claimed that eleven cases of abduction had been reported in 'the last few months' from Pakundia Thana. Official investigations, however, revealed that only one such case had occurred. And this had an ironic origin. Ramdayal Sarkar had decided to avenge himself on his rival village *matabbar* (patron) Manoranjan Sarkar. The latter had outcasted Ramdayal after a scandalous incident related to his wife. Ramdayal's form of revenge was to organize the abduction of his rival's wife. Incidentally, they had abducted the wrong girl — showing how easily one woman could substitute another in this way of thinking.[293]

It was the elements of the abductions discourse, rather than an actual abduction, that had communalized an intra-Hindu issue. As the secretary of the BPHS disarmingly observed, this had to be a communal issue since the police officer in charge of the Thana was a Muslim, and in any case it was a Muslim majority district with a reputation for abductions and riots. Not the least cruel twist of irony was that in 1930, a major riot broke out here. The power of the discourse had effaced the factuality of the event, to produce an event whose horror could not be effaced as easily by the operations of discourse itself.

[292] *Amrita Bazar Patrika*, 25 August 1925.
[293] Luckily she was released without molestation. The details regarding the meeting of 1929 and what follows after that has been culled from 'Abduction of Hindu Women', 535/29, Serial nos. 1–2, GOB: Political, 1930, WBSA.

5

War Over Music: Meaning and Implications of the Riots of the 1920s and 1930

Part I

I.i

Although separated by gender, class and ideology, Muzaffar Ahmed and Begum Shaista Suhrawardy Ikramullah echoed each other, when, out of all the many communal conflicts that serrated their past, they selected only two riots, namely those of 1926 and 1946, for remembrance. The yoking together of these two riots of Calcutta in their different minds, eloquently testifies to the importance of the earlier one, which, in contrast to the 1946 riots, is almost forgotten today. Nineteen-twenty-six was punctuated by numerous outbreaks, the most prominent of which were the April riots in Calcutta. The latter surpassed all previous riots in our subcontinent, being spread over a month (from 2 April to 9 May, with a ten-day break in between). Ahmed declares that, with the possible exception of the inmates of the Bengal Workers and Peasants Party office, everyone in Calcutta had become ultra-Muslim or ultra-Hindu during the riots.[1] The Begum is more specific. She writes: 'The Calcutta riots of 1926 were as terrible and as far-reaching in their consequences as the riots twenty years later in 1946.'[2]

Several studies of communal riots have offered comprehensive insights on the meaning and constitution of riots. This chapter

---

[1] Ahmed, *Kazi Nazrul*, p. 111.

[2] She continues, 'By 1946 the Muslims had already chosen the path, and decided on their objective — the riots only made it inevitable'. Begum Shaista Ikramulla, *Huseyn Shaheed Suhrawardy: A Biography*, Karachi, 1991, p. 24.

is, in many ways, a critical dialogue with them. Frietag and Pandey have attempted to use riots as a springboard for exploring the social conflicts which go into the making of communalism. Frietag's exploration of intra-communal rivalries as a key to communal conflict gives us a wider canvas with which to understand communalism,[3] while Pandey's work has generally been concerned with the mutation of identities. Despite their valuable insights, especially Pandey's extremely perceptive study of the translation of caste mobility into communal identity,[4] their explanatory power is limited to local conditions. The problem with the 1926 riots is that they permeated the province (in fact, the entire sub-continent). Although concentrated in cities and towns, the countryside was not untouched. Further, they possessed a common feature. This was the 'music before mosque' issue which directly motivated the violence. An understanding of the meaning and constitution of this symbolic fabrication can give us a better understanding of the rioter's motivations. In other words, a more productive starting point for approaching the riots of my period of study, is to decipher the communal meanings at stake in these outbreaks, rather than delineate the social narratives that climax in their violence.

Often, the ostentatious character of rioting leads one to see them as the terminal point of communalism. The climactic view of riots is evident in Frietag and Pandey, both of whom delineate particular social processes that culminate in riots. Another form of this understanding is embodied in the work of Suranjan Das, which deals exclusively with the history of riots.[5] Das' implicit assumption is that riots embody, in themselves, all the elements of a communal process. Such an approach may seem to be latent here in the very choice of devoting my last chapter to riots. But the thrust of my argument is different. So far, I have argued that non-communal social (I use social here as a shorthand for the multiple spheres that communalism seeks to reorient) phenomena

---

[3] Sandria Frietag, *Religious Rites and Riots: From Communal Identity to Communalism in North India, 1870–1940*, Ph.D dissertation, University of California, Berkley, 1980.
[4] Gyanedra Pandey, 'Rallying Around the Cow: Sectarian Strife in the Bhojpuri region, c. 1888–1917', in Ranajit Guha (ed.), *Subaltern Studies, II: Writings on South Asian History and Society*, Delhi, 1983.
[5] Suranjan Das, *Communal Riots in Bengal, 1905–1947*, Delhi, 1991, p. 2.

were already being, on a sustained and day-to-day basis, harnessed into symbolic structures that were reproducing and intensifying communal identities. Manifested in both the discursive sphere as well as in actions surrounding contentious events, these campaigns provided large symbolic, emotional and organizational investments in communal antagonism. If one grants that protracted and everyday symbolic reproductions of communal antagonism are crucial, then riots should be seen as a variant of communal contention. They cannot be privileged as its terminal point. Riots form one of the several, interrelated, elements of communal processes.

At the same time, riots are not simply equivalent to other kinds of communal mobilization. There is a certain specific contribution that riots make. The obvious difference with other kinds of communal mobilization is its violence. But it is not simply that: after all, communal violence is also involved in restructuring discourses, mobilizations, mental attitudes. What is significant about riots is the spectacular display of physical violence — that involves the visible and comprehensive division of society on communal lines. The network of multiple affiliations that makes up the fabric of everyday society, although not effaced completely, is suppressed by all-pervasive fears and claims of religious affiliation. It is a condition that realises the classic and unlivable ideal of communalism.

Its extreme inversion of the everyday paradoxically encourages a forgetting of riots. They are normally classified as a violent and extraordinary point of life and pushed aside by the pressures of everyday living. To live constantly with an unlivable memory is, of course, neither healthy nor possible. And yet, it is precisely because riots have a great deal to do with commonplace life, that makes it necessary for the historian to recover its impact on the everyday. One way to do this is to not only understand their transformative political power, but to also register the way they leave their traces in the manner of a memorial, exerting the influence of the past less by overt recollections than by restructuring the geography of everyday social life. This brings me to the second distinguishing characteristic of riots. Communal conflagrations have an immediate and comprehensive effect on social institutions that is different from the long-term effects of other sorts of communal mobilization. They alter, in significant ways, the very grid of social existence. Suranjan Das acutely observes that riots are transformative. However, the boundaries of his study prevents us from knowing what it is that is being transformed besides riots themselves. It is precisely this area among others that I will try to explore in the course of this chapter.

I.ii

I wish to begin my discussion of riots with a personal recollection. Researching riots was an intensely vivid experience. This sprang less from the gory details, than from the way the research allowed me to recollect and discover places and people in Calcutta which had been touched by the violence. When visiting Dhaka and Pabna, I was excited by recognizing the names of localities that I had seen in files. Sometimes I even encountered descendants of the riot-affected and direct memories of the riots. Interestingly, the subject of the fakir's burial offered a similar experience.

The experience of research pointed to a direction that I was to follow later. All the while I was trying to untangle the possible meanings of the 'music before mosque' question, my conclusion was ironically one that I had already experienced. This concerned the vital relationships that constituted living space. Above all, the 'music before mosque' question problematized the nature of social space.

In a recent essay, Michael Roberts extends the framework of colonial power-knowledge to characterize the 'music before mosque' issue as a 'cultural struggle' introduced by the semitic world-view of colonial legislation.[6] But it is not clear why this struggle, instead of taking place between the colonial administration and the objects of its legislation, occurs only amongst the latter. Moreover, if I look at my own material, then there is about sixty odd years (the span of nearly two generations of productive working life), between the enactment of the law regulating public performance of music and the creation of it as a decisive riot issue which Robert's explanation cannot explain. I emphasize the word decisive, because, although there were riots on this issue before the period of my study (particularly a cluster that took place in

[6] Michael Roberts, 'Noise as Cultural Struggle: Tom-Tom Beating, the British and Communal Disturbances in Sri Lanka, 1880s–1930s', Veena Das (ed.), *Mirrors of Violence: Communities, Riots and Survivors in South Asia*, Delhi, 1992.

the 1890s), none of these had consequences outside the localities in which they occurred. The last riot of that decade which had occurred in 1897, was remembered as a unique occasion in Calcutta,[7] clearly indicating that, even in the same city, the preceding bouts of violence had been forgotten, if at all they had been known generally. This does not mean that the issue had nothing to do with colonialism, but it was of a very different and certainly more limited sort than the encounter conceived of by Roberts.

A problem with rehearsing the epistemological 'fall' of the subcontinent is that the history prior to colonialism is devalued. Evidence indicates that contention over the music issue was present before the intervention of colonial legislators.[8] The freedom to play music publicly was celebrated as one of the many benefits of colonial rule by a loyalist editorial in 1857.[9] Clearly, the new factor that colonial law introduced was the protection of the right to play music, and not the disputation itself. The desire to take advantage of the new stipulation can be seen to lie behind the outbreak of riots in front of the Hooghly Imambara in 1865. These stemmed from a conflictual social situation, in which the upthrusting Hindu Seal bankers were attempting to redefine the privileges claimed by the old ulema smarting from the defeat of the 1857 rebellion.

There was cultural struggle involved, but it was one that permeated the history of Islam. It has been noted that the azan is based on a musical structure, while *zikr* (*zikr jali* involves remembering Allah through recitation) has been the basis for the development of Sufi musical practice, the theorization of which came from the legendary thinker and poet, Jalaluddin Rumi, whose authorization must have also helped Amir Khusrau to develop the *qawwali*. The last two Caliphs had patronized music. On the other hand, not only had music been characterized as obscene from the first

---

[7] Hemendraprasad Ghosh in his oft-quoted diary revealed his surprise by declaring it to be a 'new thing in the history of Calcutta'. Incidentally the riot was over the demolition of a mosque. 'Diary of Hemendraprasad Ghosh', in Pratul Chandra Gupta (ed.), *Bengal Past and Present*, vol. CIII, parts I–II, nos. 196–7, January–December 1984, (Calcutta Historical Society, 1984).

[8] For instance there was well-known the story of the confrontation of Chaitanya with a Kazi who had forbidden the singing of *nagarkirtan*. Hiteshranjan Sanyal, *Bangla Kirtaner*, pp. 58–62.

[9] *Sangbad Prabhakar*, 20 June 1857, in *Samayik Patrey Banglar Samajchitra*, compiled and edited by Benoy Ghosh, Calcutta, 1966.

century of the Hijra calendar,[10] but it was also a target of purification campaigns since the nineteenth century. Mansur Ahmed's ghazi grand-uncle physically intimidated musicians in his village,[11] while the campaign against the Bauls showed the continuing vitality of this campaign.

The reasons for objection to music also differed. While the Mutwalli of the Hooghly Imambara made a distinction between the 'obscene' music played by the Seals' marriage party, and the 'sombre' mournfulness of the music played by the Shi'is,[12] the fatwa cited by the Muslim residents of Salem, which was another early recorded instance of the 'music before mosque' objection, banned all sounds within the precincts of the mosque including 'loudly praising God'.[13] While this difference was moored in the different customs of the Sunnis and the Shi'is, more germane to our purpose is that the very grounds for objecting to 'music before mosque' changed. The theological orientation was inherited by Abu Bakr, who, as we have seen, issued a fatwa on the matter. However, the grounds of justification shifted with greater communalization. In his lengthy letter on the matter to *The Mussalman*, Hadi distinguished between sounds of the street which unavoidably penetrated the mosques, and music played by Hindu processions which he held was unnecessary,[14] and thus, objectionable. Wasimuddin Ahmed, probably the most prestigious Muslim leader of Pabna, admitted the novelty of the practice. But he asserted that it was an expression of the 'progressive' Muslim desire to 'advance', and should be respected by the Hindus as such.[15]

Noticeable in both ideologues was a shifting of emphasis — the first negatively and the other positively — on to the agents of

[10] Most of the details mentioned above have been culled from A. Siloah, 'The Dimension of Sound', in B. Lewis (ed.), *The World of Islam*, London, 1976.

[11] *Atmakatha*, p. 30.

[12] 'From S.K. Ali to the Lt. Governor, GOB, August 15, 1863', 91–101A/1865.

[13] 'Memorial to Lord Ripon from Syed Pasha Sahib and other Muslims of Salem'. The Salem affair arose when permission to build a new mosque was objected to by Hindus. The Muslims were influential enough to fight the case in the High Court, procuring fatwas from not only ulemas of the town, but also from Mahomedan Professors in Madras. Home Judicial A, Nos. 45–54, May 1882, NAI.

[14] *The Mussalman*, 27 April 1926.

[15] Editorial, *Amrita Bazar Patrika*, 21 July 1926.

music production. It was this change that allowed Muslim communalists to exercise a highly selective choice of prohibitions. In Lahore, a Hindu procession led by Muslim musicians was allowed to pass a mosque.[16] In Kharagpur, the Muslims promptly gave up their objections to a British flag march that played regimental music through the riot-torn town, after the authorities had dismissed their complaints.[17]

The question of music was not seen in absolutely theological terms in the twenties, but defined more by the contingent pressures of communal conflict. Theological aspects, by invoking an apparently absolute justification for the retaliatory logic of riot issues, simply provided a support. Significantly, a driving motive of the go-korbani issue was one of communal selectivity, since Hindus objected only to the slaughter of cows by Muslims.[18] 'Music before mosque' replicates the structure of go-korbani. This indicates a hidden agenda of 'music before mosque', which was to give it a status equivalent to go-korbani. Confirmation of this parity comes from the innumerable instances when go-korbani and 'music before mosque' were used as equivalent counters of communal exchange.[19]

But this pragmatism does not appear to have deflected from treating the issue as an absolute imperative. It could become more important than the threat of a common death: in Basirhat, 24 Parganas, a riot started over the singing of devotional songs by

[16] Home Poll, File no 179/1926, NAI.
[17] Home Poll, II/VII/1926, NAI.
[18] The *Mohammadi* bitterly commented, 'Cows are daily slaughtered in Calcutta, and it has never caused the Hindus' love for their mother-cow to overflow nor their religious suceptibilities to be wounded. But as soon as the Muslims slaughter a cow on the occasion of Korbani, their religious conscience becomes aggressive.' 17 July, RNP no. 30 of 1925.
[19] As early as in 1924, the BPCC managed to strike a compromise in a village in Uluberia (Howrah) on this question by getting the Hindus to renounce 'music before mosque' for go-korbani. *The Mussalman*, 25 April 1924. In his initial statement on behalf of the Bengal Muslim League, Qutubuddin Ahmed declared, with frank courage, 'I am . . . of the opinion that it [music before mosques] has nothing to do with Shariat and has been invented by self-interested persons or party as a counterblast to cow-sacrifice . . . .' *Amrita Bazar Patrika*, 3 August 1926. On behalf of the opposing side, the Nishkam Arya Sabha of Burrabazar resolved to stop 'music before mosque' in exchange for a similar gesture regarding go-korbani, 'to test fellow-feeling'. *Amrita Bazar Patrika*, 26 January 1925.

Hindus, to ward off the effects of a cholera epidemic raging there.[20] Possibly the most poignant instance of the impact of 'music before mosque' — because it has to do with feelings of attachment rather than those of hatred — is the case of Sailana State in Central India (near Indore). The Muslim population left their native place because the Darbar refused to uphold their objection to 'music before mosque'.[21]

The action of the Sailana Muslims indicates the burden of signification that 'music before mosque' carried: everyday life even become intolerable where it was allowed. This case gives us a clue to the nature of riot symbols such as 'music before mosque'. In contrast to a linguistic sign, the 'music before mosque' symbol is constituted by a complex situational structure. Its power derives from its ability to problematize the relationships of living social space. A brief elaboration of the go-korbani dispute will make this clear. The resolution to the problem of cow sacrifice (to the extent that it was resolved), was based on the principle that it was permitted, so long as it was not visible. A municipality law passed in Calcutta made it mandatory to put up screens in front of butchers stalls,[22] while the BPCC agreement in Uluberia cited above, persuaded Muslims to perform go-korbani away from 'public sight'.

At stake in the go-korbani issue was the contest over visual space. 'Music before mosque' on the other hand, rested on the notion of an acoustic space. The Salem fatwa — which is both the most extensive and representative document on the subject (many of its arguments were to be deployed in the twenties), claimed that prayer was a silent activity and the sound of music constituted an act of desanctification. The objection was to music played outside the mosque. In other words, for the anti-'music before mosque'

---

[20] *Amrita Bazar Patrika*, 18 April 1926. At times such as these, there was a general tradition of toleration of, if not co-operation with, each others practices. Waliullah remembers that in the evenings, Muslims would recite azan, while Hindus would play their percussion instruments, to drive off the cholera epidemic in Sandwip. *Yuga Bichitra*, pp. 13–14. The strength of this tradition however, did not completely die out in the mid-twenties. It was reported that in Chandpur, at this time, Muslims allowed songs against cholera to be sung publicly in front of two mosques. *Amrita Bazar Patrika*, 12 December 1926.
[21] September first half, *Fortnightly Reports*, no. 112 of 1925, NAI.
[22] *The Mussalman*, 29 June 1926.

campaigners, the sanctity of the ritual space radiated outwards to be defined by acoustic range.

The double importance of the idea of sacred space has been indicated in the controversy over the fakir's burial. On the one hand, sacred space was moored in questions of security and urban identity for groups of relatively powerless migrants. On the other hand, the N/K associated it with the desire for freedom and raised questions about future governance. It was the latter that communal formations sought to convert into a condition of anxiety through the invocation of rights over sacred space. The exercise of religious rights was allied to questions of governance by the fakir's controversy. The intertwined significance of space was carried over into the 'music before mosque' issue.

The implications of go-korbani were not simply repeated in 'music before mosque'; they were radically extended. Go-korbani was tied to ritual occasions: clashes over cow-slaughter broke out only on Bakr-Id rather than on everyday occasions. As such, the nature of this controversy was in keeping with the character of nineteenth-century riots which were tied to the ritual calendar. As early as in the 1840's, Gen. Sleeman mentions that collectively initiated riots (as opposed to ones sparked off by private vendettas such as throwing a cow's carcass into a temple) occurred every thirty–forty years, when the calendars of the Hindus and Muslims coincided to produce the simultaneous occurrence of festivals.[23] The go-korbani issue extended this 'tradition' since, in keeping with its programmatic character initiated by Dayanand Saraswati, it could potentially lead to conflicts every year on ritual occasions such as *Id ul Zuha*, thereby providing a regularity so essential to a campaign.

The 'music before mosque' issue however, could conceivably take place everyday, certainly on every occasion a Hindu procession passed a mosque. The 'music before mosque' question displaced the claim over ritual time, which in calendrically linked riot issues limited the demand over common space. The objection to 'music before mosque' could lay claim to space for all time. The contents of the Salem fatwa were echoed in the nineteen-twenties, when Muslim authorities stated that prayer was a continuous activity, for, besides the five basic congregational prayers,

[23] Major General Sir W.H. Sleeman, KCB, *Rambles and Recollections of an Indian Official*, (f.pub. 1844, revised annotated edition, Karachi, 1980), p. 131.

individuals could offer their own when they wished. On this ground they asserted that no procession with music could ever go past a mosque.[24]

'Music before mosque' was also a more portable issue. It multiplied, through analogy, the kinds of situations that could become conflictual. Objections were made to music played in houses; boats in which *sankirtan* was being sung, were stopped. Humanitarian occasions provided no insurance: a musical party collecting funds for Orissa Relief in Dhaka was attacked,[25] while the chants of a funeral procession led to riots in Kharagpur in 1926.[26] Conversely, the Hindu Sabha of Dhaka objected to the building of the Muslim Hall of Dhaka University, since they feared that Muslims would object to the sounds emanating from the nearby Dhakeshwari temple.[27] Such instances indicate an extensive spread of the issue, making it usable for everyday initiatives by small groups of people.

This spatial dispersal was anchored in mutual places of worship. Since the sites of objections were mosques, they provided the focus for attack and retaliation, spawning in consequence, counter-retaliation on temples. 'Music before mosque' encouraged the primary institutions of the two religions to be locked in battle. While Dinu Chamrawala's mosque in Calcutta furnished the site for three riots in 1926, including the April contentions,[28] the Kalitolla temple was the one favoured by Muslim rioters. A macabre token of the future was provided by the installation of a Shiv image in a dargah.[29] Interestingly, mutual desecrations were, as the police admitted, a new feature of riots.[30]

Moreover, the consequences of 'music before mosque' inflated the significance of existing practices of desecrations. The characteristic response in the mofussil to the Calcutta riots was a

[24] Home Poll, File no. 179/1926, NAI.
[25] The above incidents are taken from *Amrita Bazar Patrika*, June–October 1926.
[26] The road past Kharida mosque, which was the site for this disturbance was, as a consequence, closed to all funeral processions. Ibid., 13 July 1926.
[27] *The Mussalman*, 23 March 1926.
[28] 'Report by J.E. Armstrong, Commissioner of Police (Officiating)', Home Poll, II/VII/1926, NAI.
[29] Ibid.
[30] Ibid. Twenty-one places of worship were desecrated during the first phase of the April riots, including temples, gurdwaras, mosques and dargahs.

spate of image desecrations.[31] These were a traditional way of extracting private revenge on Hindu zamindars for whom the *pujaghar* was a symbol of conspicuous merit and family honour. But the Calcutta riots converted these forays into large, non-local communal symbols. This is what happened in Pabna, which had the highest rate of image desecrations in the province. These had not stirred too many ripples when they had occurred. However, the 1926 riots were started by mutilated images gathered from three parts of the town, which were left in front of Jogendranath Maitra's house.[32] As mentioned in Chapter 2, Maitra, the zamindar of Sitlai, was already unpopular with his Muslim tenants. But the act of desecrating images from outside his personal domain and placing them in front of his house, indicates an expansion of his individual status to make him a symbol of his religion. Certainly this was what the Hindu bhadralok of the town felt, for they rallied together immediately and retaliated by playing music as they went past the Khalifapatti mosque in an immersion procession for the images.

The time-space coordinates of the 'music before mosque' issue, which dramatically inflates the (im)possibility of everyday coexistence, corresponds to the increasing dominion of communal claims. If the go-korbani issue was the outgrowth of the Arya Samaj's internal religious reforms, the bloody plenitude of clashes over 'music before mosque' correspond to the movement of communal formations in problematizing an increasing number of subjects hitherto not included in the domain of religion. This co-relationship allows me to extend my definition of riot issues as situational symbolic structures. I can now specify their basis in particular time-space co-ordinates that have an inherent capability to interrelate with changes in communal formations. Such a definition of the meaning of riot issues, I should add, departs from seeing them as the function of a metalanguage alone. Studies of the meaning of riots have seen them as a product of either anthropological codes

---

[31] Instances: on 12 April twelve images were desecrated in Serajgunj (Pabna), after leaflets referred to the attacks on mosques in Calcutta, while there were isolated instances in Bakarganj. *Fortnightly Reports*, No 12 of 1926, April first half; In Pingna a masjid was desecrated after a letter relating the Calcutta happenings was read out. *Amrita Bazar Patrika*, 28 April 1926.

[32] 'Report on Pabna Disturbances', GOB: Political: Confidential, No. 317/1926, Serial nos 1–31, WBSA

which are inverted,[33] or as an appeal to absolute, undifferentiated values such as honour.[34] It is not as if these appeals are neither involved nor invoked. But more importantly, the character, power and flexibility of riot issues stem from their ability to problematize and even implode, the existential fabric of everyday living and relationships in shared space.

I.iii

I have already referred to Bakr's fatwa in 1923 regarding the 'music before mosque' question; he had preceded this with a fatwa prohibiting Muslims from attending Congress pandals where music was played.[35] The Muslim communalist's interest in this issue was matched by their Hindu counterparts. The *Swatantra* claimed that the 'music before mosque' involved a curtailment of religious rights that had not been seen even in the days of 'Muhammadan rule'.[36] A year later the *Dainik Bharat Mitra* darkly suggested that objections to religious slogans expressed Muslim resentment of the very inhabitation of India by Hindus.[37] Clearly the 'music before mosque' issue served the purposes of both communal parties. It was a consensual symbol through which the communalists could signal their mutual antagonism, even as they consolidated their hold over what constituted their religious communities.

Music was a crucial socio-religious institution for Hindu reformism, especially where it intersected with communal mobilization. In Chapter 1, we saw how the kirtan was seen as an institution for mobilizing low castes. Part of the reason for this understanding was that low-caste self-assertion was often mediated through music. Among the few things prescribed for the followers of the Matua cult in its initial stage, was the singing of kirtans.[38] No doubt music featured in the lives of Rajbansis who had remained Vaishnav and

---

[33] See Natalie Zemon Davis, *Society and Culture in Early Modern France*, London, 1975.
[34] See Gyanendra Pandey, '"Encounters and Calamities": The History of a North Indian *Qasba* in the Nineteenth Century', in Ranajit Guha (ed.), *Subaltern Studies III*, Delhi, 1984.
[35] Siddiki, *Furfurar Hazrat*, p. 223.
[36] 2 October 1925, RNP no. 40 of 1925, NAI.
[37] 18 April 1926, RNP no. 17 of 1926, NAI.
[38] Sekhar Bandopadhyaya, p. 323.

opposed Panchanan Barma and the Kshatriya Samaj.[39] So deeply was music involved in the lives of low-castes that, like a word, it lent itself to the expression of many relationships. On the other hand, Piyush Ghosh led a nagarkirtan in Calcutta on the eve of the HMS session in 1925,[40] while communalists in Pingna invited low castes to sing kirtans with them in a procession which went past a mosque and concluded in *hariloot*.[41] The organizers of Patuakhali Satyagraha too sang kirtans in front of the mosque there; significantly, many of them conceived the movement as a reformist enterprise that would change attitudes towards the low castes through fear of the Muslim.[42]

Of course, besides its reformist potential, music, in so far as it was crucial to Gaudiya Vashnavism, formed an important part of the Bengali Hindu identity. Sanyal argues that it provided the basic organizational mode for Vaishnavism.[43] No doubt the story of Chaitanya's quarrel with the Kazi over the permissibility of nagarkirtan would have helped its communal appropriation. Such resonances helped Hindu organizations — including both the Brahman Sabha and the Arya Samaj — to match the stubbornness of their Muslim brethren by claiming that music was a definitive and imperative aspect of Hinduism.[44] The Women's Protection League made it mandatory to attend music classes,[45] suggesting the degree to which religious associations allowed communal issues to become transferrable.

While Muslim claims on the issue of 'music before mosque' was validated by ideas of sacrosance and theological injunctions, Hindu claims did not rest exclusively, or even primarily, on religious

---

[39] According to Gautam Bhadra, 'Vaishnavism had spread among the Rajbansis and survived the onslaught of a Kshatriya movement . . . ', 'The Mentality of Subalternity: *Kantanama* or *Rajdharma*', in Ranajit Guha (ed.), *Subaltern Studies VI: Writings on South Asian History and Society*, Delhi, 1989, p. 60.

[40] *Amrita Bazar Patrika*, 11 April 1925.

[41] *The Mussalman*, 7 August 1926.

[42] See Swami Gyananda, *Patuakhali Satyagraha*, Patuakhali, 1927, p. 9.

[43] Hiteshranjan Sanyal, *Bangla Kirtaner*, p. 3.

[44] The Bengal Arya Samaj resolved that 'Nagar Kirtans formed a component part of the festivals of the Arya Samaj . . . .' The Brahman Sabha cited different Puranas in support for its contention of the imperative of music. *Amrita Bazar Patrika*, 28 July and 9 October 1926.

[45] It formed one of the eight rules prescribed for the WPL volunteers. Ibid., 9 August 1925.

grounds. The latter took recourse to the discourse of rights. Interference 'with the rights of Hindus to use the King's Highways . . . is both unjust and inexpedient . . . ', read a HMS resolution passed just after the April riots.[46] The appeal to the notion of rights was an advantage for it offered to reinforce the self-image of Hindu communalism as transcending sectarianism. On the other hand, it would allow them to characterize Muslims as fanatical and blind to reason and law, which, in turn, could evoke fears of a Bengal Pact-ruled future. This understanding lay behind the intransigent dramatization of the issue by Satin Sen, who, as we have seen, was a person who had not previously been communal. He had even led an agitation against the Laukati Union Board, in which overwhelming numbers of Muslim peasants had participated.

Sen was a terrorist, a group which, as we have seen, was specially vulnerable to communal mobilization. Equally significant was the support given by 'almost all shades of political opinion in the district',[47] to his movement. Sen ensured the general appeal of his agitation by posing it as a question of non-negotiable rights. The problem had begun with the construction of a new mosque. The Muslims then claimed an extension of the area around the old mosque where music was forbidden. With the threat of agitation, the Muslims offered to relinquish their claims on the extension. But Sen would have none of it, since it involved general 'principles'.[48] It may be remarked that the mode of action was derived from Gandhian nationalism. Although Dr Moonje and Dr Chitnavis had pioneered the use of satyagraha for the 'music before mosque' question in Nagpur in 1923, Satin Sen went further than his mentors. Volunteers and support came from as far away as Allahabad, while the issue was dramatized as an all-India question. It was also an extraordinarily prolonged affair: beginning on 30 September, 1926 it carried on through the following year and occupied a substantial part of 1928. Sen revealed the full possibilities of this new mode of communal mobilization, whereby single points of conflict provided the occasion for a widespread and prolonged campaign point — a heritage which we are still carrying in the Ram Janambhumi agitation.

The mutual commitment of Hindu and Muslim communalism

---

[46] Home Poll, File no. 179/1926, NAI.
[47] 'Situation in Patuakhali', GOB, File no. 500.
[48] Ibid., File nos 1–16.

to 'music before mosque' does not mean that the colonial policies made no contribution. However, in contrast to communal certitudes, colonial policy was marked by hesitation and apprehension. Since they were already blamed for communalism, they had to evolve policies that could encourage communalism without seeming to do so. Especially because, what was involved here was a crucial justification for the Raj, that is, the preservation of law and order.

The administration resorted to ad hocism as a panacea. A circular sent by the newly appointed Viceroy, asking for responses to his suggestion for reviving a central Conciliation Board, was uncompromisingly rejected by the provincial governments. The latter firmly supported the existing arrangement, which relegated all decisions on the 'music before mosque' question to local authorities.[49] In fact, the great fear of the government was that they might be accused of having a general policy on the matter,[50] in which event they ran the risk of being attacked by both sides.

At the same time this ad hocism had to be reconciled with the basic rules of the administration which was founded on the procedures of general applications, a framework, which, given the all-India character of the question, was all the more incumbent on this question. To get around this problem the administration took recourse to a specious and ultimately self-defeating argument. They drew a distinction between religious revivalist movements like that of the Mahdi's which challenged the State, and that of communal violence which did not.[51] This encouraged a dangerous division between the responsibilities to the State and to the society it ruled, which struck at the heart of British self-justification, posited as it had been on the beneficent aspects of providing law and, with it, social order.

However, executive ad hocism did not help them to avoid accusations. Local arbitration was based on upholding custom. But the communalization of witnesses — who recollected past practices according to the claims made by their communities — meant that the customary precedents for playing 'music before mosque' could no longer be ascertained. This gave them a self-congratulatory role

---

[49] Home Dept: Political, File no. 140/1925, NAI.
[50] Home Poll, File no. 179/1926, NAI.
[51] This was formulated when Suhrawardy's communal misdemeanours were being reviewed. Home Poll, File no. 209/1926, NAI.

as arbitrators committed exclusively to the principle of equity. However, this image had to reckon with the fact that the notion of equity lacked the general application of the law and, wanting that, could not prevent the growth of a diversity of local disaffections harboured by those who felt that a particular magistrate's adjudication went against custom. To counter this, the administration took a mechanical idea of equity, which only perpetuated controversies. Thus to assuage criticism that the administration was pro-Muslim by its actions against the Patuakhali satyagrahis, it allowed music to be played before a mosque in nearby Perojepur village in 1927. Which, in turn, raised Muslim hackles, culminating in the firing against them in Ponabalia later that year.

Colonial policy lacked the rigour that it possessed in the preceding century. Contrary to Roberts' impression, the 'music before mosque' issue was not spawned in the context of a confident and all-powerful colonial hegemony. On the contrary, the proliferation of the 'music before mosque' issue in the twenties marked the crisis of that hegemony, rather than its completion. What they did manage to accomplish, however, as a consequence, was to intensify the disseminative power of the 'music before mosque' issue.

I.iv

The 'music before mosque' issue *per se* does not explain the spread and intensity of the 1926 riots, especially those occurring in April.[52] Nor do the various elements of the violence do so. While the colonial authorities were hesitant about their overall policies, their actual handling of the April riots seemed one of encouragement by default, that is, by remaining inactive during the first three days. However, when they did deploy their armed personnel, the only thing that changed was that instead of open mass confrontations, the riots took the form of individual attacks. Organizations, such as the Arya Samaj and the HMS played an initiating role (the April riots were sparked off by an Arya Samji procession, while HMS campaigns greatly facilitated the riots at

---

[52] Besides their unprecedented duration, the April 1926 riots left one hundred and ten killed and nine hundred and seventy-five injured. A total of eleven riots took place the same year in Bengal alone. Home Poll, File no. 179/II/1926, NAI.

Kharagpur).⁵³ But the areas of their influence were not co-terminous with the spread of violence. Conversely, the Muslim leadership was divided,⁵⁴ and it was individuals like Huseyn Suhrawardy who played a prominent role.⁵⁵ Armed guards such as Marwari *darwans* and criminals played an important role, and their efforts were complemented by elements of 'nationalist organizations such as the Khilafatists and Terrorists. However, their role does not explain the enthusiasm of common people: mass participation took the form of locality based confrontations,⁵⁶ as well as clashes between members of interlinked occupations.⁵⁷ Supporting all of them were newspapers, the campaigns of which celebrated the involvement of Bengalis in riots for the first time.⁵⁸ Many of the rabid ones were run by unprepossessing youths who fronted for important communal leaders such as Sir Abdur Rahim.⁵⁹ But, like the colonial authorities who could not rein in what they encouraged, newspapers like *Amrita Bazar Patrika* that had links with the HMS, began ruing their lack of influence over plebeian elements after a week of rioting.⁶⁰

Clearly, what is required is a totality of explanation, something that approaches the scale of *zeitgeist*. Put in more palpable terms, what we are looking for is a historical formation that provides the codes and circuits, in and through which riots and their transmission derive their intensity. I suggest that it is the N/K movement to which we should look. In particular I think it lies in the syncretist implications of this movement.

⁵³ 'Report from R.N. Reid, D.M., Midnapore to Commissioner of Burdwan District', Home Poll, II/VIII/1926, NAI.

⁵⁴ The Bengal Muslim Council Party was formed during the April riots. Sir Abdur Rahim's Bengal Council Party was floated at the same time, leading the administration to comment sadly on the 'lack of union' among Muslim politicians.

⁵⁵ Although he intermittently counselled peace during the April riots, by July that year he actively helped to trigger off the Raj Rajeshwari riots in Calcutta.

⁵⁶ In Calcutta, a structuring opposition was given by the antagonism between the Marwari 'resident' and the Muslim slum 'dweller'.

⁵⁷ Thus Muslim boatmen attacked Hindu coolies in the Kidderpore Docks, Home Poll, II/VII/26, 1926, NAI.

⁵⁸ The defence of the Kalitolla temple by Bengali Hindus was reported like a battlefield narrative. *Amrita Bazar Patrika*, 6 April 1926.

⁵⁹ 16 February 1926, *Nayak*, RNP no. 8 of 1926, NAI. See also, File no. 236, Serial nos 1–3, GOB: Political, WBSA.

⁶⁰ 11 April 1926.

Two points must be made immediately. The first is that prevailing academic common sense — shared by diverse scholars such as Rafiuddin Ahmed and Ashish Nandy — has treated syncretism as a unitary phenomenon.[61] Further, narratives of syncretism have shown its demise to be inevitable, producing a sentimental penumbra around the notion of syncretism as folk practice and thereby preventing a perception of other forms to which it could be allied. Even within this overarching construction there has been no attempt at making an analytic distinction between the popular objects of common worship such as the Pirs and those of cults such as the Bauls and Kartabhajas. This undifferentiated idea of syncretism needs to be drastically altered in order to appreciate the N/K and its effects.

The N/K started as a limited alliance based on the coincidence of interests: one, for the restoration of the Khilafat, and second, for Swaraj. Nevertheless, at an organizational level, there was a close proximity between them. In continuation of a practice that had started from 1916 when the Lucknow Pact was signed, the Khilafat and Non-Cooperation conferences were held together at the same venue.[62] This obviously meant that there was a high degree of exchange of personnel.[63] Both Gandhi and Das, for instance, were office bearers of the Khilafat Conference.[64] A grand emblem of Hindu–Muslim unity was Shraddhanand's appearance in the Nakhoda Mosque in 1919. This interrelationship produced its own symbolism; a pandal in Dhaka was, for instance, decorated with an emblem that featured a mosque and a temple topped by

---

61 Syncretism in their explanations have been placed in a narrative of (tragic) defeat by the aggressive skills of superior organization (for Ahmed in the reformist movements, for Nandy in the entrenchment of the Colonial State). Ahmed, *The Bengal Muslims*. Nandy makes an implicit equation between the interlocking of Hindu and Muslim traditions spelt out in 'An Anti-Secularist Manifesto', in Hick and Hempel (ed.), *Gandhi's Significance for Today*, London, 1989, on the one hand, and the notion taken from Geertz of 'religion-as-faith' in 'The Politics of Secularism and the Recovery of Religious Tolerance', *Mirrors of Violence*, on the other hand.

62 See P.C. Bamford, 'Preface', *Histories of Khilafat and Non-Cooperation Movements*, Delhi, 1985, f.pub. 1925.

63 This spilled over into socializing between Congress and Khilafat workers. See Mansur Ahmed, *Amar Dekha*, p. 42.

64 In 1922 top Khilafatists signed a manifesto in which they declared that they 'had loyally accepted the dictatorship of that great saint and thinker — Mahatma Gandhi — in our struggle for freedom'. Ibid., p. 186.

a crescent and trishul.⁶⁵ So intertwined were the two movements, that their first comprehensive history declared that, 'the history of one would be incomplete without the history of the other'.⁶⁶

This structure of syncretist practice could, and did, attenuate into bureaucratism. In post-independence India a mechanical syncretism was promoted in the Nehruvian era, in which each official occasion was graced by a token Muslim representative to dramatize a consortium of identities. However, the N/K possessed the creativity of a mass movement and, consequently, exceeded the limits set by the idea of a federation of identities. Waliullah remembers how students celebrated Unity Day in 1919 by going around in groups, each of which was composed of a Christian, an Untouchable, a Muslim and a Buddhist representative. The normally orthodox Marwari millionaires would invite them in and partake of sweets together with them; in one case where the husband refused to dine with the non-caste, his wife shouted at him till he did so.⁶⁷ Prisoners were serviced by cartloads of food sent by both Muslim and Marwari businessmen of central Calcutta, which was an area most affected by riots.⁶⁸ The slogans 'Bande Mataram' and 'Allah O Akbar', which became spectacular signs of communal violence, were enthusiastically shouted by thousands in political gatherings.⁶⁹ In fact, so common became its usage that poems dedicated to communal unity could unselfconsciously conclude with exhortations of 'Bande Mataram'.⁷⁰

These instances indicate a sweep that exceeded the limits of inherited forms of syncretism. On the one hand, the N/K movement demanded a transcendence of religious identity; in this regard, its structure was close to the plebeian cults that had talked

---

⁶⁵ A.Y.S. Alam, p. 141.

⁶⁶ Bamford, *Histories*, p. 3.

⁶⁷ They would shout slogans of communal unity — which was made more remarkable by the fact that it included Christians and Buddhists — outside houses. Waliullah, pp. 75–7.

⁶⁸ Waliullah, *Yuga*, p. 132.

⁶⁹ Alam, p. 129. Waliullah recollects that the air was rife with 'Allah O Akbar' and 'Bande Mataram' when students joined the first school strike in Calcutta during the N/K movement. *Yuga*, pp. 105–8. In contrast 'Bande Mataram' was shouted by Hindus attacking the Khalifapatti Mosque in Pabna (D.M. deposition, *The Mussalman*, 3 August 1926.) and by Hindu demonstrators in Dhaka.

⁷⁰ Sarkar, 'Muslim Politics', p. 70.

of an Absolute which was common to Hindu and Muslim and greater than them. On the other hand, it effortlessly expanded and changed popular syncretism. The cults were confined to the religious domain; they were either marginalized, such as the Bauls, or their effects entered in a limited way in general ritual life as, for example, those occasions when women went to a mazaar to cure their barrenness. In contrast, the syncretism of the N/K was born in the mass political sphere. The result was a new identity that cut across mass religious divisions.

Syncretism acquired a new basis. The N/K was posited, above all, on the ideal of political freedom and all the longings associated with the word 'Swaraj'. The hegemony of this concept became clear by 1921 when Khilafatist leaders began to declare that their demands would be unrealisable unless Swaraj was first established.[71] The primacy of this concept implied that both Hindus and Muslims were equally necessary for the achievement of this state: they were part of the same Self (*Swa*) that was manifest in the movement. This was a very important recognition, for, through it, syncretism was grounded in the desire and possibility of political equality, which in turn, could extend to social relations. In contrast, popular, non-denominational syncretism had coexisted with the asymmetries of social power. This made it vulnerable, as we can still see in the post-reformist Improvement literature, to the reformist criticism that the 'Hindu' elements of the composite Muslim culture actually represented the hegemony of the Hindus.

But there was also another aspect to Swaraj. An official noted that it was the combination of nationalism with economic revolt that was responsible for the power of the N/K movement.[72] Two spheres should be noted. The first was that of law. The most popular institution thrown up was that of arbitration courts. This not only expressed the desire for self-governance, but did so by saving lawyers' fees. More importantly, the revenue and rent struggles gave a much larger base to the egalitarian aspirations raised in the struggle.[73] The syncretic transcendence of the N/K movement drew its power from this holistic hope of change. In the process it produced a new zone of possibilities for the creation of identities.

[71] Bamford, *Histories*, p. 166
[72] 'Histories of the Noncooperation and Khilafat Movements in Bengal, File no. 395, Serial nos 1–3, 1924, GOB: Political, WBSA.
[73] Ibid.

There were several signs of a fresh life that did not hesitate to breach social and religious conventions. The pronouncedly Hindu leader, Gandhi, was embodied as the Mahdi,[74] while Azad extended the sphere of Koranic injunctions by enjoining alliance with Hindus on religious grounds.[75] Further, the implications of caste reform were extended to Hindu–Muslim relations. For instance, untouchability rules relating to Muslims, which had never been addressed by the reformist movements, were now spontaneously opposed. Once, upon seeing a bearded prisoner serving them, a Hindu boy, imprisoned for his N/K activities, threw out his food. He was immediately berated, while other students spontaneously broke out into a song celebrating Hindu–Muslim unity.[76]

Moreover, a new area of experimentation opened up in which the signifiers of different identities were amalgamated in new practices. There was, for instance, Nazrul Islam's poetic idiom of religious polyimagism. This was one of the highest achievements of the N/K, for not only did Nazrul's activist romanticism celebrate its unity, but also, when the momentum of the movement was no longer available, his poetry kept generating its own energies to rage against the tide of communal ambitions. In the course of acquiring affiliation with the masses of the N/K movement, his verse detached its polyimagism from its source in religious identities, and relocated it in working-class struggles. That the general tendency evident in Nazrul was not exceptional, is shown by two incidents which occurred in the midst of the intense communal antagonism of the mid-twenties. The first took place in Dhaka in 1926, when a procession commemorated C.R. Das's first death anniversary by taking out a coffin. The other occurred in Howrah when a mohurrum procession took out tazias that bore the portraits of both Gandhi and Das.

Although lasting for a limited period, the N/K produced a profound transformation that invested the political, social and

[74] Sarkar, 'Muslim Politics', p. 73.
[75] Azad divided non-Muslims into friendly and non-friendly and cited verses from the Koran to state that it approved of those who had no record of trying to invade Muslim lands or of opposition to Muslims. Hardy argues this represents a complete break with classical jurists since they never put 'parity of reasoning (*qiyas*)' on par with 'divine prescription (*nass*)'. Peter Hardy, *Partners in Freedom — and True Muslims: The Political Thought of Some Muslim Scholars in British India 1912–47*, Lund, 1971, pp. 28–9.
[76] Waliullah, *Yuga* pp. 121–2.

economic spheres with a culture of innovativeness and transgression, accompanied by notions of interdependence and equality. At bottom was a shared trust in a common, though not undifferentiated, collective Self. All of this acquired the beginnings of an institutional framework in the Bengal Pact. The Pact combined the objectives of mutual accommodation (on ritual matters) with equity (on economic issues). Although limited and defensive, the Pact nevertheless testified to the mutual trust forged in the course of the N/K. It provided an emotional bonding to reconceive social relations.

Unfortunately, it was precisely this deep relationship of trust and hope that turned into its opposite, once charged with the profoundly negative energy of betrayal which the intensifying conflict over communal issues introduced. The N/K had produced a shared politico-cultural code, and its power demanded a commensurate charge of antagonism in order to split it along the fault line of religious distinctions. The negative power is evident in Sarat Chandra Chattopadhyaya's denunciation of the N/K as meaningless and untrue.[77] The *Matwalla* ranted, 'Satan seems to have possessed the Hindus at that time, and their attitude towards the Muslims at that time seems inexplicable'.[78]

In many ways the 'music before mosque' was an ideal trigger to implode the heritage of the N/K. It involved, within its structure, some of the basic issues of the N/K, which concerned the relationship between space, identity and governance. More importantly, it released a spiralling movement of violence that ripped apart the large and intertwined circuits of social relationships that the N/K had imbricated into the everyday. Obviously, given the comprehensive scope of syncretist desires created by the N/K, the effect of this inversion would be correspondingly large. And this destructive charge was increased by drawing upon an ensemble of long established practices of antagonism. Understanding this explosive process will show how the riots restructured social life in Bengal.

I.v

Any riot derives its fundamental source of power from the dangers posed to the body. This is obvious enough. But what needs to

[77] 'Bartaman Hindu-Musalman Samashya', p. 151.
[78] 30 April, RNP no. 19 of 1926.

be stressed in this context is the fact that riots take to their [il]logical conclusion the process we had observed in Chapter 2, namely the burden of meaning placed by the urban gaze on the communal signifiers of the body. Immediate communal recognition of the body is necessary when unknown victims/attackers are instantly killed/ beaten/ fled from. The absolute semioticization of the body was regarded as an obvious fact by someone who actively participated in the 1946 riots of Calcutta. When asked how he recognized a Muslim, he answered exasperatedly, 'By his *lungi* or beard of course'.[79] What this common sense suppressed was the possibility of being wrong. And if my interviewee did happen to be right on this score, then it only went to show the success of the whole process by which the body had become completely communalized by 1946. In the April riots there were cases of fatal misrecognition. A bearded Hindu was assaulted by his co-religionists; a Bengali Hindu wearing a lungi was likewise beaten up.[80] Obviously, the fears generated by such punishment consolidated the symmetry btween the body and its communal significations. At the same time, the signifiers themselves became a source of contestation: thus riot actions included both the exhortation to shave victims, as well as acts that fulfilled these incitements.[81]

The existential importance of these physical markers were specially important during the April riots. The second phase of these riots was marked predominantly by killings.[82] Normally this took place through individual attacks. But a more horrifying method was that of throwing kerosene drenched rags through the windows of an antagonist's house and then ganging up to protest against, and even actively oppose, the intervention of fire engines.[83] In contrast, physical extinction was much less evident in the mofussil riots of Pabna; in fact, only one person was killed in the whole course of the riots and he was attacked on the first day in the town. A larger distinction appears to have been made

[79] Interview with Rabindranath Ghosh, June 1989.
[80] Home Poll, II/XXV/1926, NAI.
[81] One of the slogans of the riots went as follows (as translated by the correspondent) 'Shave your beard and keep a top lock instead/ the prayer has been abrogated, now wind up your prayer carpet: Letter from Mohammed Shafi, *The Mussalman*, 13 May 1926.
[82] Home Poll, II/XXV/1926, NAI
[83] Home Poll, II/VII/1926, NAI.

there between the existential and the semiotic, which indicates the simultaneous operation of other appeals that were responsible for containing the intensity of violence. The violence is qualified by a personal quality, and seems allied more to punishment than to extinction. In many cases, the victims knew their attackers: during the Pabna riots, Khudiram Mistry, a carpenter, actually tried to talk to the belligerent crowd.[84] Some victims occasionally managed to wrest concessions from them; for instance Benode Sutradhar Mistry a carpenter, was given back his saw by the rioting crowd.[85] The main imperative was to rob the Hindu of the symbols of his wealth and status. Thus a characteristic action was to mix up the stored grain in the house,[86] thereby inflicting a blow to the investment oriented Hindu (a stereotype we had encountered in Chapter 2). There were also instances of compelling bhadralok to share a hookah with Muslims, thereby violating the pretensions to exclusiveness that pollution rules gave them. Clearly, the distinction between the semiotic and the existential meant that direct signifiers of the body were not attacked, or rather, they were attacked only in extreme cases. In rural contexts Hinduness was defined more in terms of the social and economic attributes imputed to the figure of the Hindu.

In an earlier chapter, I had indicated the political-ideological moorings of the body semiotic, which had characterized rural Islam from the nineteenth century. This semiotic acquired a new significance during the N/K. One of the mainstays of the N/K's popularity was the appeal of charkha: among the provinces, Bengal had the second highest number of charkhas that were distributed.[87] Consequently, an overwhelmingly Hindu semiotic was

---

[84] The D.M's description remains a very moving indictment of the inhumanity of riots: 'He [Khudiram] told them that he worked for them and that for this reason his house should be spared but no heed was paid . . . the accused were known to him from before and are thus not strangers to him.' Lalon C. Sarkar vs 1. Basir Shaikh, 2. Mojhir Shaikh, 3. Nasim Khan alias Lachman Khan, Home Poll, II/XI/1926, NAI.

[85] Benode Gobinda Sutradhar vs Patu Khan and Meser Mollah. Ibid.

[86] The D.M. talked of the 'wanton destruction of cooking utensils, the scattering of grain, tearing of cloth and bedding'. Lalon C. Sarkar vs. 1. Basir Shaikh.

[87] Bamford, *Histories*, p. 27. According to Waliullah, one lakh charkhas were distributed free in Bengal, the greater number of beneficiaries being Muslims. *Yuga*, p. 141.

converted, by the process of mass mobilization, into a sign of shared affirmation. Khadi threw up its own heroes. For instance, the story of Khaddar Mian was widely celebrated.[88] This idealization of 'shared-dressing' provides another, more intense, signification to the attacks on 'cross-dressing' during the time of riots. For, in that context, the former became a sign of common betrayal.

Almost naturally, the antagonism spilled over into spaces shared with the other. Road intersections, possibly because of their logistical advantage in affording speedy escape, provided a particularly fertile ground for bellicosity.[89] This acquired a larger significance because of the 'music before mosque' problem. From the introductory section of this chapter it is clear that the site of the 'music before mosque' quarrels were roads, where places of worship were normally situated.

Dinu Chamrawalla's masjid — a site of repeated contests — was located on an intersection of important arteries of Calcutta. Roads are the lifeline, the key to the topography of all modern cities, and Calcutta was no exception. But it had its own distinctive salience there. Roads provided the most palpable, everyday testament to the possibility of a culturally heterogenious life in the city. While more people were beheld by gaze than by name, not all contacts were necessarily anonymous. Roads were also mapped out by the public intimacy of known shopkeepers, business encounters and places of male sociability like the *adda* and tea shops.

The implications of the attack on the heterogeneity of street life becomes profounder when we look at the residential pattern of Calcutta. In addition to divisions fostered by class, the layout tended to follow regional, professional and religious divides. Although neighbourhoods were mixed, the proportions tended to be overwhelmingly weighed towards one collectivity or another. In the context of riots, this imperfectly segregated residential pattern was given a communal clarity. Migrations betrayed the fear of common spaces and contributed to geographical polarization. There was an exodus from Calcutta during the April riots

[88] He was originally from a poor family in Noakhali. After joining the boycott of schools, he went around the countryside with his charkha, until he finally settled into a stationery shop in Sandwip. Waliullah, *Yuga Bichitra*, p. 141.

[89] Home Poll, II/VII/1926, NAI.

which accelerated in the second phase.[90] On the other hand, villagers in Pabna tended to leave for the town where there was a Hindu majority.[91] The intensity of rioting led many, especially in the context of Pabna and Kharagpur, to consider establishing permanently separate localities.[92] Clearly the riots had begun to complete what the 'music before mosque' had started.

The process of antagonistic separation goes into the making of, what bears for me, the chief institutional impress of the riots on social relations. Many elements of this remained operational for months, while some became permanent features. This was the phenomenon of social boycott. Possibly because of its widespread impact during the N/K, it was used by the administration as an index for measuring the extent of communal feeling.[93] However, this diagnostic disposition overlooked the fact that social boycott was also constitutive of communal relations. For, in its repudiation of existing relations of sharing, it acted as a precise institutional homologue of the bitterness spawned by the death of the N/K movement. It may not be a coincidence that the area that saw the greatest amount of N/K activity, namely Eastern Bengal, was also the special locus of social boycott. Through its alliance with communal antagonism, social boycotts spread into networks of little conflicts. These were at times left by riots, or sometimes preceded them and played an important role in generating violence.

The phenomenon of social boycott is generally held to be indicative of a mechanism by which caste relations are readjusted through collective pressure, exerted by boycotting specific services or social relations with another or ones own collectivity/ies. Its aim is, as Guha notes in his analysis of its application to nationalist movements, a coercive one, in addition to (as his argument implies) being an instrument of (re)integration.[94] Communalization extended the functions of social boycott. The aims of discipline and readjustment began to co-exist with the idea of economic autonomy. In the survey of Improvement literature, we have already

[90] See sections on 'Migration' in II/VII and II/XXV, NAI.
[91] Home Poll, II/XI/1926, NAI.
[92] Report of the Relief Committee, *Amrita Bazar Patrika*, 13 July 1926. Administrators in Kharagpur also toyed with the idea of establishing separate Muslim mohallas. Home Poll, II/VIII/1926, NAI.
[93] For instance see Home Poll, II/XXIII/1926, NAI.
[94] Ranajit Guha, 'Discipline and Mobilise', in Partha Chatterjee and Gyanendra Pandey (eds), *Subaltern Studies VII*, Delhi, 1992.

encountered the logic of dissociating from the Hindu as part of the process of advancing one's religious and material lot. While this was not designed to be anti-Hindu, in practical terms it caused a great deal of bitterness. To take an instance from the purely religious sphere, Mansur Ahmed's forefathers decided to repudiate their Madari background not out of antagonism for Hindus, but due to their conversion to the Faraizi faith. However, the unintended consequence of this conversion, as Mansur Ahmed recalls, was antagonism with their Hindu neighbours that followed their withdrawal from the common festivities, participation in which had been a feature of their earlier practices.[95]

At the same time, Improvement literature did not take into account the possibility of the socially superior using economic segregation as a disciplinary weapon. This happened in the boycott of many Muslim professional groups by the economically superior Hindus of Calcutta and Dhaka. The bitterness caused by this disciplinary mode fed into the ideal of social and economic self-dependence, to produce a mutually reinforcing spiral of antagonism. The bitterness was submerged by joy when a red sheet, circulating during the April riots, celebrated the violence for arousing the 'latent spirit of the Mussalmans'. It declared that, 'We are supremely happy at the decision of the Marwaris to boycott us. A few such shocks and time will show whether India will remain a land of the Hindus or become a stronghold of the Mussalmans.'[96] In the context of riots, this may reflect simple bravado. But a more complex affectivity is produced in other contexts. This can be seen in the response to a boycott imposed by Hindus on the Muslims of Kushtea. The speaker was Ashrafuddin, who had been an 'extreme non-cooperative' [sic] and still proclaimed himself to be a Swarajist. On the one hand, the sense of betrayal was palpable when he characterized the boycott as showing: 'the arrogance of wealth, the arrogance of learning, it is to put you down, nothing else'. On the other hand, the complicated emotional texture of this antagonism was supplemented by his moorings in the discourse of Improvement. Beginning his speech by criticizing Muslims for producing their poor and helpless state, he went on to exhort his audience to use self-reliance as a weapon. He concluded by declaring: 'Sell to the

[95] *Atmakatha*, p. 22.
[96] *Amrita Bazar Patrika*, 24 April 1926.

Hindus but do not buy from them. The Hindus are saying, "we won't buy from the Muslims". What further declaration of war can there be?.'[97]

Precisely because of its emotional and institutional groundings, social boycott was rarely a one-shot affair. It tended to go through a long and tortured process of breakdown and integration. The Janmashtami festival of Dhaka, in keeping with the general practices of rural Bengal, was observed by Muslims: it was customary to employ Muslim musicians and labourers in the procession, while wealthy Muslims lent elephants and horses. Other Muslims, including villagers, came to watch. There was then a complex configuration of economics, neighbourliness, common symbols of prestige, and the shared excitement of a grand ritual. In common with some other mofussil conflict spots, social boycott preceded the Dhaka riots (in contrast with Calcutta), undergoing a tortuous process of antagonism and disentanglement that culminated in direct violence. A careful campaign was conducted by the mohalla sardars to boycott the Janmashtami procession in 1926, since Hindus had planned to play music in front of two mosques. Amongst those who participated in the boycott were hackney carriage drivers who, in their wit and vitality, had provided an emblem of the shared 'life' of the city.[98] After the attack on the procession, the Hindus started a boycott of the carriage drivers and included the masons and cartmen in it. In turn, this created more economic hardship and bitterness and led to another round of violence.[99] Similarly, the popular support for the Patuakhali satyagraha was preceded by a comparable history of boycotts of *tamashas* and of Saraswati puja.[100]

Social boycott also provided a low-temperature alternative to riots. It could extend the embattled psyche of riots without inflicting physical damages. We may recall the last clause of Ashrafuddin's injunctions equating boycott with war. By the latter part

[97] Home Poll, Confidential, File no. 140, Serial nos 1–9, WBSA.

[98] S.K. Datta, a victim of the Partition who spent his childhood and early part of his maturity in that city, remembered the phaeton drivers with affectionate respect, especially their sharp repartees, much in the same way a Calcutta resident will proudly tell you of its street humour to vindicate the superiority of that city's life. Interview with S.K. Datta, June 1992.

[99] All details on the Dhaka riots in this paragraph, except where otherwise cited, is drawn from Home Poll, II/XX/1926, NAI.

[100] GOB, File no. 500/1–16/1926, WBSA.

of 1926, social boycott had spread to many districts, concentrated mainly in Faridpur, Bakarganj, Bogra and in two Mymensingh towns[101] while, during the riots, Hindus formed a separate bazar in Pabna town.[102]

However, it was the direct violence of riots that produced the most lasting effects of boycott. Even in October, it was reported that the Marwaris still abstained from using Muslim bandsmen, coachmen and syces in Calcutta.[103] Although, boycott could not remain a permanent feature,[104] unerasable changes occurred in the compositional structure of the economy. The Muslim domination of the dyer trade was broken after Marwaris imported Hindu dyers.[105] It is also after the April riots, that Muslim butchers, who embodied Muslim violence, were boycotted and Hindu butchers entered the trade for the first time.[106] Moreover, since Hindus were the main customers of Muslim dominated trades such as carpentry, tailoring, binding, carriage driving, the withdrawal of their patronage meant that many Muslim traders had to change their occupation. The consequence was a mushrooming of saloons, laundries, *mudi* (grocery) shops, repair workshops in Muslim areas. On the other hand, Hindus took to carpentry, tailoring, binding, fruit selling and horse-carriage driving.[107] More traumatic were the scars left by simple acts of brutality that extended the principle of boycott. The most notable of these was when Hindu doctors refused to attend to Muslim patients during the April riots. This motivated the founding of the Islamia Hospital.[108] Which, like the butcher's shops, became another silent reminder of that horror.

The principle of social segregation was carried over into the sphere of governance. Pressurizing the administration involved

---

[101] Home Poll, II/XXII/1926, NAI.

[102] *Amrita Bazar Patrika*, 13 July 1926.

[103] Home Poll, II/XXII/1926, NAI.

[104] For instance it was reported that the boycott of a mela, started two years earlier in Pabna, was being eased. *Fortnightly Reports*, October second half, No. 1 of 1928.

[105] Ibid.

[106] Waliullah, *Yuga* p. 17.

[107] Ibid., pp. 235–7.

[108] Ibid. This was in contrast to Pabna, where despite being beaten up earlier and deprived of his umbrella and stick, Pranbandhu Chakrabarty, a non-registered medical practitioner went to treat a Muslim patient. See Emperor vs Umir Pramanik and 86 others. Home Poll, II/XI/126, NAI.

criticism of its executive functioning. The highly communalized Relief Committees[109] methodically campaigned against the police, a process which culminated in the controversy following the transfer of P.C. Lahiri, the deputy commissioner in charge of North Calcutta, where the riots had occurred. He was an obvious scapegoat for the general indifference of the police (in contrast, Armstrong, the white police commissioner, was praised!). But he was an effective one for producing more controversy. While the *Amrita Bazar Patrika* led the chorus of criticism against this move, the *Mussalman* took exception to his replacement by another Hindu. Of profounder import than the squabble over individual transfers was the implications of the criticism of the police.[110]

They provided the most widely encountered face of the administration. The police constable was — and remains, as a walk in Calcutta today will show — close to the poor in class and culture while being their most brutal, daily oppressor. In other words, his position could be aspired to by the largest number of common people, while the imperative to do so (given his powers) during the riots would be at its most intense. Not surprisingly, many demands were made to appoint Muslims as policemen. This extended the quota principle and emerged as another subject of communal controversy.[111] By extension, the magistrate's post, since it involved judging rioters, became communally sensitive; something which the administration consciously realized and tended sometimes to

---

[109] Just after the outbreak of the April riots a Muslim Relief Committee was set up, followed shortly by a Hindu Relief Committee. The objectives included providing for the families of those killed, distributing food to those in want. But the Police Report goes on to observe, 'Both the committees were . . . intensely communal in spirit . . . ', with some of their pamphlets having a distinctively 'provocative' edge. Home Poll, II/XXV/1926, NAI.

[110] Editorial, *The Mussalman*, 13 April 1926. Police personnel were communally involved from the Talla riots in 1897. Rafiuddin Ahmed, *The Bengali Muslims*, p. 181. In 1926 there were reports of police involvement in looting (corroborated by official investigations, Home Poll, II/VII/26, NAI), and targeting of Muslim bustis, *The Mussalman*, 8 May 1926.

[111] The Dhaka Muslim Association, in response to the April riots, called for an increase in the number of Muslims in the Police. *The Mussalman*, 4 May 1926. The Marwari Federation condemned the victimization of Hindu policemen, stating that this was an outflow of the Muslim attempt to 'affect the efficiency and purity of administration. Letter to the private secretary to the Viceroy from the Marwari Association, Calcutta, 29 June 1926, No. 205/1926, NAI.

manipulate.[112] The communalization of the legal wings of the Executive added another link between the fight over job reservations and the conditions of ordinary folk. This crystallized into the desire for a communally sensitive, if not segregated, administration.

I.vi

So far, I have been attempting to understand the contribution of riots in constructing communal identities. In this, I have followed the normal course of studies of the meaning of riots which begin from and terminate in, the binarization of identity they produce. These include the work of Natalie Zemon Davis and Suranjan Das. The assumption that participation in collective violence is premised on belonging to one or the other group is undoubtedly true, even if it is tautological. What is overlooked is that the process of constructing identities involves relationships with rival identities, even within the course of riots themselves. These other claims sometimes syncopated their assertions. In Hajinagar, Naihati, at the beginning of June 1926, a quarrel which started on caste lines, transformed itself in minutes, into an intense communal battle.[113] The specific ways in which communal identity associates with other claims in my period will, I suggest, give us an understanding of logic and operational strength of communalism itself.

But before exploring that subject, it may be worthwhile to see the limits imposed on communal riots by the violence itself. Even as the April riots were cheered on by the antagonistic communities, they bred, at the same time, a sense of oppressiveness. Both sentiments sometimes coexisted. A few days after the celebratory report on the defence of the Kalitolla Temple, the *Amrita Bazar Patrika* carried a set of headlines that read: 'CITY IN DISMAL SILENCE/ DREARY ISOLATION REIGNS EVERYWHERE/ Unprovoked Attacks on Citizens/All Talks of Conciliation Fail'. It was followed by a story of how festivities in a house were suspended after it

---

[112] The administrators deliberated a long while over the religious identity of the legal personnel who would be involved in the adjudication of cases of rioting in Pabna. While it was decided to have an Anglo-Indian for a magistrate, it was suggested that a Muslim lawyer should be used to prosecute Muslim accused, and vice versa. Letter from Marr to Moberly, 10 July GOB: Political: Confidential, No. 317/1-31/1926, WBSA.

[113] *The Mussalman*, 3 June 1926.

produced false alarms. The city was reborn in fear, creating an utter individuation of life. This was intensified by comprehensively negating the throbbing and intoxicating life of Calcutta's streets. The apprehension of isolation in such circumstances could assume the quality of non-being. 'The monotony of death-like calm in those localities [riot affected] would suddenly be disturbed by the howl of a goonda suddenly coming out of a lane and stabbing the stray passerby . . . . Silence reigns supreme till another hooligan repeats the bloody trick', wrote the *Patrika* in its editorial. The near expressionistic power of this passage derives from the analogy drawn between the stricken passerby and the lifelessness of the street, which is generalized by the rhythms of communal violence.

If isolation was the precondition for the creation of a seamless community, then it followed that its oppressiveness would breed initiatives in cross-communal collectivities. This took place under the aegis of appeals to locality based identities — which, as we have seen, were also a source of mobilization for violence. The *para* (neighbourhood) was an important component of Calcutta's residential geography, and pride in its distinctiveness provided the organizing impulse. The young men of Muraripur in Calcutta formed a Defence Party to repulse outsiders, irrespective of their religious affiliation; in Narkeldanga, Muslims came to the help of the defending Hindus because they were neighbours. Equally heartening was the resistance provided to communalists even when both sides hailed from the same locality. It testified to the demands made by a simple and comprehensive commitment to human relationships. In Nikashipara, local Hindus restored peace when co-religionists of that place attacked a mosque; their efforts at initiating peace by forming a joint Defence Committee spread to neighbouring Shyambazar as well, resulting in Hindu and Muslim leaders of both localities jointly conducting a door-to-door campaign.[114]

Nevertheless, in the absence of any larger ideological consolidation of these efforts, they simply remained signs of hopeful efforts, rather than anything more. Incidentally, it is a token of the comparative powerlessness of these initiatives that even my narrative has been dependent on the mercies of press policy. It was only after an editorial appeared in the *Patrika* which talked of the need for conciliation that such efforts were reported at all.

[114] *Amrita Bazar Patrika*, 1926, April issues.

A more effectively implosive range of identities were those that sprung from a paradoxical characteristic of communalism itself. In order to generalize its appeal, communalism perforce had to appeal to other identities. We have seen this being done in the case of gender as well as for regional affiliations. The HMS campaign, begun in 1925, to involve the Bengalis, bore fruit, as we have seen, in the riots. But Bengali identity also revealed its dangerous autonomy.[115] During the Maniktalla 'Spur' incident, Bengalis stoutly refused to be goaded into violence because they did not wish to host riots during the Durga Puja.[116] The most important instance of this paradoxical relationship concerns caste. There was an active, symbiotic relationship between riots and caste. Caste reform activity carried out under the auspices of the Hindu Mahasabha was an established feature of Pabna and Mymensingh.[117] The Hindu bhadralok initiators of the Pabna riot toured the district and held forth on the problems of untouchability.[118] Communal polarization afforded the prospect of mobilizing low castes, as we have seen in the context of Patuakhali. Nevertheless, the hurdle of upper-caste superiority refused to disappear. For instance, far from offering the slightest hint of social equality to the lower castes, the Patuakhali Satyagraha Committee merely called attention to the contribution of untouchables in the movement and requested the upper castes to spread the Vedantic vision.[119]

[115] According to a letter from B.F.Bharucha, Mina Peshawari appealed to Bengalis to desist from rioting since Muslims had a quarrel only with the Marwaris. *Amrita Bazar Patrika*, 30 April 1926. The fear of language-based unity among Bengalis had prompted a massive diatribe against its possibility in the *Arya Jivan*. 3 December, RNP no. 49 of 1925, NAI.

[116] 'Report by C.S. Fairweather, 17.10.1926', Home Poll, II/XXIII/1926, NAI.

[117] This was probably due to the influence of Digindranarayan Bhattacharya. For instance many meetings were held in 1923 to extend the services of Napits and Dhopas to Malis. These places included, (besides Tangail where a meeting was held in 1910), Muktagacha, Gourepur and Serjegunje. *Serajgunj Malijatir Udbodhan (Srotriya Narasundar Praptir Bibaran): Kaokola, Serajgunj Hindu Mahasabha Birat Adhibeshan*, (Chairman and Coordinator, Digindranarayan Bhattacharya), Calcutta, 1925.

[118] The chief guests in the first general meeting of the Sujanagar Hindu Sabha included Jogendra Nath Maitra, Indujyoti Majumdar and Ashutosh Lahiri; the last named was Secretary of the Hindu Relief Committee. The meeting culminated in high-class Hindus accepting water from the hands of untouchables, *Amrita Bazar Patrika*, 5 November 1926.

[119] Swami Gyananda, *Patuakhali*, p. 6.

As we have seen, despite Namasudra–Muslim riots in 1926, the Namasudras, along with the Rajbansis, dissociated themselves from Hindu communalism. The unifying power of riots was obviously a limited one. The interests of participants was sometimes limited to just rioting. The process of communal identity formation is subject to the vicissitudes of time, and its apprehensions of the antagonistic other is moulded by the particular condition it finds itself as a collectivity at any given period. Interests may not be shared even when there are common affiliations of identity and ideology. This is evident in the case of the working class.

It was in this period that communalism showed it could disrupt working class action. The workers of Kharagpur established a history of united struggle when they struck work against the policy of retrenchment in 1923.[120] The class-based union, however, faced competition from the Hindu communal union, once a branch of the Sabha had been started there. The impact of the latter was evident in the repeated rioting that took place throughout the late twenties in that town.[121] In Calcutta the working class areas were located at the peripheries and thickly clustered with migrants from the United Provinces and Bihar. They provided the main conduit for the spread of riots into Bengal. In 1925, a series of intense riots broke out in Kidderpore, Kankinarrah and Titagarh, involving dock and jute mill workers. There were also riots in these areas in 1926, notably in Naihati and Kidderpore. What is significant, however, is that while these riots did not coincide with the main city based riots, the latter also did not spread to these places. Although there were constant apprehensions during the April riots that workers from Howrah and the mill areas would be joining up with their co-religionists, this did not take place.[122]

What occurred were attacks on European personnel of the Gauripur Jute Mills, after a European manager, in the exercise of his traditional prerogatives, kicked a native worker.[123] The

[120] *Fortnightly Reports*, January second half, 1923, NAI.
[121] The existing Labour Union, it was said, was antagonistically disposed towards the Hindu Sabha, since 'it is intended to embrace all communities'. 'Report from R.N. Reid, D.M. Midnapore to commissioner of Burdwan Division, 30.5.1926', Home Poll, II/VII/1926, NAI. A year earlier the Kankinarrah Labour Union had been divided because of communalization. *Amrita Bazar Patrika*, 29 December 1925.
[122] Fortnightly Reports, April first half, No. 112 of 1926, NAI.
[123] *Amrita Bazar Patrika*, 9 April 1926.

spontaneity of the worker's reaction stemmed from a non-economic protest against the racist dehumanization of the workers. But this gesture also provided an analogue of the equally brutal fact of the dispensability of the workers by the uncompromising machinery of racist capitalist profit. The new shift system was being introduced around the same time as the riots took place, throwing thousands of workers out of their jobs and reducing the working week to four days.[124] It takes little effort of sympathy to realise the implications of this on migrants whose condition of deprivation, sacrifice and hope could critically intensify in this situation, creating concerns that could not be dovetailed into communal conflict.

Part II

II.i

On the one hand were communal riots, and, on the other, class-based, anti-colonial strikes. The relationship between working-class identity and communal mobilization was a highly fluctuating one. Working-class mobilization could both resist communalization as well as become its active constituents. Incidentally, it is interesting that the peaks of working-class communal mobilization did not always coincide with the high points of province-wide communal mobilization. Clearly, class could create temporal differentiations within the communal process. This unstable and differentiated relationship is an important clue to examining a dominant strand of understanding on communalism in Bengal, namely, that it translates class identities into communal ones.

A great deal of the persuasiveness of the idea that rural class relations of Bengal can be simply translated into communal cleavages stems from the ability of this equation to service many arguments. Ideologues of Muslim separatism like Waliullah drew on the overall correlation of composition between Hindu (landlord) and Muslim (peasant), to prove their point.[125] The Bengal Congress used precisely this equation to prove that disturbing the social status quo in the countryside would sponsor communal divisions.[126] A

---

[124] Ibid., 8 April 1926.
[125] Waliullah, *Yuga* p. 287.
[126] These were the arguments trotted out to Mansur Ahmed by his Congress friends. *Amar Dekha Rajnitir*, p. 71.

more precise specification of the general understanding was provided by Muzaffar Ahmed in 1926, when he wrote that class conflicts were given a communal nomenclature by vested interests.[127] The idea of (re)naming as the basis of communalism crops up in an unexpected guise in the sophisticated model construction of Partha Chatterjee. His assertion of communalism as a linguistic conspiracy of the secularist State,[128] when put beside his parallel contention of a 'relatively undifferentiated ryoti peasantry' in predominantly Muslim Eastern Bengal,[129] suggests that communalism is a matter of redesignating the experience of an integrated peasant community.

Two assumptions underpin this approach. The first is that the relationship between class and communal identities is fairly simple and unvaried. One is simply transposed on to the other in a process that is implicitly undifferentiated. The second important assumption is that there is a symmetry between class and communal divisions, which implies that both sets of groupings were monolithic. Without an assumption of the symmetry between these two, the act of renaming cannot be fluently accomplished. I will try to examine these assumptions in the light of two focal issues, that is, of the voting on the Bengal Tenancy Amendment Bill (BTAB) in the Legislative Council in 1928, and the riots in Dhaka and Kishoreganj.

Chatterjee's painstaking disclosure of the voting pattern in the Legislative Council between (Hindu) pro-landlord Swarajist votes and the (Muslim) pro-ryot/bargadar votes on the Amendment question, makes the debate an emblem of his overall argument. At the outset it should be noted that the existence of a few stubborn voters who could not be discounted as Hindus, prevents a fluent translation of Hindu into landlord.[130] Nor could these voters be dismissed as mere exceptions who proved the rule. For instance, J.L. Bannerjee, who took a consistent stand on voting for ryots,

---

[127] 'Sampradayikatar Bisham Parinam', *Nirbachita Rachana Sankalan*, Calcutta: 1986, f.pub. 1976, p. 17.

[128] Chatterjee, *Bengal*, p. lii.

[129] Ibid., p. 61.

[130] A typical instance of the way the exceptions interrupted the communal symmetry can be cited from the report of the debate on the Transfer Fee, which started with, 'On the question of percentage the Government as also all the groups in the House except Mahomedans and three Hindus supported the 20 per cent'. *Amrita Bazar Patrika*, 28 August 1928.

played a prominent role. He was the first to raise an objection to the provision for a twenty-five per cent transfer fee to be given to the landlord, which later became a rallying issue for the pro-ryot lobby. In the immediate context of the BTAB, Bannerjee, along with K.C. Raychaudhury who had been the Secretary of the Tenants' Party within the Legislature, addressed a joint meeting with Sir Abdur Rahim who was hated as the chief individual symbol of Muslim communalism in Bengal. The assembly focussed on the *salami* question in the BTAB.[131] On the other hand, Bannerjee was the first to begin a serious debate within the Council on the question of landlordism in general. Not the least significant fact of this intervention was that it was launched as a criticism of the praise that had been showered on landlordism by Sir A.K. Ghuznavi. The latter, as we know, had played a leading role in mobilizing objections to 'music before mosque'.[132]

Bannerjee had behind him the authority of a political formation composed of multiple strands which, despite their differences, had constantly complicated the simple translation of class into communal mobilization. There was firstly the repudiated heritage of the Swarajist mobilization of ryots. Under the leadership of prominent Muslim leaders like Akram Khan and blessed by C.R. Das himself, it had been associated with mobilizing objections to *nazar* (transfer fee) payment to the landlords.[133] While quickly aborted, it nevertheless provided an impetus for Hindu tenants to mobilize themselves. The Howrah District Tenants Conference demanded many of the key provisions of the BTAB, ending with the invocation of 'Bande Mataram'.[134] Hindu and Muslim leaders often conferred together on the ryot question in forums such as the Krishak O Rayat Sabha.[135] More importantly for the politics of this period was the fact that this nearly still-born heritage of Swarajist ryot mobilization was carried on by the opposition within the party, led by Birendranath Sasmal. Sasmal was very close to

[131] Ibid., 12 August 1928.
[132] *Amrita Bazar Patrika*, 7 August 1928.
[133] *Fortnightly Reports*, March first half, June second half, 1924, NAI.
[134] *Amrita Bazar Patrika*, 1 November 1925.
[135] For instance an open air meeting of this organization, was graced by the following individuals: Wahed Hossain, Shah Emdadul Huque, both MLCs, Bhuban Mohon Ghosh, Bhagirath Das, Pt Shyamlal Goswami. *Amrita Bazar Patrika*, 1 March 1925.

J.L. Bannerjee, and, in fact, went beyond him to press unsuccessfully for bargadari rights in 1929 at Contai.[136] Sasmal signified the low-caste response on this question. Interestingly, the only representative of the Rajbansis in the Council is counted amongst the most consistently pro-ryot members in the table compiled by Partha Chatterjee.[137] Finally, proximate to these groups, but going away from them ideologically, were the leftists who changed the name of their group from that of the Labour Swaraj Party to the Labour and Peasant Party in 1925 in order to emphasize their concern with the proceedings of the BTAB.[138] Not the least significant aspect of this group was that they both showed the near impossibility of automatically translating class into communal affiliation; of the sixteen members who made up the Peasants and Workers Party in 1926, twelve were Muslims.

Equally complicating was the response of the urban bhadralok to the Tenancy Bill. This may be seen in the unexpected response of the *Amrita Bazar Patrika* to the Bill when it was first mooted in 1925. The *Amrita Bazar Patrika* characterized the Amendment as adversely affecting the interests of the poor, middle classes.[139] This did not prevent it from supporting the Amendments; it even criticized the landlords for their intransigence. Their overall view implied that the proposals were not particularly dramatic.[140] It is interesting to note here that the BTAB did not become a major issue among the Calcutta middle class in 1925. The Calcutta professionals did not subsist on their rent from land alone; after all, this was the reason why they were in Calcutta. It was the Pact that had affected their interests in a more fundamental manner, and opposition to the latter was crucial in motivating communal bitterness in the province.

[136] Tanika Sarkar, *Popular Movements*, p. 83.
[137] His name was Nagendra Narayan Ray. *Bengal*, p. 89.
[138] February second half, 1926, *Fortnightly Reports*, No. 112, NAI.
[139] It stated 'that under the category of landlords [were included] practically the entire middle class of *Bhadralogs* of Bengal'. Although it said that nothing should be done to 'bring about the ruin of this poor middle class', it also upheld the need for providing protection to the ryots. 26 November 1925.
[140] For instance it said the provisions on sharecroppers 'though important are not drastic'. In a later editorial, it bemoaned the 'unpleasant spectacle' of bitter internecinal war, but concluded that it blamed the landlords more than the tenants'. Ibid., 10 and 17 August 1928.

Instead of resorting to communal appeals, the Swarajists, in their opposition to the Bill, defended class interests — but, as a sub-set of regional ones. Here another facet of the debate needs underlining, that is, the interlinkage between class and region. The Tenancy debate provided the occasion for a great deal of explicit idealization of the landlord. He was held up to be a patriarchal exemplar who cared for his tenants. More importantly, his wealth also provided the guarantee that the interests of agriculture would be safeguarded by preventing the land from slipping out of the hands of agriculturists, an eventuality that would take place if land was made easily transferrable by unreliably poor and ignorant ryots. The preying non-agriculturists, it was repeatedly specified in newspaper articles, primarily denoted Marwari moneylenders and European capitalists.[141] In other words, the antagonism between landlords and moneylenders was overlaid by a strong appeal to provincial sentiment.

The Swarajists were using this occasion to crystallize a political constituency. Nalini Ranjan Sarkar, the Chief Whip, led the Swarajist defence of the status quo. His speech defended the interests of the mofussil bhadralok and, by extension, the big zamindars. It was not simply aimed at satisfying the prior economic demands of his basic constituency, but also at crystallizing its popular self-image. The latter was constituted by a combination of poverty and cultural attainment of the mofussil bhadralok. Nalini Sarkar argued for the protection for their interests negatively, by talking of their lack of wealth, and positively, by invoking their apparently immense contribution to the cultural life of the villages. This discourse tried to displace peasant claims on two fronts. On the one hand, it bestowed the halo of economic victimhood on itself, thereby detaching the idea of poverty from that of oppression; on the other hand, it replaced the traditional yoking of rural Bengal (with its powerful evocations of authenticity) with the peasantry and the notion of labour, by an invocation of cultural pride. The two elements of this discourse, that of poverty and of cultural pride, were linked together by the threatening figure of the moneylender. The latter emerged as a danger to provincial identity. Nalini Sarkar was engaged in producing a defence of landlordism that could disarm the appeal to

---

[141] See for instance, *Amrita Bazar Patrika*, 14 August 1928.

the interests of the (Muslim) peasant by appealing to the 'Bengali'.[142]

The Swarajist interest in this cannot be explained only by reference to the issues raised by the BTAB. The political consolidation of a mofussil class through this more comprehensive discursive appeal makes sense in the context of what was happening elsewhere. That year was dominated by agitation against the Simon Commission. In February there had been a highly successful hartal against the Commission in Calcutta, and the Congress manifesto announcing the ambition for Dominion status was circulated in the middle of the Amendment debate. It was followed by the release of the Nehru Report which spelt out the Congress stand on the nature of representation to be provided in the new post-independent state. Clearly, a new round of nationalist agitation was in the offing. In this context it made sense to prepare the grounds for the mobilization of rural Bengal, which, as the N/K had shown, was where the agitation could really shake the Empire.

The fact that an anti-communal possibility was unrealized, points to the absence of adequate political intervention. The presence of Leftists was far too small. On the other hand, the Swarajist stand was bondaged to history. They may have announced their non-communal intention, but this was not enough. The repudiation of the Bengal Pact had already given them a communal aura. Further, the appeal to Bengaliness lacked credibility. Their claim to a supra-communal regional identity had been ruptured along with the Pact. Consequently, the specific stand of the Swarajists in the Tenancy Bill debate had to carry the burden of a history which had to be explicitly addressed if its position was to be prevented from being interpreted by a communal framework. And this was crucial, for the communal frame of reference had spread from the staunchly communal Muslims to those who had earlier pinned a great deal of hope on the Pact. Mansur Ahmad's reaction is a case in point. Ahmad, who describes himself as a 'Congressi' Muslim, remembered the BTAB issue as one in which the Hindus were ranged aginst the Muslims.[143]

Given the nature of Muslim responses to their stand, the

---

[142] Sarkar said that although the middle class was poor, 'they hold up the banner of culture in the villages; it is this class that has contributed to all that our province can take pride in'. *Amrita Bazar Patrika*, 9 August 1928.

[143] *Amar Dekha Rajnitir*, p. 63.

Swarajist 'mistake' can be seen as the consequence of not so much negligence as an ostentatious indifference to an obvious political fallout. What was clearly revealed in the Swarajist stand on the BTAB was that it refused to recognize any consequences that the Muslim identity of the peasantry may have on its policies. It is a communalism of silence produced by the historical sub-text of the action, rather than of overt mobilization. In general, the mid-twenties presented a situation of hybrid identity formation which was produced by both the N/K as well as the communal mobilization that followed it. Any identity mobilization in these circumstances had perforce to be hybrid, that is, it had to reiterate its hold by addressing, whether silently or explicitly, the force and claim of other identities and the opportunities for counter-mobilization that they possessed.

Nevertheless, the BTAB was an issue in which communal categories could at best reinforce class ones, not replace them. It is worth noting that the main fallout of the mobilization around the BTAB was the formation of the Nikhil Banga Praja Party, which was to be later renamed the Krishak Praja Party (KPP). It was based on class identity. Consequently, it could tap the possibilities opened up by the language of class, and ally with the low castes in a bid to gain political power. It is this alliance that we see consolidated by the end of this period in 1930, when a combine of Proja and low-caste legislators battled against Swarajist opposition and much communal propoganda, to pass the Primary Education Bill in the Council.[144]

However, the KPP was not based exclusively on class, but rested on an unstable heritage. The KPP was constituted solely of Muslim members (although supported by J.L. Bannerjee) and emerged from the recently established Muslim group in the Council. This was because of its mooring in the discourse of the Muslim peasant. As we have seen in Chapter 2, this was a hybrid formation in which the two terms of this identity — Muslim and peasant — gestured at alternate avenues of social and political possibilities, even as they were present together within the same discourse and often in the same text. The hybridity was not a matter of simple co-presence alone, for, by drawing upon the economic concepts of Islam, primarily those concerning strictures on moneylending,

---

[144] McPherson, *The Muslim Microcosm*, p. 115.

class elements could be inserted into an anti-Hindu campaign. This was evident in the anti-Saha moneylender agitations centred in Manikganj and Dhaka from 1924. This outbreak provided the space for communally minded preachers to attempt a reorientation of basically class issues for a communal aim. We will encounter a similar campaign in Kishoreganj during 1930.

Nevertheless, distinctions were never completely bridged. An individual like Mansur Ahmad, who was dedicated to the class basis of the KPP, found himself in conflict with communal interests.[145] The schism was apparent in movements as well. Regarding the sustained struggle between (Muslim) ryot and (Hindu) moneylenders in the two places just mentioned, the colonial authorities had to admit that 'in spite of agitations to convert it into a communal dispute, [it has] been confined to its original economic aspect, and the result is . . . a considerable improvement in the status of the Muhamadan cultivator in these districts'.[146] The mobilizations on ryot and Muslim identities were kept separate even by those anti-Swarajists who forefronted the importance of Muslim identity in ryot mobilization. Thus, as an analogue of the federated character of the N/K which had signalled its unity-in-separation by holding their conferences in different but adjoining spaces, an Ulema and Ryot conference was held in Gaffargaon, Mymensingh, where one part of the conference engaged with the question of Islamic education, while the other directed itself to a detailed consideration of ryoti demands that coincided with the concerns of the BTAB.[147] Although this gap posed no china wall, and there were constant overlaps, it seems to have shaped district-level politics of this period. This can be seen by a cursory comparison of Mymensingh with Pabna.

Along with Pabna, Mymensingh was a district with the highest incidence of image desecrations in the twenties. Nor did it lack other features of communal enthusiasm, such as disputes over 'music before mosque' and go-korbani. Even more suggestively, at the end of 1926, almost as if in imitation of the events in Pabna, there was a procession organized by Hindu landlords led by Shashikanta Acharya Chaudhury, an important HMS supporter, which passed the principal roads while ostentatiously

---

[145] *Amar Dekha Rajnitir*, p. 66.
[146] July first half, *Fortnightly Reports*, No. 25 of 1925, NAI.
[147] *Amrita Bazar Patrika*, 7 January 1925.

playing music.[148] Yet no communal riots took place here in this period. A possible reason was the intense class struggle between Muslim cultivators and Hindu landlord/moneylenders in many places. On the one hand, the Hindu landlords there acted as the vanguard of mobilization against the BTAB. On the other hand, the district was a site for a massive spate of ryot meetings, especially in Hindu landlord-dominated areas such as Gaffargaon and Muktagacha. In contrast, Pabna did not rank as a site for proja/ryot movements,[149] although, as we will see, it had a class struggle of a different sort. It should be emphasized that the Pabna riot was basically communal. The poor were indiscriminately targeted, and the principle of conflict was not determined by class solidarities.[150] While the immediate trigger was the April events in Calcutta, the riots had already been prepared for by a spate of image desecrations and meetings that stressed Muslim exclusiveness. The Muslim intelligentsia of a number of villages in Serajgunj had got together to organize a branch of the Tanzeem, the manifesto of which made no reference to class demands.[151]

If the Swarajist response to the BTAB debate suggested that the conversion of class into communalism could proceed via an absence of consideration of the Other, the Muslim initiative evolving from the contention reveals a complex and unstable inter-articulation of class and communal formations. Class and communal mobilization within the framework of the Muslim peasant can be mutually distinctive, yet also allow its interlinkages to appropriate class categories by communal ones. This is a far cry from the effortless translation of categories that commentators have assumed.

What we have in this period of composite identity formation is a relationship of political inter-articulation between different identities. The latter are distinct from each other since they unravel

[148] The procession was about a mile long, and included no less than twenty music parties with about one thousand processionists in uniform, armed with guns, swords, spears and lathis. It was held in Muktagacha, Acharya Chaudhury's seat. *Amrita Bazar Patrika*, 19 October 1926.

[149] Tanika Sarkar lists Dhaka, Mymensingh, Barisal and Faridpur as the main bases of the Proja movement, *National Movement*, p. 108.

[150] The objects and modes of attack did not reveal economic motivations. GOB: Political: Confidential, 317/1–31/1926, WBSA.

[151] *The Mussalman*, 1 June 1926.

different social and political possibilities. At the same time, each contains — whether explicitly, as the case of moneylending which allows an easy communalization of class appeals, or inferentially, such as the historical sub-text of communalism that the regional-cum-class appeals of the Swarajists carries with it — opportunities for appropriation by alternate identity formations. Another important instance of this process is the ryot–Muslim–bargadari relationship. Incidentally, this problem also raises questions about the assumption of a homogeneous Muslim ryot class that props up the translation approach.

This assumption is based on seeing the Muslim consolidation at the Council as representative of, for all practical purposes, an undifferentiated Muslim peasantry. In this connection, the findings of Nakazato regarding the active prevalence of bargadari tenanacies throughout Eastern Bengal is important, if not crucial.[152] Certainly the programmes of the ryot meetings that proliferated in the mid-twenties, spanning a vast range of places such as Calcutta, Mymensingh and Nadia, all point to an almost uniform opposition against the bargadari provisions.[153] When the question of granting the bargadars occupany rights came up in 1933–34, the KPP opposed it![154] Given this context, it seems likely that the pro-ryot legislators' support to the bargadari provisions in the Council stemmed from a realization of political benefits to be acquired from supporting proposals they knew would be voted out.

In fact, the bargadari question suggests the complexity of the

---

[152] Nakazato has shown the central importance that Tenancy legislations had for bargadari system in general (to which must be added the fears raised by possible legislations, such as those that led to the widespread eviction of bargadars after the Kerr Committee's recommendations). Nakazato points out the way bargadars also farmed rayati/underrayati land, which concealed the actual amount of land under this system and the numbers working under it. See Naraiki Nakazato, *Agrarian System in Eastern Bengal, c. 1870–1910*, Calcutta, 1994, pp. 81–8.

[153] Anti-Bargadari resolutions were passed in Rayat meetings in Calcutta (*Amrita Bazar Patrika*, 21 January 1925), Mymensingh (Ibid., 4 February 1925), and Nadia (Ibid., 9 February 1925).

[154] As early as 1925, Huq had presided over a rayat meeting in Dhaka which asked the government to maintain the status quo regarding the Barga question, Ibid., 11 February. For KPP opposition, see Adrienne Cooper, *Sharecropping and Sharecroppers Struggles in Bengal, 1930–1950*, Calcutta, 1988, pp. 126.

communal process.[155] We had seen in the case of the Rajbansis, that the turn to communal mobilization coincided with the problem of confronting the bargadari issue. A similar relationship is observable in Pabna. Among the Eastern districts, it was distinguished by the highest number of bargadars who possessed the most stable and advantageous arrangements.[156] And, along with Jessore, Pabna had the largest number of recorded instances of bargadar movements in this century.[157] The announcement of the BTAB appears to have motivated a fresh round of agitation amongst them. Significantly, a year before the riots, a bargadar movement had broken out in which both Hindus and Muslims had participated in Pabna; it was correspondingly pacified by Hindu and Muslim leaders. This had taken place in Chatmohar which was one of the epicentres of the riots.[158] In an earlier chapter I have referred to a similar incident that happened in Hadal in 1925, where a bargadar struggle was succeeded by a communally oriented Anjuman meeting held under the auspices of the Bakr establishment, that did not refer to bargadari rights at all. This provides yet another instance of this mutually reinforcing relationship between communal mobilization and bargadari movements. It was a process that was repeated in Jessore in 1928 when, alongside a huge bargadari movement which spread into nearby Khulna and Faridpur, there was an intensive communalization of the local Board elections[159]

[155] Tajul Islam Hashmi does talk of the bargadars as a separate category, but his argument suggests that they were integrated with the Muslim rayats in a seamless process of communalization. 'Communalization of Class Struggle'.

[156] The number of those living mainly on bargadari as a proportion of the number of agricultural families, was the highest in Pabna amongst the Eastern districts, Chatterjee, *Bengal*, p. 43. For stability and advantageousness of arrangements in Pabna, see ibid., p. 45.

[157] While the earliest recorded instance of a bargadar movement is in Jessore, 1909, in 1913 a similar struggle broke out in Serajgunj where Muslim bargadars refused to carry the harvested crop to the landlords house, and accept barga contracts. In 1918 the bargadars of Ullapara in Pabna again rose in protest. Cooper, *Sharecroppers*, pp. 115–16.

[158] *Amrita Bazar Patrika*, 12 January 1925. There had also been an instance of bargadar mobilization in Shahzadpur the same year, Cooper, ibid. It should be added here that all the places mentioned till now as hosting bargadar movements in Pabna, were also major centres for the riots in 1926.

[159] The Bargadar movement continued from March till the end of the year, *Fortnightly Reports*, 1/1928, NAI. For reference to the local Board elections, see ibid., December, first and second halves.

While class is implicated in communal identity, the latter can also be deployed to suppress and/or supercede class struggles. What we see then in the twenties is a picture of interlocking identities, even as they mutually contest each other. One cannot escape implying the Other. What we really have in this unstable condition is the conjunctural dominance of one over the other. In this process, the outcome is ultimately determined by the nature of the political intervention. Of course, the overall corelationships of social and political forces at any given period contributes to the success or failure of a particular identity formation to emerge as the definitive feature of the age. But, it is the ideological character of any intervention, more specifically, the way communal formations exploit favourable conjunctures by appropriating other identities to themselves, that provides the decisive factor to understand its growth. It is the twin aspects of this process — the instability and the nature of ideological intervention — that I will elaborate by a quick look at the Dhaka and Kishoreganj riots of 1930.

II.ii

These riots, which took place only a year after the formation of the KPP, pose an enigmatic mix of class and communal motivation. In retrospect, this appears to signify the transition from the communally volatile twenties to the more class-based politics of the KPP in the thirties. However, while this may supply the general frame of reference, it was the effects of the world-wide depression, particularly on the price of jute, along with the fears raised by Sarda Bill (that led to a spate of marriages before the Bill came into effect, thereby increasing indebtedness as a consequence of the expenses involved),[160] which gave these riots their specific animus against moneylenders. But even within this overall

---

[160] The effects of the Sarda Bill that have been observed by T. Sarkar, *National Movement*, p. 246, must be tempered by the fact that the authorities in their Fortnightly Reports do not include either Dhaka or Mymensingh among the main areas affected by mass marriage of daughters before the Bill came into effect; the districts mentioned are the more Northerly ones of Dinajpur, Rangpur and Bogra. Of course this does not mean that such marriages did not take place or that these did not contribute to a general sense of economic oppression. See March first and second halves, *Fortnightly Reports*, Home Poll, 18/IV/1930, NAI.

characterization, there were differences. These will become clear when we look at the Dhaka riots which occurred in May, 1930.

The main points of these two riots have been covered by Tanika Sarkar[161] and Suranjan Das,[162] while Sugata Bose[163] and Partha Chatterjee[164] have also contributed to our knowledge of the Kishoreganj riots. I really wish to add some qualifications and new angles to this already exhaustive discussion. Schematically put, the main points covered by Sarkar and Das on the Dhaka riots are that they occurred in the city as well as in surrounding villages and, in both areas, communal conflict, as suggested by its objects of attack, coincided with class struggle. The only difference was that, in the city, the class character could be extrapolated from the concentration of the attack on Hindu houses of Keyatulli where the palatial houses of businessmen were located, while in the villages it was apparent in the fact that the main object of loot for the Muslim crowds were the debt-bonds held by their money-lenders. The other important point with which we shall be less concerned here, is the mass involvement in the Civil Disobedience movement in the city. While the observance of 26 January as Independence Day occasioned the first communal incident in the particular chain of events leading to this riot, the former movement was supported by a great many Muslims despite the tension.[165] This had two consequences; firstly, it encouraged the powerful, loyalist section of Muslims led by the Nawab of Dhaka to unite the factions against the pro-Disobedience sections. This prepared the grounds for the eruption of communal conflict.[166] Secondly, it prompted the British to encourage anti-Hindu mobilization amongst the Muslims. The

[161] *National Movements.* pp. 233–55.
[162] *Communal Riots in Bengal*, pp. 107–33.
[163] 'Communal Riots in Agrarian Bengal', pp. 463–91.
[164] *Bengal*, pp. 135–9.
[165] See T. Sarkar, pp. 232–4. K.C. Neogy's questions in the Legislative Assembly asserted that many Muslims from Dhaka went to Contai to break the Salt laws there; later, on the 15 April, many Muslims joined the hartal to protest against the arrest of Jawaharlal Nehru, and (less than a month later) against the arrest of Gandhi and Kitchlew. Home Poll, X/IV/1930, NAI.
[166] There was a proposal for the three Muslim organizations of Dhaka, the Anjuman, the Muslim Association and the Bais Panchayet, to be amalgamated on 18 May, a mere four days before the outbreak of the riots. A.H. Clayton, Commissioner, Dhaka Division to Chief Secretary, GOB, 3/6/1930, File no. 10/30.

administration aided the Muslims further by their inactivity during the riots and even overtly encouraged the rioters.[167]

The imperative to counter the nationalist promise of intercommunal co-operation through communal mobilization was absent in the rural areas of Dhaka. This fits in with a reservation that I have on the first formulation: a distinction ought to be made between the rioting in the city and the villages. In the latter, the overriding preoccupation with debt-bonds indisputably points in the direction of dominantly class mobilization.[168] A similar observation is not however possible to make for Dhaka city. To begin with, a proof advanced for the non-communal character of the riot is that temples were not attacked. While attacks on temples are not an essential ingredient of communal riots — they certainly did not occur before the Calcutta riots of 1926 — it is also likely that they were generally ignored because of the *modus operandi* employed.[169] More importantly, the class argument holds only in the event of poor Muslims attacking rich Hindus. But there was an (almost) equally large number of cases in which poor Hindus attacked the not so rich Muslims. In other words, the rioting did not suffer from the effects of class cleavages within the Hindus and Muslims. This conjunctural unity within religious collectivities during these riots was reinforced by the sustained history of communal conflicts in the city from 1926.

The asymmetry between the rioting in city and village in Dhaka is significant when we compare Pabna in 1926. In both cases, the rioting interlinked two spaces by flowing over from the urban to the rural. The difference was that in Pabna the population of surrounding villages threatened to invade the town on the very first day; town and country tended to form a continuum during the riots, an impression which is reinforced by the fact that the character of the riots in the villages did not diverge qualitatively from the town. On the other hand, the relationship between town and country in Dhaka was established only through the news

---

[167] See T. Sarkar, pp. 234–5, 242–3, and Das, *Communal Riots*, p. 111.

[168] Das, *Communal Riots*, p. 114. At one place the Union Board President specified that only Saha houses could be attacked, Sarkar, *National Movement*, p. 251.

[169] There was a general avoidance of fights at close quarters. No. 495/1930, LP & J/6/1996/IOL. This pattern does not encourage raiding of each other's places of worship, which would entail the likelihood of hand-to-hand battles.

carried by individuals, which provided a sanction for the Muslim peasantry to express their own version of class justice.[170] The case of Dhaka villages presents yet another instance of a crowd using self-justifying rumours to authorize their actions.

Class consciousness played a dominant role in the Kishoreganj riots. But these riots, more than any other, pose a teasing ambiguity regarding their identities and motivations. This ambiguity is counterfactually confirmed by the Hindu Mission report, when it says that one of its objectives was to counter the propoganda, which it ascribes to the Government — that these riots were fought on class lines.[171] The enunciation of such an aim publicly acknowledged the power and relevance of its rival interpretation of class conflict, even as it discovered within the interstices of the event, a space for its own intervention.

But the Report did more; it set the terms of the way that this ambiguity would be treated, that is, as a debate regarding the particular motivation actually involved. In recent times the debate has been premised on an opposition between economic and religious motivations, corresponding to a division made between utilitarian attitudes and those wrought by belief.[172] The approach appears fruitless on two counts. First, any history of institutional religion, if not of observable religious practice, will show that religious beliefs do not preclude manipulation of those beliefs or the harbouring of material motivations. Second, it is hard to see the point of emphasizing the utter importance of religion in rural Bengal in the early twentieth century; this may have served some purpose if one was convinced that the number of atheists there, if any, amounted to a socially significant force.

---

[170] Apparently two or three Muslims went from Dhaka town to the villages, to proclaim that the Nawab had ordered Hindus to be attacked. No. 495/1930, LP & J/6/1996/IOL. The Nawab's name was invoked to authorize looting in Keraniganj, 10/4/30, LP & J, IOL.

[171] *Mymensigh–Kishoreganj Hindur Durgati*, collected by Hindu Mission (pub. details absent), IOL, vol. II, pp. 71–2.

[172] See Chatterjee, *Bengal 1920–1947*, pp. 136–7. It should be remarked that Bose is rather less definite than Chatterjee, but nevertheless ends on a note which indicates a speculative preference for the religious, put in the following psychological terms: ' . . . The satisfaction of an irrational and perhaps subconscious passion can conceivably be a stronger human motive than the satisfaction of a material interest'. Sugata Bose, 'Roots of Communal Violence', p. 491.

However, highlighting one set of obvious factors can obscure the recognition of another. The invocation of religion by both Chatterjee and Bose, suppresses the issue of communal motivation. Communalism, as I have tried to show, involves not simply religious belief per se, but particular attitudes to ones 'own' religion as well as to the other's. This includes the indeterminate, interpenetrating zone of customs, beliefs, rituals which we normally designate as syncretist. Conversely, the phenomenon of communalism dramatizes the problem of the multiplicity of affiliations that is the common feature of this society.[173] The problem, as I have stated earlier, is really one of trying to discover the structures of this ambiguity.

A reminiscence of this period could flag off our enquiry. Shantimoy Roy (cited earlier), during his sojourn in Mymensingh jail in this period, recalled that they interacted intimately with the accused of the Kishoreganj riots there. From them he gathered that the riots were initially agrarian in character, led by middle-level peasant leaders, including some Communists. It later turned communal through the influence of communally minded maulvis and, more importantly, by the unremitting characterization of them as communal by the HMS and sections of the Congress.[174] Roy's impressions are borne out by an overwhelming mass of evidence. The almost exclusive object of attack in Kishoreganj were the debt-bonds of the moneylenders, and it was only in a

---

[173] The evidence Chatterjee offers is scant, and points in fact to the co-presence of multiple affiliations among the peasantry, rather than one monolithic community as he would have it. He cites a Hindu representation that claimed the use of 'holy Khargos' by Muslim rioters. If indeed this was the case — and there is more than a slight element of doubt here, for no other source mentions that the instruments used were in fact 'holy' — it reveals the notion that the Hindus were seen as insiders to their sense of community. What would be the point of sacrifice, if one does not part with something of one's own? And if this was the case, we then have a more complicating instance in which the language of one religion is used in order to express a much more inclusive notion of a community that cannot be elided into the one denoted by that religion. In other words what we have here is really a dramatization of the multiplicity of affiliations. Rather than the singular community which he defines in the very next paragraph: 'The very nature of peasant consciousness, the apparently consistent unification of an entire set of beliefs about nature and about men in the collective and active mind of the peasantry is religious.' *Bengal*, pp. 136–7.

[174] Interview with Shantimoy Roy, part I, 2 August 1988.

single case that a moneylender was killed along with his family. The case of this particular lender, Krishna Ray, will occupy us later, but it must be said here that this was an exceptional occurrence, for the man had sought to repulse the crowd by gunfire.[175] As in Dhaka, the Civil Disobedience had struck a positive response here before the onset of the riots. More significant was the intensity of class mobilization: the Communists already had a base here.[176] Moreover, Muslim moneylenders were targeted along with their Hindu counterparts — an added proof of the class motivations involved[177] Significantly, the riots began with an attack on a Muslim taluqdar.[178] But, as Roy recalls and Sugata Bose observes, the riots took on a communal character as it progressed, including in its objects of attack, the low-caste Namasudras and poor peasants.[179] The influence of the religiously bellicose elements was also evident in attempts at conversion.[180]

The class-communal ambiguity had a sequential character. This is not new; we have encountered an analogous phenomenon in the Hajinagar riots of 1926. The consecutive structure of this ambiguity was immensely aided by Hindu communalism, which, after 1928, insistently attempted to remove the paradox of the Muslim peasant by communal clarification. Such efforts were evident in the debate on the Primary Education Bill. The logic of this was best noted by those who had the most to gain from a communal rupture. Observing, in 1930, that the Praja Party was the nucleus of the opposition to the Ministry, colonial strategists felt that it might not remain in that position for long if the intensified communal campaign of the Hindu Sabha against the Ministry had an effect; in that case it said, the KPP could split on the question of support to the ministers.[181] And this, it is worth remarking, would also establish the value of Hindu communalism to the Hindu landlords of Eastern Bengal. A greater ambition is evident in the attempt to colonize the memory of the Kishoreganj riots, which I will try to show through some of the texts produced

[175] Nine members of the family were killed. Bose, 'Roots of . . . ', p. 476.
[176] The Young Comrades League was already established here, Sarkar, *National Movement*, p. 238.
[177] Ibid., p. 244.
[178] Ibid., p. 251.
[179] 'Roots of Communal Violence', p. 485.
[180] This was obviously highlighted by the Mission report, vol. II, pp. 63–4.
[181] *Fortnightly Reports*, 18/III/1930, February first half, NAI.

by Hindu communal forces. What was involved here was not only the endeavour to break the duality of the Muslim peasant formation by simply suppressing the question of class but more sophisticatedly, it tried to appropriate issues of class into the internal structure of its ideology.

I will study three texts that were published in 1931. Two of these are poems written by individuals bearing upper-caste names. One of them called *Loter Gan* (Song of Loot) is fairly well-known amongst the texts proscribed by the Government. It is penned by Laksmikanta Kirtanya and Kumuda Bhattacharya, both of whom hailed from a Mymensingh village.[182] However, the care taken by the authorities to censor communal propoganda did not extend to other texts, which were equally pernicious. One of these, called *Hindur Durgati* (The Misfortune of Hindus), is a poem written by Jogendrachandra Acharya of Kumarpur in Mymensingh.[183] These ballad-like poems were meant to be sung in the kirtan style in order to create a community of Hindus through evoking empathy with the sufferings of their co-religionists in Kishoreganj. We have already seen that the kirtan was deployed for Hindu unity, in addition to carrying the charge of conflictual energies accruing from the 'music before mosque' question. Its simultaneous links with low-caste mobilization were also underlined a year earlier, when it was used to popularize the Munshiganj Temple Satyagraha in Dhaka.[184]

This imprint of the latter is evident in the discourse of *Mymensingh-Kishoreganje Hindur Durgati*.[185] This is a series of reports on different village riots, compiled by the Hindu Mission. The Mission was headed by Swami Satyananda, who was active in the Patuakhali Satyagraha. He seems to have been carrying on the tradition of Swami Shraddhanand in Eastern Bengal, which, in later years, rested on a radical reformist attitude to untouchability, necessitated by a paranoic fear of Muslim supremacism and Hindu annihilation. An able organizer — the Hindu Mission had, by 1931, established permanent offices in Mymensingh, Bogra and Dhaka, in addition

[182] Laksmikanta Kirtanaya and Kumuda Bhattacharya, *Ganera Bahi: Lotera Gan*, Village Kagarcaram, Mymensingh, 1931.
[183] Jogendrachandra Acharya, *Hindur Durgati*, vol. I, Kumarpur, Mymensingh, nd.
[184] Buddhadev Bhattacharya, *Satyagrahas in Bengal, 1921–1930*, Calcutta, 1977, p. 177.
[185] *Mymensingh-Kishoreganje Hindur Durgati*, vols. I and II, Hindu Mission.

to those established in the riot affected areas,[186] — Satyananda had successfully led the movement by Namamsudras to enter the Kali temple in Munshiganj in the face of local upper-caste opposition. Significantly, while trying to persuade his opponents in the upper-caste, local Bar, he had invoked fears of low-caste vulnerabilities to Muslim designs.[187]

Such independent initiatives gathered enough support to communalize Kishoreganj.[188] A great deal of this was probably due to the urgency felt by sections of Hindu landholders after the BTAB. The Mission report explicitly defines the Hindus of Eastern and Northern Bengal — specifically the districts of Chittagong, Comilla, Noakhali, Rajshahi, Pabna and Bogra — as its target audience that ought to be forewarned by the events of Kishoreganj.[189] These riots are depicted in terms of Muslim oppression and Hindu victimhood. They are given a status that emblematizes the apparently powerless condition of all Hindus in Eastern Bengal. I have earlier asserted that this feeling of victimhood was ironically located among the privileged. This is reiterated by the organizing principle of these texts, which is the tragedy of the moneylender, Krishna Ray.

We shall return to Ray later. At this point it is important to note that these texts comprehensively orchestrate the main motifs of communal antagonism of the twenties, clustering them around the riots. There is no theoretical elaboration of the kind we had seen in the ideologues of the early part of the century. These texts use the conclusions of the earlier ideologues as motifs that can be given new symbolic meanings through placement in fresh contexts. For example, the condition of Hindus in these texts is defined by riots. While the old association with population growth differential remains one of the guiding concerns of the Hindu Mission, Hindu propoganda no longer has to wrestle with the problems posed by the immense length of time that census indicators dictated. The riots dramatically pose the problem of

---

[186] *Mymensingh-Kishoreganje Hindur Durgati*, vol. I, p. 3.

[187] Bhattacharya, *Satyagrahas*, p. 169.

[188] Satyanand had links with the HMS from the time of Patuakhali Satyagraha. During the Munshiganj agitation, Padamraj Jain, the then secretary of the BPHS, gave supportive action by forming a Satyagraha Committee in Dhaka. *Satyagrahas*, p. 169.

[189] *Mymensingh-Kishoreganje Hindur Durgati*, vol. I, p. 4.

immediate genocide by the Muslims. In contrast to the superiority accredited to the Muslims by Mukherji, the Mission claims that Islam harbours a historical hatred for the Hindus, which can only be restrained by the State.[190]

The imperative to remove the shackles of untouchability from the low castes who had occupied a place of self-interested patriarchal concern in the early years of the 'dying Hindu', is now directly connected to the immediate survival of the upper castes. It is of course helpful for this discourse that many of the moneylenders — and there were many petty ones who were attacked — were low caste.[191] Not surprisingly there are many positive references made to low-caste involvement in these texts. For instance, one of the versions of the Ray incident in the Mission Report says that two low-caste servants of the Ray family persuaded the Muslims not to harm the females; further, the only instance of a fightback provided by the report concerns a stand made by Namasudras.[192] Yet the latter are described as being generally quiescent. This characterization is then used to argue that, if untouchability rules were suspended, the upper caste could receive the benefits of the physical power of low castes. An interview with Namasudra representatives regarding their general failure to fight the Muslims, yielded the reply that they lacked the confidence to do so, being deprived of it by the contempt embedded in untouchability rules.

Further, the association between maleness and violence tended to attenuate the role provided to women in the discourse of abductions. In fact, as I have mentioned in chapter 4, the riots had been preceded by a controversy over alleged cases of abduction in Pakundia in 1929 — and this provided the immediate motive for the anti-abductions campaign by the Mission. Surprisingly, however, the most important palliative advanced for abductions was the Shuddhi movement. It does not take much effort to realize

---

[190] The Report ends with a section called 'Our Plea', in which its interpretation of the events are offered. *Mymensingh-Kishoreganje Hindur Durgati*, vol. II, p. 70.

[191] Bose observes that while the big taluqdars-mahajans were drawn from the upper castes, many intermediate Nabasakh castes, like Sahas, Telis, Baniks supplied traders (and petty lenders). 'Communal Violence', p. 472. Obviously attacks on low castes were highlighted by the Mission report, which specifically mentions attacks on Jogi and Karmakar lenders. *Mymensingh-Kishoreganje Hindur Durgati*, vol. I, pp. 28–30 and vol. II, p. 41.

[192] *Mymensingh-Kishoreganje Hindur Durgati*, ibid.

that Shuddhi is not directly related to the problem of abductions. On the other hand, it does relate quite fundamentally to the more instrumentalist problem of the Hindu males, that is, of population depletion. The forefronting of Shuddhi here is an indicator of the way this discourse behaves when faced with panic; it dispenses with women altogether! When the figure of a woman occurs, she is shown as being engaged in communal combat, and is moulded in the image of Sati. Not the existential empowerment of women, but their death is seen as their heroic contribution. Ray's wife is called Sati, and in an emblematic posture, while the Muslims and the fires they had alighted rage around her, she clings to her husband. But he is pulled away from her and hacked into two.[193] In other contexts, women are seen to be preparing themselves for the fire much in the manner of the Rajput practice of *jauhar*, a grand enterprize that incidentally masks the lack of actual cases of rape in Kishoreganj.

The key trope is that of the *Kali Yug*, the belief in the end of a temporal cycle which would be betokened by the inversion of caste and gender relations.[194] These texts frame their paranoia with the emotions and associations latent in this trope, adeptly insinuating the figure of the Muslim to replace those of the Shudra and women. By the same token, these two groups cease to act as signs of internal threat. In a more significant move, it uses the Kali Yug to warn rather than prophesy.[195] Social hierarchy thereby functions as a sign of normality, of the preservation of the species that can ward off the apocalypse. But the Kali Yug trope is also modified to include the non-traditional question of class. This is done by embodying the Kali Yug-as-warning in the tragedy of one of the wealthiest moneylenders of that region, Krishna Ray. This tale provides the central structure and emotional heart of all three narratives. And in its telling can be seen the kind of efforts made by Hindu communalism as it sought to appropriate class divisions to itself.

[193] This version is given by both *Hindur Durgati*, p. 5, and *Lotera Gan*, p. 3.
[194] *Hindur Durgati*, p. 2. talks of the riots as the handiwork of 'Kalir lila'. For an extended discussion of the operation of the Kali Yug myth in modern Bengal, see Sumit Sarkar, 'The Kalki-Avatar of Bikrampur: A Village Scandal in Early Twentieth Century Bengal', in *Subaltern Studies VI*, Ranajit Guha (ed.), Delhi, 1989.
[195] Thus *Mymensingh-Kishoreganje Hindur Durgati*, exclaims at the wrath shown by God, and concludes that the latter was teaching Hindus to be physically prepared. p. 2.

The exemplary story is one in which Ray gives shelter to his neighbours, and along with his son heroically tries to ward off Muslims who set fire to his mansion. Together with other members of their family, they are finally killed when they run out of bullets. It is an ideal story about courage. A photograph of Ray which adorns the report of the Hindu Mission, bears a legend stating that he had died fighting the Muslims.[196] Which is in sharp and studied contrast with the actions of the Hindu neighbours of Ray and the other affected victims. They had confirmed the stereotype of the cowardly Hindu male — which was an object of communal reform — by failing to organize counterattacks.[197]

This exemplary story seeks to rework the significations of wealth itself. It is indeed striking that these texts provide an inflated figure of the losses sustained by Ray. Not only is his palatial house celebrated (*Hindur Durgati* gives out that it had twenty-two rooms, *Loter Gan* that it had a mere thirteen),[198] but his two motor-cars are also mentioned.[199] The volume of his monetary possession excites even greater enthusiasm. The texts provide figures of the huge amount he had lost and their estimates far exceed the official figures.[200] By framing his wealth in a representative context of oppression and extinction, this intervention seeks to remove the signification of wealth as a sign of social hierarchy and exploitation. It may be

[196] *Mymensingh-Kishoreganje Hindur Durgati*, vol. II.
[197] The Mission report says that even if fifty Hindus had organized themselves with lathis, they would have been able to stave off the Muslims, vol. I, pp. 8–9.
[198] Ibid., pp. 1, 3. The celebration of the house employs almost identical language in both poems, to the effect that it was rare to find such house in villages.
[199] It is interesting that what T. Sarkar observes were the things that offended the moral economy of that village, namely, the recently built house of palatial proportions and the acquisition of a motor car which Muslim peasants were not allowed to touch, are the thing that are celebrated here. *National Movements*, pp. 249–50.
[200] According to the *Durgati* texts Ray had offered them Rs 40,000; all three texts are agreed that the total amount of loss amounted to Rs 3 lakhs of which, according to *Hindur Durgati*, Rs 80,000 was accounted for by debt-bonds, p. 2. Das states that Ray had lost only Rs 11,251 in cash and ornaments, although his house was also burnt down (which is not reckoned by the Report). There is one case in Kumarpur, where 3 lakhs worth of debt-bonds was looted. *Communal Riots in Bengal*, pp. 124–5. Obviously the two sets of facts have been brought together, to produce the particular effects described above.

recalled that all the instances of Muslim oppressiveness in both the *Durgati* texts concern the confiscation and destruction of debt-bonds. And this — if we take into account the rhetoric of genocide — is inextricably bound with the attack on their physical existence. This coupling makes Ray's case even more important, for it is the only instance which allows such a connection to be persuasively dramatized. By this token, these debt bonds signify the secret power that the Muslims seek to appropriate, the importance of which is demonstrated by the fact that Ray chooses to resist rather than give up his money. The oppressiveness of the Muslims is as expansive as the inconceivable extent of Ray's possessions: his wealth becomes an index of the degree of their domination.

We come close then to a structure of social arrangement which we had encountered in Chapter 3, where the wealthy Muslim is valued because he is a representative of his community. There is a major difference however. In the case of the Muslim community there was a notion of obligation attached; wealth was important because it was subject to the demands of affiliation. As stated, this ideological claim was ratified by the acts of some important Muslim landlords, such as A.K. Ghuznavi and Panee. Both of them preempted some of the provisions of the BTAB by conceding them in their own estates.[201] In contrast, these texts made no demands of social obligation. On the contrary, we have here an uncompromising insistence on preserving privileges which is not foreign to the spirit displayed in the BTAB vote. Consequently, only a relatively simple structure of pathos protects the story of Ray from the alternate, unfavourable reading of martyrdom to personal greed. When the Muslim peasants surround him, he tries to fob them off by offering a sum of money, which appears miserly in comparison to the full amount of his worldly assets (which were

---

[201] I have already referred to Ghuznavi's initiative in ch. 2. Maulvi Wajed Ali Khan Panee, the famous zamindar of Karatia, Mymensingh, converted a major portion of his zamindari into a endowment under a Waqf Board, which would look after various charitable institutions, especially devoted to education. A special feature of this Waqf deed was that tenancy right holders within the Waqf property would be given unrestricted rights to trees, sink wells and tanks, and raise pucca buildings. *The Mussalman*, 27 February 1926. In contrast, the idealization of Hemchandra Chaudhury, the Zamindar of Ambaria (Mymensingh) by *Amrita Bazar Patrika* did not refer to any act of granting rights to his subordinates. 18 August and 8 September 1925.

looted). And rather than surrendering his debt-bonds he chooses to use his gun and take human lives.

It is then, in the context of the Kishoreganj riots that the landlord emerges as the lynchpin of communal discourse, expanding his undoubtedly important, but not central, position in the communal mobilization of the mid-twenties. In retrospect, it may be stated that the Swarajist idealization of the landlord as representative of Bengaliness provided the grounds on which Hindu communalism could appropriate class categories to make them a constitutive part of its vision. The symbolic generalization of the landlord could allow his death, as presaged by ryoti mobilization, to embody a condition of disaster and, by simple extension, the beginnings of a communal holocaust. In everyday terms, this implied an unremitting fear of the Muslim peasant: this is the implication of the constant underlining of the fact that the rioters were known neighbours of their victims.[202] The degree of success attained by Hindu communalism is an index of the degree to which privileges had become important to the very notion of the Self among the Hindu rural upper class. Like their hero, Krishna Ray, they preferred death to surrendering the comforts of their biases and luxuries.

But the clinging to greed as the only resource for making sense of a collapsing world, is less an expression of confidence than of desperation. As we have seen, although the BTAB debate did prepare for the communalization of issues involving class contradictions, traces of different affiliations remained even within the immediate context of the riots of 1930. At another level, the Congress remobilization for nationalist activity, which featured the leadership of Bose (who had, by being jailed at the outset of the burial controversy, stayed outside the sphere of communal controversy), gathered together the political imagination of the period into non-communal channels.

Moreover, it is worth reminding ourselves that this reflects only a particular moment in the history of communalism. Communalism, as we have seen in the course of this survey, had developed a flexible, accessible and permeable ideological structure that could service the needs of multiple social collectivities at key conjuctures.

---

[202] Thus the Mission report begins by conjuring up the fearful situation in which known Muslim neighbours with whom politenesses had been exchanged only an hour earlier, turned murderers and looters. *Mymensingh-Kishoreganje Hindur Durgati*, vol. I, p. 3.

Although not necessarily shackled to any particular social group, it was the privileged — drawn from both landholding and middle-class sectors — who displayed greater initiative in producing communal campaigns, adhered more unwaveringly to its worldviews and, consequently, deployed more resources in promoting its many conflicts. Not surprisingly, the all-encompassing character of communal bitterness of the 1920's left a permanent mark. The Civil Disobedience movement, unlike that of the N/K, did not encompass Muslims. The moments when it did so remained momentary, for the communal bitterness of the previous decade made it all too easy to abort their participation.

Bibliography

Private Papers

Baker Papers (CSAC)
C. Tegart Papers (CSAC)
Donald Macpherson, Memoirs (IOL)
E.F. McInerny, Memoirs (IOL)
F.O. Bell Papers (IOL)
J.H.M. Mills *Biography of Charles Tegart* (handwritten) (IOL)
J.T. Donovan Papers (CSAC)
J.V. Hodge Papers (CSAC)
M.M. Stuart, Memoirs (IOL)
O.M. Martin Papers (CSAC)
P.D. Martyn, Memoirs (IOL)
S.G. Taylor Papers (CSAC)
S. Rahamatulla, Memoirs (IOL)
Veronica Westmacott, *We Were Survivors* (IOL)
W.H.J. Christie, Memoirs (IOL)

Records of Organizations

Akhil Bharatiya Hindu Mahasabha Papers (NMML)
Wesleyan Methodist Missionary Society (London) Archive Correspondence (SOAS).

Official Records

India Office Library and Records, London.
Public and Judicial Department Papers, (L/P & J series).
National Archives of India, New Delhi.
Proceedings of the Home (Political) Department, Government of India.
Proceedings of the Home (Public) Department, Government of India.

Proceedings of the Home (Judicial) Department, Government of India.
West Bengal State Archives, Calcutta.
Proceedings of the Home (Political: Confidential) Department, Government of Bengal.
Proceedings of the Home (Police) Department, Government of Bengal.

Official Publications

Bamford, P.C., *Histories of Khilafat and Non-Cooperation Movements* (Delhi: 1985, f.pub. 1925).
Calcutta Corporation Minutes (1924–1928).
Census of India, 1891, 1901, 1911, 1921, 1931, Bengal volumes.
Hunter, W.W., *A Statistical Account of Bengal, Vol. IX: Districts of Murshidabad and Pabna* (Delhi: 1974, f.pub. 1876).
—— *A Statistical Account of Bengal, Vol. VIII: Districts of Rajshahi and Bogra* (Delhi: 1974, f.pub. 1876).
Municipal Administration Report, 1924–1925.
O'Malley, L.S.S., *Bengal District Gazetteers*, Pabna (Calcutta: 1923).
Rangpur District Gazetteer: B Volume, Rangpur District Statistics, 1911–12 to 1920–21 (Calcutta: 1923).
Report on the Administration of Bengal, 1925–1926 (Calcutta: 1927).
Report of Native Newspapers (Selected Years).
Report on the Working of the Reformed Constitution in Bengal, 1921–1927 (Calcutta: 1928).
Vas, J.A., *Eastern Bengal and Assam District Gazetteers: Rangpur* (Allahabad: 1911).

Interviews

Abdul Rahman (Laloo Mian), December 1993.
Abdullahil Rasul, June 1988.
Anandita Datta, July 1990.
Bejoy Bhattacharya, June 1988.
Dhritikanta Lahiri Chaudhury, July 1988.
Ghulam Rasul, December 1993.
Moidul Islam, December 1993.
Mohammed Maksud Ali, June 1990.
Mohammed Yusuf Warsi, December 1993.
Nilima Mukherji, June 1988

Nuruddin Siddiki, December 1993
Pratibha Basu, January 1993.
Rabindranath Ghosh, June 1989.
Sadhana Bhattacharya, June 1988.
Saibal Gupta, September 1988.
Shantimoy Roy, August 1988
S.M. Islam Qureshi, December 1993
Shaukat Ali, June 1990.
S.K. Datta, June 1992.
Sourendra Mohon Roy, January 1989.
Usha Guha Roy, June 1988.

Newspapers, Journals

Ahmadi
Amrita Bazar Patrika
Bengalee
Forward
Hindu Musalman
Jana Sevak
Modern Review
Prabashi
The Mussalman
The Statesman

Contemporary Literature/Commentary

Begum Rokeya Rachanabali, Abdul Qadir (ed.) (Dhaka: 1993, f.pub. 1973).
Chattopadhyaya, Sarat Chandra, 'Bartaman Hindu–Musalman Samashya', in Sukumar Sen (ed.), *Saratsahityasamagra* (Calcutta: 1392[1985]).
—— 'Muslim Sahitya — Sadhana', in Sukumar Sen (ed.), *Saratsahityasamagra* (Calcutta: 1392[1985]).
—— *Palli Samaj* (rpt. Calcutta: 1364[1957]).
Chattopadhyaya, Bankim Chandra, *Anandamath, Bankim Rachanabali*, vol. I, Jogeshchandra Bagal (ed.) (rpt. Calcutta: 1397[1990])
—— *Debi Chaudhurani, Bankim Rachanabali*, vol. I, Jogeshchandra Bagal (ed.) (rpt. Calcutta: 1397[1990])
Deb, Mahesh Chandra, 'A Sketch of the Condition of Hindu Women', in Goutam Chattopadhyay (ed.), *Awakening in Bengal in Early 19th Century (Selected Documents)*, vol. I (Calcutta: 1965).

Gandhi, M., *Collected Works of Mahatma Gandhi*, vols. XXX and XXXI, 1926 (Ahmedabad: 1968).
Ghosh, Hemenprasad, 'Diary of Hemenprasad Ghosh', in Pratul Chandra Gupta (ed.), *Bengal Past and Present*, vol. CIII, parts I–II, nos 196–7, January–December, 1984.
Meerza, Delawarr, *Muslim Modernism in Bengal: Selected Writings of Delawarr Hosaen Ahmed Meerza 1840–1913*, Sultan Jahan Salik (ed.) (Dacca: 1980).
Mitra, H.N. (ed.), *Indian Annual Register*, vol. IV and V (Calcutta: 1923, 1924)
Pal, Bepinchandra, *Nabajuger Bangla* (Calcutta: 1964).
Rai, Lala Lajpat, 'The Depressed Classes', in Vijay Chandra Joshi (ed.), *Lala Lajpat Rai: Writings and Speeches, Vol. I, 1888–1919* (Delhi: 1966).
Savarkar, V.D, *Hindutva: Who is a Hindu?* (Poona: 1949, f.pub. 1923).
Smiles, Samuel, *Self-Help* (London: 1935, f.pub. 1859)
Swami Vivekananda, 'Bhakti–Yoga', *The Complete Works of Swami Vivekananda*, vol. III (Calcutta: 1964).
—— 'Modern India', *The Complete Works of Swami Vivekananda*, vol. IV (Calcutta: 1964).
—— 'My Plan of Campaign', *The Complete Works of Swami Vivekananda*, vol. III (Calcutta: 1964).
—— 'The Future of India', *The Complete Works of Swami Vivekananda*, vol. III (Calcutta: 1964).
Tagore, Rabindranath, *Gora, Rabindra Rachanabali*, vol. IX (Calcutta: 1961).
—— 'Hindumusalman': Letter written to Kalidas Nag, 1329[1922], *Rabindra Rachanabali, Vol. XIII: Prabandha [Essays]*, (Calcutta: 1368[1961]).
—— 'Kabuliwala', *Galpaguccha* (rpt. Calcutta: 1368[1961]).

Pamphlets

Abedin, Munshi Mohammed Jainul, *Atmakahini* (Kochiamor, P.O. Birampur, Dinajpur: 1926). (NL)
Acharya, Jogendrachandra, *Hindur Durgati*, vol. I (Mymensingh). (IOL)
Ahmad, Afsaruddin, Abdussamad, *Hazrat Ali O Bir Hanumaner Larai* (Calcutta). (IOL)
Ahmed, Moulvi Reazuddin, *Baul Dhangsha Fatua* (Rangpur: 1925). (NL)
Ahmed, Moulvi Reazuddin, *Phakiri Dhoka Rod* (Rangpur: 1926). (IOL)

Ali, Mohammed Ansur, *Shud Nabaran Samiti* (P.O. Lakshmia, Mymensingh: 1926). (NL)
Ali, Mohammed Maksud, *Narendrapurer Bahase Bedaite Dalan* (Jessore: 1924). (NL)
Ali, Mohammed, *Sahtiya Sangrakshan: Bangiya Musalmaner Sahitya Raksha Upay* (Dhaka: 1927). (NL)
Ali, Mohammed Yakub, *Mussalmaner Jatibhed* (Hooghly: 1927). (NL)
Ali, Syed Mahabub, *Chirosthayee Bandobasto O Bangiya Rayat* (Calcutta: 1924). (NL)
—— *Jamidarer Bajeaday ba Abwab* (Calcutta: 1924), (NL)
Ali, Sayyid Shah Mohammed, *Mithya Pir* (Dinajpur: 1919). (NL)
Al-Islam, Khondakar Ain, *Garu O Hindu-Musalman* (Calcutta: 1910). (IOL)
Amin, Ruhul, *Nafaol Mocchelmein ba Mashayal Tattva* (Khulna: 1925), (NL)
Anjuman i Ulemaya Report 1913–1916 (Calcutta: 1918). (NL)
Annual Report of the Women's Protection League for the Year 1938 (publishing details destroyed).
Auyiyal, Abdul, *Mahila Bandhab*, (trans.) Moulana M.A. Shilani, Moulvi S. Hossain (Dhaka: 1925). (IOL)
Aziz, Abdul, *Najat* (Noakhali: 1925). (NL)
Badiazzaman, Khodakar Mohammed, *Banger Zamindar* (Pabna: 1925). (NL)
Bagura Hindu Sabher Nibedan (IOL).
Bannerji, Kader Baksh, *Amar Islam Dharma Grahan* (Burdwan: 1921). (IOL)
Bari, Abdul, *Furfurarer Isal i Soab Darshan* (Noakhali: 1924). (NL)
Bari, Mohammed Abdul, *Gyanonmodana* (Jalpaiguri: 1923). (NL)
Barma, Harachandra Das, *Kayastha Samalochana: Kayastha Utpatti, Bangiya Kayasther Upabita Tyag Abong Asaucher Bibaran O Sriharachandra Das Barmar Bangsha Parichay Itibritta Alochana* (Dinajpur: 1926). (NL)
Bhanu, Hasena, *Shazadi Ara O Khorshed Alam* (Noakhali: 1931). (IOL)
Bhattacharya, Digindranarayan, *Jatibhed* (Serajgunj: 1924, f.pub 1912). (NL)
—— *Shudrer Puja O Vedadhikar* (Serajgunj: 1924, f.pub. 1915). (NL)
—— *Go-Korbani ba Atmabali* (Serajgunj: 1923). (NL)
—— *Bange Vaishya Khatriya* (Basirhat: 1926). (NL)
—— *Biplabi Sri Gouranga* (Srinabadwip: 1953). (NL)
Bhattacharya, Girindra Narayan, *Hindur Naba Jagaran* (Calcutta: 1931). (NL)

Bhaumik, Madanmohon, *Muktir Pathe* (Calcutta: 1924). (NL)
Bhayali, Abdul Hayy, *Adarsh Krishak* (Mymensingh: 1921, f.pub. 1920). (NL)
Bikrampuri, Fakir Mohammed Hossein, *Kalimah Samashya* (P.O. Goapara, Dhaka: 1924). (NL)
Bisi, Saileshnath Sharma, *Hindusamajer Bartaman Samashya: Address of the Reception Committee at the Serajgunj Provincial Hindu Mahasammilani* (1923). (NL)
Biswas, Mohammed Baccher, *Lakshmipurer Hanafi O Mohammadider Bahas* (Jessore: 1921). (NL)
Chattopadhyay, Amarendranath, *Dhaka Zilla Jubak Sammilani Abhibhashan* (Dhaka: 1926). (NL)
Chattopadhyay, Kshirodechandra, *Amina* (Calcutta: 1927). (NL)
Chaudhury, Pramatha, *Atma Katha* (Calcutta: 1946).
Dasgupta, Abhayananda, *Mayer Dak* (Calcutta: 1920). (NL)
Das, Mukunda, *Karmakhetrer Gan* (Barisal: 1932). (IOL)
Das, Sanatan, *Bidobha Bibaha* (Calcutta: 1926). (NL)
Debi, Shantishudha, *Krishak Udbodhan* (Mymensingh: 1926). (NL)
Deuskar, Sakharam Ganesh, *Bangiya Hindu Jati Ki Dhangshanmukh?* (Calcutta: 1910). (NL)
Gani, Abdul, *Jibon Sapna* (Tripura: 1921). (NL)
—— *Islam Bilap* (Malda: 1924). (NL)
Gupta, Nalinikanta, *Bharate Hindu O Musalman* (Calcutta: 1925). (NL)
Hadal Khilafat Committee, *Sabhapatir Abhibhashan, Anjuman i Waizin i Hanafiya Banglar Tritya Barshik Calcutta Adhibeshane Pathite*. (IOL)
Hamid, Abdul, *Pir-Muridi-Samashya ba Bapbetar Takrar* (1924). (IOL)
Hamidi, Mohammed Moazuddin, *Krishaker Unnati O Dukho Durdasher Pratikar* (P.O. Kolaroa, Khulna: 1929). (NL)
Hossein, Maulana Mohammed Golam, *Bhul-Sangshodhan* (Calcutta: 1927). (NL)
Ibrahim, Mohammed, *Nafaol Mocchelmein ba Mashayal Tattva* (Calcutta: 1925). (NL)
Indian National Congress, *Cawnpore Riot Enquiry Committee* (Allahabad: 1933).
Kabyabakarantirtha, Madhusudan, *Nimna O Patit Jati* (Calcutta: 1921). (NL)
Kanjilal, Amaresh, *Bektigata Artha–Niti* (Calcutta: 1921).(NL)
Kanjilal, Amaresh, *Manush Tairir Masala* (Jessore: 1921). (NL)
Karim, Abdul, *Hazrat Bahman Shaheed* (Calcutta: 1917). (NL)

Khan, Abdul Karim, *Taraf Gourangir Itihas* (Tangail, Mymensingh: 1935). (NL)
Khan, Ali Akbar, *Moslem Mohila Charit* (Calcutta: 1920). (IOL)
Khan, Mohammed Akram, *Samashya O Samadhan* (Calcutta: 1930). (NL)
Khilafat Sangeet, vol. I (Mymensingh: 1921). (NL)
Kirtanaya, Lakshmikanta, Kumuda Bhattacharya, *Ganera Bahi: Lotera Gan* (Mymensingh: 1931). (IOL)
Malijatir Udbodhan (Srotriya Narasundar Praptir Bibaran): Hindumahsabher Birat Adhibeshan (Calcutta: 1925). (NL)
Mandal, Manindranath, *Arya Poundrik* (Midnapore: 1910), (NL)
—— *Bangiya Jana Sangha* (Midnapore: 1923). (NL)
—— *Banger Digindranarayan* (Burdwan: 1926). (NL)
Mian, Abedali, *Krishak Boka* (Mymensingh: 1921). (IOL)
—— *Kalichitra* (Rangpur: 1926). (NL)
Modern Book Agency, *Deshpriya Jatindramohon Sengupta: His Life and Work* (Calcutta: 1933).
Mukherji, U.N., *A Dying Race* (rpt. Calcutta: 1910). (NL)
—— *Hindu Samaj* (Calcutta: 1910). (NL)
—— *Hinduism and the Coming Census: Christianity and Hinduism* (Calcutta: 1911). (NL)
Mymensingh-Kishoreganje Hindur Durgati, vols I and II, compiled by Dhaka Hindu Mission. (IOL)
Nazirabadi, Mohammed A., *Islam O Bigyan* (Mymensingh: 1924). (NL)
Nariraksha Samiti: 1938 Shaler Karyabibarani (publishing details destroyed)
Nazir, Abbasali, *Kalir Fakirer Khela: Alimganer Nasihat* (Lakhpur, P.S. Shibir, Dhaka: 1327[1920]). (NL)
Qureshi, Moulvi Hakim Masheer Rahman, *Narir Pabitrata ba Purda Raksha* (Calcutta: 1924). (NL)
Rahman, Ahmader, *Nari Tirtha* (Calcutta: 1931). (IOL)
Rahman, Fazlur, *Go-Korbani* (rpt. Calcutta: 1924). (NL)
Rahman, Mohammed Abdur, *Ittefaq ba Moslem Bandhutwa Sutra* (Dinajpur: 1926), (NL)
Rahman, Mohammed A., *Dari Kata Fatwa Arthat Je Parimane Dari Kata Sharanushare Haram O Je Parimane Dari Kata Jayez Tahar Bibaran* (Barisal: 1327[1925]). (NL)
Rahman, S., *Fakirer Keramat: Darbesher Ascharya Jibon Katha* (Calcutta: 1924). (NL)
Rashid, Mohammed Abdur, *Musalmaner Arthasanket O Tahar Pratikar* (Calcutta: 1938, f.pub. 1929). (NL)

Ray, Motilal, *Hindur Jagaran* (Calcutta: 1926). (NL)
Ray, Prafulla Chandra, *Faridpur Pradeshik Hindu Sabha* (Calcutta: 1925). (NL)
Sattar, Abdus, *Imamaul Mocchelmein Hazrat Mohammed Abubakr Siddiki: Pir Kablar Jiban-Charit* (Calcutta: 1939). (IOL)
Sayer, Garib, *Krishak Bandhu* (Calcutta: 1910). (NL)
Sengupta, Amritlal, *Jugodharma* (Calcutta: 1914). (NL)
Shah, Mohammed Emdad Ali, *Fakir Sambal* (Chittagong: 1926). (NL)
—— *Koo Riti Barjan* (Barisal: 1922). (NL)
—— *Milan Jug ba Niti Rahashya* (Barisal: 1922). (NL)
Shamsuddin, Abul Kalam, *Atit Diner Smriti* (Dhaka: 1968), p. 12.
Sharma, Aghorenath, *Haridas Thakur* (Bolpur: 1895). (NL)
Shusen, Abul, *Banglar Bolshie* (Dhaka: 1925). (NL)
Speech of the Chairman, Chittagong Islamia Conference, (Chittagong, 1925). (NL)
Swami, A.S. Narayan, *Arya Samaj Kahake Bole?*, trans. R. Bandopadhyaya, (Calcutta: 1926). (IOL)
Swami Gyananda, *Patuakhali Satyagraha* (Patuakhali: 1927). (NL)
Swami Icchananda, *Kaler Ingit* (Burdwan: 1924). (NL)
Tangail Hindu Samaj, *Bangla Hindu Jatir Khoy O Tahar Pratikar* (Tangail: 1924). (NL)
The Women's Protection League: Report of the Years 1935–37 (publishing details missing).
Vandopadhya, Annadacarana, *Harinam Panchali* (Calcutta: 1925). (NL)
Wadud, Kazi Abdul, *Hindu Musalmaner Birodh* (Shatiniketan: 1935). (NL)

Biographies, General Works

Amin, Shahid, *Event, Metaphor, Memory: Chauri Chaura 1922–1992* (Delhi: 1995).
Ahmed, Abul Mansur, *Amar Dekha Rajnitir Panchas Bachar* (Dhaka: 1975).
—— *Atmakatha* (Dhaka: 1974).
Ahmed, Muzaffar, *Kazi Nazrul Islam Smritikatha* (Calcutta: 1985, f.pub. 1965).
—— *Nirbachita Rachana Sankalan* (Calcutta: 1986, f.pub. 1976).
Ahmed, Rafiuddin, *The Bengal Muslims 1871–1906: A Quest for Identity* (Delhi, 1981).
Ahmed, Sufia, *Muslim Community in Bengal 1884–1912* (Dacca: 1974).
Al Azmeh, Aziz, *Islam and Modernity* (London: 1992).

Ali, Syed Ameer, *Memoirs and Other Writings of Syed Ameer Ali* Syed Razi Wasti (ed.), (Lahore: 1968).

Bandopadhyay, Bibhutibhushan, *Diner Pare Din* (Calcutta: 1986).

Banerjea, Surendranath, *A Nation in the Making: Being the Reminiscences of 50 Years of Public Life* (Calcutta: 1963, f.pub. 1925).

Basu, T., P.K. Datta, S. Sarkar, T. Sarkar and S. Sen, *Khaki Shorts Saffron Flags: A Critique of the Hindu Right* (N. Delhi: 1993)

Bhattacharyya, Buddhadeva in collaboration with T.K. Banerjee and D.K. Das, *Satyagrahas in Bengal: 1921–1939* (Calcutta: 1977).

Bose, Sugata, *Agrarian Bengal: Economy, Social Structure and Politics, 1919–1947* (Cambridge: 1986).

Broomfield, John, *Elite Conflict in a Plural Society: Twentieth Century Bengal* (Berkeley and Los Angeles: 1968).

—— *Mostly About Bengal* (N. Delhi: 1982).

Chakravarty, Papia, *Hindu Responses to Nationalist Ferment* (Calcutta: 1992).

Chatterjee, Partha, *Bengal 1920–1947: The Land Question* (Calcutta: 1984).

—— *The Nation and Its Fragments: Colonial and Postcolonial Histories* (Delhi: 1993).

Chaudhuri, Nirad C., *The Autobiography of an Unknown Indian* (London: 1951).

Chaudhuri, Sukanta (ed.), *Calcutta: The Living City*, vol. I, *The Past* (Calcutta: 1990).

Chowdhury, Hamidul Huq, *Memoirs* (Dhaka: 1989).

Cooper, Adrienne, *Sharecropping and Sharecropper's Struggles in Bengal, 1930–1950* (Calcutta: 1988).

Cotton, H.E.A., *Calcutta: Old and New* (Calcutta: 1907).

Das, Girindranth, *Bangla Pir-Sahityer Katha* (Barasat, 24 Parganas: 1976).

Das, Pulin Behari, *Amar Jiban Kahini*, Amalendu De (ed.) (Calcutta: 1987).

Das, Suranjan, *Communal Riots in Bengal, 1905–1947* (Delhi: 1991).

Das, Veena, *Critical Events: An Anthropological Perspective on Contemporary India* (Delhi: 1995).

Davis, Natalie Zemon, *Society and Culture in Early Modern France* (London: 1975).

De, Amalendu, *Bangali Buddhijibi O Bicchinatabad* (Calcutta: 1971).

Dutta, Abhijit, *Muslim Society in Transition: Titu Meer's Revolt (1831)* (Calcutta: 1986).

Eaton, Richard, *The Rise of Islam and the Bengal Frontier, 1204–1760* (N. Delhi: 1994).

Engels, Dagmar, *Beyond Purdah?: Women in Bengal 1890–1939* (Delhi: 1996)
Fazl, Abul, *Rekha Chitra* (Chattagram: 1968).
Ghosh, Shantishudha, *Bir Sangrami Satindranath Sen* (Calcutta: 1978).
Gordon, Leonard A., *Bengal: The Nationalist Movement, 1876–1940* (Delhi: 1974).
Gramsci, Antonio, *Selections from the Prison Notebooks*, Quintin Hoare and Geoffrey Newell Smith (eds and trans), (New York: 1971).
Grunebaum, Edmund von, *Muhammadan Festivals* (London: 1981, f.pub. 1951).
Hardy, Peter, *Partners in Freedom — and True Muslims: The Political Thought of Some Muslim Scholars in British India 1912–1947* (Lund: 1971).
—— *The Muslims of British India* (Cambridge: 1972).
Hunter, W.W., *The Annals of Rural Bengal* (rpt. Calcutta: 1965)
—— *The Indian Mussalmans: Are They Bound in Conscience to Rebel Against the Queen?* (rpt. Lahore: 1968).
Ikramulla, Begum Shaista Suhrawardy *Huseyn Shaheed Suhrawardy: A Biography* (Karachi: 1991).
Islam, Nurul Mustafa, *Muslim Public Opinion as Reflected in the Bengali Press, 1901–1930* (Dhaka: 1973).
Jabbar, Abdul, *Banglar Chalchitra* (Calcutta: 1395[1988], f.pub. 1377 [1970]).
Jordens, J.F.T., *Swami Shraddhanand* (Delhi: 1981).
Khan, Tamizuddin, *The Test of Time: My Life and Days* (Dhaka: 1989).
Krishna Kumar Mitrer Atmacharit (Calcutta: 1937).
Mandal, Tirtha, *Women Revolutionaries of Bengal, 1905–1939* (Calcutta: 1991).
Mcpherson, Kenneth, *The Muslim Microcosm: Calcutta, 1918–1935* (Weisbaden, 1974).
Metcalf, Barbara Daly, *Islamic Revival in British India: Deoband, 1860–1900* (Princeton: 1982).
Mitra, Krishna Kumar, *Atmacharit* (with afterword by Kanai Chattopadhyaya), (Calcutta: 1386[1979]).
Nakazato, Nariaki, *Agrarian System in Eastern Bengal c. 1870–1910* (Calcutta: 1994).
Newell, H.A., *Calcutta the First Capital of British India: An Illustrated Guide to Places of Interest with Map* (Publishing details absent).
Pandey, Gyanendra, *The Construction of Communalism in Colonial India* (Delhi: 1990).
Prakash, Indra, *Hindu Mahasabha: Its Contribution to India's Politics* (N.Delhi: 1966).

Ray, Acharya Prafulla Chandra, *Life and Experiences of a Bengal Chemist* (Calcutta: 1932).
Ray, Rajat Kanta, *Social Conflict and Political Unrest in Bengal, 1857–1927* (Delhi, 1984).
Samaddar, Sivaprasad, *Calcutta Is* (Calcutta: 1978).
Samayik Patrey Banglar Samajchitra, Benoy Ghosh (ed. and comp.), (Calcutta: 1966).
Sanyal, Hiteshranjan, *Bangla Kirtaner Itihas* (Calcutta: 1989).
Sarkar, Sumit, *The Swadeshi Movement in Bengal, 1903–1908* (New Delhi: 1973).
—— *Modern India 1885–1947* (New Delhi: 1983).
Sarkar, Tanika, *Bengal 1928–1934: The Politics of Protest* (N.Delhi: 1987).
Savarkar, V.D., *Who is a Hindu?* (rpt. Poona: 1949)
Shamsuddin, Abul Kalam, *Atit Diner Smriti* (Dacca: 1968).
Seshadri, H.V. (ed.), *Dr Hegdewar the Epoch Maker: A Biography*, compiled by B.V. Deshpande and S.R. Ramaswamy (Bangalore: 1981).
Siddiki, Allahma Saifuddin, *Furfurar Hazrat* (Hooghly: 1993).
Sleeman, Major General Sir W.H., *Rambles and Recollections of an Indian Official* (revised ed. 1980, f.pub. 1844).
Southard, Barbara, *The Women's Movement and Colonial Politics in Bengal: The Quest for Political Rights, Education and Social Reform Legislation, 1921–1925* (N. Delhi: 1995).
Sur, Atul, *Shatabdir Pratiddhani* (Calcutta: 1986).
Sufi, Mohtar Hossein, *Begum Rokeya: Jiban O Sahitya* (Dhaka: 1986).
Waliullah, Mohammed, *Yuga Bichitra* (Dhaka, 1967).

Articles

Aggarwal, Purushottam, 'Surat, Savarkar and Draupadi: Legitimising Rape as a Political Weapon', in T. Sarkar and U. Butalia (eds), *Women and the Hindu Right* (N. Delhi: 1995).
Ahmed, Rafiuddin, 'Conflict and Contradictions in Bengali Islam: Problems of Change and Adjustment', in Katherine P. Ewing (ed.), *Shari'at and Ambiguity in South Asian Islam* (Delhi: 1988).
Amin, Sonia Nishat, 'The Early Muslim *Bhadramahila*: The Growth of Learning and Creativity, 1876 to 1939', in Bharati Ray (ed.), *From the Seams of History: Essays on Indian Women* (Delhi, 1995).
Bhadra, Gautam, 'The Mentality of Subalternity: Kantanam or Rajdharma', *Subaltern Studies VI: Writings on South Asian History and Society* (Delhi: 1983).
Bhattacharya, Neeladri, 'Myth, History and the Politics of

Ramjanambhumi', in S. Gopal (ed.), *Anatomy of a Confrontation: The Babri Masjid–Ramjanmbhumi Dispute* (Delhi: 1991).
Bose, Sugata, 'Class, Nation and Religion in Peasant Politics: East Bengal from Noncooperation to Partition', *Bengal Past and Present*, vol. CIII, parts I–II, nos 196–7, January–December 1984.
—— 'The Roots of Communal Violence in Rural Bengal: A Study of the Kishoreganj Riots, 1930', *Modern Asian Studies*, vol. 16, no. 3, 1982.
Carroll, Lucy, 'Colonial Perceptions of Indian Society and the Emergence of Caste(s) Associations', *Journal of Asian Studies*, vol. XXXVII, no. 2, February 1978.
Chakrabarty, Dipesh, 'Modernity and Ethnicity in India: A History for the Present', *Economic and Political Weekly*, 30 December 1993
Chaytor, Miranda, 'Husband(ry): Narratives of Rape in the Seventeenth Century', *Gender and History*, vol. 7, no. 3, November 1995.
Datta, P.K., '"Dying Hindus": Production of Hindu Communal Common Sense in Early 20th Century Bengal', *Economic and Political Weekly*, vol. XXVIII, no. 44, 1993.
—— 'VHP'S Ram at Ayodhya: Reincarnation through Ideology and Organisation', *Economic and Political Weekly*, vol. XXVI, no. 44, 1991.
—— 'War Over Music: The Riots of 1926 in Bengal', *Social Scientist*, vol. XVIII, nos 6–7, 1990.
Frietag, Sandria B., 'The Roots of Muslim Separatism in South Asia: Personal Practice and Public Structures in Kanpur and Bombay', in Edmund Burke III and Ira M. Lapidus (eds), *Islam, Politics and Social Movements* (London: 1988).
Gallagher, John, 'Congress in Decline 1930–1929', in John Gallagher, Gordon Johnson and Anil Seal (eds), *Locality, Province and Nation* (Cambridge: 1973).
Gordon, Richard A., 'The Hindu Mahasabha and the Indian National Congress, 1915 to 1926', *Modern Asian Studies*, vol. IX, no. 2, 1975.
Guha, Ranajit, 'Discipline and Mobilise', Partha Chatterjee and Gyanendra Pandey (eds), *Subaltern Studies VII: Writings on South Asian History and Society* (Delhi: 1992).
Haque, Mozammel, 'Impediments which Delayed Muslim Progress in Education 1900–1911: An Analysis', *Studies in Islam*, vol. XVIII, nos 3–4, July/October 1981.
Hashmi, Tajul Islam, 'The Communalisation of Class Struggle: East Bengal Peasantry, 1923–1929', *Indian Economic and Social History Review*, vol. XXV, no. 2, 1988.

Jones, Kenneth W., 'Religious Identity and the Indian Census', in N.G. Barrier (ed.), *The Census in British India: New Perspectives* (N. Delhi: 1981).

Metcalfe, Barbara Daly, 'Maulana Ashraf Ali Thanavi and Urdu Literature', in Christopher Shackle (ed.), *Urdu and Muslim South Asia; Studies in Honour of Ralph Russell*, (Delhi: 1991).

Nandy, Ashis, 'An Anti-Secularist Manifesto', in John Hick and Lamont C. Hempel (eds), *Gandhi's Significance for Today*, (London: 1989).

—— 'The Politics of Secularism and the Recovery of Toleration', in Veena Das (ed.), *Mirrors of Violence: Communities, Riots and Survivors in South Asia* (Delhi: 1992, f.pub. 1990).

Pandey, Gyanendra, 'Rallying Around the Cow: Sectarian Strife in the Bhojpuri Region, c. 1888–1917', in Ranajit Guha (ed.), *Subaltern Studies II: Writings on South Asian History and Society* (Delhi: 1983).

—— '"Encounter and Calamities": The History of a North Indian Qasba in the Nineteenth Century', in Ranajit Guha (ed.), *Subaltern Studies III* (Delhi: 1984).

—— 'In Defence of the Fragment: Writing about Hindu Muslim Riots in India Today', *Economic and Political Weekly*, vol. XXVI, nos 11 and 12, March 1991.

Ray, Rajat Kanta, 'Colonial Penetration and the Initial Resistance: The Mughal Ruling Class, the English East India Company and the Struggle for Bengal 1756–1800', *The Indian Historical Review*, vol. XII, nos 1–2, July 1985–January 1986.

Roberts, Michael, 'Noise as Cultural Struggle: Tom-Tom Beating, the British and Communal Disturbances in Sri Lanka, 1880s–1930s', in Veena Das (ed.), *Mirrors of Violence: Communities, Riots and Survivors in South Asia* (Delhi: 1992, f.pub. 1990).

Sarkar, Chandiprasad, 'Bengali Muslim Politics, Society and Culture during the Khilafat — Noncooperation Movement', *Bengal Past and Present*, vol. CIII, parts I–II, nos 196–197, January–December 1984.

Sarkar, Sumit, 'The Kalki-Avatar of Bikrampur: A Village Scandal in Early Twentieth Century Bengal', in Ranajit Guha (ed.), *Subaltern Studies VI: Writings on South Asian History and Society* (Delhi: 1989).

Sarkar, Tanika, 'Jitu Santal's Movement in Malda, 1924–1932: A Study in Tribal Protest', in Ranajit Guha (ed.), *Subaltern Studies IV: Writings on South Asian History and Society* (Delhi: 1985).

—— 'Rhetoric Against the Age of Consent: Resisting Colonial Reason and the Death of a Child-Wife', *Economic and Political Weekly*, vol. XXVIII, no. 36, 1993.

Sengupta, K.K., 'The Agrarian League of Pabna, 1873', *Indian Economic and Social History Review*, vol. VII, no. 2, 1970.
Sen, Samita, 'Honour and Resistance: Gender, Community and Class in Bengal, 1920–1940', in Sekhar Bandopadhyaya, Abhijit Dasgupta and Willem van Schendel (eds), *Bengal: Communities, Development and States*, (New Delhi: 1994).
Shiloah, A., 'The Dimension of Sound', in Bernard Lewis (ed.), *The World of Islam* (London: 1976).
Siddiqui, M.K.A., 'Caste among the Muslims of Calcutta', in Imtiaz Ahmed (ed.), *Caste and Social Stratification among the Muslims* (Delhi: 1973).

Dissertations

Alam, Abu Yusuf Shamsul, 'Khilafat Movement and the Muslims of Bengal', M.Phil. Thesis, Jawaharlal Nehru University, 1979.
Bandopadhyaya, Sekhar, 'Social Mobility in Bengal in the Late 19th and Early 20th Centuries', Ph.D. Thesis, Calcutta University, 1985.
Basu, Swaraj, 'The Rajbansis of North Bengal: A Study of a Caste Movement 1910–1947', Ph.D. Thesis, Calcutta University, 1992.
Frietag, Sandria B., 'Religious Rites and Riots: From Communal Identity to Communalism in North India 1870–1940', Ph.D. Dissertation, University of California, 1980. (NMML Microfilm).
Sarkar, Tanika, 'National Movement and Popular Protest in Bengal 1926–1934', Ph.D. Thesis, Department of History, Delhi University, September 1980.

Index

Ahmad, Mansur 68, 77, 83–6, 101–6, 220–1, 243, 264, 277, 279
Ahmad, Muzaffar 196, 233, 238, 273
Ahmed, Rafiuddin 68, 74, 255
Ali, Ameer 26, 65, 112, 199, 212
Azad, A.K. 141–2
Arya Samaj 48, 50, 199, 225, 248, 250, 253

Banerjea, Surendranath 40–1, 126, 134, 162, 232, 234
Bannerjee, J.L. 273–5, 278
Bakr, Pir Abu 49, 66, 87–90, 105, 124, 136, 139, 142–7, 171, 215–16, 243, 249, 282
Barma, Panchanan 158, 163–4, 168, 170–1, 250
Bauls 97–9, 171, 255
Bengal Pact 97, 102, 128, 132, 146–7, 155, 157, 174, 181–2, 233–4, 259, 275, 277
Bhattacharya, Digindra 40–4, 52–4, 56, 61, 67, 163
Bisi, Sailesh 51, 56, 58, 60–1
Boards, District\Local 51, 66, 176–82, 190–1
Bose, Subhash 124, 128, 132–4, 210, 235
Bose, Sugata 75, 166, 284, 286–8
Brahmin\Brahminism 33–6, 43, 46, 170
Brahmo Samaj 41, 53, 205, 221
BTAB 80, 82, 156, 174–6, 197, 273–82, 290, 294–5

Calcutta Riots 194, 223, 238, 247–8, 253–4, 260, 262, 267–72
Census 23–5, 35, 37–40, 45–7, 50, 58–9, 61–3, 113, 116–18, 158, 162
Chatterjee, Partha 66, 174, 273, 275, 284, 286–7
Chattopadhyay, Bankim 84–6, 159, 228
Chattopadhyay, Sarat Chandra 64, 85, 259
Chaudhury, Nirad 117, 172, 227, 229, 235
Civil Disobedience 197, 284, 288, 296

Das, C.R. 42, 56, 96, 110, 133–5, 143–4, 147, 155,. 233, 255, 258, 274
Das, Pulin 173, 206, 226–9, 231–2, 234
Das, S.R. 150, 154, 234
Das, Suranjan 239–40, 268, 284
Deuskar, Sakharam 26, 37–9
Dhaka 103, 105, 159, 197, 205–7, 241, 247, 255, 265, 283–9

Frietag, Sandria 239

Gandhi, Mahatma 55, 96, 134, 196, 207–8, 255, 258
Ghosh, Piyush 48–9, 62–3, 160, 226, 230–2, 250
Ghaznavi, A.K. 78, 89, 92, 175, 274, 294

Gupta, Nalini 51, 57–9

HMS 22, 44, 48–52, 54–6, 62, 108, 137, 154–7, 164, 175, 197–8, 204, 212, 225–6, 231, 250–4, 270, 279, 287
Hindu Mission 289–91
Hindu Sabha 159, 164, 173, 176, 204, 237, 247, 271
Hossein, Rokeya 215–20, 224
Huq, Fazlul 40, 82, 97, 102, 114, 124, 128, 143–4, 174

Islam, Nazrul 79, 84, 87, 196, 219, 233, 258

Karmi Sangha 233–4
Khan, Akram 82, 94–7, 100–2, 223, 236, 274
K.P.P. 80, 82, 94, 212, 278–9, 281, 283, 288
Kishoreganj Riots 283–4, 286, 288–9, 292, 295. *See also* Ghaznavi

Malaviya, M.M. 21, 48, 49, 126, 154, 164, 203
Mandal, Manindranath 42–3
Mitra, K.K. 150–3, 162, 169, 183, 210, 214
Mukherji, U.N. 22, 24, 26, 34–46, 52, 62–4, 108, 162–3, 229–30, 291
Mymensingh 59, 172–4, 177, 181, 204–5, 227, 237, 270, 279–80

Namasudras 31–2, 40, 43, 48, 60, 79, 158–9, 161–2, 166–7, 200, 229, 271, 288, 290–1
Nehru Report 197–8, 277
N\K 40, 50–1, 75, 83, 85, 96–7, 102, 110, 123–4, 126–7, 131, 133, 139, 148, 157, 163–6, 208, 230, 234, 246, 254–9, 261, 263, 277–9, 296

Pabna 41, 56, 93, 178, 248, 279–80, 282
Pabna Riots 172, 178, 194, 223, 241, 260–1, 263, 266, 285
Pandey, Gyanendra 25, 238–39
Patuakhali Satyagraha 105, 253, 265, 270, 289

Rai, Lajpat 21, 27, 63, 126, 155, 226
Rajbansis 32, 160–3, 167–9, 249–50, 271, 275, 282. *See also* Rangpur
Rangpur 151, 155, 157–9, 166, 169–71, 176–7, 183, 214
Ray, P.C. 40, 51, 52, 55, 59–62
Roberts, Michael 241–2, 253

Sarkar, Sumit 74, 87
Sarkar, Tanika 75, 77, 150, 188, 283–4, 293
Sasmal, Birendranath 233, 274
Sen, Satin 105–6, 251
Southard, Barbara 207, 219
Shuddhi 49, 99, 291–2
Suhrawardy, Huseyn 134–5, 140–2, 145–6, 254
Swadeshi 26, 28–32, 39
Swami Shraddhanand 22, 40, 48, 50, 62, 136, 209, 211
Swami Vivekananda 32–3, 36, 41–4, 53–4
Swarajists 56, 110, 122, 127–28, 132, 134–5, 143–5, 147, 156, 178–82, 264, 274, 276–81, 295
syncretism 77, 99, 133, 255–9

Tagore, Rabindranath 29, 40, 46–7, 84, 137, 231

Vaishnav 31, 41, 44, 52–5, 250

Wahabi\Faraizi 69, 76, 90
Waliullah, Mohammed 73, 82, 114, 139, 149, 221–2, 256, 272